LOOMPANICS'

GOLDEN RECORDS

Articles and Features from

THE BEST BOOK CATALOG

IN THE WORLD

LOOMPANICS'

GOLDEN RECORDS

Articles and Features from

THE BEST BOOK CATALOG

IN THE WORLD

Edited by
Michael Hoy

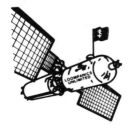

Loompanics Unlimited
Port Townsend, Washington

Loompanics' Golden Records
Edited by Michael Hoy
© 1993 by Loompanics Unlimited

Cover by Mark Zingarelli

Published by:
Loompanics Unlimited
PO Box 1197
Port Townsend, WA 98368
Loompanics Unlimited is a division of Loompanics Enterprises, Inc.

ISBN 1-55950-092-1
Library of Congress Catalog Card Number pending

Contents

Introduction

by Michael Hoy

Welcome to ***Loompanics' Golden Records***, a collection of articles and features that have appeared in the Loompanics Unlimited Book Catalog — *The Best Book Catalog In The World.* We strive to have the articles and features we publish be as good as the books we sell. We want these items, like our books, to clear your head, to incite and provoke, and make you think about your life in strange new ways.

More than 40 articles and features are collected herein, including two commissioned especially for this book: *Circus of the Scars,* by Jim Hogshire, and *Early Release,* by G.J. Shaefer.

Ladies and gentlemen of America and all the ships at sea, Loompanics Unlimited proudly presents: ***Loompanics' Golden Records.***

— *Michael Hoy, Pres.*
   15 March 1993

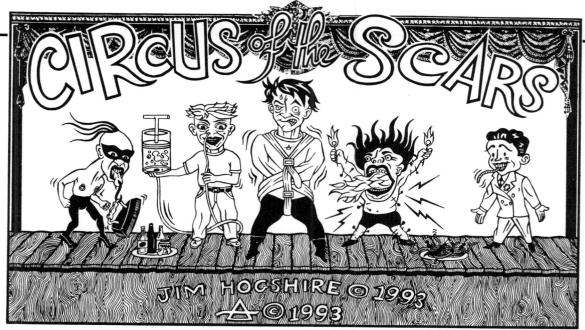

CIRCUS of the SCARS

JIM HOGSHIRE © 1993
△ © 1993

One of the more atrocious things the audience sees while watching Jim Rose's Circus Sideshow is The Amazing Mr. Lifto. Although he rarely causes people to vomit in disgust he always elicits a chorus of oohs and ahs as he calmly inserts a coat hanger through a self-inflicted hole in the head of his penis and attaches it to a steam iron.

By this time, the audience has already seen him use his pierced tongue and pierced nipples to pick up similar heavy objects — such as concrete blocks — but this... this is too much. There is silence as naked Mr. Lifto squats down, hooks dick and iron together, then slowly stands up.

His penis stretches. It stretches some more. The audience starts to moan and then, when his dick is stretched long and thin, the iron rises from the floor and Lifto straightens up. The iron sways gently beneath his knees. Then, triumphantly, he raises his arms into the air and begins to swing the iron back and forth between his legs, as showmaster Jim Rose chants, "Liff-*toh*, Liff-*toh*, Liff-*toh*."

If not the most atrocious, the scene is certainly the most popular with journalists who cover the show, especially since, to avoid breaking the law, Lifto has sometimes resorted to "covering" his dick with a long stripe of shaving cream — which of course just makes his act that much more appalling.

"That's the toughest part of the show," says Rose, "making atrocities palatable."

Jim Rose has probably never said anything as revealing as this, since any interview with him is likely to be part of the show itself. Other members of the troupe, Lifto, Tim the Torture King, the Tube, the Slug and the rest are not supposed to talk to the media. This is because Jim Rose — the man who rubs his face in broken glass — is terrified of being labeled a fraud. He couldn't stand having to prove his atrocities are real (although, so far, nobody's asked).

But then again there are those killjoys who go around saying that fire-eating is easy since there's a special protective chemical fire-eaters smear inside their mouths. Even though none of these guys who make claims like this reveal just what the protecting salve might be nor are they willing to eat a little fire themselves, it can ruin a showman's reputation. So Rose keeps a tight rein on his freaks, and his version of the show and its history is the only one available for public consumption. That's all in the sideshow tradition where performers didn't used to tell even *each other* their real names. "Truth" is a relative word at best in the sideshow world.

> *Jim Rose and his "marvels" don't employ any of the typical sleight-of-hand techniques used by magicians. With the exception of one trick..., Rose's stunts are real. The darts thrown at his naked back really do stick in there, quivering in his flesh.*

(Continued next page)

But his fear is exaggerated. Jim Rose and his "marvels" don't employ any of the typical sleight-of-hand techniques used by magicians. With the exception of one trick (the swallowed razor blades on a thread — a trick as hackneyed as sawing a lady in half), Rose's stunts are real. The darts thrown at his naked back really do stick in there, quivering in his flesh. "The Slug" really does chew up mouthfuls of live maggots, crickets and, of course, slugs. And Rose goes to great lengths to ensure authenticity — inviting audience members (not shills, either) to help out. They stand on Rose's head as he buries his face in the broken glass. They pounce on his chest while he lies bare-backed on a bed of nails. And when he gets up, it is obvious that the nails were sharp. Even the razor blade "trick" is hardly a fake. Do it wrong and you'll cut your tongue off.

He passes a steel sword around the crowd so they can grip it, feel it, and assure themselves that this long spike (after a quick wipe-down with alcohol) is the very one the Slug slides through his esophagus into his stomach, to barely prick his duodenum.

> *Still, it is hard to believe that anyone would really use a staple gun to fasten a dollar bill to his forehead (as Rose does) or run long steel pins into the orbit of his eye (as Tim the Torture King does) or brand himself (as Lifto does). After all, that's gotta hurt.*

Still, it is hard to believe that anyone would really use a staple gun to fasten a dollar bill to his forehead (as Rose does) or run long steel pins into the orbit of his eye (as Tim the Torture King does) or brand himself (as Lifto does). After all that's gotta hurt.

Yes, it hurts. Officially, the troupe won't admit to more than mild discomfort. Unofficially, one of Rose's freaks admits that if he isn't high before he gets on stage, he certainly is by the time he gets off. The endorphins released by skewering both cheeks with a long piece of steel about the size of a bicycle spoke are as powerful as opium. Especially if you do this shit night after night as Jim Rose's Sideshow has been doing the last year. And learning to eat fire means you *will* be burned over and over again. Your mouth blisters up, the roof of your mouth peels away. Even once you learn to eat fire correctly, to tilt your head just so and spit the gas out evenly so as

not to catch your face on fire, there is still the very real danger of gasoline vapor exploding in your lungs.

And there's no way to avoid swallowing some of it. Luckily, today's gasoline is unleaded, so modem fire-eaters don't slowly poison themselves while searing their mouths. Still, sometimes they do blow up. And many a sword-swallower has died trying to break some silly record.

★ ★ ★

Once just a Seattle oddity, the group has gained official stardom status by appearing on Sally Jessy Raphael and respectability by telling Geraldo Rivera to fuck off. All through the summer of 1992, the group cruised the country with the Lollapalooza tour and by the beginning of 1993, they will have finished their first tour of Europe. Who knows, maybe they will launch a revival of the sideshow? But for now, however famous they may be, they remain the one and only circus sideshow in the country. The only heir to a once popular form of entertainment that died out in the early fifties, when it became declasse to gawk at people with deformities, or applaud people who would degrade themselves by deliberately doing things they know are going to make people faint, things that really would be called "torture" if anybody did it to you.

To punch a hole through your tongue and suspend a brick from it... doesn't that sound like something Amnesty International would heartily condemn? Or using someone as a human dart board? Or running a tube through a man's nose into his stomach and forcibly pumping him full of a half-gallon of beer, toothpaste, ketchup, chocolate syrup, raw eggs and who knows what else? That's sick. Even sicker is to pump it out, swirl it around, squeeze the chunky, reddish fluid into plastic cups and drink it. Not just sip it. Drink it. Come to think of it, the Italian fascists used a similar technique to torture their opponents.

Small wonder Jim Rose double-talks the media. Who wants Sally Struthers or Ted Danson on your case? Rose has had his share of do-gooders, especially some PC clowns in Portland who panned his act, calling it an offense to human dignity and a grotesque example of the lows people will stoop to just to make a buck. Imagine what they must have thought of Dolly, the Doll Lady, a 63-year-old midget woman who was part of a real-live circus sideshow until the advent of thorazine, mental hospitals and human dignity. Her role in the show is as traditional

(Continued next page)

as it ever gets. She is the midget lady, adored by troupe and fans. She is to be gawked at as she feeds broken glass into the waiting mouths of her freak boys. And just like the sideshows of yesteryear she is treated like a queen. They even put her on a pedestal.

She eats it up. She loves it. Her granddaughter comes to watch the show and is proud of her. She comes from the end of a long line of sideshow performers, some of whose lives seem truly ghastly.

Not too long ago, it was a sideshow staple to set up a row of deformed people in a tent while a barker outside lured customers in with promises to see the results of incest or venereal disease. Armless men sipped tea with their toes, guys with horrid skin diseases made a living as "the spotted boy" or "the human alligator." And pinheads! Pinheads were dressed up in smocks with mystical signs embroidered on them and billed as "Ancient Aztecs." It was also considered great entertainment to force pinheads to box each other, or if not another pinhead, then at least an ugly negro who could be billed as a "wild man from Borneo." Circus sideshows went as far as to catch pygmies in Africa and put them on display as "missing links" — one of these pygmies was even made a permanent fixture in the Monkey House at the Bronx zoo!

Siamese twins were a guaranteed draw, as were any people who could be advertised as half animal half human ala the "mule-faced woman" or the "Ostrich boy." The tiny, the giant, the obese and disfigured were all there along with the "manufactured freaks." These were generally the tattooed men who told tales of shipwrecks on South Sea Islands where savages spent their time alternately forcing them to mate with their daughters and torturing them. Women teased their hair, yellowed their skin, put on exotic costumes and told horror stories of their days before their escape from some faraway eastern harem.

And the knife-throwers with human targets, the serpent women and their death-defying python dances! Here is where the sword-swallower came in. In fact, all kinds of regurgitators gained fame, some by swallowing poison, others by gulping down live frogs or mice, then bringing them back up alive. There were human "claw hammers" who used their teeth to extract iron spikes driven into thick planks.

It is in the tradition of the manufactured freak that Jim Rose's show goes. People who deliberately do painful or ugly things for the money.

Which brings us back to the atrocities and making them palatable.

In a way, Jim Rose's dilemma is the same any other entertainment show faces. Network news programs are an example. They really don't feel the viewing audience can stomach any true pictures of human beings with half their faces blown off. And high-quality video of recently limbless — but not lifeless — people in agony is just too... too. That's why we got to watch the same bomb go down the same black and white chimney in Iraq and didn't get to see charred people writhing around or bloated little kids shitting themselves to death.

Still, there is an atavistic appeal to viewing atrocities (maybe even an intellectual appeal) sometimes known as the "car wreck syndrome," and so they must be made "palatable." In the case of TV shows and movies, one way is to allude to scenes "too graphic to be shown on television" or issue a disclaimer at the beginning of the show.

> *Jim Rose sort of issues a disclaimer at the beginning of his show. He walks out on stage, says hello to the audience, then slowly rams an eight-inch screwdriver up his nose... "If you can't take that," he tells the audience, "you may as well leave right now." And a number of people who have laid down ten bucks or more to see the show do just that.*

Jim Rose sort of issues a disclaimer at the beginning of his show. He walks out on stage, says hello to the audience, then slowly rams an eight-inch screwdriver up his nose. Lots of people gasp right away. More keep gasping as Rose turns from side to side to show just how deep inside his head he's pushed this screwdriver. Then he slowly pulls it out, glistening with mucus.

"If you can't take that," he tells the audience, "you may as well leave right now." And a number of people who have laid down ten bucks or more to see the show do just that.

(Continued next page) **3**

> *One time in Montreal, Tim the Torture King stuck a needle up into his eye socket and hit an artery. Blood spurted out.*

True to his word, it just gets worse. No show is exactly like another, so anything can happen. One time in Montreal, Tim the Torture King stuck a needle up into his eye socket and hit an artery. Blood spurted out. It pulsed out. He slid the needle out and stanched the flow then ran the skewer through his cheeks. The same thing happened, blood began gushing out of the Torture King's face and some of the people closest to the stage started fainting. But the place was so crowded the only way to get the people to fresh air was to lift them up and let the crowd pass the bodies back toward the door. The unconscious bodies floated over a sea of revolted people, there was screaming and hysteria.

"It looked like Khomeini's funeral," recalls Rose, "You know, when that mob got ahold of his corpse and just started passing it around, grabbing at it, and the shroud was coming off."

Jim Rose's show is easily as captivating as Khomeini's funeral. At times it is as gross as the most violent of homo-biker-fisting-videos, or scenes of gallon-sized red wine enemas, or watching some wretched drunk puke globs of bile onto an afternoon sidewalk. Mostly it's the timing. Rose uses the audience as more than a prop, they are an integral part of the show. His constant narration, full of bullshit stories about the origins of his characters, or jokes about someone who is obviously in pain and danger, keeps his audience right with him. Sometimes he lets up a little and everybody settles down while one of the performers merely eats a light bulb or walks up a stairway of swords.

But they beg for more. Jim Rose sweats and the audience begs. So he brings on the gruesome stuff. "The Tube" pokes a bright green string into one of his nostrils, runs it through his sinuses and out the other nostril. Then he flosses his head.

★★★

What were these guys doing before they became manufactured freaks? One of them washed dishes for a living and walked on broken glass and hot coals in his spare time... for fun. One of them used to be a kindly pharmacist quietly counting out pills in Montana. Jim Rose was always a street character, making his living by being bizarre in public and passing the hat. He did it in Europe, he did it in California and finally managed to get a Seattle Restaurant to book him as oddity entertainment while the belly dancer took her breaks. He charged everybody a buck.

> *What will they do in the future? One of them is already teaching himself to suck all his organs up behind his rib cage so his spine will be clearly visible from the front.*

What will they do in the future? One of them is already teaching himself to suck all his organs up behind his rib cage so his spine will be clearly visible from the front. One of them is in the process of having his entire body, from head to toe, tattooed blue. It is his aim to become the first such completely tattooed man in history, and the first mostly-tattooed man since "The Great Omo" of 75 years ago. One of them has already begun to train his stomach muscles to move in such a way that it appears he has a living struggling animal in his belly.

Some ideas incorporate animals into the act, but certain laws will probably prevent them from ever being staged. Another is to catch bullets in their teeth. But once again, laws regarding the discharging of firearms in crowded places where alcohol is served will probably thwart them here, too. Still nothing is out of bounds.

And of course they are thinking of things to regurgitate. One fascinating idea is to swallow a chunk of something radioactive and put a Geiger counter up to the belly to record the destruction. Another trick, inspired by a tabloid story, is to create "The Human Crockpot." For this trick the performer plans to pour a can of stew into a plastic bag, tie it off with a string and then swallow it, keeping it in his stomach until it reaches the proper temperature. Then he should be able to pull out the bag and pour a hot, steaming meal into a plate.

Undoubtedly, they will come up with some way to make even this disgusting act even more repulsive but still palatable. ★★★

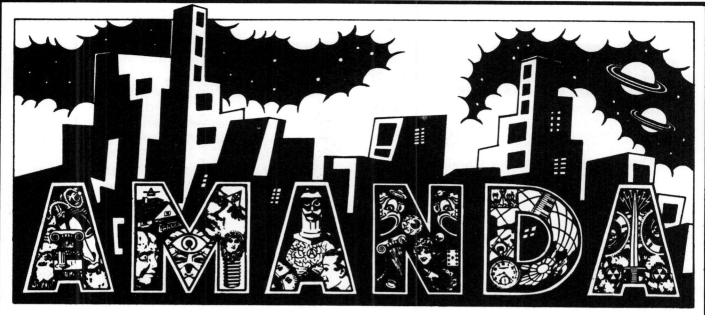

BY MICHAEL E. MAROTTA
Illustrations by △   © 1990

"Fuck a duck, Mom, do I hafta?" whined 10-year-old Amanda.

"Yes, you have to. Gramps needs the new memory threads for his next software release and I hafta go to Anchorage to make a video."

"Whydntchajus splice it on Vidnet?"

"Cause it's too touchy for Vidnet. This is art, kid."

Amanda went to her room and took five barbies from a shelf. Then she pried open her misspiggybank and seized a fistful of Eurodollars. From a dresser drawer, she chose extra sets of barbie clothes. She stuffed all of this, along with a stack of CDs, into one of the many purses from under her bed and ran full tilt upstairs. At the door to the garage, she collided with Mom.

"Bye, Mom, love you!" she stretched up for a kiss.

"Right. Here, take your wand and I made you a thermos of algae."

"Oh, god, Mom!"

"Stop arguing and go. Do a complete on that zep, don't just take off. I'll be back Wednesday. Use Skylink..."

"Yeah, yeah, yeah," Amanda sneered under her breath as she moved out of hearing range.

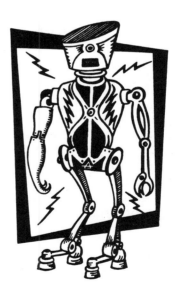

Her pet robot, Beardsley, was waiting at the hangar door. "Tough luck, fuck a duck. Gonna make a buck?" it chirped.

Her pet robot, Beardsley, was waiting at the hangar door. "Tough luck. Fuck a duck. Gonna make a buck?" it chirped.

Amanda sighed a pouty snort through her nose. "Not this trip. We're taking some KNA to Gramps and then back home. Let's start the countdown. In you go." The robot attached itself to the cargo hoist and activated

First published in 1990 Spring Supplement

(Continued next page) **5**

the block and tackle. Once inside, it scooted off toward the rear of the zeppelin. Amanda leapt for the ropes and hauled herself inside then walked forward to the cockpit. Twenty minutes later, she was sure the 50 meter, semi-rigid, hot air and helium, solar-powered ship would fly to Cleveland and back.

Beardsley fluted at her over the intercom. "Don't take a nap. Check the flaps!"

"The flaps report nominal."

"Go by the book. Go out and take a look. You can't fly with my beam on the eye."

"Oh shit. Disengage that."

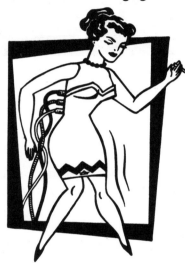

Wired to the computer, the 35-cm dolls moved about stiffly but be-lievably.

"No way, Jose. I'm voicelocked and Mom's the word."

"Fuck!" Amanda did a complete walk-around, checking the flaps, the rudder and the landing gear. She cupped her hands over the running lights she could reach to check the bulbs. She even dipped her finger into the emergency fuel tank although the cockpit readout and the gauge on the tankcap both showed full.

At 70 kph, the trip from Michigan's "Little Finger" to Cleveland was tedious. Amanda began filling the time by scanning up and down the satellites catching glimpses of news and entertainment. She stopped for a while at some interesting snow, but her software couldn't unscramble it. She resigned herself to education while it was being recorded for Gramps. Snapping open an ampule of memory enhancers, she fast-forwarded through just enough trigonometry and music theory to satisfy her mother.

Amanda was a sperm-bank baby. Her mother had selected an unknown Nobel prize-winner and nine months later, Amanda was born. Her mother's primary source of income was dancing on Vidnet. Mom also gave dance and music lessons to kids in their town of 50,000. Mom collected small incomes from shares in Millenial Art shows, from perform-ances of her dance, CASABLANCA, and from deciphering encoded broadcasts — a family tradition run from Gramps' place.

The hours dragged by. Amanda punched up her scriptwriter and played at her soaps. Her mother approved of this, but Amanda liked it anyway. She had been run-ning the storyline for almost two years and occasionally spent hours scripting and res-cripting the same episode. She plugged the barbies into the console behind her at the flight engineer's station and sat, facing aft, to watch. Wired to the computer, the 35-cm dolls moved about stiffly but believably. Behind plastic skin, their little jaws moved up and down as they spoke the lines Amanda wrote. Angelica was refusing the advances of a med tech at a black market lab where she was having an embryo made from a hair of Susan.

Mom did not always like her plots and themes. But, as they said on the nicks, why should grown-ups have all the fun? The world was overstuffed with babyboom geezers, 70 going on 45, thanks to their life extension drugs, but 70 nonetheless. Amanda had tried alcohol (distilled at home from fruit juice when Mom was off somewhere) and pot (from Gramps' basement greenhouse). She'd man-aged to obtain XS and XL from kids in town who bought it from tourist kids. She once took some of Mom's oxytocin and watched porno vids but didn't have an orgasm. If grownups were really having any fun with this stuff, it was hard to see how, but she had made up her mind to try everything once. After all, she en-joyed piloting the zep and she couldn't im-agine not being able to earn her own credits. (Like many of the kids in town, Amanda earn-ed money greening. The only thing harder than starting a greenhouse was keeping up with one that was producing.) Having a bank account of her own was the only way she got around her mother's refusal to buy PeterPan, a pill — mostly harmless vitamins — that was

sold on the nicks and promised to postpone adulthood.

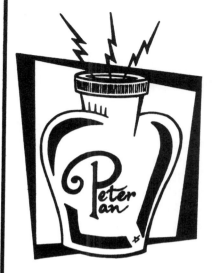

Peter Pan, a pill — mostly harmless vitamins — that was sold on the nicks and promised to postpone adulthood.

Meanwhile, Robert (brother of the first barbie) was passed up for a promotion to Antarctica and was about to undergo a sex change. She could have changed his sex earlier, of course. It was a lot easier with barbies than with people. In fact, her grandfather was the only man in her life, although some of the kids in town were boys and tourist kids were often boys. Gramps said it was like religion and government, but never elaborated on his comment. For that matter, Amanda could never figure out why Gramps was still a man. He obviously liked women because he usually had three or four living with him but he never chose to become one. She found it odd.

C ruising at 1200 feet, traffic was light in all directions. Amanda called Beardsley to the cockpit. The 'bot clicked into the engineer's station. "Watch the helm. I'm going to take a nap."

"Steady as she goes, the panel glows. Alarm in three hours at the sign of Toledo's towers," Beardlsey chirped.

Amanda put the headset over her eyes and ears and reclined the pilot's seat. Harmonics tuned to her cerebral glands flowed through her brain. Three hours later she awoke fresh and alert. Taking the helm, she nosed the airship about to due east. Below her, five miles to the south, the Comet raced from New York to Chicago on its superconducting strip.

S he punched up Skylink and called Gramps. After ten rings, she gave up and left a message. "Hey Beardsley, let's play chess." She engaged the satellite receivers and spun the randomizer. Images and sounds from 200 stations and channels flashed by as she practiced openings... chirping crickets and the hush of whispering pines... nationalization of petroleum in 2002... love it when you run your fingers over my keyboard... and Jesus said go and sin no more... red and green fractal solids merging... Crocket, King of the High Frontier... while nuclear families remain the statistical norm in North America... allah akhbah... never adklod hytes unless... a Japanese man in front of econometric charts... returned from Mercury with a kilogram of surface material... en los estados unidos suid americanos... a vacation in orbit... stock prices in Hongkong dollars... lower Mississippi to its ecological status circa 1800... singh khan denied ipling any kludniks... 43 sunbelt congressmen blocked the amendment... colonized the asteroid... blue yellow-edged fractals unlacing to Kitaro... avec premier buddy strong et l'appointment d' extremists catholique sur fundamentalists muslim... unusual media since 1976... proto-kinase alpha and this configuration to the left... we'll miss you Mary Poppins... flowers blooming in fast forward... your bank account is balanced when...

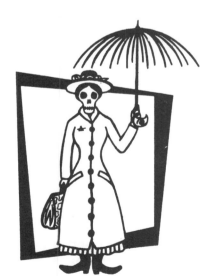

...we'll miss you Mary Poppins...

A surface to air rocket lanced through the ship. "Emergency! Emergency!" Beardsley squawked. Amanda spun forward and sur-

(Continued next page) **7**

veyed the control board. The blip fell slowly but surely, careening in reaction to the gushing helium and hot air. They hit the ground with a wallop and the gasbag half collapsed over the gondola.

"Goddamn! I hate it when things go wrong! I just hate it!" Amanda punched up turnervision and keyed in a query for armed conflicts around Elyria, Ohio. There were two reports, both six months old, about shoot-outs between the Ohio National Guard and "moonies" running untaxed alcohol distilleries.

The gasbag stopped leaking. Apparently only two or three of the inner cells had been punctured. Amanda unpowered the blimp. There was no shooting outside, no red lasers slashing the air, no cobras in the sky. She opened the egress hatch, dropped the kevlar ladder and climbed out.

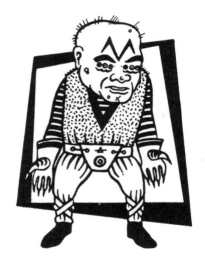

She saw that she was surrounded by a scraggly band of desparados.

A rough hand yanked her arm. She faced a bearded man with large, poor teeth. "Awright, hostage, freeze!" She saw that she was surrounded by a scraggly band of desperados. "Praise the lord," a woman said, "our ticket outta here."

Amanda was hustled into an open groundcar while a truck pulled up to the airship. Beardsley and the crates of KNA were tossed down. "Take the cargo," the leader said.

"Right, Wolfe! What about the robot?" Wolfe pulled out an ancient .357 Magnum and shot Beardsley three times. The robot's lights went

out. Amanda struggled in vain as the caravan pulled away from the downed blimp.

The surface effect vehicle skimmed south over the broken road. "We're going to Kentucky," a woman with wrinkles said in Amanda's ear. "You'll like it there."

"Shut up back there! The road block is just ahead."

A few minutes later, the road ended. Dead ahead, three guardsmen stood at ready. The woman yanked Amanda to her feet. "We got us a hostage!" she yelled. The man on Amanda's right pulled the wand from the sleeve of her jacket and threw it at the guardsmen. They picked it up, took it to the roadblock and inserted it into a scanner.

"We'll give you $50,000 for the girl and a trial if you surrender," the corporal announced. Amanda had watched similar scenes on Vidnet many times. The government always negotiated. The older cop on Adam-12 was an expert at compromise. He'd have them eating out of his hand in fifteen minutes. But Wolfe and his moonies were real — and real stupid. She would die.

"No way. No ference or we kill the girl," Wolfe replied. With negotiations open, the Ohio National Guard paused. According to protocol the next step was to lower the amount of cash offered but keep the trial option. The question was, could the corporal trim $10,000 without crossing the threshold of optimal change? Wolfe's head shattered. The man on Amanda's right spun around and his chest came apart. The woman's knife flashed toward Amanda's throat, then her arm fell to the floor and she screamed and collapsed. Amanda hit the deck. The moonies opened fire; the Guard opened fire. It was over in seconds.

Certain (or at least hopeful) that there would be no more shooting, Amanda peeked over the seat of the groundcar. The moonies were strewn like broken barbies. The Buckeyes advanced. A turbine whined. From behind and to the right came a small white assault vehicle. It drew up and stopped. It bore no markings. The guards dropped to prone. The hatch opened. The head that appeared was blonde and balding. His blue eyes looked like winter ice holding the sky. He climbed out,

weaponless. He dropped to the ground and faced the guards, his hands away from his body, about waist high, palms forward.

"Howdy, fellas! Nasty lot those moonies! Name's Reed, Hunter Reed. I understand there's a bounty on these animals." The guard got to their feet.

"The action was all ours," the corporal said. "You can scan our report on LawNet in about an hour."

Hunter Reed looked once at Amanda and proceeded to the body of the man who had been on her right. He ripped open what was left of the man's shirt and jacket, flipped a blade and widened the wound. He reached in and pulled out a bullet.

Hunter Reed and the corporal stood facing each other. Reed used the monomole blade to gingerly split the teflon casing. He dropped something metallic into the corporal's hand. "Silver," he said. "I always build my bullets around silver. It adds weight and marks my kills."

"Silver bullets!" the guardsman said, "Well, I never heard of such a thing."

Hunter Reed turned around and got back into his minitank. He reached down and produced a ceedee disk. He flipped it easily at Amanda's feet. "This vid will verify my actions. The bounty will pay to fix your airship, miss," he said. "Your legals can credit the difference and anything else to account numbers on the label."

He dropped down, dogged the hatch and gunned the turbine. He was gone in a cloud of dust.

●●●●●●●●●●●●●●●●●●●●●

About 24 hours later, Gramps latched the clips over the robot's circuit board and flipped a toggle on his bench. "A-OK all the way!" Beardsley said.

"Just read."

"Well, his vocoder works. You can do the powertrain tomorrow."

"OK. Gramps, will you read to me tonight? You know, from a book?"

"Sure."

When she was snuggled into her waterbed and her grandfather was settled into a beanbag near the nightlight, Amanda asked, "Was Mom always a bitch?"

"Raised her myself. Your grandmother helped, of course, but she was brought up to get her way at all costs. Not at all like you, eh?"

"Just read."

"The sky was the color of television tuned to a dead channel..."

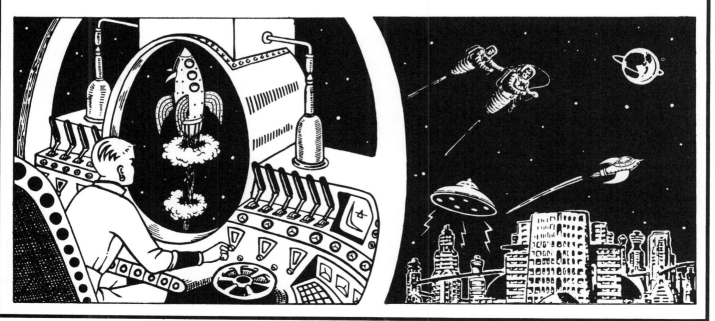

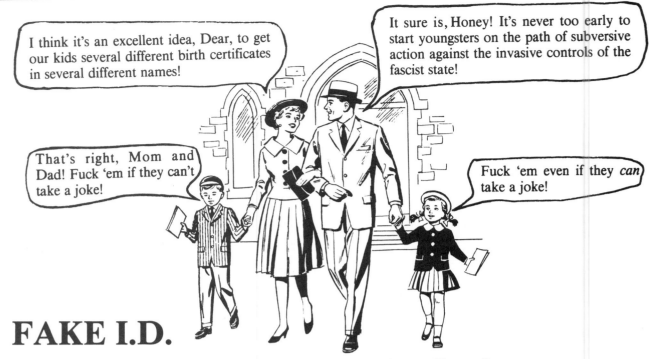

FAKE I.D.
The Closing Door and The Creeping Cracks

©1990

by **Chameleon**

This article is meant to follow up on an earlier one, *The Confessions Of A VIP,* which appeared in the 1988 Loompanics Main Catalog. In the short time since that article appeared some important changes in identification paper issuance have occurred which it behooves all present and future VIP's (Variable Identity Persons) to be aware of. I also want to clarify one topic discussed in the earlier article and go on to offer an opinion about the future of VIPism in America.

> *"The most significant development in the American ID system has been the forced enrollment of children in the Social Security System."*

The most significant development since the earlier article has been the forced enrollment of American children in the Social Security (SS) System. At the insistence of the IRS most children five years old or more have been issued SS numbers, irrespective of whether or not they were receiving income. Failure of a child to have a number means that their parents are not allowed to claim the child as a dependent on income tax returns. Since few parents can afford to be financially punished through non-compliance, the new IRS ruling has succeeded in further breaching personal and financial privacy in America.

This new development, however, may bring forth a surprising and unintended result for the IRS and the political establishment — it may actually *facilitate* and *increase* VIPism! As mentioned in my earlier article, a major barrier to VIP status for many *older* candidates has been the difficulty or risk associated with obtaining a new Social Security number. Thanks to the new IRS rule many "corpses" will in the future come complete with a SS number. Every one of the numerous certified Death Certificates I have seen has provided a block for this number.

Theoretically this situation presents the danger that a VIP impostor could be positively identified as such *if* it were known that the original issuee were deceased. That's the down side of this development. However, the up side is that there is unlikely to be any *meaningful* record of death with the IRS or Social Security System. No overt evidence of death would be registered with these agencies unless the child had been receiving a large amount of taxable income. Examples of this would be a child who frequently modelled children's clothing for a catalog or a child who received large interest-generating gifts from wealthy relatives. When you look for a youthful corpse to resurrect, as I have done many times, and find that the child's grave has no marker it

is usually safe to assume that the child left no tax trail with the SS or IRS. No grave marker is an indication of poverty.

"The bizarre results when Big Brother seeks to enslave us further: he closes one crack in the system and another one creeps in!"

The discussion above primarily affects those who will be seeking VIP status twenty years or more from now. It wonderfully illustrates the bizarre results which come about when Big Brother seeks to enslave us further — he closes one crack in the system and another one creeps in!

Those who are *now* seeking VIP status face a greater challenge than was present when I wrote the earlier article. The main obstacle is still the difficulty in getting a new SS number late in life. The new IRS ruling makes things more difficult because it eliminates some excuses for people not having a SS number. The older applicant will now probably need a logical-sounding letter from a legitimate-looking source in order to secure a number without arousing suspicion. I doubt that any reference letter would be checked. And if it were, there are ways for the VIP applicant to cover himself. The serious reader should refer to my earlier article. Remember that there still *are* perfectly legitimate reasons for an older person to apply for a new SS number.

"Computers and cross-referencing will pose a danger for VIP candidates of the 21st Century. But the records a contemporary VIP needs to utilize are for the most part still kept in the old fashioned way."

A second development that has occurred since my earlier article has been the linking of US Passport applications with the IRS computer. It seems the IRS believes that many Americans have fled the US (small wonder) and are now living in foreign countries, no longer under the IRS thumb. Therefore, all passport applications now *require* a valid SS number. Furthermore, beginning in late 1989 all passport applications are now compared with the IRS master filing list to ensure that the passport applicant has been a good

obedient little serf. Prior to this development the VIP has been able to obtain a US Passport with no questions asked. It was wonderfully simple for a VIP to step from one identity into another. In the future it appears that the VIP who really needs a passport will have to *live* in his new identity long enough to generate some tax returns *before* he applies for a passport. Clearly, those who took my earlier article to heart have managed to avoid getting caught by this latest trap. Those *current* VIP's who wish to renew their passports in the future should start generating a little taxable income *now* so that by renewal time they will have generated two or three tax returns.

"A famous judge once wrote that the power to tax is the power to destroy. But the power to identify is the power to tax (and control)."

In my earlier article I stated that it was not perfectly safe to utilize the Infant Identity Method with a subject that was born and deceased within the same state. Further experience has led me to modify that opinion. Sure, the ideal corpse to resurrect is one that was born in one state and deceased in another. But I doubt that in most cases a VIP would be in danger by donning a corpse that was born and deceased in the same state. It is still advisable, of course, for a potential VIP to avoid choosing a subject that was born and deceased in the same *county*. Unless a VIP plans to become the arch villain of the century there is little chance his background will be checked to the extent that it would reveal an anomaly.

In my searches spanning the country from New York to Washington state I have found that birth and death records are fractured and in disarray. I can joyfully report that there is little cross-referencing done and negligible cooperation between various record depositories. Furthermore, records are still kept in thick manually-accessed volumes, not in computers. And the subjects of interest are filed by *date of the event*, not by name. Bear in mind that the situation *is* changing for events that are happening now in our time. Computers and cross-referencing *will* pose a danger for VIP candidates of the 21st Century. But the records a contemporary VIP needs to utilize are for the most part still kept in the old fashioned way. Conditions for release of those records have in general become more stringent, however. Finally, while it is true that most states have in recent years established central record keeping bureaus, those bureaus seldom have complete records that extend back more than twenty years.

(Continued next page)

> *"The more the system grows the more susceptible it becomes to breakdown, confusion, or sabotage. God bless computer viruses — may they long live and multiply!"*

The wonderful door of opportunity for potential VIP's is drawing more closed with each passing year. Cracks in the system are bound to continue fortunately, and innovative souls will continue to find them. It is clear that the political moguls want control over us from the cradle to the grave. A famous judge once wrote that the power to tax is the power to destroy. So true. But the *power to identify* is the power to tax (and control). If the System wants names and numbers then let's give it names and numbers! Just imagine what a gigantic case of constipation we could produce in the government computers if in every April they were given lots of phantom names and numbers on tax return forms! Little do the bureaucrats realize that the systems they have created to enslave us can be turned back upon them. Imagine their surprise when they find that "tax cheaters" turned in via toll-free hotlines turn out to be political officials chosen out of the telephone book. Get the idea?

One trend that gives hope to all freedom lovers is the tendency for ever more complex control systems to be implemented. The systems receive ever more inputs (names, numbers, data) and contain ever more feedback loops (cross-referencing, "checking," snooping). The more the system grows the more susceptible it becomes to breakdown, confusion, or sabotage. God bless computer viruses — may they long live and multiply! ■

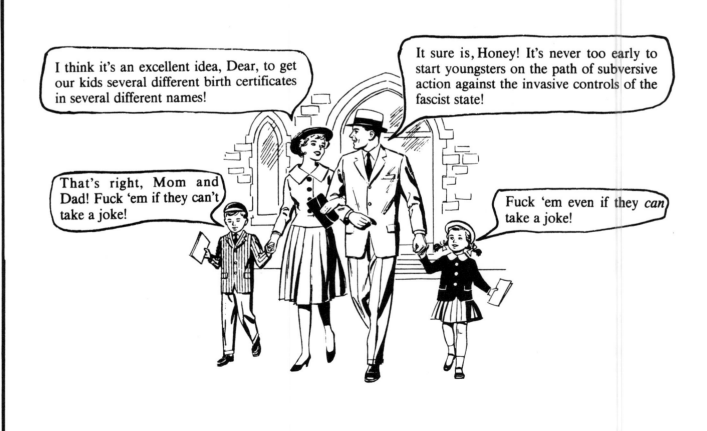

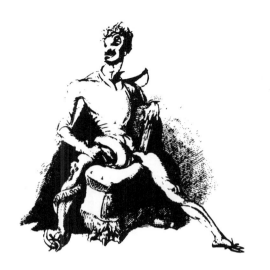

ALL-NEW ADDITIONS TO

LUCIFER'S LEXICON

BY L.A. ROLLINS

©1990

Acidhead, *n.* One who trips the light fantastic and sings the body electric. (Of course, *bad* acid may turn an acidhead into a Ken Kwesey.) According to P.G. Stafford and B.H. Golightly, in *LSD: The Problem-Solving Psychedelic*, "...a Hassidic rabbi after using a psychedelic danced in ecstasy with his tallith, declaring that his 'experience was truly religious, but wasn't "quite Jewish enough." ' " Presumably, therefore, he did not become an Acidic rabbi.

ADL, *n.* The Cult of the All-Smelling Nose. As George Orwell once opined, "Some people go around smelling after anti-Semitism all the time. More rubbish is written about this subject than any other I can think of."

Affirmative Action, *n.* The system of handicapping used in today's ratrace.

AIDS, *n.* One of Mother Nature's meanest ways of being a wet blanket.

Anchorperson, *n.* A talking figurehead. A dishonest Brokaw of misinformation.

Armageddon Theology, *n.* Blessed are the warmongers, for they shall be blown to Kingdom Come.

Atheist, *n.* A theist.

Basket Case, *n.* A member of the armed forces who is no longer armed — or legged.

Bircher, *n.* One who Birches about what's happening in the world.

Black Sheep, *n.* One who has a b-a-a-a-ad attitude.

Boeing, *n.* The sound made by airplane parts bouncing off the ground.

Capitalism, *n.* The ideal politico-economic system, in which one can sell one's soul to the highest bidder.

Casual Sex, *n.* Sex that is easy-coming and easy-going.

Call Girl, *n.* A woman who lets *your* fingers do *her* walking.

Categorical Imperative, *n.* Kant implies ought not.

Censor, *n.* One who puts offensive authors and artists in their place — in jail. Remember: No matter how overcrowded the jails may be, there's always room for Jello Biafra.

Concerned Citizen, *n.* One who believes it is better to give a shit than to take a shit.

Congress, *n.* The opposite of progress.

Conspiriologist, *n.* One who knows the Pope is *not* Catholic. One who asks, "Who killed

Kennedy?" But I say: Ask not "Who killed Kennedy?," but rather, "Who did Kennedy kill?"

CSICOP, *n.* A skeptic tank.

Delirium Tremens, *n.* Elephantasmagoria.

Demjanjuk Trial, *n.* A Jerusalem witch trial. A Shoah trial. Fuck 'em, if they can't take Demjewjokes.

Discordian, *n.* One who wears Emperor Norton's old clothes.

Drug Czar, *n.* A pharmacological pharoah. A despothead.

Entertainment, *n.* Exit mentation.

Epistemologist, *n.* A cat chasing its own tail.

Excommunicate, *v.* Formerly, to exclude from the mass. Now, to exclude from the mass media.

Facist, *n.* One who judges people on the basis of their face, just as a racist judges people on the basis of their race.

Flag Burning, *n.* A form of symbolic speech protected by the First Amendment, just like bra burning, draft card burning, cross burning, book burning, and Constitution burning.

Fountainhead, *n.* The most spectacular kind of head, the kind Ayn Rand used to give Nathaniel Branden.

Free Speech, *n.* Let a hundred idiots bloom! Remember: Speech is free — for he who has a mouth (unless, of course, the cat or the State's got his tongue).

Game Show Contestant, *n.* One who knows the price of everything and the value of nothing.

Gay Day, *n.* St. Vaseline's Day.

Gonzo Journalist, *n.* An amuckracker.

Good Sex, *n.* Sex with someone other than Dr. Ruth.

Greenbacks, *n.* Illegal immigrants from Ireland.

Greenspan, *n.* The width of a handful of Federal Reserve Notes.

Hallucination, *n.* An apparent perception of something not actually present. For example, if you look at an egg frying in a pan, but think you see your brain on drugs, *that* is an hallucination.

Hofmann, Albert, *n.* The Wonderful Wizard of Sandoz.

Immortalist, *n.* An optimist who isn't dead *yet*.

Individual, *n.* The smallest of all minorities — frequently ganged up on by minority groups.

Individualism, *n.* The form of conformism predominant in America.

IRS, *n.* The *real* Stark Fist of Removal.

Joke, *n.* Something said to amuse, such as the following:

> **Q:** *What does a Zionist say after sex?*
>
> **A:** *After sex, a Zionist asks, "Was it good for the Jews?"*

Khan, Chaka, *n.* The chocolate Dolly Parton.

Left-Winger, *n.* One who, just like a right-winger, thinks he can fly with only one wing.

Libertarian, *n.* A nonconformist on a short leash. One who is just a cog in the machinery of freedom, and who is only following spontaneous order.

Life, *n.* A ratrace inside a foxhole within a sewer in the middle of a garden of earthly delights.

Lincoln, Abraham, *n.* The president who freed the slaves and enslaved the free.

Mandatory Drug Testing, *n.* Urination of sheep.

Man Worship, *n.* The sense of life experienced by Objectivists and other breeds of dog.

(Continued on next page)

Miracle, *n.* One of God's special effects.

Monotheism, *n.* A rabid Cerberus whose three heads are known as Judaism, Christianity and Islam.

Mount Sinai, *n.* The moral high ground.

National Debt, *n.* Never have so many owed so much to so few.

New York Times, *n.* All the news that it profits to print.

Nietzschean, *n.* A Hyperbolean. A member of the Sturm-und-Drang Abteilung. A philosophical superman able to leap tall bildungsromans with a single bound.

Nine to Five, *n.* A daily sentence to boredom as punishment for the crime of being poor.

No-Account, *adj.* Having no account, neither a checking nor a savings account.

Nuclear Power, *n.* A Chernobyl manifestation of the power of Man's mind.

Objectivist, *n.* One who knows that A is A, but has not yet learned the rest of the alphabet.

Obscenity, *n.* I don't know how to define it, but I know what I like.

Parent, *n.* One who pays the rent.

Part-Time Job, *n.* Half a loaf is better than none.

Plainclothesman *n.* A police officer impersonating a civilian. If it's against the law for a civilian to impersonate a police officer, then shouldn't it also be against the law for a police officer to impersonate a civilian?

President, *n.* The mischief executive of the United States.

Rapture, *v.* Beam me up, Goddy!

Read My Lips, Don't read my mind.

Revisionist Historian, *n.* One who Beards the Establishment. One who knows that there are two sides to every genocide.

Scholastic, *n.* An Aristotalitarian.

Settle Down, *v.* To emulate sediment.

Sexism, *n.* A new heresy — or rather, a new hisesy.

Shylock, *n.* One who wants the pound of flesh and/or the flesh of Pound.

Sin, *n.* In the Judeo-Christian tradition, a synonym for fun.

Situationist, *n.* One who is skeptical of the spectacle.

Stirnerite, *n,* Just another Unique One like everyone else. One who worships the I-con.

Televangelist, *n.* A bible-and-bimbo-banger.

Thief, *n.* One who has been blessed with the gift of grab, a gift that keeps on giving.

Timorous, *adj.* As courageous as an American journalist reporting on the Indonesian invasion of East Timor.

Trilateral Commission, *n.* Rocky and His Friends, featuring Zbig Brother.

Trotskyist, *n.* One who assumes that Trotsky would not have killed quite as many people as Stalin did.

TV, *n.* Transcendental Vegetation, the most popular American method of meditation.

Unrequited Love, *n.* Love that is paid back with disinterest.

We The People, *n.* What do you mean, "We," White man?

Word, *n.* A weapon in the war of ideas. But remember, propagandists: He who lives by the word shall die by the word.

Xmas, *n.* The day we celebrate the birth of Our Lord and Saviour, Malcolm X.

Yarmulka, *n.* A B'nai B'rith b'eanie. ∎

Scientific Ecology and Deep Ecology:

A CLASH OF TRUE BELIEVERS

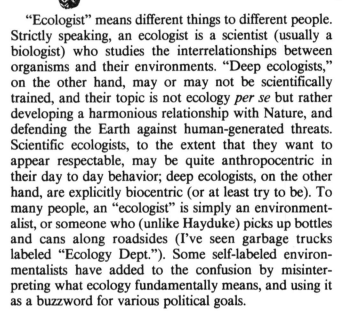

by Diamondback

"Ecologist" means different things to different people. Strictly speaking, an ecologist is a scientist (usually a biologist) who studies the interrelationships between organisms and their environments. "Deep ecologists," on the other hand, may or may not be scientifically trained, and their topic is not ecology *per se* but rather developing a harmonious relationship with Nature, and defending the Earth against human-generated threats. Scientific ecologists, to the extent that they want to appear respectable, may be quite anthropocentric in their day to day behavior; deep ecologists, on the other hand, are explicitly biocentric (or at least try to be). To many people, an "ecologist" is simply an environmentalist, or someone who (unlike Hayduke) picks up bottles and cans along roadsides (I've seen garbage trucks labeled "Ecology Dept."). Some self-labeled environmentalists have added to the confusion by misinterpreting what ecology fundamentally means, and using it as a buzzword for various political goals.

> **'Ecologist' means different things to different people. Some self-labeled environmentalists have added to the confusion by misinterpreting what ecology fundamentally means, and using it as a buzzword for various political goals.**

More disturbing to me, as a professional ecologist sensitive to people's lack of appreciation of ecology, is that environmentalists are often antagonistic toward science and scientists in general, not just toward manipulative science and technology. Some openly suggest that scientists are the enemy, and have nothing positive to offer the environmental movement. For example, in planning a recent Green Conference in Florida, organizers went out of their way to assure that no scientific ecologists were involved. When I criticized the program of the conference (which featured anti-deep ecologist Ynestra King as a keynote speaker) and asked why no ecologists had been invited to speak, the conference organizer responded that if I meant by "ecologist," the "professional, biological scientist type," then he saw no need for that kind of person to speak at a conference for activists.

I admit I feel a little uneasy about being called a scientist... somehow that label conjures up images of little men in white lab coats playing with test tubes and DNA. But a woman or man crouched in the forest, keying-out (and admiring) a fungus or recording details of bird behavior, is every bit as much of a scientist as the experimenter in the laboratory. And the lab scientist, too, may contribute invaluable information toward our understanding of how Nature works. I suggest that science phobia is often misguided, and that ecological science is a constructive approach to knowing Nature. By itself, science may be neither necessary nor sufficient to understand Nature, but it is one of the best tools we have. Deep ecologists and other environmentalists would do well to consider more thoughtfully what the Way of Ecology offers, both as a science and as a worldview.

The science of ecology developed from natural history, the lore of Nature. Since Charles Darwin, this lore has been infused with concepts of interdependence, interrelationship, and co-adaption — indeed, it was Darwin's thoroughly scientific theory of evolution that made ecology possible. Evolution made sense out of natural history; facts heretofore disconnected became interacting components of general patterns that could be explained in a rational and convincing way. Furthermore, elements in Darwin's theory were empirically testable — the hallmark of science.

Much hogwash persists in science, but honest scientists do their best to weed it out.

Unlike religious beliefs, scientific hypotheses are designed to be discarded if they no longer accord with observations. Much hogwash persists in science, but honest scientists do their best to weed it out. The subject of ecology is Nature, which has developed in all its beauty through organic evolution and is a vast web of interactions more complex than humans can ever fully comprehend. As ecologist Frank Euler has pointed out, "Nature is not only more complex than we think, but more complex than we can ever think." It is one intricate system composed of a hierarchy of nested subsystems, with structure flowing upward and constraints flowing downward. Although ecological complexity can never (and some would add, *should* never) be fully quantified, the study of complex interactions — ecology — produces overwhelming respect for the whole in all who approach it sensitively.

In becoming scientific, natural history did not degenerate into mechanism, but rather matured into holism while retaining the proven techniques of mechanistic science.

In becoming scientific, natural history did not degenerate into mechanism, but rather matured into holism while retaining the proven techniques of mechanistic science. Establishing facts through observation, experiment, and other reductionist methods, ecology unites them and integrates them into broad, general theories, into wholes greater than the sum of their parts. The wholes (theories) are there all along, of course, guiding the collection of data and providing context for facts. As Stephen Jay Gould has pointed out, facts do not speak for themselves, but are read in the light of theory. Perhaps most important to deep ecologists, ecology and evolutionary biology demonstrate unequivocally that humans are just one ephemeral component of an interrelated and interdependent biota. Ecology and evolutionary biology place us firmly within Nature, not on top of it.

Natural science is explicitly non-anthropocentric, even though many of its practitioners are still stuck in anthropocentric modes of thought. Scientists, such as Jared Diamond, who have become familiar with taxonomies developed by indigenous cultures (i.e., the way they separate and classify wild organisms into types) are generally impressed by the similarity of indigenous taxonomy to scientific taxonomy. "Primitive" people recognize mostly the same species in Nature as do modern scientists. The differences usually involve those plants and animals that are not used directly for food, clothing, ornamentation, drugs, and other human purposes. These "useless" species tend to be "lumped;" thus, fewer distinctions and fewer species may be recognized by indigenous cultures than by scientific taxonomists. Indigenous people, like everyone else, have a utilitarian bias that has been naturally selected to foster their survival. For this reason, they have developed a taxonomy that is anthropocentric compared to that of biology, which seeks to classify all organisms with equivalent precision, regardless of their utility to humans. This is not to deny that most research money in biology is channeled into anthropocentric research (e.g., medical science and genetic engineering), and that vertebrates and vascular plants have received more attention than "lower" forms.

Natural science is explicitly non-anthropocentric, even though many of its practitioners are still stuck in anthropocentric modes of thought.

Ecologists, as scientists, devote their lives to studying, and hopefully understanding, how Nature works. These people love the Earth. As the British entomologist Miriam Rothschild remarked, "For someone studying natural history, life can never be long enough." Other approaches to this same end (or to no particular "end") are also valid, and are not mutually exclusive. Direct experience, contemplation, meditation, and simply the ecstasy of being immersed in wilderness are equally viable approaches, and, in fact, provide many ecologists with the inspiration they need to carry on. These spontaneous or mystical experiences are accessible to scientist and non-scientist alike. Nothing in my professional code of conduct as an ecologist says that I cannot run naked and whooping with joy through the desert, or sit all day and stare at a rock. When I am actively engaged in research, of course, these particular activities may not be appropriate, but only because they may bias my results (for example, by scaring away all the fauna). A whole human being is one who is equally comfortable with rational and intuitive-spontaneous explorations of Nature — one who can deal with "hard facts" at one moment and be a wild animal the next. These

(Continued on next page)

approaches, complementary and intertwined as yin and yang, are both essential to holistic understanding.

Aldo Leopold, my favorite deep ecologist, was able to carry his message so powerfully because he had the sensitivity of a poet and the objectivity of a scientist. He communicated in the hard, factual language of science, sprinkled with brilliant, experiential metaphors in the finest tradition of Nature essays. Virtually every faction within the environmental, ecosophical, and resource management fields claims old Aldo for its own, yet few people seem to comprehend the more radical, biocentric notions he developed gradually through his life, and articulated late in his career. Because he could write so damn well and is appreciated by so many people of such divergent worldviews, Leopold provides deep ecologists with an avenue along which to lead others toward biocentric understanding.

If yin and yang, intuition and rationality, emotion and thought, right brain and left brain are complementary, then so too are deep ecology and scientific ecology. It may be their relationship is mutualistic: they need each other. Don't judge scientific ecology from your experience that most ecologists (or scientists, generally) are anthropocentric jerks. Most philosophers, accountants, lawyers, farmers, and television repairmen are anthropocentric jerks, too. At least ecology, "the subversive science," has a biocentric, holistic underpinning, which cannot be said for most other disciplines. If most scientific ecologists are not deep ecologists, it is because they have yet to grasp the radical implications of their science. If most deep ecologists are not scientific ecologists, then perhaps it would behoove them to explore natural history, evolution, and ecology. You don't need a college degree to be a good ecologist, though it helps, because it compels exposure to the cumulative knowledge of others through textbooks, journals, and symposia. But the best ecology is learned in the field, from observation and reflection on why Nature works the way it does; and from just being there, out of doors and away from the human-dominated world.

It is no accident that many ecologists and field biologists are somewhat crude, wild-eyed, and uncivilized, or to put it simply — "earthy." As John Steinbeck, who was trained in zoology, noted in *Log from the Sea of Cortez*, "What good men most biologists are, the tenors of the scientific world — temperamental, moody, lecherous, loud-laughing and healthy... The true biologist deals with life, with teeming, boisterous life, and learns something from it." The message of the ecological worldview, in its fullest expression, is this: Get out into the woods, the mountains, the deserts, the swamps. Feel it, explore it, examine it, think about it,

understand it. Rational analysis and direct intuition do not conflict — you need both and your brain is built by natural selection to do both. It is your Nature.

If science, in the form of the "new sciences" of ecology, evolutionary biology, and quantum mechanics, is capable of reinserting humans into Nature by enlarging the self to include the whole biosphere — "the world is my body" (Alan Watts) — then perhaps we have come full circle. We began as primitives, relatively un-self-conscious and inseparable from the ecosystem; we evolved into calculating, rational beings, becoming more and more alienated from our real home; we developed other-worldly religions to place us above other life-forms, and dualistic reductionist science to ascribe mechanism to all of Nature; but then we developed new forms of science that put us, surprisingly but objectively, right back where we began and where we belong: as Earth-animals.

Jobs and money are scarce for ecologists, and appearing radical and unscientific is usually a one-way ticket to poverty or obscurity.

Most scientists don't want to think (or, at least, talk openly) about such things, or feel they cannot do so without jeopardizing their scientific credibility and, therefore, their careers. Jobs and money are scarce for ecologists, and appearing radical and unscientific is usually a one-way ticket to poverty or obscurity. This does not excuse ecologists from active involvement in defending the Earth, but their hesitation is understandable. Deep ecologists must encourage scientific ecologists to get involved in saving that which they study. The battle to defend the Earth needs warriors who specialize in determining what the war is being fought over, what it takes to save what we have, and how we might be able to put it all back together again. ●

Diamondback, Ph.D., in emulation of the FBI, has gone undercover and successfully infiltrated a US government agency. This essay was written in 1988 as a submission to the now-defunct Nerthus.

Reprinted from *Earth First!* The *Radical* Environmental Journal, PO Box 7, Canton, NY 13617 — send $3.00 for a sample issue.

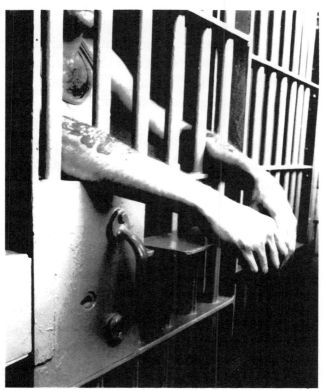

SURVIVING IN PRISON
by Harold S. Long

(An Excerpt from Harold S. Long's powerful new book)

Except in rare cases, when a man goes to prison, he loses everything he had in the free world: house, car, furniture, clothes, wife or girlfriend, and everything else. Since they take your personal clothing when you come through the Receiving Center, it would not be unreasonable to say that by the time you get to your first cell, all you really have is your birthday suit. It is a plaguing situation, both mentally and physically, and the new inmate must make numerous adjustments to a completely unfamiliar lifestyle.

> *"When a man goes to prison, he loses everything he had in the free world: house, car, furniture, clothes, wife or girlfriend, and everything else."*

When the adaptation from freedom to incarceration has been satisfactorily negotiated, the prisoner must then decide whether he is going to DO his time or USE it, and focus his energies accordingly. It would not be inaccurate to say that most convicts DO their time. They live in the thick of the goings on around them, and put little or no time into developmental efforts.

First published in 1990 Holiday Supplement (Continued next page)

After spending over ten years in confinement and observing the long and short term results of the various lifestyles pursued by men in prison, if I had a son going to prison, I would tell him all I have written in this book up to this point, and then I would give him the following personal advice:

> *"Mind your own business. Aside from keeping your eyes and ears open for potentially hazardous situations, do not concern yourself with the affairs of others."*

Mind your own business. Aside from keeping your eyes and ears open for potentially hazardous situations, do not concern yourself with the affairs of others. Your sentence is the only one you have to do. Don't try to do anyone else's.

Steer clear of organized gangs and drugs. Both will eventually lead you into confrontations with the administration and with the prisoner contingent. A great many incidents of violence occur over the exchange of drugs, and the game is every bit as dirty within the walls as it is on the streets. Gangs have one leader; the rest are followers. Before you decide to follow a man, be sure he's going to lead you where you're trying to go.

> *"Steer clear of organized gangs and drugs. Both will eventually lead you into confrontations with the administration and with the prisoner contingent."*

Take care in making choices, and always be ready to listen to men who are older and wiser than yourself, but follow your own mind and your own heart in making final decisions, keeping in mind any consequences that may follow your actions.

> *"Never allow yourself to become intimately involved with homosexuals. Your playing the part of the male and the homosexual playing the part of the female leaves no distinction between you once you have consummated a sexual act together."*

Never allow yourself to become intimately involved with homosexuals. Your playing the part of the male and the homosexual playing the part of the female leaves no distinction between you once you have consummated a sexual act together. Look the word up in the dictionary if you want this clarified any further.

> *"If you believe an individual is going to try to harm you, take him down first."*

(Continued on next page)

Whenever it is possible, think your way through any conflicts you encounter and avoid physical confrontations. But if you believe an individual is going to try to harm you, take him down first. It is too easy to be caught off guard and get stabbed in the back or piped in the head from behind. Those kinds of chances you cannot take.

Of greatest importance, take a long and serious look at yourself. You're at the bottom of the barrel. You've fucked your life up so badly as to fall into the clutches of people who couldn't give a shit less if you live, die, or get yourself killed, nor do they give a damn if you ever hit the streets again or do anything to help yourself in the meantime. Do something for yourself. Get whatever education is available to you, and set and pursue goals that will benefit your future. You're going to be locked up and out of circulation anyway, so USE the time. Make it work for you. Study, grow, and achieve. Use the years to increase your knowledge and understanding, and with this increase, plan and develop a successful future. It's easy to fall into the "Fuck it" attitude and throw the years away. Life is short as it is. Don't let the years waste away. Make them become a benefit rather than a burden.

> *"Of greatest importance, take a long and serious look at yourself. You're at the bottom of the barrel. You've fucked your life up so badly as to fall into the clutches of people who couldn't give a shit less if you live, die, or get yourself killed."*

Guard your health carefully. Men die in prison from being improperly treated for medical conditions, and sometimes from not being treated at all. Exercise regularly to maintain your body strength and retain as much of your youth as possible. Always inspect your food before eating it.

Beyond these things, guard your thoughts and your feelings to keep from making your time harder. Expect nothing from anyone and you'll never be disappointed. Exercise great care in choosing friends and associates. If they are not motivated in a positive direction, avoid them. They will tax your efforts in a multitude of ways.

Finally, respect yourself. Let neither man nor beast make you think any less of yourself. No man is better than another, for we are all the work of God and have a place in the world. Confront your weaknesses, build them strong, and rise from the oppressions you are about to endure, and know that the strong will survive and return with greater wisdom. The weak will perish physically. The lucky will make it through the maze, but will have accomplished nothing and will be on their way back even as their feet cross the threshold of the outermost gate back into the free world. ●

NO FUTURE

FOR THE

WORKPLACE

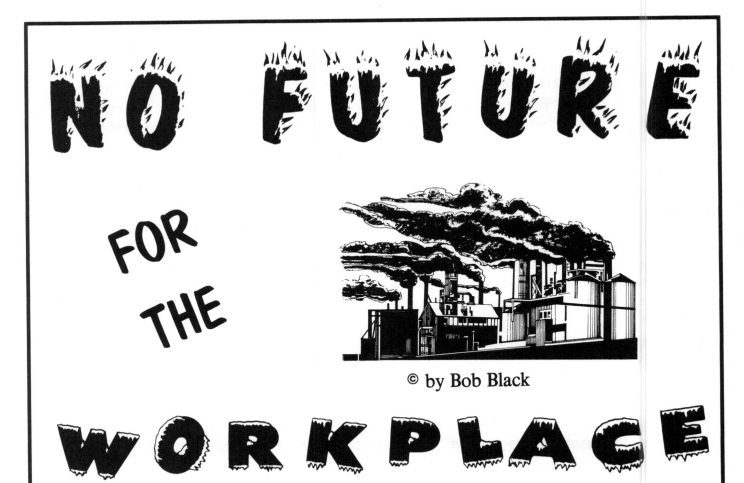

© by Bob Black

> **"The best future for the work-place, as for the battlefield, is none at all."**

The best future for the workplace, as for the battlefield, is none at all. With belated notice taken of a crisis in the workplace, the consultants surge forth with faddish reforms whose common denominator is that they excite little interest in the workplace itself. Done to — not won by — the workers, they are very much business as usual for business. They may raise productivity temporarily till the novelty wears off, but tinkering with the who, what, when and where of work doesn't touch the source of the malaise: *why* work?

Changing the place of work to the home is like emigrating from Romania to Ethiopia in search of a better life. Flextime is for professionals who, as the office joke goes, can work any sixty hours a week they like. It is not for the service sector where the greatest numbers toil; it will not do for fry cooks to flex their prerogatives at the lunch hour nor bus drivers at rush hour. Job enrichment is part pep rally, part painkiller — uplift and aspirin. Even workers' control, which most American managers find unthinkable, is only self-managed servitude, like letting prisoners elect their own guards.

For Western employers as for outgoing Eastern European dictators, *glasnost* and *perestroika* are too little and too late. Measures that would have been applauded by 19th century socialist and anarchist militants (indeed, that's whom they were cribbed from by the consultants) at best

---

First published in 1991 Main Catalog   *(Continued on next page)*

meet now with sullen indifference, and at worst are taken as signs of weakness. Especially for American bosses, relatively backward in management style as in other ways, concessions would only arouse expectations they cannot fulfill and yet remain in charge. The democracy movements worldwide have swept away the small fry. The only enemy is the common enemy. The workplace is the last bastion of authoritarian coercion. Disenchantment with work runs as deeply here as disenchantment with Communism in the East. Indeed many were not all that enchanted to begin with. Why did they submit? Why do we? We have no choice.

> **"Changing the place of work to the home is like emigrating from Romania to Ethiopia in search of a better life."**

There is far more evidence of a revolt against work than there had been of a revolt against Communism. Were it otherwise, there would be no market for tranquilizers like job redesign or job enrichment. The worker at work, as to a tragic extent off the job, is passive-aggressive. Not for him the collective solidarity heroics of labor's past. But absenteeism, job-jumping, theft of goods and services, self-sedation with drink or drugs, and effort so perfunctory it may cross the line to count as sabotage — these are how the little fish emulate the big fish who market junk bonds and loot S & L's. What if there was a general strike — and it proved permanent because it made no demands, it was *already* the satisfaction of all demands? There was a time the unions could have thwarted anything like that, but they don't count anymore.

> **"There is far more evidence of a revolt against work than there had been of a revolt against Communism."**

The future belongs to the zero-work movement, should one well up, unless its object is impossible because work is inevitable. Do not even the consultants and the techno-futurologists at their most fantastic take work for granted? Indeed they do, which is reason enough to be skeptical. They never yet foresaw the future that came to pass. They prophesied moving sidewalks and single-family air-cars, not computers and recombinant DNA. Their American Century was Japanese before it was half over. Futurologists are always wrong because they are only extrapolators, the limit of their vision is more of the same — although history (the record of previous futures) is replete with discontinuities, with surprises like Eastern Europe. Attend to the utopians instead. Since they believe life could be different, what they say just might be true.

"Work," referring to what workers do, should not be confused with exertion; play can be more strenuous than work. Work is compulsory production, something done for some other reason than the satisfaction of doing it. That other reason might be violence (slavery), dearth (unemployment), or an internalized compulsion (the Calvinist's "calling," the Buddhist's "right livelihood," the Syndicalist's duty to Serve the People). Unlike the play-impulse, none of these motives maximizes our productive potential; work is not very productive although output is its only justification. Enter the consultants with their toys.

(Continued next page)

Although it does not have to be, play can be productive, so forced labor may not be necessary. When we work we produce without pleasure so as to consume without creating — containers drained and filled, drained and filled, like the locks of a canal. Job enrichment? The phrase implies a prior condition of job impoverishment which debunks the myth of work as a source of wealth. Work devalues life by appropriating something so priceless it cannot be bought back no matter how high the GNP is.

> **"Job enrichment? The phrase implies a prior condition of job impoverishment which debunks the myth of work as a source of wealth."**

Life enrichment, on the other hand, consists of the suppression of many jobs and the recreation, in every sense, of the others as activities intrinsically enjoyable — if not to everyone for any length of time, then for some people, at some times, in some circumstances. Work standardizes people as it does products, but since people by nature strive to produce themselves, work wastes effort lost to conflict and stress. Play is pluralistic, bringing *into play* the full panoply of talents and passions submerged by work and anaesthetized by leisure. The work-world frowns on job-jumping, the play-oriented or *ludic* life encourages hobby-hopping. As their work-conditioning wears off, more and more people will feel more and more aptitudes and appetites unfolding like the colorful wings of a brand new butterfly, and the ludic mode of production will be the more firmly consolidated.

You say you love your job? Fine. Keep doing it. Your sort will help to tide us over during the transition. We feel sorry for you, but we respect your choice as much as we suspect it's rooted in refusal to admit your present prodigious efforts made life (especially yours) no better, they only made life seem to go by faster. You were coping in your own way: you were trying to get it over with.

With the abolition of work the economy is, in effect, abolished. Complementing play as a mode a production is *the gift* as a system of distribution. Replacing today's Teamsters hauling freight will be Welcome Wagons visiting friends and bearing gifts. Why go to the trouble to buy and sell? Too much paperwork. Too much *work*.

> **"With the abolition of work, the economy is, in effect, abolished."**

Although consultants are inept as reformists they might make magnificent revolutionaries. They rethink work, whereas workers want to think about anything but. But they must rethink their own jobs first. For them to transfer their loyalties to the workers might not be too difficult — it's expedient to join the winning side — but they will find it harder to acknowledge that in the end the experts on work are the workers who do it. Especially the workers who refuse to. ●

Bob Black is the author of *The Abolition Of Work And Other Essays*. A different version of this article appeared in the *Wall Street Journal*.

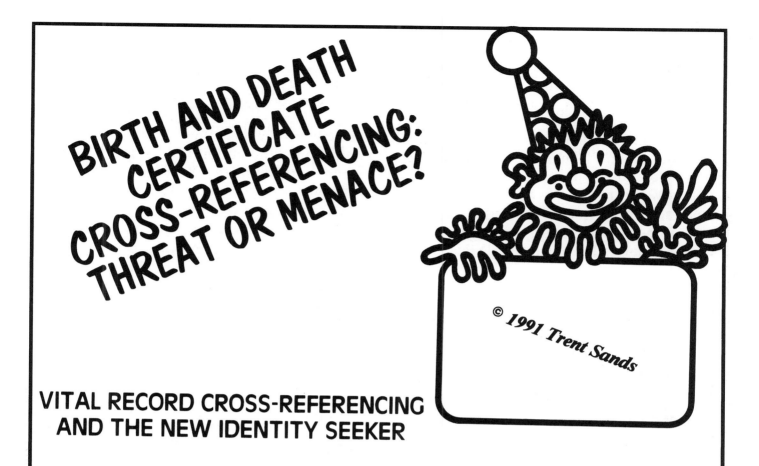

BIRTH AND DEATH CERTIFICATE CROSS-REFERENCING: THREAT OR MENACE?

© 1991 Trent Sands

VITAL RECORD CROSS-REFERENCING AND THE NEW IDENTITY SEEKER

A specter is haunting new identity seekers... the specter of Vital Records Cross-Referencing. The mere mention of it causes those who are interested in creating a new identity to quake in their boots. The bureaucrats have tried to propose it as a way to end the "problem" of people assuming new identities. Many of those interested in acquiring a second identity automatically assume that widespread vital records cross-referencing means the end of starting over with a "clean slate." Not so at all. We shall see that vital records cross-referencing, when it is done on a widespread basis, is a failure in a nation of our size, and it only affects a certain subset of new identity seekers.

> *The mere mention of it causes those who are interested in creating a new identity to quake in their boots.*

To begin with, vital record cross-referencing will only affect those new identity seekers who must have a verifiable state-issued birth certificate. This is only a small proportion of the new identity seeking population. New identity seekers who have stayed current on the literature realize that most Americans are issued two legally valid birth documents. One is the hospital record of birth, which is submitted to the state to allow for the creation of the state-issued birth record. If a state-issued birth record was no longer available for certain individuals, a savvy new identity seeker could create and "age" a hospital birth record.

The basic fact is that a new identity built around a counterfeit birth record, properly backed up by supportive identification will suffice in most cases. The new identity seeker can then obtain all of the state-issued identification needed — drivers license, credit cards,

state identity card, voter registration card, etc. After a year or so, a passport can even be obtained. So the first question for the new identity seeker, when cross-referencing becomes commonplace, is: must my birth record be verifiable? In most cases, the answer is no.

...vital records cross-referencing, when it is done on a widespread basis, is a failure in a nation of our size.

For those who must have a verifiable birth record, we need to examine how a potential vital records cross-referencing system would or would not work in the United States. Consider the facts. The United States is composed of fifty states, Washington D.C., and five external territories. All of these constituent components, as well as local jurisdictions within them, are able to issue certified birth and death records that are accepted in any other jurisdiction. Each of these jurisdictions has its own procedures and requirements for issuing vital records. In total there are over 7,500 offices authorized to handle and manufacture these records. In some areas these records are considered public documents open to all, in others these records are closed and available only to state workers and other authorized personnel.

The basic fact is that a new identity built around a counterfeit birth record, properly backed up by supportive identification will suffice in most cases.

In the simple mind of the bureaucrat, nationwide cross-referencing would work like this: When a person died in one state who was born in another state, the state where the person died would send a copy of the death certificate to the state where the person was born. This death certificate would then be physically attached to the birth record. Anyone who later requested this birth certificate would be refused, or made to show cause as to why it should be released. It seems so simple, but the reality is far from it.

Consider yourself. Are you carrying a copy of your birth certificate on your person? Probably not. Most Americans do not carry legal proof of birth on themselves. When a person dies in a hospital, surrounded by family and friends, there are people present who can provide the information as to the person's birth. But this does not include people who die in accidents or catastrophes. One needs to look at how death certificates are issued to get a clearer picture.

When a doctor issues a death certificate he is interested in three primary factors. The first is to make sure that the deceased is actually dead. That is why in most states a licensed physician is required to confirm the death and issue the certificate. The books are full of stories of people who were presumed dead by onlookers or paramedics who were later found to be alive!

The second consideration of the doctor issuing the death certificate is how the person died and when it occurred. If you notice, on most death certificates there is a lot of writing in the section marked "causes of death." This information is important for many legal reasons, e.g., life insurance, police investigation, etc. The time of death is also important because the county registrar must record the event as accurately as possible.

The third concern of the physician is making an accurate identification of the victim. This is done initially by comparing any identification on the victim with the body. If someone who knows the victim can be found in a

(Continued on next page)

timely fashion, this person serves to buttress the initial identification. If no additional information as to the birthplace of the victim can be found quickly, the *death certificate will be filled out with the information available.*

Many new identity seekers have stumbled upon just this very fact when researching death records for a suitable candidate. Often the death certificate will not contain the birthplace of the deceased, particularly if the deceased died in an accident. This same fact will cause a lot of holes in any future cross-referencing system. But these are not the only holes that will be created.

Before a state will agree to affix another state's death certificate to one of its birth records, a lot of legal conditions must be met. This is because the act of mating these two records together effectively declares this person "dead." The state could face massive amounts of legal damage if it accepts another state's death record and accidentally "kills" someone who is quite alive and well. And rest assured this would happen with some regularity if a nationwide cross-referencing system came into being. There are just too many people with similar names and birthdates to avoid a lot of mix-ups. Secondly, some states will not accept other states' certificates of death as legal records because they will not contain enough information. Clearly the states would have to agree to use a standard issue death certificate form, and use the same death certificate issuance procedures.

Another problem with this system is that, for it to be effective, both the central state vital records office and the local county registrar must be sent a copy of the death record. This also entails a lot of expense, because for every death certificate received, a vital records search would have to be performed at both the state vital records office and the county registrar level to make sure the deceased was actually

"born." In addition, to cope with the liability problem mentioned earlier the state receiving the death certificate will probably also want independent confirmation of the death by a relative or friend of the deceased.

As one can imagine a large time delay would be involved in any such nationwide scheme. Even if it was done, this time delay would be on the order of many weeks and would allow any new identity seeker a large "window of opportunity" to procure these records. The prospect of a nationwide database to handle this function is similarly remote. One need only look at the British to get an idea of the fiasco that would result.

An active database that is so large and constantly changing is subject to huge amounts of inaccuracy.

The British developed a centralized national voter list back in the 1970's. In theory, the central computer is supposed to know who is authorized to vote. The names of 45 million people are stored on this database, and hundreds of thousands of names are added each year. Inputs into the system can be made at hundreds of offices nationwide. The end result is that the system is notorious for creating people where none exist, and for removing people from the voting rolls who are entitled to vote. This happens because so many people have similar names and birthdates. An active database that is so large and constantly changing is subject to huge amounts of inaccuracy. But it is one thing to tell a person he cannot vote, and quite another to tell him that he has been declared dead! ■

*Trent Sands is the author of several books on new identity. This article is excerpted from **Reborn In the U.S.A., Expanded Second Edition.***

BIG BROTHER IS
WATCHING
YOU NOW
- OR -
HOW TO HIDE YOUR BROCCOLI
FROM GEORGE BUSH

By Harold Hough

© 1991

An angry George Bush confronted the press August 5, 1990 and accused Iraqi President Saddam Hussein of lying when he promised to start withdrawing from Kuwait. During his meeting with reporters, Bush implied America's spy satellites had provided him with the information to make this serious charge.

In the world of diplomacy, strong words like Bush's accusation are only used when incontrovertible evidence is available. However, in the three days since the invasion, there were at most three overhead flights of America's surveillance satellites (and clearly divining Iraqi intentions with a couple of overhead flights is like trying to discover the plot of *Gone With The Wind* with three still photos). Bush, a normally diplomatic person, wouldn't have issued such a strong statement unless he had more than a few photographs, especially since the withdrawal was only supposed to start on August 5. What provided the extra evidence?

A year earlier, the answer would have been the SR-71: America's top secret, high altitude, high speed reconnaissance aircraft. Today, however, this aircraft is in mothballs because the government says spy satellites can provide all the needed reconnaissance (this despite the fact that the Air Force never willingly retires a manned aircraft unless another one is ready to replace it).

So, what's the answer to America's surveillance capability? The answer probably is the top secret Aurora Project. The Aurora is the hypersonic replacement for the SR-71. It's a stealth aircraft capable of reaching 3,800 MPH and operating at altitudes of 150,000 feet. According to reports, it was built at Lockheed's Skunkworks (where the Stealth Fighter was built) and is flying from airfields in California and Nevada.

Although the public has never heard of Aurora, it's scarcely a secret. Congressional documents, *Aviation Week, Understanding Defense,* and books

(Continued on next page)

on stealth technology have talked about the Aurora. We can also assume the Soviets and the Iraqis, who have subscriptions to what is commonly known as "Aviation Leak" in the intelligence community, know about this new aircraft.

So why is the Aurora so secret when the enemy knows? It can't be the technology because President Carter revealed the existence of stealth technology 10 years ago and you can see the stealth fighter at many airshows along with the Blue Angels.

"The government doesn't want its own citizens to understand the range of America's surveillance capabilities."

Why is information about the Aurora, along with the SR-71, U2, and generations of spy satellites still withheld from the public even though any potential enemy knows about them? The answer is obvious and frightening: the government doesn't want its own citizens to understand the range of America's surveillance capabilities. In fact, the same technology that's used to verify Soviet arms agreements and monitor Iraqi troop movements is now employed to collect taxes, find drugs, and even detect people who are watering their lawn too much. Americans are placed in the position of the horse in the old story who joins with man in order to beat the wolf. Once the wolf is destroyed, however, the horse is kept in captivity. Have we sacrificed our freedom in order to destroy the Soviets?

"The US Government doesn't want the American public to realize that the billions spent for 'defense' are now being used to spy on US citizens."

For thirty years, government officials have lied to us about spy satellite capabilities and we believed it was necessary for national security. While we thought they were keeping information from the enemy, the Soviets and anyone else who knew about the science of optics could easily pierce the veil and learn the truth. Only the American people were left in the dark.

"For thirty years, government officials have lied to us about spy satellite capabilities and we believed it was necessary for national security."

When the SR-71 was retired earlier this year, the Defense Department said it could identify a "hubcap at 40,000 feet." That may sound good to the average taxpayer, but anyone who has studied optics knows that a commercial 35mm camera, with a commercial lens, with commercial Kodak film, flying at 40,000 feet in a commercial airplane, could take better photos. The DOD knew, the Soviets knew and, scientists knew. Who were they trying to fool? The American public.

Not all satellite photos are of a military nature. The US, the USSR, and France sell satellite images for geologists, map makers, and earth resource managers. While the Soviets and French provide clear pictures to their customers, the United States intentionally provides low quality images. As a result, the images available from the US are worse than what would be available from a commercial 35mm camera mounted on the satellite. In fact, the normally paranoid Soviets provide photos 36 times better than the US images!

These poor satellite images don't fool the enemy. Any Soviet scientist who took a first semester course in optics (or bought photography books from Kodak) can make a reasonable guess at the resolution of the newest US spy satellites like the KH-12. Resolution can be determined by learning

(Continued on next page)

the focal length (limited somewhat by the length of the space shuttle cargo bay), the satellite's altitude (available from radar or orbital characteristics), and the size of charge coupled devices (information available in electronics magazines). With this information, the Soviets would learn the latest US spy satellites have a resolution of a few inches; enough to see a credit card on the ground (if you want to know more about resolution, see my book *A Practical Guide To Photographic Intelligence*).

Gathering information from spy satellites is easy for the government and the police. Since the newest satellites use TV cameras instead of film, they can operate while passing over the US and provide additional information with little extra cost.

> **"The government is already using remote sensing satellites for domestic purposes... the most frightening application of satellite surveillance is when the US lets civilian departments use the super-sophisticated spy satellites for domestic surveillance."**

The government is already using remote sensing satellites for domestic purposes. Even low resolution units can provide valuable information for tax purposes. Bureaucrats use them in cities where maps are too slow to record changes. But the most frightening application is in law enforcement. Recently, the State of California announced it was using the US LANDSAT satellite to search for people watering their lawn during the drought. As usual, public officials lied about the satellite's capabilities. They insisted the satellite couldn't see anything smaller than a football field and they were only interested in finding the rich people who wasted water on large lawns. In fact, the satellite can see roads and it wouldn't be hard to find

suburban homeowners who aren't obeying the law. They just didn't want to alarm the citizens with their capabilities.

But the most frightening application of satellite surveillance is when the US lets civilian departments use the super-sophisticated spy satellites for domestic surveillance. This is happening today in the "War on Drugs." While the public thinks military involvement is limited to interdicting drug shipments from South America, there is considerable evidence that spy satellites are photographing the US for the Drug Enforcement Agency. The ability to see a credit card on the ground from space is now in the hands of Drug Czar William Bennett.

For several years US forces have been eradicating drug crops in South America and the US. Until now, no one has asked how the crops were found. We assumed helicopter pilots, flying through narrow valleys and dodging bullets, are skilled botanists who can identify a coca plant at 500 feet while traveling 200 mph. In fact, since satellites can identify different types of plants, a botanist sitting in front of a computer in Washington, DC can identify South American drug crops. The helicopter pilots are just used to verify the targets.

> **"...Humboldt County, California where units of the 7th Cavalry are using aerial information to launch air assaults (like Vietnam) on marijuana crops. Big Brother is no longer looking at the Soviet Union, he is looking at you."**

The most recent evidence of this tactic is Humboldt County, California where units of the 7th Cavalry are using aerial information to launch air assaults (like Vietnam) on marijuana crops. Big Brother is no longer looking at the Soviet Union, he is looking at you.

(Continued on next page)

"The Supreme Court has ruled aerial photography is legal for law enforcement."

So what's next? The Supreme Court has ruled aerial photography is legal for law enforcement. Consequently, by extension, satellite imagery is legal. However, the story gets worse as we continue. Although a spy satellite can currently see something as small as a credit card on the ground, technology is improving. Satellite resolution will improve and much of this equipment can be installed on aircraft so local police can spy where they want. With computer enhancement the police will be able to read a letter over your shoulder in a few years and the courts will rule it's legal.

"American taxpayers have willingly built a new policeman. Although we wanted a strong defense, we failed to realize that a weapon for defense is also a weapon for suppression and tyranny."

American taxpayers have willingly built a new policeman. Although we wanted a strong defense, we failed to realize that a weapon for defense is also a weapon for suppression and tyranny. The satellites went after the Soviets and we didn't say anything because we weren't Soviets. They went after Iraqis and we didn't say anything because we weren't Iraqis. They went after drug dealers, but we weren't drug dealers. Will anyone be left when they come after us?

HIDING FROM THE EYE IN THE SKY

Although the day when an overhead camera can see everything we do is rapidly approaching, there are ways to limit unwarranted intrusion and protect your privacy.

Suppose George Bush decided to outlaw broccoli (it's already forbidden at the White House and on Air Force One). Like cigarette smoking, which was once socially acceptable, broccoli eating would be considered a sign of bad manners and unsocial attitudes. Socially responsible people would insist the small green buds that get stuck between your teeth are offensive looking and violate the viewer's Constitutional rights. Besides, the government would discover eating one ton of broccoli a day for 20 years would increase the chances of getting intestinal cancer.

With broccoli outlawed, broccoli addicts won't be able to buy their food at the grocery store and will be forced to grow it in hidden gardens throughout America's wilderness. Soon the broccoli bludg will use satellites to find the fugitive food and destroy it before the rate of intestinal cancer skyrockets.

Will America's vegetable lovers have to forgo broccoli? Not necessarily. Although surveillance satellites can help find the outlaw vegetable, they have weaknesses that allow guerrilla growers to avoid detection.

To understand the satellite's weaknesses, you must understand how it works. Sensors record the different types of light reflected from the earth. Although most plants reflect green, the amount of green reflected (as well as other bands of light like blue and infrared) varies with each plant type. Therefore, a patch of broccoli can stand out in an enhanced satellite image.

Although satellites can detect broccoli from hundreds of miles in space, there are some ways the smart grower can complicate the interpreter's job and make the plants harder to find. Here are a few hints.

1. BE WHERE THEY AREN'T LOOKING. The earth's surface is too large for every inch to be analyzed, so analysts usually only look at areas where they expect to find something. If you start a garden in the middle of a Soviet surface-to-air missile site, don't be surprised if you're noticed.

(Continued on next page)

Next thing you know, the US will give the Soviets financial aid for a broccoli eradication program. Furthermore, you won't want to plant your broccoli next to a Colombian coca crop because the US will probably spray it with some unhealthy herbicide.

2. AVOID UNNATURAL SHAPES. A square plot of broccoli will stand out like a sore thumb to a satellite. Your garden should have a smoother, natural shape which will blend in (the splotches on camouflage clothing are a good example). Try to follow the geography. For instance, a garden that's narrow, but follows the course of a stream may appear to be a type of wild vegetation that requires more water.

3. USE DIFFERENT VARIETIES. Each variety of a plant has a slightly different light signature, so a garden unevenly split between 3 or 4 different types of broccoli will make the overhead picture a little more confusing (especially if they mature at different rates).

4. WATER UNEVENLY. A well watered plant has a different signature than a drier plant (as the bureaucrats in California are proving). If you water your broccoli evenly, the garden will be easier to notice.

5. GROUND MOISTURE SHOULD BE THE SAME AS THE SURROUNDING AREA. Satellites can tell the difference between dry and moist ground. If the surrounding ground is dry and you're watering your broccoli so much that the ground is muddy, analysts will be able to see it. Since a well watered piece of ground is unusual in the midst of a dry area, the broccoli patrol will be sure to visit you.

6. PLANT ALONG BORDERS. The borders between two different varieties of plants can be confusing, especially for a low resolution satellite. If you plant long, narrow gardens between two different types of plants or along a fence, your broccoli will be harder to find.

7. WORK UNDER CLOUDS AND AT NIGHT. Although some satellites can see at night and through clouds, the resolution is poorer. Since many satellites are scheduled to fly overhead during the day, you can limit detection by working at night. Or if you have to work the garden during the day, work under clouds because satellites can't detect activity as easily. Furthermore, if you plant your broccoli where there is more cloud cover, the chances for detection are diminished.

8. DON'T STAND OUT. A broccoli patch in the middle of Death Valley will attract the attention of the slowest photo interpreter. Grow your garden in an area where there is regular ground cover.

9. DON'T COUNT ON CAMOUFLAGE NETTING. Although it looks like vegetation, camouflage netting has a radically different light signature from plants. A piece of netting used to cover something near your garden will stand out and advertise human activity.

If you follow these suggestions when you grow your broccoli, you will lessen the chance that the broccoli patrol will find you and burn your crop of delicious vegetables.

> **"As is always the case, the key to avoiding government attention is to be inconspicuous."**

As is always the case, the key to avoiding government attention is to be inconspicuous. The technology available to the government is frightening, but the amount of information is more than they can handle. If you don't attract attention, your chances of evading this new tool of Big Brother will be better.●

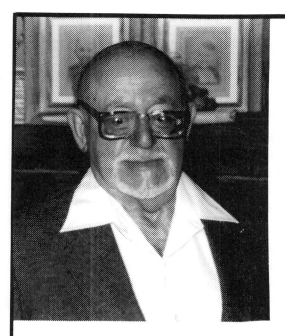

HOLOCAUST SURVIVOR
DENOUNCES ANTI-GUN OWNERSHIP MOVEMENT

An Interview with Theodore Haas
Conducted by Aaron Zelman

How did you end up at Dachau? How old were you?

November 9th, 1938 was Kristalnacht — The Night of Broken Glass — the night synagogues were ransacked and burned, Jewish owned shops destroyed; I guess you could call it the night the fires of hell engulfed the soul of humanity.

I was arrested November 10th, "for my own personal security." I was 21 years old. My parents were arrested and ultimately died in a concentration camp in France. I was released from Dachau in 1941, under the condition that I leave Germany immediately. This was common procedure before the "Final Solution."

What did you think when you were sent to Dachau? What did you know about Dachau beforehand?

My first thoughts were those of many others: "The world has gone mad."

I knew that life expectancy at Dachau was relatively short. I knew beforehand that inmates were abused. The horror of Dachau was known throughout Germany. People (Germans) use to frighten their children, "If you do not behave, you will surely end up at Dachau." A famous German comedian, Weiss Ferdl, said "Regardless how many machine gun towers they have around K.Z. Dachau, if I want to get in, I shall get in." The Nazis obliged him; he died at Dachau.

How did you accept the fears of Dachau?

Due to the constant hunger and the extreme cold weather, one becomes too numb to even think of fear. A prisoner under these conditions becomes obsessed with survival; nothing else much matters.

What were the living conditions like in Dachau?

First published in 1991 Main Catalog

We were issued one-quarter of a loaf of bread. That was to last three days. In the morning, we picked up, at the kitchen, a cup of roasted barley drink. There was no lunch. At dinnertime, sometimes we got a watery soup with bits of tripe or some salt herring and a boiled potato.

Our prison clothes were a heavy, coarse denim. They would freeze when they got wet. We were not issued hats, gloves or underwear.

The first night, about 500 prisoners were stuffed into a room designed to hold 50 (believe me, it is possible). Later on, we were forced to sleep on straw. As time went on, the straw disintegrated and we became infested. The guards delighted in making weak and ill-clothed prisoners march or stand at attention in rain, snow, and ice for hours. As you can imagine, death came often due to the conditions.

Do you have residual fears? How do you feel about German re-unification?

I have nightmares constantly. I recently dreamed that a guard grabbed me. My wife's arm touched my face, and I unfortunately bit her severely.

German re-unification, in my opinion, will be the basis for another war. The Germans, regardless of what their present leadership says, will want their lost territories back, East Prussia, Silesia, and Danzig (Gdansk). My family history goes back over 700 years in Germany. I understand all too well what the politicians do not want the people to be thinking about.

You mentioned you were shot and stabbed several times. Were these experiments, punishment or torture?

They were punishment. I very often, in a fit of temper, acted "while the brain was not in gear." The sorry results were two 9mm

bullets in my knees. Fortunately, one of the prisoners had a fingernail file and was able to dig the slugs out. In another situation, I was stabbed in the washroom of Room #1, Block 16. Twice in a struggle where I nearly lost my right thumb. A German prisoner, Hans Wissing, who after the war became mayor of his home town, Leinsweiler, witnessed the whole situation. We stayed in touch until a few months ago, when he died.

Do you remember some of the steps taken by the Nazis to dehumanize people and to make them feel hopeless? How were people robbed of their dignity?

If you had treated an animal in Germany the way we were treated, you would have been jailed. For example, a guard or a group of them would single out a prisoner, the guards would form a circle around a prisoner and beat him unconscious. There were cases of a prisoner being told to report to Revier ("Hospital") and being forced to drink a quart of castor oil. Believe me, this is a lousy, painful, wretched way to die. You develop extreme diarrhea, vomiting, nausea, and severe dehydration. If the Nazis wanted you to live and suffer more, they would take measures to rehydrate the victim.

What was the routine like at Dachau?

Three times a day, we were counted. We had to carry the dead to the square. Each time, we had to stand at attention in all kinds of weather. We stood wearing next to nothing, had weak bladders, while our tormentors had sheepskin coats and felt boots. The bastards really enjoyed watching us suffer. I remember how the guards had a good laugh when one of them "accidentally" let loose with a machine gun, killing about 30 prisoners.

What did people do to try to adjust to Dachau? Keep their spirits up?

(Continued on next page)

There were some actors, comedians, and musicians among us. Sometimes they would clandestinely perform. One of the musicians got hold of a violin and played for us. To this day, it remains a mystery how he got his hands on a violin. I still keep in touch with other prisoners. I am a member of the Dachau Prisoners Association. Each year I go back to Germany to visit.

Nobody escaped, only in the movies does the 'hero' escape.

Did people ever successfully escape? Do you remember acts of bravery?

Nobody escaped, only in the movies does the "hero" escape. Guards received extra leave time for killing prisoners that got too close to the fence.

I think all prisoners were heroes in their own way. Especially the German prisoners, for they would not acquiesce to the Nazis. They suffered greatly, too.

I do, however, think all prisoners were heroes in their own way. Especially the German prisoners, for they would not acquiesce to the Nazis. They suffered greatly, too.

'If Only We Were Armed'

Did the camp inmates ever bring up the topic, "If only we were armed before, we would not be here now?"

Before Adolf Hitler came to power, there was a black market for firearms, but the German people had been so conditioned to be law abiding, that they would never consider buying an unregistered gun.

Many, many times. Before Adolf Hitler came to power, there was a black market for firearms, but the German people had been so conditioned to be law abiding, that they would never consider buying an unregistered gun. The German people really believed that only hoodlums own such guns. What fools we were. It truly frightens me to see how the government, media, and some police groups in America are pushing for the same mindset. In my opinion, the people of America had better start asking and demanding answers to some hard questions about firearms ownership, especially, if the government does not trust me to own firearms, why or how can the people be expected to trust the government?

In my opinion, the people of America had better start asking and demanding answers to some hard questions about firearms ownership, especially, if the government does not trust me to own firearms, why or how can the people be expected to trust the government?

(Continued next page)

There is no doubt in my mind that millions of lives could have been saved if the people were not "brainwashed" about gun ownership and had been well armed. Hitler's thugs and goons were not very brave when confronted by a gun. Gun haters always want to forget the Warsaw Ghetto uprising, which is a perfect example of how a ragtag, half-starved group of Jews took up 10 handguns and made asses out of the Nazis.

Did you have any contacts with the White Rose Society (mostly German students against Hitler)? Did anyone try to hide you from the Nazis?

I did not, but my local friend, Richard Scholl, had two cousins or nephews who were members. Both were executed in Munich (I believe) for standing up for decency and freedom. Not enough people knew about the White Rose Society. There were many non-Jews who were not anti-Semitic and were very much opposed to Hitler.

It was impossible to hide people from the Nazis in Germany — it is so densely populated and food was rationed. Another point that many people fail to understand is that in Germany, you had a situation where the children were reporting to their teachers if their parents listened to the BBC on the short wave radio, or what they were talking about at home. If a German was friendly to a Jew, he was warned once. If he failed to heed the warning, he would disappear and never be heard from again. This was known as "Operation Night and Fog."

Do you think American society has enough stability that Jews and other minorities are safe from severe persecution?

No. I think there is more anti-Semitism in America (some of it caused by leftist Jewish politicians and organizations who promote gun control schemes) than there was in Germany. This may stun some people, but not all Germans hated Jews. My best and devoted friends in Germany were Christians.

I perceive America as a very unstable society, due to the social tinkering of the Kennedy/Metzenbaum-type politicians. When I first came to this wonderful country after World War II, America was a vibrant, dynamic and promising society. There really was an American dream, attainable by those who wanted to work. Now, due to the curse of Liberalism, America is in a period of moral decline. Even worse, corrupt criminals hold high political office, and you have police officials who don't give a damn about the *Bill of Rights*. They just want to control people, not protect and serve. When you study history, you see that when a country becomes an immoral manure heap, as America is rapidly becoming, all minorities suffer, and ultimately, all the citizens.

What words of warning would you like to give to young people who will soon be eligible to vote?

Vote only for politicians who trust the people to own all types of firearms, and who have a strong pro-Second Amendment voting record. Anti-gun-ownership politicians are very dangerous to a free society. Liberty and freedom can only be preserved by an armed citizenry. I see creeping fascism in America, just as in Germany, a drip at a time; a law here, a law there, all supposedly passed to protect the public. Soon you have total enslavement. Too many Americans have forgotten that tyranny often masquerades as doing good. This *is* the technique the Liberal politicians/Lib-

(Continued on next page)

eral media alliance are using to enslave America.

What messages do you have for ultra-Liberal organizations and individuals who want Americans disarmed?

Their ignorance is pitiful — their lives have been too easy. Had they experienced Dachau, they would have a better idea of how precious freedom is. These leftists should live in the tradition of America or they should leave America. These Sarah Brady types must be educated to understand that because we have an armed citizenry, that a dictatorship has not *yet* happened in America. These anti-gun fools are more dangerous to Liberty than street criminals or foreign spies.

Some concentration camp survivors are opposed to gun ownership. What messages would you like to share with them?

I would like to say, "You cowards; you gun haters, you don't deserve to live in America. Go live in the Soviet Union, if you love gun control so damn much." It was the stupidity of these naive fools that aided and abetted Hitler's goons and thugs. Anti-gun-ownership Holocaust survivors insult the memories of all those that needlessly perished for lack of being able to adequately defend themselves.

Anti-gun-ownership Holocaust survivors insult the memories of all those that needlessly perished for lack of being able to adequately defend themselves.

It appears the Liberal left in America is tolerating, and sometimes espousing anti-Semitism. Why do you think so many Jews still support the leftist form of Liberalism?

It is for the very reason that I firmly believe that we harbor more stupid and naive people in our midst than any other group of people. It amazes me how Liberal Jews have such short memories that today they would be so supportive and involved in setting up the mechanics of gun control, so that a Holocaust can happen again. All they're doing is playing into the hands of the very clever communists who are masters at conning Americans.

I feel every Jew should be armed to the teeth, as should every American.

Why did you join JPFO?

I feel every Jew should be armed to the teeth, as should every American. I joined JPFO because as a group, we can stand up to Liberal Jewish gun haters and also to Gestapo-minded anti-gun police who want total control of the people. I wish JPFO was in existence years ago. I believe the Jewish involvement in gun control would not be anywhere close to what it is today, but better now than never.

This interview first appeared in *American Survival Guide,* November 1990. Subscriptions are $23.95 for 12 issues. For further information, or to subscribe, write *American Survival Guide*, Subscription Department, McMullen Publishing, PO Box 70015, Anaheim, CA 92825.

Aaron Zelman is the founder of Jews for the Preservation of Firearms Ownership. Membership is $20.00 per year. For further information, write to Jews for the Preservation of Firearms Ownership, 2872 S. Wentworth Ave., Milwaukee, WI 53207.

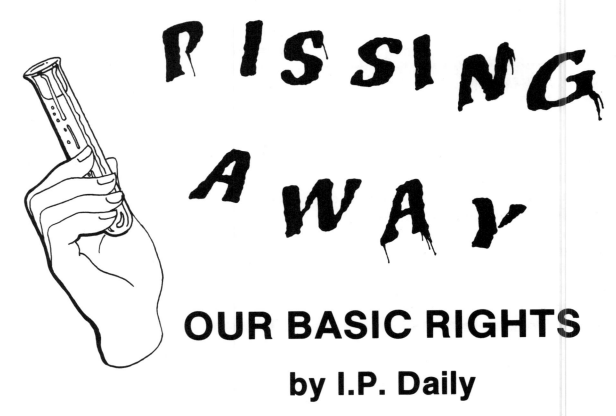

PISSING AWAY

OUR BASIC RIGHTS

by I.P. Daily

© 1991

The decade of the 90's may bring an unprecedented erosion of our constitutional rights. Once these rights have been restricted, it may be impossible to ever win them back.

A dangerous movement is underway in the United States. The people behind this movement believe that the only way to control the crime and gangs and addiction associated with illegal drugs is to suspend or eliminate many of our fundamental freedoms. This movement was carried in on the conservative tide of the 1980's; the decade of the 90's may bring an unprecedented erosion of our Constitutional rights. Once these rights have been restricted, it may be impossible to ever win them back. With the demise of these freedoms we will lose much of what has made the United States so attractive to the oppressed people of this planet. We will be left with the crime and gangs and addiction to drugs and no civil liberties.

There is no question that illegal drugs have caused a rip in the fabric of many of America's largest cities. Gangs battle for control of drug distribution in inner city streets. The number of drug addicted and drug dependent people grows every year. The damage caused by these druggies escalates: they steal to support their habits, they endanger the lives of others at work or on the road, they wreak havoc on our medical and educational systems with their crack babies and overdoses. The fact that AIDS can be and often is spread by intravenous drug users adds to the fear of drugs. But is it necessary to strip away the rights and free-

First published in 1991 Main Catalog

(Continued on next page)

doms of all Americans to combat this problem? Has it ever helped?

The drug issue became political paydirt during the 1980's. Let's examine what happened with cocaine to see how attitudes and policy changed. In the late 70's, cocaine was a glamor drug. It was a socially acceptable drug for upper middle class white professionals. It was widely available at parties. The people who used it were clean and attractive; the poor could not afford it. The distribution network for cocaine was decentralized, without the violence so closely associated with drug dealing today. The addictive properties of cocaine were not appreciated, nor was there any evidence of the damaging medical effects of long term usage. This situation began to slowly change.

A growing pool of wealthy "snowblowers" created a larger market for cocaine. More and more money flowed into the inner-city where dealers sold their wares from vacant houses, back alleys and run-down apartments. The decentralized market for cocaine was begging for consolidation and organization. What started as a recreational drug had become an addictive drug, and the people hooked on cocaine would pay any price. As the laid-back 70's gave way to the uptight 80's, the whole drug issue changed.

All over the country, inner city groups went toe-to-toe in battles over the drug distribution market. The poor and disenfranchised youth of America's urban wasteland saw an answer in drugs: here was a chance to make good money, to buy the trappings of a capitalist society, to get prestige and respect. When you take a group of restless teenagers and add money, weapons and a sense of sport, you get gangs. Gangs moved in to take over the distribution of drugs. On the west coast, the infamous Crips and Bloods grew in power and influence. With the growth in gangs battling for territory, financed with drug money and armed with deadly weaponry, America saw a huge

increase in drug related violence. For the first time, armed street gangs weren't just confined to Chicago or Detroit — they spread out to Seattle, Omaha, Peoria and countless urban and rural communities all over the country.

The legal system in the United States was at a loss to combat drug-related violence. Our system's leniency toward children was established at a time when no one imagined how violent and deadly youth gangs could be. Drugs were not only available in schools — the drug lords were school-aged kids themselves. They wore beepers to school so they could transact business between classes: the "earn while you learn" plan. Every day there were news stories linking blatant killings to drugs. As the criminal justice system tried to grapple with the drug problem, we heard more and more stories about criminals set free without serving a day for their crimes. The media reported story after story about the "drug cartel" in South America that produced the illegal drugs and how they were immune from prosecution and terrorized the governments and people where they lived.

Politicians moved farther and farther to the right as the contest became, not whether you were against drugs, but *how much* you were against drugs.

During this period there was a change in our federal administration. We went from a Democratic president to one of the most conservative politicians in the country: Ronald Reagan. The age of "neo-conservatism" had begun, and drug policy was shifting from the top down. Sensing a groundswell of public concern over drugs, politicians from both parties jumped on the

(Continued next page) **39**

anti-drug bandwagon. It was an issue tailor-made for the American political process: there was an obvious villain (drugs) and only one side to the issue. Politicians moved farther and farther to the right as the contest became, not whether you were against drugs, but *how much* you were against drugs. The police complained that they couldn't handle the drug problem because the Supreme Court had tied their hands. Now the Bill of Rights had become a villain, and the politicians took aim.

> **The police complained that they couldn't handle the drug problem because the Supreme Court had tied their hands. Now the Bill of Rights had become a villain, and the politicians took aim.**

One of the first casualties in the War on Drugs was the "exclusionary rule." The exclusionary rule prohibits police from using illegally obtained evidence in court. If you are subjected to an illegal search, anything found as a result of that search cannot be used against you in a court of law. The police argued that this rule was allowing guilty persons to go free. The media reported cases of people caught with pounds of drugs — just because a few "i's" weren't dotted and "t's" weren't crossed, they were set free. The rightward-leaning Supreme Court obliged. They provided for a "good faith" exemption to the exclusionary rule. The police can now use illegally obtained evidence if they are acting in "good faith." So much for freedom from unreasonable searches and seizures.

Next to go was the right to bail. The Constitution guarantees a right to reasonable bail. Police argued that because the drug dealers had access to so much cash, they would take advantage of the right to bail and flee prosecution. It seems that no amount of bail was too high for the crime of selling drugs. Congress responded with the Crime Control Act in 1989 — the right to bail in federal court was essentially eliminated. The Act says that suspects have a right to a bail hearing on any felony charge. However, if the prosecutor alleges that the defendant might flee prosecution, or might be a danger to "*any* person" in the community, bail can be denied. So much for the right to bail.

Here are some of the other restrictions on civil liberties that have come as a result of the War on Drugs: The government can tap your phone more easily. Bank account records may be examined more freely — without your knowledge or consent. All government records are open to examination by law enforcement officials on a much more lenient basis. New seizure and forfeiture laws allow a defendant's assets to be taken before conviction. This last measure makes it much more difficult for the accused to pay for an adequate defense. Where will all of this end?

There is a reason we have the civil liberties we do. The right to bail is an essential recognition that a person charged with a crime is still considered innocent until proven guilty. Restrictions against illegal evidence are there for many reasons. They protect people from coerced confessions and police-planted "evidence." They also protect the millions of innocent people whose lives could be ruined by searches and seizures that had no basis other than cops on fishing expeditions. The removal of civil liberties cuts across the whole spectrum of society. Nowhere is this more evident than in the growth of drug testing.

Drug testing for everyone seems to be latest assault in the war on civil liberties. Hundreds of thousands of people are now being told that if they want to continue their

(Continued on next page)

employment they must submit to random drug tests. In our system, you aren't allowed to arrest someone without suspicion, yet now you can test without suspicion. The concept of individual suspicion is a cornerstone of civil liberties law. Random drug testing shifts the law so that people are guilty until tests prove them innocent. It is a dangerous erosion of the principle of individual suspicion.

There are many lessons to be learned from the War on Drugs. The first is that governments are more often the cause of problems than the solution.

Random drug testing is hailed as the path to a "drug free workplace." That's an admirable goal, if it can be accomplished without destroying an individual's civil liberties and privacy rights. There are only a few jobs where the danger from drug usage seriously threatens public safety. Airline pilots are an example. And it seems that some sort of drug testing is appropriate in these situations. But such jobs are few and far between, and it is vital that testing be on a voluntary basis. Once we lose the concept of individual suspicion, it will be very difficult to regain it.

Drug testing itself is hypocritical. We test for illegal drugs such as cocaine, LSD and marijuana, but an alcoholic airline pilot would pass the test with flying colors. Certainly an alcoholic pilot is just as dangerous to public safety as one who is addicted to cocaine. There are many, many dangerous, mind-altering drugs that are perfectly legal. Airline pilots can be addicted to prescription narcotics just as easily as illegal drugs. Whether a substance is legal or illegal tells you little or nothing about how it affects people. All the drugs that are currently illegal were at one time legal to use in this country, and many legal drugs, such as alcohol, were illegal at one time. Alcoholism destroys more lives in a year than illegal narcotics, but because it is legal there is not a criminal infrastructure surrounding its production, distribution and use.

The war against civil liberties is not over, and there are some signs that our basic freedoms may withstand some of the recent attacks. There have been several court challenges to random drug testing and the courts are still divided on the issue. Many of the new seizure and forfeiture laws are also the subject of pending court challenges. Many Americans have seen that the drug problem has not improved, even with all the money thrown at it. They have seen the slow-down in the justice system, the prison overcrowding and the premature release of violent criminals, the grip that gangs have on their schools. And they are starting to resist the call for yet more money and the lure of the politician's easy solution.

Civil liberties protect all of us and it is our expansive view of individual rights that makes America unique among nations. Let's not piss it all away.

There are many lessons to be learned from the War on Drugs. The first is that governments are more often the cause of problems than the solution. Politicians will bark out simplistic solutions for any problem, as long as that solution means more money, more power for them. It is very appealing to say that the damage of illegal drugs can be halted by removing civil liberties that only criminals use. But civil liberties protect all of us and it is our expansive view of individual rights that makes America unique among nations. Let's not piss it all away.★

DID THOMAS JEFFERSON WEAR

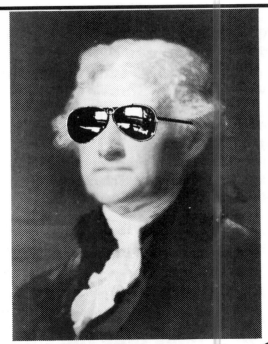

MIRRORSHADES?

-or- Why is the Secret Service Busting Publishers?

© 1991 by Michael E. Marotta

Operation Sundevil is a Secret Service action that has led to at least 28 arrests in over a dozen states. Their targets: computer hackers.

Patriotism is the last refuge of a scoundrel, warned Samuel Johnson in 1775. His words have been underscored once again. Dennis DeConcini has been fingered as a "Keating Five" Senator. The Arizona Democrat accepted campaign contributions from Savings and Loan swindler Charles Keating. Then the Senator attempted to block or stall federal investigators. So, we know he is a scoundrel. What makes him a patriot? Operation Sundevil.

Operation Sundevil is a Secret Service action that has led to at least 28 arrests in over a dozen states. Their targets: computer hackers. Said DeConcini, "This criminal case may account for losses of over $50 million in 14 cities." However, he must have been speaking of his own crimes because *no juried convictions* have come from Operation Sundevil.

Which is not to say that Sundevil is unsuccessful. Indeed it has been. Operation Sundevil resulted in raids, arrests, seizures, indictments and press conferences. It killed a magazine. Mothers were held at gunpoint, waiting while their children came home from school to be busted for crimes that never took place.

The chief speaker for Operation Sundevil is Gail Thackeray, assistant Attorney General for the state of Arizona. Thackery says things like "We're going after people who use computers to commit financial fraud" and "Some of these people who are loudest on the bandwagon may just slink into the background." She has been quoted often in *News-*

week and appeared on National Public Radio's "Heat" with John Hockenberry.

Operation Sundevil resulted in raids, arrests, seizures, indictments and press conferences. It killed a magazine. Mothers were held at gunpoint, waiting while their children came home from school to be busted for crimes that never took place.

GAMES
PEOPLE PLAY

Steve Jackson publishes games. He calls his method GURPS, for Generic Universal Role Playing System. While games like Monopoly and Scrabble require well-defined rules and equipment, GURPS defines only the broad outlines and you make up your own rules. You can bring markers, maps, characters, and pieces into the game if and when you choose. Whether you play *Carwars* or *Witch World* or *Flight 13,* the game starts with a basic world view or scenario. Characters have powers and limitations. You gain or lose hits, points, credits, and strengths by rolling dice. Play is moderated by a Game Master.

Steve Jackson thought it would be neat to make a game based on the science fiction worlds of William Gibson, Bruce Sterling and John Shirley. The game *Cyberpunk* is set in a near future of intense personal technologies from computers and boom boxes to neural implants and bionic attachments. To write the game book, Steve Jackson hired Loyd Blankenship.

Loyd Blankenship is also known as The Mentor to people whose handles include Necron 99, The Prophet, Knight Lightning and Fry Guy. These are the Legion of Doom. A self-styled coterie of hackers, the Legion of Doom has struck fear into the hearts of establishment authorities. So the Feds went after them.

Since Loyd Blankenship was a fringe member of the Legion of Doom, he was busted. At 7:00 am on Thursday, March 1, 1990, he was awakened by the Secret Service. After having their way with him and his house, they moved on to his employer.

"The Secret Service seized all the computers *Cyberpunk* was being written on. They took all the files and all the backups and all the copies of the game. The warrant was without a judge's signature and many lines were blank. They did significant damage to the premises and property. With employees standing around offering them keys, they forced open a footlocker, they used boltcutters to cut locks, they tore open lots of boxes in the warehouse."

Calling *Cyberpunk* "a handbook for hackers" the Secret Service trashed Steve Jackson Games.

According to Steve Jackson, "The Secret Service seized all the computers *Cyberpunk* was being written on. They took all the files and all the backups and all the copies of the game. The warrant was without a judge's signature and many lines were blank. They did significant damage to the premises and property. With employees standing around offering them keys, they forced open a footlocker, they used boltcutters to cut locks, they tore open lots of boxes in the warehouse."

Interestingly enough, Steve was never interrogated. The one-hour interrogation of Loyd Blankenship bordered on the absurd. For instance, the Secret Service asked him how long his wife worked at Lawrence Livermore Labs when in fact she has never worked there, something the Secret Service should have been able to determine on their own.

The government was less than careful with the equipment they seized. The computers were disassembled and returned to Steve Jackson in that condition. One computer was returned with visible damage and has not been reassembled. The motherboard was exposed and two half-height hard disks bounced around inside the machine.

> **The government was less than careful with the equipment they seized. The computers were disassembled and returned to Steve Jackson in that condition.**

Jackson requested access to the materials so he could run his business. "After weeks of promises, we still couldn't get to the files. They said we could get about nine files. We started out with the business files, addresses and contracts." The Secret Service let Steve stand behind an operator who accessed the files Steve asked for; he could not operate the computer himself. Meanwhile "others were standing around laughing and making jokes about what they saw on the screen."

Eventually, he gave up. "We went back to old files and test copies of the game and worked from there. The game's debut was delayed six weeks. My attorney's advice was to tell the world about what's happened." And he did. The gamebook for *Cyberpunk* proudly displays an eye-in-pyramid symbol and the words, "The book that was seized by the US Secret Service."

Lawyer Sharon Beckman traced the blank search warrant to U.S. Magistrate Stephen H. Cabelle.

Because the US Attorney's office in Austin, Texas, contends that the investigation is still in progress, its affidavits are still sealed. We do not know what evidence Special Agent Tim Foley presented to Judge Cabelle to obtain the warrant.

HAVE GUN, WILL TRAVEL

Steve Jackson was not the only publisher to be hassled. Craig Neidorf published *Phrack,* a news service for techies interested in computers and telephones. Someone sent him a BellSouth memo on 911 services. He published it and was busted. Also busted for the same reason was Rich Andrews, owner of the JOLNET BBS. Interestingly enough, it was Andrews who alerted the authorities, asking Bell if it was okay to publish the memo, since it was labeled "proprietary" but was not copyrighted.

> **The goal of Mitch Kapor's Electronic Frontier Foundation is to bring law and order to cyberspace. Rule of law, according Kapor's theories, will mean that hackers are prosecuted when they damage property and rule of law will also mean that the government cannot violate the rights of computerists. Unsigned warrants, arrests without trials, and the trashing of publishers will not be tolerated on the electronic frontier.**

(Continued on next page)

The cases of Craig Neidorf and Steve Jackson came to the attention of another computerist, Mitch Kapor. (Kapor resigned as president of Lotus when the work was no longer fun for him.) He came up with a model of "cyberspace as an electronic frontier." Joining him were Apple retiree Steve Wozniak, Grateful Dead lyricist John Perry Barlowe and computer security guru, Dr. Dorothy Denning.

According to this model, or paradigm, the West was settled because of the railroad and the telegraph. Today, we have computers to carry the freight of an information-based economy. One difference is that the railroad and telegraph had to conform to the physical geography of the lands they passed through while the computer has created its own landscape. Cyberspace is the sum total of all computer-to-computer connections. Most people do not even know it exists.

The goal of Mitch Kapor's Electronic Frontier Foundation is to bring law and order to cyberspace. Kapor has pledged a minimum of $275,000 of his own money. His generosity was at least matched by Steve Wozniak. Their contributions went to hire lawyers. The Boston firm of Silverglate & Good supplied Sharon Beckman to work with Steve Jackson. The New York firm Rabinowitz Boudin assigned their own Terry Gross and hired Chicago lawyer Sheldon Zenner to defend Craig Neidorf.

Rule of law, according Kapor's theories, will mean that hackers are prosecuted when they damage property and rule of law will also mean that the government cannot violate the rights of computerists. Unsigned warrants, arrests without trials, and the trashing of publishers will not be tolerated on the electronic frontier.

COLD TYPE
AND COOL MEDIA

Craig Neidorf's trial in Chicago during late July and early August of 1990 demonstrated the shift in the powers of the various mass media. The Feds took early control of the printed page. As long as they could convince the press that the nation's 911 Emergency Phone System was at risk, their assertions were printed as facts.

Marshall MacLuhan defined television as "cool" because it is a participatory medium. In that sense, nothing is cooler than a computer bulletin board network.

On Monday, January 15, 1990, AT&T suffered a software failure and long distance service was disrupted. When Secret Service agents later made Sundevil arrests, they alluded to this disruption. The Big Lie was furthered by an *Infoworld* columnist who spread the "rumor" to thousands of corporate readers. In fact, no charges relating to the AT&T event were ever filed.

"The indictment portrays one of the most extensive attacks yet by so-called computer hackers and is likely to raise new fears about the vulnerability of the nation's computers and the computerized phone system," said the *New York Times* on January 18, 1990 about a West Coast case. On February 12, 1990 *Telephony* claimed that the Legion of Doom stole Emergency 911 programs. "Four alleged computer hackers were indicted last week on charges that they schemed to steal and publish proprietary BellSouth Corp. emergency 911 data. The alleged activity could have produced disruptions in 911 networks nationwide, according to federal officials."

The government was lying.

Marshall MacLuhan defined television as "cool" because it is a participatory medium. In that sense, nothing is cooler than a computer bulletin board network. Word went out on the networks. Facts (as opposed to government allegations) spread along Bitnet and Usenet. Among the people who responded was John Nagle.

(Continued on next page)

Nagle found a book called *The Intelligent Network* in the Stanford Bookstore in Palo Alto. The book contained a chapter on emergency phone service and a reference to a document called "Bellcore TA-TASY-000350, E911 Public Safety Answering Point: Interface Between a 1/1AESS(tm) Switch and Customer Premises Equipment." In fact, anyone can order these specifications. List price: $13.00. Of course, the memo in question is neither a program nor data nor software documentation. The government's tissue of lies was thin indeed.

> ## It is easy to see that the real purpose of Operation Sundevil is to bully people out of their equipment and away from hacking.

In fact, it is easy to see that the real purpose of Operation Sundevil is to bully people out of their equipment and away from hacking. On May 8, 1990, 28 arrests in 14 states brought in 42 computers and over 20,000 floppy disks. Three months later, on August 16, New York State police seized $50,000 in equipment from 13 hackers, five of them juveniles. They were charged with "stealing" phone numbers for toll-free 800-service. They allegedly stole (copied) several computer games from a university system. And they were charged with the theft (copying) of "a $1.2 million dollar computer program." The price tag of this UNIX subroutine was based on the estimated *development* cost — just as it costs millions to develop a new car model, though, obviously, no individual auto is worth the whole amount of the process.

In both the Sundevil and Gotham raids, police told some parents that their kids were responsible for the January 15, 1990 AT&T long distance outage. In fact, AT&T has accepted sole responsibility for this snafu. And so far, no one has been formally charged in court with this non-existent crime. Some "convictions" were obtained against Legion of Doomers and others who plea bargained. When Craig Neidorf held his ground, he blew the government out of the water, and they dropped their charges.

CRIMES AND MISDEMEANORS

The Secret Service, being a branch of the US Treasury, is responsible for protecting both the President and the Money Supply. (Who says we're not a capitalist nation?) So why are they busting publishers?

According to prosecuting attorney Kirk Tabbey, "Treasury Agents protect the credit of our nation. With the advent of credit problems, credit card fraud, and an incredible array of computer problems," 18 USC 1029 and 1030 empower the Secret Service to pursue hackers. In fact, there have been cases of so-called "hackers" carrying out acts of credit card fraud. Computer-literate criminals are here.

> ## The Secret Service, being a branch of the US Treasury, is responsible for protecting both the President and the Money Supply. (Who says we're not a capitalist nation?)

However, there is a difference between computer hackers who happened to break the law and criminals who use computers to carry out traditional crimes.

Consider the case of Kevin Mitnik. He was accused of breaking into computers at AT&T and NORAD, the North American Air Defense Command. Seemingly serious, these actions are no more criminal than those of peacenik protestors who

(Continued on next page)

occupy establishment buildings for political publicity. The protestors are arrested, fined and sent home. Kevin Mitnik was held "incommunicado" — the judge ordered him held for trial with no access to a telephone.

Mitnik was singled out. Craig Neidorf and Rich Andrews were targeted. Steve Jackson was fingered. The Legion of Doom is persecuted. Why? Because most of the people who are responsible for law and order do not understand, and therefore fear, computers.

By contrast, Kirk Tabbey, assistant prosecutor for Washentaw County (Ann Arbor) Michigan, actually uses his Zenith TurboSport 386 laptop computer. As a participant in Operation Sundevil, Tabbey has busted his share of hackers. (One preteen from suburban Detroit had cracked the TRW Credit database.) Even so, he takes a very narrow view of the problems that other people paint with a broad brush.

According to Kirk Tabbey, we live in a world of inter-connected computer networks. Tabbey maintains that to be considered truly private property, a computer system connected to the phone lines must post a "no trespassing" sign of some sort. Digital Equipment Corporation recently lost a prosecution against a hacker because many nodes on their Easynet show "Welcome to VMS 5.1" as a login message.

JEFFERSON IN MIRRORSHADES

Three years ago, Admiral John Poindexter called press conferences to announce that from now on private databases were going to be regulated by the government. The Soviets, he claimed, were using CompuServe, GEnie and other bulletin board services to collate information about high technology. In retrospect, this national security advisor must have known how close the USSR was to unraveling. Yet, he raised the specter of international Communism to throttle the electronic press.

John Poindexter's dreams of control were shattered when he was indicted for his role in Iranscam/Contragate. Today, we have Senator Dennis DeConcini. He claimed that hackers stole $50 million and today he is exposed as the lackey of a banker who bilked investors for $200 million.

> **Changes in machinery do not over-ride the self-evident principles upon which rational societies are based. Computers are the printing presses of the modern world. The now-defunct *Creative Computing* once featured a poster of Thomas Jefferson composing the Declaration on a DEC-Writer terminal. He would have liked that image.**

In 1787 Thomas Jefferson wrote, "A free press is the only safeguard of public liberty... and were it left to me to decide whether we should have a government without newspapers or newspapers without a government, I would not hesitate a moment to prefer the latter."

The First Amendment did not evaporate when Mergenthaler invented the Linotype. Changes in machinery do not over-ride the self-evident principles upon which rational societies are based. Computers are the printing presses of the modern world. The now-defunct *Creative Computing* once featured a poster of Thomas Jefferson composing the Declaration on a DEC-Writer terminal. He would have liked that image.

Michael E. Marotta is a freelance writer. Several of his articles on computers and freedom appear in Loompanics' Greatest Hits.

BOB'S HOPELESS DESERT CLASSIC

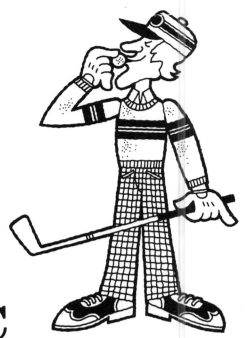

© 1991 by Bob Black

Ladies and gentlemen of Operation Desert Shield, welcome to Bob's Hopeless Desert Classic. I never miss a war, it's great to be on the side that's always right. I know I speak for all Americans, especially the op-ed columnists, when I say we're behind you — thousands of miles behind you. So get out there and golf us out of this sand-trap.

We have a great show for you today. I'm sorry that Andrew "Dice" Clay couldn't join us, but he was vetoed by the Saudi authorities. They said, "Too feminist." They also asked me not to tell you any jokes about getting stoned. Saudi culture doesn't permit

me to bring along the usual bevy of starlets, but I know later in the show you'll give a big hand to the Ballet Trockadero.

> I never miss a war, it's great to be on the side that's always right.

With Operation Desert *Sword* only two days away I know you're a little

First published in 1991 Spring Supplement

(Continued on next page)

jittery. The recruiters never said any-thing about *fighting*. You joined the army to learn marketable skills, like standing at attention. I'm not saying your underprivileged backgrounds are a military disadvantage, let's just say that Iraq has some crack troops and we have some *crack* troops. You joined the army to be somebody. Chances are you will be some body.

I'm not saying we have a morale problem, but tomorrow the medics will be looking at a *lot* of scorpion bites.

I'm not saying war is inevitable, but when I played golf with General Colin Powell the other day he said they'd have the Gulf veterans' memorial set up before you even go home! If you do. This war shows how far we've gone toward equal rights for all. The first time I saw General Powell on a golf course he was a caddy.

And while I'm on the subject, we have a coed mercenary army now. You've come a long way, baby — could be the end of the line — and girls, you look great in those jungle camouflage fatigues! The Iraqis might mistake you for a reforestation project. Sweet-hearts, you make the desert bloom.

How many of you out there are Reservists? I bet *you're* surprised to be here. I was golfing with Vice President Quayle last week. Now he wants to get *out* of the Reserves. But he won't be called up. He's doing such important work.

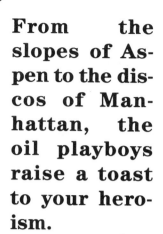

From the slopes of As-pen to the dis-cos of Man-hattan, the oil playboys raise a toast to your hero-ism.

And don't think the Emirate of Kuwait isn't worth dying for. I was playing golf with some Kuwaiti refu-gees in Palm Springs recently and they appreciate the sacrifices you'll be making to restore their traditional way of life. As Arabs go, Kuwaitis are a lot like us. Well, maybe not like *you*, but they're a lot like *me*. Kuwait has its own time zone: Miller Time. Kuwait makes *The Bonfire of the Vanities* look like *The Grapes of Wrath*. Kuwaitis are very different from Iraqis. A Kuwaiti plays blackjack, an Iraqi carries one. Kuwaitis are the only Arabs if you mention the sands they think you mean a casino. From the slopes of Aspen to the discos of Manhattan the oil playboys raise a toast to your heroism.

Now some people say the case for starting this war is as leaky as an Israeli ferryboat. They say why die for

a place so far away even Domino's doesn't deliver. Now stop me if you've heard this one, but the joke going around the homefront goes like this:

How is the President's war policy like a Gulf War veteran? Hasn't got a leg to stand on. Guess you were stumped by that one. Now you know why it's called a *gag*.

I'd like to conclude this part of the show with a musical tribute inspired by Allan Sherman, the guy they named the tank after, and by Tom Lehrer. I am in fine voice tonight but you'll just have to take my word for it.

*Holy terror, **Intifada**,*
This war won't be like
*   Grenada*
Soldiers thirsting
Car-bombs bursting
Saudi women aren't much
*   fun*
And that's the worst thing.

Foes turn friends in ways
*   that are mysterious*
Lebanon was hopeless and
*   now it is Syria's.*

Our Islamic allies hate us
*Though we're there to **quo***
*   their **status***
*In a **jihad***
We will be had
Even with William Safire to
*   masturbate us.*

It's time for me to go, but I'll be back, I'll always be back, until you turn the guns around. Till then, or till next time, remember — where there's war, there's Hope.

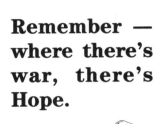

Remember — where there's war, there's Hope.

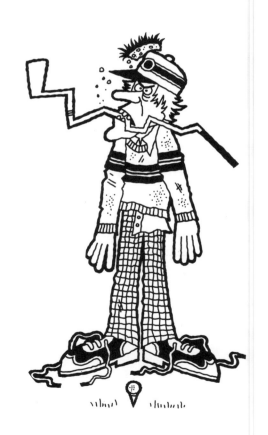

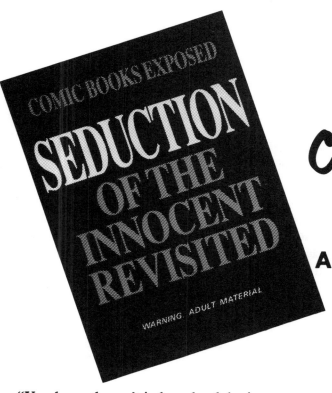

THE WAR AGAINST COMIC BOOKS REVISITED

A Special Review/Article
by Steve Schumacher

"You honestly can't judge a book by its cover — especially a comic book!" is the warmed-over cliche used to promote *Seduction Of The Innocent Revisited,* a new Christian Fundamentalist attack on (you guessed it) comic books. Author and hatchetman John Fulce reproduced without permission over a hundred pages of artwork, many of them covers, for the express purpose of judgement. But that's OK — he wasn't being honest, anyway.

A casual reader may wonder why there's a lot of white boxes floating over the female bodies Fulce picked to photocopy. Early on he explained, "I used censor tape to cover nudity and certain objectionable images for obvious reasons" (p. 11). Fulce's censored examples might deceive if possible even the elect, but they can't fool me, for I've read and still own most of the originals. It's clear from reviewing a sample that Fulce has largely whited out such god-awful smut as lingerie, naked thighs, and bare behinds.

Consider the double-page spread (pp. 60-61) depicting a coterie of wacked-out hooded cultists muttering mumbo-jumbo over a woman they've captured and stripped. Fulce whited out her breasts and genitals to suggest the obvious, but a glance at the unexpurgated original reveals that the artist was modest enough to drape the damsel in darkness —

there's literally nothing to see! What is Fulce covering up?

This example is hilarious because Fulce brought it up to show how comics "glorify the more popular forms of quasi-religion" (p. 45) and "how deep into occultism comic book readers really are" (p. 59). Of course, these cardboard cultists are unmitigated bad guys; the scene reads like an overheated outtake from a Jack Chick bible tract comic strip. Cartoonists are hardly glorifying New Agers here!

Other examples of willful misinterpretation are rampant. A long-running plotline in Wonder Woman's comic has been the testing and gradual undermining of her faith in her native Greek gods; Fulce stupidly lumped this careful treatment of religion under the heading "Occultism and New Age Philosophy" (p. 70, 74). In one story Superman succeeds in deprogramming a dopey cult that has formed around him; Fulce got things exactly backward to complain of "idolatry:" "Even Superman is a candidate for 'godhood'" (p. 46, 73). And so on, and so on, throughout this foolish book.

In fairness, Fulce makes a few astute observations about gratuitous violence, and this isn't one of those pointless cases where someone from the outside criticizes a genre for which he has no sympathy or understanding. Fulce loved comics for much of

---

First published in 1991 Summer Supplement

(Continued on next page)

his life; he was a collector for 23 years and ran his own comic store for another seven before something apparently snapped. This background makes it hard to understand and excuse his book's glaring omissions, material that Fulce almost certainly knows about and wishes the reader not to know about.

The back cover copy proclaims that in today's comics, "there is a constant and alarming anti-Christian theme similar to the anti-Semitic theme found in German literature during the 1920s and 1930s." Fulce indeed harps on the notion that comic books are out to get Christianity (pp. 76-109), though the self-serving and unfounded Nazi analogy is nowhere to be seen in the body of the book. It's certainly true that several individual comic writers are no fans of organized religion, but Marvel and DC's ownership by giant corporations guarantees that very little gets published by these companies that would offend mainstream congregations (as opposed to extreme fundamentalists like Fulce).

In 1989, DC disrupted its publishing schedule, lost several of its best writers in protest, and caught a lot of flak from fans (including myself) when it abruptly aborted a time-travel storyline that in part involved Swamp Thing attending Jesus' Passion. Although the story was by all accounts well-written, respectful, and consistent with the Gospel accounts, DC probably didn't want to risk any kind of bad publicity at a time when Swampy was being marketed to television and toy stores and the Batman movie was about to be released.

Fulce neglected to mention this incident, concurrent with his book's writing and well-known in the trade, which tends to contradict his paranoid thesis; instead, he just rattled on for page after page with lines like, "Comics are part of the New Age consensus that is determined to wipe out every trace of what was formerly called decency, goodness, kindness, and truth" (p. 77).

Blindingly obvious is the converse proposition: Christians like Fulce are definitely out to get comic books. He concludes his book with a blueprint for hassling local authorities into harassing comic dealers (pp. 190-193) and with contact addresses for various national organizations ready to "fight to purge obscene materials from the shelves of comic stores" (pp. 194-197) as part of a larger campaign to police all media to suit their own tastes. Their pretext is generally the importance of protecting children by raising them in a vacuum.

There have been several legal skirmishes already in this campaign of persecution; Fulce doesn't report any of these instances of his ideas being carried out into practice by law officers out to make political hay. The first and longest-running case was that of Friendly Frank's Comic Shop in Lansing, Illinois, whose manager was arrested in December, 1986, for possession of obscene magazines. These were underground comics, among them the beloved and artful *Omaha* comic, all marked as clearly for adults, and the spurious issue of selling them to minors wasn't even raised.

Nevertheless, the manager and his employer were dragged through the mill for this victimless crime: related zoning violations, conviction in January 1988, prolonged appeal procedures, and eventual reversal in November, 1989. This was something of a Pyrrhic victory; in the interim the store lost its lease because of its criminal reputation and was closed. The Comic Book Legal Defense Fund was founded to pay some of Friendly Frank's legal expenses, and it continues to support other comic shops victimized by this kind of harassment (see *Comics Journal* #133, pp. 13-15).

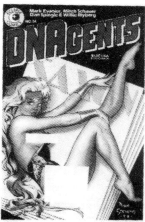

*The lady on this comic book cover is **not** naked — no nipples, pubic hair, or other "private parts" are shown, but Fulce has censored it anyway. What is he hiding?*

The same Florida obscenity statute whereby 2 Live Crew rappers were prosecuted has been used in a series of comic shop crackdowns throughout the conservative northern part of the state.

(Continued on next page)

Xeno's in Jacksonville was entrapped in July, 1990, for selling the store's only copy of a *Cherry* anthology to an undercover cop; the issue had been special-ordered by an anonymous caller but not picked up. A few days earlier a district court judge had ruled *Cherry* obscene; in these medieval proceedings, artists and publishers aren't notified of the hearing date in case they'd like to be there to defend their work, and retailers aren't notified which comics have been declared obscene until they're arrested for them.

Another shop, Novel Ideas in Gainesville, was stung in September, 1990, when it sold an issue of *The Score* (a hard-boiled though hardly hard-core crime comic) to a cop's 17-year-old son. The store's owner called the police to turn himself in; instead, sheriff's officers opted to haul this dangerous criminal out of his store during business hours, handcuffed before the cameras of invited newsmen, charged with a third-degree felony for selling harmful material to someone under 18 (*Comics Journal*, #139, pp. 9-10).

These assaults have obviously had a chilling effect. For example, every comic shop in Jacksonville has now "voluntarily" withdrawn any adult material (*Comic Buyer's Guide*, 11/30/90). The biggest chill is the vicious federal RICO act, which absurdly defines two felony convictions by an "enterprise" as a "pattern" of "racketeering," permitting imprisonment for up to 40 years and forfeiture of all assets to the government before appeal. Theoretically, Warner Communications (which owns DC) could be seized by the feds if some hick town judge found two things he didn't like in a *Batman* comic. RICO prosecutors have so far restricted themselves to beating up on such big-time gangsters as mom-and-pop video rental stores.

Unfortunately, this new wave of repression cheered by Fulce really isn't new. Early in 1954 psychiatrist Dr. Fredric Wertham capped his crusade against crime comics with the publication of the original *Seduction Of The Innocent.* Wertham made comic books a burning issue for a while around the country, inspiring bonfires and legislation, and he testified in April, 1954, at the Senate Judiciary Subcommittee on Juvenile Delinquency which was investigating his charges with an eye toward federal action.

Comics publishers reacted by cobbling together the Comics Code Authority in September, 1954, as a self-policing and public-relations mechanism. The Comics Code succeeded in deflecting the feds long enough for the nation's attention to shift to other manufactured enemies, but the great EC line of comics and over 300 other titles were casualties (*Comics Journal* #133, pp. 76-87).

Wertham was convinced that comics cause crime because most of the juvenile delinquents he asked told him they read comics. Of course, if Wertham had asked non-delinquents, he'd have gotten the same response, because in those pre-TV days just about every kid read comics. While Wertham produced meaningless correlations to prove that comics are harmful, Fulce's new *Seduction* provides no hard evidence at all, just scary assertions and armchair (should I say, "electric chair"?) psychologizing by such esteemed authorities as Ted Bundy (pp. 181-184).

Although Fulce cribbed its title and concept, there isn't one reference in his entire book to either Fredric Wertham or *Seduction Of The Innocent.* I find this almost incredible, though maybe understandable considering that Wertham was a political liberal, considered himself non-religious, and had little in common with conservative fundamentalists like Fulce (paraphrasing Dr. Mark West, *Children, Culture, And Controversy,* chapter 5). It does go to show that censors come in all stripes.

Not only doesn't he mention Wertham, Fulce erroneously rewrites history to omit the crime and exploitation comics that Wertham fought against. Instead he presents a saccharine history of comics, headed "The Age of Innocence," which starts with Superman and ends with Archie (pp. 14-17); only with the advent of the 1980's comics that he abhors does Fulce see any evil.

Wertham would hardly have agreed with Fulce that "comic books in those days were more positive and wholesome in their depiction of society" (p. 17). Where Wertham viewed the 1950's Batman and Robin team as "a wish dream for two homosexuals living together" (*Comics Journal* #133, p. 87), Fulce idealized the good-old-days by saying, "The Robin of thirty years ago would never have behaved in such a fashion" (p. 145). By not presenting either the facts or Wertham's view of them, Fulce conveys the bogus impression that

(Continued on next page)

controversial comics are a new phenomenon. Is he trying to justify his own love for comics during the "innocent" years?

Some of Fulce's arguments are totally incoherent. He repeatedly maintains that comics are for, always have been for, and always should be for kids, yet he also rants about a parallel stream of "Underground Comics" (oddly defined here to include crude 8-page "Tahitian bible" [*sic*] stroke/ joke books along with the real counter-culture undergrounds like *Zippy the Pinhead*), which "have been around for years; indeed, comic book historian Les Daniels suggested they were the first comic books ever published, making their appearance as early as the 1920s" (p. 25). It's patently obvious that comics for children and comics for adults have coexisted from the start, just as they have in other forms of literature.

How about this one: Fulce asserts throughout that comics are a great danger to the moral fiber of America's youth, at the same time citing ho-hum U.S. Youth Indicator statistics to show that there's been a slight improvement in juvenile propriety during the 1980's. In his own words, "comic books worsened at precisely the moment when America and its young people began to get better" (p. 21). Fulce doesn't seem to realize when he's shot himself in the foot.

Fulce must be credited for presenting a rousing free speech argument against his own position. To quote in part, "Any attempt to legislate what can or cannot be produced and sold to comic book fans is a violation of the First Amendment and the denial of a basic right to people who should be able to make up their own minds about what materials they buy and read. If narrow-minded parents don't want their children to patronize comic book stores, it's up to them to set and enforce rules in their families. But, don't try to make decisions for other families!" (p. 180).

Well, he's convinced me; this seems like a good argument. Fulce was playing devil's advocate and indicated that he would answer the free speech argument in its turn, after what he called the "no harm" argument, but he never got around to it, another bizarre omission.

Despite and because of its many flaws, *Seduction Of The Innocent Revisited* is a true nutball classic. It's a fun fast read, mainly because of all the pirated pictures. These represent a fair selection of the more lurid extremes of today's overground comics fare, suitable for the curious and the censorious alike.

It's jam-packed with incredible quotes like, "...anything that diverts people from the worship of the True God is by definition evil...." (p. 46; sounds like Fulce can't stand other people having fun; what's his next target, baseball?). Here's another: "We must drive these kinds of rats out of the marketplace so America's young people can grow up with clear heads..." (p. 28; the technical term for this is "brainwashing").

Fulce writes clearly and unself-consciously, so his book provides a revealing view into the mind of a bluenosed busybody. As long as he and his kind don't get into power, we can laugh.

Additional information may be obtained from:
The Comic Book Legal Defense Fund
Box 501
Princeton, WI, 54968
and
The Comic Legends Legal Defense Fund
5335 Yonge St, Ste 120
Willowdale, Ontario
M2N 6M2
Canada

These organizations gladly accept donations to support those on the front lines of the free speech war. Publications mentioned in the review:

The Comics Journal
7563 Lake City Way NE
Seattle, WA 98115

Comics Buyers Guide
700 E State St.
Iola, WI 54990

Between Iraq And A Hard Place
A Preamble To
The Brave New World Order
by Ben G. Price

Act I
Stage Dressing
For
The Comedy of Terrors

The "First World" war didn't quite end all wars, but it began with the process of drawing up a global roster of industrialized countries capable of manufacturing finished products from pirated raw materials on high adrenalin. The "Second World" war was fought to precipitate from a cloud of mustard gas, nuclear fallout and smog the one giant of manufacture that would dictate the course of development to all the others by serving as a watershed of technological innovation. The others: those too weak to object and those immolated for the cause would follow in step. Note: The victor of the Second World war demonstrated its superior industrial competence by manufacturing incomparable weapons of destruction.

Keep this in mind, because the waging of the Second World war did not end with the military defanging of Germany and Japan. The profit taking continued under cover of darkest national security, with only a brief hiatus following the recent demoralization of the Soviet Union. With this astonishing capitulation, the last credible challenger of America's intention to define a "Second World" of mutually indentured industrialized franchises was whisked, whimpering, off the stage of history. And while this would seem to untutored minds a great victory for the "West," the military industrial complex upon which the American economy is based began to falter and, at a feverish pace, search for a new marketing strategy to make its primary export viable again. Until the fall of the Berlin Wall, the Second World war continued on simmer heat. Left-over imperial colonialism was rehashed into a carnivorous pate' of raw ideology. It boiled down to anti-communism, which meant "containing" the Soviet Union and its expanding empire, "at all costs," including the psychological threat of mutual annihilation, which was made credible by terrorizing taxpayers into funding the manufacture of the very weapons at the core of their neurosis.

During the era of nuclear "peace," the war to establish the priorities of globalism continued. "Pockets" of indigenous resistance to world Capitalism were turned into guerrilla battlegrounds. Fascist regimes were propped-up with a constant flow of military "aid." And a gullible populace gobbled up the news of America's slow burning battle to make the world safe for democracy. Anti-communism was the little snack of commentary in all the school books and all the "news" reports. We were educated to call the whole unappetizing gruel "The Cold War." It was the war of nuclear feint and hypnotism. It was the war that made us fear Big Brother so much that we created our own, before a foreign one was imposed on us.

The First World, with its Marshall Plan-born entourage of second "worlds," emerged as the victor, but continues to act with impunity as if still

(Continued on next page)

at war, on the unassailable premise that the world-at-large has learned nothing. It has learned nothing because it has been shown nothing worth learning. All matters of importance concerning people being told to kill each other on the battlefield, which should have been matters of open public debate, were kept secret throughout the "Cold War." That kind of information became the essence of the term "state secret." Democracy was flushed out of the system by the very concept of secrecy.

The Second World war was such good business that it was never brought to an end. Politically, the Cold War was the endgame maneuvering of a strategy that was to consolidate the "second world" into a manageable marketplace. The whims of any particular nation's citizenry would be tolerated in inverse proportion to the degree of their ability to hinder or slow the process of world Capitalization.

Act II
The Opening Shots
of
The *Third World* War

Reality is two-tiered where power is concerned. The C.I.A., which hired Manuel Noriega as a regional snitch, got its money's worth when it persuaded him to take a fall for a "drug running" operation (done under the watchful nose of drug-running American heroes like Colonel "Ollie" North, who, protected by Ronald Reagan's useful amnesia, invented cover stories with which to wrap magazines of bullets for importation into the bodies of dissidents in foreign lands opposed to the emerging "New World Order"). Today the U.S.A. controls Panama without dispute, and Manuel Noriega says he received the American version of Jesus Christ as his personal savior one day in his prison cell. Reality on this level is first defined by the consultants, then experienced by the masses.

The second layer of reality, the one recognized by anyone who finds the use of raw power suspect (that means, apparently, everyone but the average American citizen), does not mistake the cover story for the actual goal. In the case of the Panama invasion, for instance, the hidden agenda was the retaking of the Canal *before* the negotiated turn-over of the Zone, arranged by President Carter, could take effect. Conservative outrage over President Carter's settlement with the Panamanian government went so far beyond opposition within the democratic process that it extended to the treasonous arena of drugs for arms in Central America, and arms for hostages in Iran. Unfortunately, the felons now run the government.

Washington outsiders like Jimmy Carter, who was elected president "by mistake" in an election against America's first appointed president Gerald Ford, have not been privy to the redneck blueprint for the "New World Order" being slipped around our necks like a Press Club tie. But skull and crossbone pirates like the C.I.A.'s own George Bush well understand why an up and coming world dictatorship shouldn't give up control of the Panama Canal. Nor should it allow agrarian anti-industrial democracies to go a-borning where once cooperative banana republics, like Nicaragua and El Salvador, have in the past given American fruit wholesalers plenty of elbow room.

The invasion of Grenada, always a "puzzlement," as the King of Siam used to say, makes as little sense as the Vietnam War did, if one insists the events must fit into the surface level of official "reality." If, as linguistics might suggest, we explore the "deep structure" of events, a whole new reality stands in the foreground, in stark contrast to the groundwork of deceit laid by the propagandists.

Act III
The Saddamizing
of
The American Mind

The Iraqi invasion of Kuwait triggered a high-tech booby trap that was set for the purpose of catching Saddam Hussein in his own troglodytic zipper. Questions about specific diplomatic signals allegedly passed directly to Hussein through American Ambassador April C. Glaspie indicating that the U.S. would "look the other way" if such an invasion took place are not entertained as valid by the government that hid Ms. Glaspie from public access all during the so-called "war."

56

(Continued on next page)

To call it a "war" at all is rationally suspect, though not politically. Politics, as suggested, is less picky about defining reality. In a sad display of human folly, over three hundred Americans lost their lives crashing into each other, rolling jeeps off the desert roads, and strafing each other with "friendly fire." Most American deaths were accidental, non-combat glitches.

For that matter, most of the Iraqi 100,000+ deaths (that is a "conservative" figure) were as impersonal, though not accidental. The counting of the dead is even more impersonal for being withheld as a post war extension of domestic psychological manipulation. The ally-sponsored civil war in Iraq is the perfect ploy to camouflage war damage as self-imposed and make it impossible to verify the number of deaths attributable to allied bombings of civilian areas.

"Career" journalists, shivering in their boots and afraid to go up against the nationalist fever sweeping the country on a tide of tax-bought propaganda, didn't seem interested in the political machinations that put America in the forefront of a major military invasion, or they'd have asked the hard questions when they needed to be asked: before the first sortie was flown. What *does* seem to have captured the interest of reporters is the vicarious thrill of looking through the video crosshairs as "smart bombs" swooped into the front doors, elevator shafts and ventilation ducts of targeted buildings where people, to whom the bombs and reporters were indifferent, would die.

There is no comparable interest in exploring why the Star Wars style SDI spy satellites launched under a veil of secrecy by NASA, "failed" to reveal (at least so far as *public* policy goes) the seriousness of the Iraqi military build-up and thus telegraph the planned invasion of Kuwait. Orbital reconnaissance is so secret, apparently, that reporters thought it was useless to ask what specific role it played in the Iraqi-American charade. But the "brass" knew far in advance what was coming. And even if they were asked, they "legally" wouldn't have to tell reporters anything, because of national security. Hence, the legality of everything they did subsequently becomes moot. Where there is no accountability, law is moot. And democracy is a farce buttressed by symbols and banners that are not to be

violated in public displays of dismay, under penalty of the law.

When Iraq moved against Kuwait, the United States' shadow government tripped the trap. It called in the chips owed to the U.S. by its franchises, cornered the Soviets and suggested a moderate protest over the crackdown on the Baltic, then went to the U.N. and wrapped up a deal that resulted in the international acceptance of an occupying army of over half a million heavily armed troops perched on top of the bulk of the world's known oil reserves. What surprised everybody but the Soviet government, the European governments who jumped on the bandwagon, and the rest of the governments that went along at least in principle with the scheme, was just how heavily invested in warfare the American government had become. So who does that leave out? I mean besides the American people and Saddam Hussein.

The nightly blather on the airwaves saw countless interviews with military "experts" who reiterated the conventional wisdom that an air war against Iraq would not be enough to loosen its hold on Kuwait. This "wisdom" followed the dogma that sanctions, blockades, and all other non-violent means of persuasion would be pointless. And since the air war would be inadequate, strategists planned for a massive ground war, which the rest of the experts promised would be long and bloody and psychologically devastating to the delicate American psyche. That was before the gee-whiz entertainment value of mechanized war at a distance met its audience: the industrialized, corporate citizens of the Brave New World Order.

The American psyche has been twisted beyond the recognition of its identification with humanity. George Bush likes to pretend it was "Vietnam Syndrome" that was ailing us before he "cured" our national malady by giving carte blanche to vicariously and collectively kick some foreign ass. A more believable explanation of our malaise suggests that a natural weariness of war has been repressed and denied to the point of communal stupidity, a dirt ignorance that was purchased with hard-earned tax money diverted to the propaganda machine.

Sanctions and blockades, had they been anything but expedient, calculated pre-war measures, might have worked to get Iraq out of Kuwait. But they assuredly would *not* have worked to get a massive,

(Continued on next page)

credible U.S. military presence established in the region. Was there any connection between the decision to abandon sanctions and establish just such a military presence and the shift in the balance of power precipitated by the crumpling of the U.S.S.R.? Was the "peace dividend" that Congress "threatened" to convert from war and arms preparations to social needs too much of a good thing for defense contractors to swallow?

Act IV
Cross Hairs
and
Ex-Marx Enthusiasts

The U.S.S.R., like the reactor at Chernobyl, has been in hot water with the "community of nations" ever since that power plant coughed a cloud of radioactivity across Europe and the Soviet Republics. It was a big day for everybody concerned. It was the first case of public accountability to which the Soviets had succumbed. And maybe there was a reason.

Not long before that time, Ronald Reagan was telling the American taxpayers about his Strategic Defense Initiative, for which they would be paying, sight unseen, a thrift-bailout-style fortune. He promised to share the technology from the development of the system with the Soviets, while at the same time maintaining absolute secrecy about the details where taxpaying Americans were concerned. Americans "illegally" trading secrets about the technology could be tried as traitors, while Politburo members being "briefed" on the same information would be wined and dined and slapped on the back. At least that was the weird scenario defined by the Reagan demented government. To our credit, few believed, though to our shame, few challenged this blatant crappola.

It may be of interest that "Star Wars" surveillance and microwave focused beam weapons already in orbit and under U.S. command are up to the task of triggering just such a catastrophe as occurred at Chernobyl. But why speculate? The world got a taste of the American military's high-tech destructive capacity by watching Iraq Around The Clock on CNN. Baghdad was surgically

returned to the neolithic era. Tanks, towns, and trench-burrowing soldiers disappeared into desert mirages that, for all the news media told us, might never have existed in the first place.

A few years ago, a young German man piloted a single engine plane, undetected, and landed it in Red Square, causing well-publicized embarrassment to the Russian old-guard. His feat prefigured the next advance in American air weaponry, which was in the area of "stealth" technology. Throughout the Reagan term of presidency, if one theme of emphasis could be identified, it would have to be military research and development. And Reagan promised to share this technology with the world. It appears the Bush era will be one of deployment and engagement of that technology, and it seems that the level of "sharing" we can expect will be on the order of that experienced recently by Iraq and perhaps the Soviet Union, on the receiving end.

At the beginning of the end of the Second World war, the U.S. used Nagasaki and Hiroshima as international visual aids to demonstrate what technological superiority on the field of battle means. The U.S. shadow government was not so much re-defining the nature of warfare in Iraq as it was reinforcing a forgotten lesson of power.

Act V
Cartoon Khartoum:
America Caricatures Itself

With the mania over national pre-eminence raging and with euphoria over the disproportionate slaughter of Iraqis, the flag has become the drug of choice, the only reality filter commercially available in America without a prescription or a jail sentence.

If there is a national conscience, it has lost heart and backed itself up the rump of history looking for an untried bowel from which high vantage point it hopes to one day represent the sphincter-pinched opinions of those who secretly object to the notion of war merely for the sake of the empire's hidden agenda. Objectors who remain silent will, no doubt, whistle dixie out their asses with deep conviction when the time is right and the risks of refusal are lowered. But until then expect the usual moral constipation recorded in all eras of tyrannical rule.

(Continued on next page)

The heir to the "Great Communicator," George Bush, mispronounced Saddam Hussein's name religiously up until the military humiliation of Iraq. The Bush-whacker called him "Sodom," as if to enlist every bible-thumper to the national cause by mere reference to the moral affront (or is that a-back?) of Saddam Hussein's earthly existence.

There is no doubt that among America's most influential anal retentives George Bush made his point amply clear: he was rejecting the wimpy image of his past by projecting it on someone he holds in less esteem than himself. In the rubble of Iraq a miracle blossomed: George Bush was "born again." Just thank God he wasn't cloned! The immediate cause of "the war" was presidential over-confidence, bought and paid for by over-taxed laborers in the fields of industry and patty-flipping. George Bush's transcendence of his wimpy past came not from "within" his self-earned reserve of character, but rather from a reserve of unused weapons burning a hole in the pocket of his overall disdain for humanity.

Ill-will and compulsion drove Bush to release a torrent of destruction upon the first Third World upstart he could throttle and pretend was a real threat. Grenada and Panama weren't credible victories, so a Blitzkrieg on Iraq (the "fourth largest army in the world!") was arranged. American soldiers and their parents financed the whole thing. They supplied the arms... and the legs. As luck and good P.R. would have it, they left their hearts and minds out of it, except for a puppy-like morality that wanted to see their own cuddly familiars returned safely. No humanity was wasted on the abused and afflicted soldiers of Iraq. As enemies, they were classified as spots in the field to be denatured. And the citizens of Baghdad were just collateral on the loan of our new technology.

Act VI
Endgame

The real news from the Iraqi front, filtered through the flag with the rest of the censored reality, was that the Russians weren't there. It was the only news that the official silence made more obvious. That the Soviets would sit this one out meant the apocryphal Third World War prophesied in all the revival meetings would have to wait another millennium to trigger the rapture. One can credibly predict there will be a series of Iraq-style moves against strategic Third World countries, but not a global conflict to be given a number. The remaining big question is whether the republics of the Soviet Union will gain membership in the Brave New World Order as a unit, and hence as a Second World franchise, or rather as separate Third World labor pools.

A few other myths have fallen by the wayside in the wake of the invasion of Iraq. First, the myth of "mutually assured destruction," the militaristic catechism by which politics was guided for over forty-five years has been, for some rather mystifying reasons, abandoned. It's as if the Soviets no longer have nuclear missiles, though we "know" they do and we "know" America does too. What's changed that the citizens of a free democracy shouldn't know about? Apparently everything.

The myths of "massive U.S. casualties in a ground war," "no new taxes," and "a kinder, gentler nation" seem almost too trivial to mention once you realize there's nothing new about just plain lies.

So where does it all take us? The end of history has yet to be written, but an overview of this peculiar era in the interplay of global power centers might read:

The Cold War was dead and buried; the war for the Second World was done. But the Brave New World Order was on its way, and the Third World war had just begun.

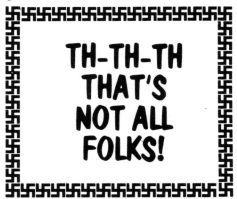

TH-TH-TH THAT'S NOT ALL FOLKS!

WHAT IS THE FIJA?

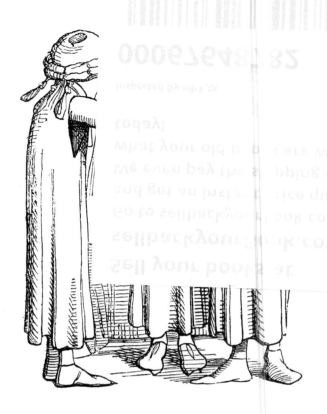

"FIJA" means Fully Informed Jury Amendment, Act or Association.

FIJA would require by state law that judges resume telling jurors about their right to vote their consciences when deciding on a verdict. Jurors would have to be told they have the right to acquit someone because they believe that the law itself is wrong, or is being wrongly applied, even when the facts of the case would support a conviction.

FIJA is also the name of the organization sponsoring this and related jury-rights amendments. But FIJA's ultimate goal is to tell everyone the truth about the rights of jurors, whether or not laws requiring that judges "read them their rights" are ever passed.

Accordingly, FIJA, publishes both informational and political materials, assist grass roots effort to inform jurors of their rights, assists state-level lobbying and/or ballot-issue efforts to put FIJA up for a public vote, and sponsors conferences toward these goals.

WE WANT EVERY POTENTIAL JUROR IN AMERICA TO KNOW THE TRUTH!

NEW HOPE FOR FREEDOM: FULLY INFORMED JURORS
by Don Doig

America's Founders were worried that the government they created might someday grow too powerful, and begin to pass laws which would violate the rights of the very people the government was supposed to protect: ordinary, peaceful, productive Americans. But they had an "ace in the hole" which they believed would suffice to hold the government in check. That was the right to a trial by jury of one's peers.

Since when, you might ask, can a jury protect people from arbitrary and unjust prosecutions, or from being forced to obey bad laws? Legislatures create our laws. Aren't we supposed to follow them, and lobby our legislatures for any changes that need to be made?

Yes, we can surely lobby. But we Americans have access to a more direct, less political, and much less expensive means by which to protect ourselves against governments which grow too ambitious, and any oppressive laws they enact.

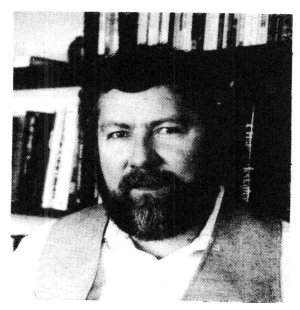

Don Doig - FIJA National Coordinator

America's Founders fully realized that the temptations of power would be too great to leave it up to the legislative, executive, and judicial branches of government to define what the rights of the citizens of this nation were. Ultimately, citizens at the local level, acting according to the dictates of individual conscience, were going to need to have the final say, the final check and balance. *The people would need veto power over bad laws.*

That is why they provided just such a veto, a centuries-old tradition carried over from England to the colonies, which held that jurors could judge whether a law was a good law, a law that did not violate the rights of the free men and women. If, according to the dictates of conscience, jurors did not think a law was just, or if they thought the law had been misapplied, they could refuse to convict an otherwise "guilty" defendant. Even a single juror could prevent a conviction, by voting "not guilty."

And if the jury as a whole decided to acquit the defendant, its decision was and is final. A verdict of not guilty cannot be overturned, nor can the judge harass the jurors for voting for acquittal. Juror's cannot be punished for voting according to conscience.

These principles date back to the time of the Magna Charta. In 1670, William Penn was arrested for preaching a Quaker sermon, and in so doing breaking the law of England, which made the Church of England the only legal church. The jurors in his trial, led by Edward Bushell, refused to convict him, and were as a result locked up without food, water, tobacco and toilet facilities.

Four were put in prison for nine weeks. When they were finally released by the Court of Common Pleas, the decision established that jurors could no longer be punished for their verdicts. This case helped establish freedom of religion, as well as the right to a trial by a jury of one's peers — a jury free from government coercion.

The sedition trial of John Peter Zenger, in the American colonies, was another landmark case. Zenger had been arrested for publishing some materials critical of the Royal Governor of New York colony and his cronies, accusing them of corruption. While the charges were true, under the law, truth was no defense. Zenger's attorney, Andrew Hamilton, argued to the jurors, that they were judges of the merits of the law, and should not convict Zenger of violating such a bad law. This jury agreed. Zenger was acquitted, and this case helped establish the right of freedom of speech.

The Founding Fathers were clear about where they stood on their issue of rights of jurors. In 1771, John Adams stated unequivocally that a juror should ignore a judges' instruction on the law if it violates fundamental principles:

"It is not only... (the juror's) right, but his duty in that case, to find the verdict according to his own best understanding, judgment, and conscience though in direct opposition to the direction of the court."

According to "The Changing Role of the Jury in the Nineteenth Century," (Anonymous, *Yale Law Review* 74.174, (1964):

"There is much evidence of the general acceptance of this principle in the period immediately after the Constitution was adopted."

Thomas Jefferson said in a letter to Thomas Paine in 1789: "I consider trial by jury as the only anchor ever yet imagined by man, by which a government can be held to the principles of its constitution."

And yet, during the nineteenth century, judges chipped away at this fundamental right of free citizens, transferring more and more power to themselves, contending that jury review of law was no longer necessary, now that democratic elections had "replaced monarchy." By the end of the century, the Supreme Court had decided to leave it up to the judge to decide if the jury should be told of its right to judge law as well as fact.

Today, jurors are generally told that they must accept the law as the judge explains it, and may not decide to

(Continued next page)

bothered by what seems to them an unjust law. Judges falsely tell them that their only role is to decide if the "facts" are sufficient to convict the defendant. Defense attorneys are not allowed to encourage jurors to vote to acquit because they believe the law is unjust or unconstitutional, and defendants are generally not allowed to even discuss their motives.

In plain words, in what comes down to a protracted power struggle between the people and the judicial system, the people have been losing.

In fact, jurors still, to this day, have the right to veto, or "nullify" bad laws. They are just not told this by the courts. And both judges and prosecutors exclude people from serving on juries who indicate a willingness to nullify the law. This violates the protection jurors were supposed to be able to give their fellow citizens against unjust prosecutions. A jury is properly a cross section of the community as a whole.

What can be done? The Fully Informed Jury Amendment/Act (FIJA) can be passed into law. As a state constitutional amendment or as a statute, it will require judges to inform jurors that if they think a law is unjust or unconstitutional — or even just misapplied — they need not convict an otherwise "guilty" defendant.

FIJA does not give jurors the right to act as a legislature, since their decisions affect only the case at hand and do not set precedents for future cases. Nor can jurors create new offenses on which to find the defendant guilty. Should a jury convict a defendant unjustly, the judge may set aside the conviction, and in addition the defendant always has the right of appeal...

People from all walks of life and from across the political spectrum are organizing as "FIJA activists," either lobbying state legislators to support FIJA legislation, or seeking to put the issue to a vote via referendums and initiatives. FIJA bills have been introduced in Alaska, Arizona, California, Louisiana, Iowa, Massachusetts, Montana, Nevada, New York, Oklahoma, Tennessee, Texas, Utah, Washington and Wyoming. In Alaska and California FIJA activists are doing citizen initiatives along with their legislative efforts. And in all areas of the country, people are spreading the word with literature, bumper stickers, t-shirts, tapes, talk shows, and conversation.

Judges and others within the government's courts have for years been waging a campaign of disinformation, so that modern day jurors very rarely know what their rights are. We think it's past time that the people themselves begin to demand that their rights as jurors be respected.

It's not just the jurors whose rights are being denied. Defendants, in the first place, have the right to a fair trial by a jury of their peers, but have often not been getting fair trials because of judges who won't tell juries the truth about their rights, powers, and responsibilities.

In fact, this campaign to deny juror's rights has been going on for so long that nowadays many attorneys (and probably some judges) are not even aware that the rights exist!

With FIJA we the people have an opportunity to resume control of this country and again to take responsibility for the protection of our rights. *Please become a FIJA activist — join us in the campaign to require that every trial jury be fully informed!*

As a participant in the debates over the ratification of the Constitution put it, in 2 Elliot's Debates, 94, Bancroft, *History of the Constitution,* 267, 1788:

"If a juror accepts as the law that which the judge states, then that juror has accepted the exercise or absolute authority of a government employee, and has surrendered a power and right that once was the citizen's safeguard of liberty.... For the saddest epitaph which can be carved in memory of a vanished liberty is that it was lost because its possessors failed to stretch forth a saving hand while yet there was time."

ANSWERING THE HARD QUESTIONS
by Larry Dodge

While on my road trips, in meetings, talk shows, and media interviews, the same or similar questions come up again and again, which has encouraged me to come up with a repertoire of satisfying answers. These I want to share with you, since you many need to respond to similar questions during the campaign ahead, though I make no claim that mine are the best or only answers.

Won't FIJA lead to anarchy, with juries judging the law?

FIJA is actually an antidote to "anarchy" we've already generated as a byproduct of too many laws for people to obey, and which helps explain both soaring crime rates and overcrowded prisons. When juries consistently refuse to convict people

(Continued on next page)

of breaking a certain law, the incentive is for lawmakers to change or erase it — lest they lose the next election. When the law books become cleansed of unpopular or confusing laws, the rate of compliance with the remaining laws will be high, thus *reducing* anarchy.

Likewise, whenever jurors feel compelled to apologize to a defendant for convicting him (which is quite often, nowadays), and then later find out they had the authority to vote according to conscience, but weren't told about it, their own respect for the law and our legal system can only diminish. In other words, failure to inform juries of their rights breeds anarchy.

Four states (Indiana, Oregon, Maryland, and Georgia) already have general provisions in their constitutions acknowledging that juries may judge law, and twenty-two other states have the same provision included in their sections on freedom of speech or libel. To my knowledge, no chaos has resulted because of these provisions.

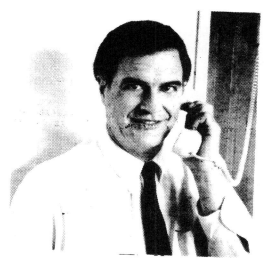

Larry Dodge is the National Field Representative for the Fully Informed Jury Association.

Couldn't the jury convict someone of a worse crime than the one is charged with?

No. Juries do not and would not have the power to escalate or invent charges against a defendant. Their power may only be exerted in the direction of mercy, never of vengeance. Nor can juries "make law" by which to convict a defendant. That remains the job of the legislature. They may, however, reduce the charges against an accused person, provided the lower charge is a less serious form of the same crime he was originally charged with. The decisions of juries do not and would not establish precedent for future cases.

What if the jury is prejudiced in favor of the defendant, and lets him go even though he's clearly guilty?

This is the "corrupt jury" problem, and happens periodically with or without jury instruction in their right to judge the law. Jury members should be randomly selected from the population as a whole. If, instead, a jury is selected so that all its members come in determined to acquit a guilty person, it is likely to do just that, no matter what it's told or not told. For this to happen virtually requires that both the prosecutor and judge be corrupt, as well, taking no steps to see that at least some of the jurors are not prejudiced. In short, if the defendant faces fourteen people, all of whom favor letting him go free regardless of whom the evidence, he will go free.

Even under these circumstances, if jurors were instructed that each of them could vote according to his own conscious, as FIJA provides, there is at least a possibility that one or more jurors would not go along with the rest, thus hanging the jury with one or more **guilty** votes. Chances for justice might then improve, via another trial, perhaps a change of venue, or a different judge, and certainly another jury.

Further, victims of crimes who do not find satisfaction in a criminal trial verdict have with fair success, been able to sue perpetrators for damages. In other instances, crime victims who were unhappy with verdicts handed down in state courts have been able to have defendants tried in federal courts on other charges, often for violating their civil rights.

Do jurors have the right, or just the power, to judge the law?

They have *both.* They have the power, because in a jury system, no one can tell the jury what verdict it must reach, nor restrict what goes on in jury-room deliberations, nor punish jurors for the verdict they bring in, nor demand to know why they reached that verdict. It is no accident that our nation's founders provided for appeals of guilty verdicts, but not of acquittals: they intended the jury to have the power to halt a prosecution.

They have the right, because each juror is partially responsible for the verdict returned, thus

(Continued next page)

for the fate of the accused individual — and for every responsibility there is a corresponding right. In this case, that is the right to consider everything necessary for him or her to vote for a just verdict. That includes evidence, the defendant's motives, testimony, the law, circumstances — whatever, including the juror's own *conscience*.

Finally, when one gets down to it, there is precious little difference, except in academic legal discourse, between a right and a power. Most dictionaries recognize this by listing them as synonyms.

Wouldn't our courts be flooded with jury trials if the FIJA were to become law?

It's probable that the number of jury trials involving some of the least popular and most frequently broken laws would increase, until prosecutors began choosing not to attempt convictions on them any more, police began letting up on enforcement, and legislators began reading the writing on the jury-room walls. But the peak should soon pass. And a reduced number of costly appeals to higher courts is expectable, because more people would feel they'd received justice at their original trials.

Ultimately, though, one must ask what's more important, fast service at your local courthouse, or **justice** for accused individuals, and real-world feedback to the lawmakers?

Wouldn't there be a lot of variation from place to place in jury verdicts, according to local community standards?

Perhaps, though it could hardly compete with the variations in verdicts and sentences already being handed down by different judges...

It might prove true that informed-jury verdicts would vary more than they do now from place to place with respect to ceratin types of offenses. Tolerance of abortion, drugs, pornography, gun ownership, etc. might be higher in some communities than others. But then, what's the merit in trying to force-fit a diverse society into one huge homogeneous mold, in obliging every person or every community to conform to some central authority's notion of how to behave? We suggest that if your act doesn't go over locally, walk.

Actually, the overall trust and effect of FIJA should be to promote consistency — in the form of *tolerance* — everywhere. It is already happen-

ing, as different kinds of Americans are joining together in coalitions to make FIJA into law. Most people, it turns out, would rather secure their own liberty than damage someone else's — it's just that our political system spawns and promotes rancor between competing special-interest groups, where one group's gain is usually another's loss.

FIJA will also make it more difficult for majorities to deny the rights of minorities, because any minority (and we're all minorities) will be able to defend itself via jury veto powers.

The real payoff is that government, which grows in power and intrusiveness with every escalation of distrust and intolerance between warring factions of citizens, may lose its grip as trial juries resume their check-and-balance function, and "live and let live" re-emerges as the American ethos.

What happens if the jury nullifies a good law?

This is not generally a problem. We have centuries of experience with jury veto power, and generally laws that protect people against invasions of their property or threats against their safety, are supported by the community as a whole, and are enforced by jurors. Maryland and Indiana report good success and nullification instructions.

It is both *elitist* and *erroneous* to accuse the ordinary citizens of this country of not being able to govern themselves when the opportunity or need arises. Political science studies show that people become extremely conscientious, cautious and responsible when they sit on a jury — more so than at practically any other time in their lives.

What would become of the practice of basing verdicts upon legal precedents?

The role of case law, or precedent, would remain useful as advice for all parties to a trial, but its use as a basis for verdicts in current jury trials would end. A major objection in fully informing juries of their rights and powers is to provide ever-evolving *feedback* to our legislators, so that regular adjustments can be made in the rules that we live by.

The idea is to match our laws to our standards of right and wrong on an ongoing basis, so that gaps will no longer develop between them. This kind of consistency cannot be had when "precedent requires" that the same verdict be found for

(Continued on next page)

a modern case as was found in similar cases in the past. When gaps between what's moral and what's legal get too large, we risk "anarchy" on the one hand, totalitarian intervention on the other.

Would FIJA violate our Fourteenth Amendment right to equal protection under the law?

"Equal protection" is already tough to guarantee, given the differences in quality between judges, prosecutors and defense attorneys who may become involved in any given case. Add to them our media-assisted fads and fashions in law enforcement, and the very unequal kinds of deals which are regularly pushed upon defendants by the prosecutor and/or the judges outside the courtroom (too often based upon the accused person's appearance, background, and ability to pay), and "equal protection" takes on the appearance of an ideal which draws a lot more lip service than real concern.

Juries generally become part of the problem only to the extent that both the prosecution and the defense have done everything in their power to select the least knowledgeable and most manipulable jurors possible. If those making an equal protection argument really cared, they'd ask for laws ensuring *random selection* of jurors from as broad a base as possible.

FIJA may provide a partial answer, because chances of equal treatment of defendants would appear to increase if the jury were to receive complete and accurate instruction in its veto powers, not because information begets fairness, but for at least two other reasons: (1) if jurors are lied to about their right and powers, a certain percentage of them can be expected to see through the falsehood, then to rationalize reciprocating that dishonesty by lying to one or both attorneys and the judge during the selection process. Just what they may be covering up or misrepresenting, and why, will certainly vary from jury to jury, and that's exactly what the doctrine of equal protection rails against;

(2) When both prosecution and defense know in advance that the jurors will be fully informed of their power to judge both law and fact, their jury selection criteria can be expected to change accordingly. Both sides would face an incentive to find jurors able and willing to consider not only factual but also moral-philosophical questions in search of justice, especially in those cases where the merits or the applicability of the law may be at issue. The result should be both better-quality juries and more equality under the laws that they work with.

Wouldn't FIJA cause a great increase in the number of hung juries?

In the short run, perhaps, as laws which are hard for people to understand, identify with, or apply are evaluated by juries. As "mercy buffers" between the power of the state and the accused individual, and between majorities and minorities, a certain frequency of inability to reach a consensus is to be expected. But that's the point: it's important for that there remains at least one institution of government which must achieve unanimity to make a decision, since most series of usurpation of rights in general begin with attacks on the rights of unpopular minorities or individuals.

On the other hand, juries always have a responsibility to identify, and sometimes to determine an appropriate punishment for people who damage the social fabric of their communities. When the trial is over, other members of the community often want to know how and why the verdict was found. This exception provides a strong incentive for the jurors to make a serious attempt at unanimity.

When that incentive isn't strong enough, and a long series of hung juries on cases involving a particular law occurs, it sends a powerful message to lawmakers that reform is necessary. Such a series may reflect public demand for more precision, fairness, latitude, appropriateness or other features in the law. But the beauty of feedback for juries is that it is rarely a statement of special interest: hardly ever do all twelve people on a jury share a single political goal or viewpoint, and the chances that all the people on a series of juries will do so are utterly remote.

The relative frequency of hung juries can therefore be read as a measurement of true public sentiment about the law. The more *responsive* our legislatures become to that measurement, the stronger the association between community moral standards and the law will become, and the fewer hung juries there will be. ●

This material was reprinted by permission from the Special Outreach Issue of *The FIJA Activist, the Newsletter of the Fully Informed Jury Association.* For more information, write FIJA, PO Box 59, Helmville, MT 59843.

THE WAR
AND
THE SPECTACLE

The orchestration of the Gulf war was a glaring expression of what the situationists call *the spectacle* — the development of modern society to the point where images dominate life. The PR campaign was as important as the military one. How this or that tactic would play in the media became a major strategical consideration. It didn't matter much whether the bombing was actually "surgical" as long as the *coverage* was; if the victims didn't appear; it was as if they didn't exist. The "Nintendo effect" worked so well that the euphoric generals had to caution against too much public euphoria for fear that it might backfire. Interviews with soldiers in the desert revealed that they, like everyone else, depended totally on the media to tell them what was supposedly happening. The domination of image over reality was sensed by everyone. A large portion of the coverage consisted of coverage of the coverage. The spectacle itself presented superficial debates on the new level of instant global spectacularization and its effects on the spectator.

Nineteenth-century capitalism alienated people from themselves and from each other by alienating them from the products of their own activity. This alienation has been intensified as those products have increasingly become "productions" that we passively contemplate. The power of the mass media is only the most obvious manifestation of this development; in the larger sense the spectacle is everything from arts to politicians that have become autonomous *representations* of life. "The spectacle is not a collection of images, but a social relation among people, mediated by images" (Debord, *The Society of the Spectacle*).

Along with arms profits, oil control, international power struggles and other factors which have been so widely discussed as to need no comment here, the war involved contradictions between the two basic forms of spectacle society. In the *diffuse spectacle* people are lost amid the variety of competing spectacles, commodities, styles and

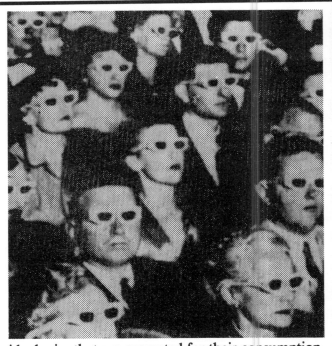

ideologies that are presented for their consumption. The diffuse spectacle arises within societies of pseudoabundance (America is the prototype and still the unchallenged world leader of spectacle production, despite its decline in other regards); but it is also broadcast to less developed regions — being one of the main means by which the latter are dominated. Saddam's regime is an example of the rival *concentrated spectacle*, in which people are conditioned to identify with the omnipresent image of the totalitarian leader as compensation for being deprived of virtually everything else. This image concentration is normally associated with a corresponding concentration of economic power, state capitalism, in which the state itself has become the sole, all-owning capitalist enterprise (classic examples are Stalin's Russia and Mao's China); but it may also be imported into Third World mixed economies (such as Saddam's Iraq) or even in times of crisis, into highly developed economies (such as Hitler's Germany). But for the most part the concentrated spectacle is a crude stopgap for regions as yet incapable of sustaining the variety of illusions of the diffuse spectacle, and in the long run it tends to succumb too the latter, more flexible form (as recently in eastern Europe and the USSR). At the same time, the diffuse form is tending to incorporate certain features of the concentrated one.

The Gulf war reflected this convergence. The closed world of Saddam's concentrated spectacle dissipated under the global floodlights of the diffuse

First published in 1991 Fall Supplement
(Continued on next page)

spectacle; while the latter used the war as a pretext and a testing ground for implementing typically "concentrated" methods of control — censorship, orchestration of patriotism, suppression of dissent. But the mass media are so monopolized, so pervasive and (despite token grumbling) so subservient to establishment policies that overtly repressive methods were hardly needed. The spectators, under the impression that they were expressing their own considered view, parroted the catch phrases and debated the pseudoissues that the media had instilled in them day after day, and as in any other spectator sport, loyally "supported" the home team in the desert by *rooting* for it.

This media control was reinforced by the spectators' own internalized conditioning. Socially and psychologically repressed, people are drawn to spectacles of violent conflict that allow their accumulated frustrations to explode in socially condoned orgasms of collective pride and hate. Deprived of significant accomplishments in their own work and leisure, they participate vicariously in military enterprises that have real and undeniable effects. Lacking genuine community, they thrill to the sense of sharing in a common purpose, if only that of fighting some common enemy, and react angrily against anyone who contradicts the image of patriotic unanimity. The individual's life may be a farce, the society may be falling apart, but all complexities and uncertainties are temporarily forgotten in the self-assurance that comes from identifying with the state.

War is the truest expression of the state, and its most powerful reinforcement. Just as capitalism must create artificial needs for its increasingly superfluous commodities, the state must continually create artificial conflicts of interest requiring its violent intervention. The fact that the state incidentally provides a few "social services" merely camouflages its fundamental nature as a *protection racket.* When two states go to war the net result is as if each state had made war on its own people — who are then taxed to pay for it. The Gulf war was a particularly gross example: Several states eagerly sold billions of dollars' worth of arms to another state, then massacred hundreds of thousands of conscripts and civilians in the name of neutralizing its dangerously large arsenal. The multinational corporations that own those states now stand to make still more billions of dollars restocking arm-

aments and rebuilding the countries they have ravaged.

Whatever happens in the Middle East in the complex aftermath of war, one thing is certain: The first aim of all the states and would-be states, overriding all their conflicting interests, will be to crush or coopt any truly radical popular movement. On this issue Bush and Saddam, Mubarak and Rafsanjani, Shamir and Arafat are all partners. The American government, which piously insisted that its war was "not against the Iraqi people but only against their brutal dictator," has now given Saddam another "green light:" to slaughter and torture the Iraqis who have courageously risen against him. American officials openly admit that they prefer continued police-military rule in Iraq (with or without Saddam) to any form of democratic self-rule that might "destabilize" the region — *i.e.,* that might give neighboring peoples the inspiration for similar revolts against their own rulers.

In America the "success" of the war has diverted attention from the acute social problems that the system is incapable of solving, reinforcing the power of the militarist establishment and the complacency of the patriotic spectators. While the latter are busy watching war reruns and exulting at victory parades, the most interesting question is what will happen with the people who saw through the show.

The most significant thing about the movement against the Gulf war was its unexpected spontaneity and diversity. In the space of a few days hundreds of thousands of people all over the country, the majority of whom had never even been at a demonstration before, initiated or took part in vigils, blockades, teach-ins and a wide variety of other actions. By February the coalitions that had called the huge January marches — some factions of which would normally have tended to work for "mass unity" under their own bureaucratic guidance — recognized that the movement was far beyond any possibility of centralization or control, and agreed to leave the main impetus to local grassroots initiative. Most of the participants had already been treating the big marches simply as gathering points while remaining more or less indifferent to the coalitions officially in charge (often not even bothering to stay around to listen to the usual ranting speeches). The real interaction was not between

(Continued on next page)

stage and audience, but among the individuals carrying their own homemade signs, handing out their own leaflets, playing their music, doing their street theater, discussing their ideas with friends and strangers, discovering a sense of community in the face of insanity.

It will be a sad spirit if these persons become ciphers, if they allow themselves to be channeled into quantitative, lowest-common-denominator political projects — tediously drumming up votes to elect "radical" politicians who will invariably sell them out, collecting signatures in support of "progressive" laws that will usually have little effect even if passed, recruiting "bodies" for demonstrations whose numbers will in any case be underreported or ignored by the media. If they want to contest the hierarchical system they must reject hierarchy in their own methods and relations. If they want to break through the spectacle-induced stupor, they must use their own imaginations. If they want to incite others, they themselves must *experiment.*

Those who saw through the war became aware, if they weren't already, of how much the media falsify reality. Personal participation made this awareness more vivid. To take part in a peace march of a hundred thousand people and see it given equal-time coverage with a prowar demonstration of a few dozen is an illuminating experience — it brings home the bizarre unreality of the spectacle, as well as calling into question the relevance of tactics based on communicating radical viewpoints by way of the mass media. Even while the war was still going on the protestors saw that they had to confront these questions, and in countless discussions and symposiums on "the war and the media" they examined not only the blatant lies and overt blackouts, but the more subtle methods of media distortion — use of emotionally loaded images; isolation of events from their historical context; limitation of debate to "responsible" options; framing of dissident viewpoints in ways that trivialize them; personification of complex realities (Saddam = Iraq); objectification of persons ("collateral damage") etc. These examinations are continuing and are giving rise to a veritable industry of articles, lectures and books analyzing every aspect of media falsification.

The most naive see the falsifications as mere mistakes or biases that might be corrected if enough members of the audience call in and complain, or otherwise pressure the mass media into presenting a somewhat wider range of viewpoints. At its most radical this perspective is expressed in the limited but suggestive tactic of picketing particular media.

Others, aware that the mass media are owned by the same interests that own the state and the economy and will thus inevitably represent those interests, concentrate on disseminating suppressed information through various alternative media. But the glut of sensational information constantly broadcast in the spectacle is so deadening that the revelation of one more lie or scandal or atrocity seldom leads to anything but increased depression and cynicism.

Others try to break through this apathy by adopting the manipulative methods of propaganda and advertising. An antiwar film, for example, is generally assumed to have a "powerful" effect if it presents a barrage of the horrors of war. The actual subliminal effect of such a barrage is, if anything, prowar — getting caught up in an irresistible onslaught of chaos and violence (as long as it remains comfortably vicarious) is precisely what is exciting about war to jaded spectators. Overwhelming people with a rapid succession of emotion-rousing images only confirms them in their habitual sense of helplessness in the face of a world beyond their control. Spectators with thirty-second attention spans may be shocked into a momentary antiwar revulsion by pictures of napalmed babies, but they may just as easily be whipped into a fascistic fury the next day by different images — of flag burners, say.

Regardless of their ostensibly radical messages, alternative media have generally reproduced the dominant spectacle-spectator relation. The point is to undermine it — to challenge the conditioning that makes people *susceptible* to media manipulation in the first place. Which ultimately means challenging the social organization that produces the conditioning, that turns people into spectators of prefabricated adventures because they are prevented from creating their own.●

Bureau of Public Secrets
PO Box 1044
Berkeley, CA 94701
No copyright, 3 April 1991

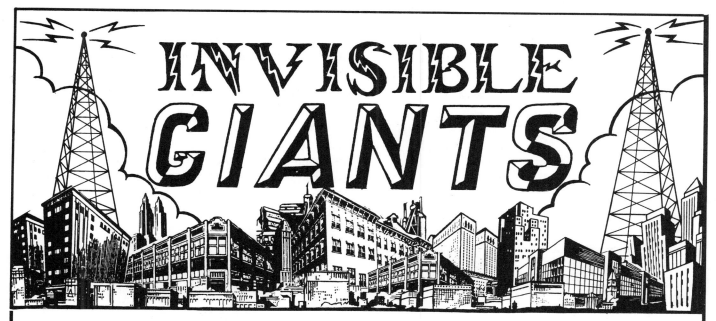

INVISIBLE GIANTS

The Tabloids and the Mainstream Media

© 1991 by Jim Hogshire

Illustrations by A-

Even when feeding off them, the mainstream news likes to pretend the supermarket tabloids don't exist. When NBC wanted to reveal the name of the alleged rape victim at the Kennedy's Palm Beach estate, they used the excuse that the woman's name was well-known within Palm Beach society, *not* because her name and photo had already been published in the *Globe*.

When Ted Koppel wanted to rhapsodize on the ethics of revealing rape victim's names, *Nightline* acknowledged the tabloid's existence but illustrated the *Globe* by holding a copy of the *Enquirer* in front of the camera. Koppel then solicited the opinions of NBC News president Michael Gartner, who made damn sure nobody thought he would ever take the *Globe* into consideration when making a decision of such journalistic moment.

"Well, we didn't do it because the *Globe* had done it, Ted," Gartner reassured us. "The woman's name had become quite well-known in the Palm Beach community."

With these words Gartner spilled the elitist beans. The knowledge of the bejeweled matrons of Palm Beach meant more to him than the five million people across the country who had read the woman's name and seen her picture in the *Globe* that week. From then on, in the show, the *Globe*

became the Newspaper With No Name — referred to only as "the tabloid." Nobody from ABC or any of the network news programs asked a representative from Globe Communications to come onto their hallowed shows. When *Globe* editor Wendy Henry pointed out to AP reporters that there was no crime in being a rape victim, her philosophy was assumed to be a flimsy cover for her gross sensationalism. When Gartner or the anonymous *New York Times* editors rambled on about their soul-wrenching debates we were expected to believe them. That is because we are not so gullible, so cretinous as tabloid readers.

The reality is that supermarket tabloids are closer to mainstream America than either Ted Koppel or the *New York Times* and by ignoring them we ignore an enormous influence on the public mind. Furthermore, the supermarket tabloids have begun to reshape mainstream media almost against their will — and it's not because nobody is reading them. There are at least 50 million supermarket tabloid readers in America. Who knows how many more absorb their messages while standing in line at the checkout counter? Nobody is immune. *New York Times* columnist Russell Baker referred to *National Examiner* headlines as often as he did John Updike's novels when describing his summer vacation. *Newsday* ran a story on the *Examiner's*

treatment of Saddam Hussein and even the *Nation's* Alexander Cockburn devoted about a third of his column to an *Examiner* story.

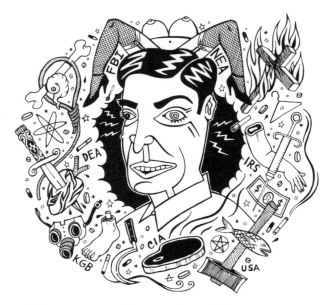

There are at least 50 million supermarket tabloid readers in America. Who knows how many more absorb their messages while standing in line at the checkout counter? Nobody is immune.

The typical tabloid reader buys more than one tabloid at a time and reads no other newspaper, supplementing his or her views with television only. Their devotion to their tabloids is marvelous. When the *National Examiner* reported that Polident commercial star Martha (Bigmouth) Ray was hospitalized, she received more than 1,000 get well cards. The *Examiner's* Tony Leggett gets more than 200 letters every day seeking his psychic assistance. Only Ann Landers and Abigail Van Buren get more mail. Crates of letters are carted into the tabloids' offices every day and reader's service personnel make sure each person receives an answer to his question —no matter how bizarre.

The tabloids take their readers seriously, and the readers return the favor.

Often relying on the tabloids as their main source of news and opinion, tabloid readers learn of the pitiful birth of a dog baby in Romania, the discov- ery that vinegar can cure cancer and that being struck by lightning can transform a woman into a man.

Tabloid readers also learn that Muslim countries routinely flog and execute foreign visitors for trivial crimes. They learn that "druggies" are best served with life in prison, homeless people are secret millionaires, nagging wives can be handled by super-glueing their mouths shut, and lately, that Allah demands women submit to gang-bangs for "his greater glory."

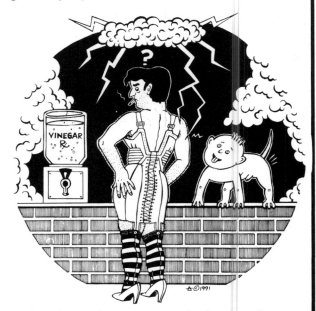

Tabloid readers learn of the pitiful birth of a dog baby in Romania, the discovery that vinegar can cure cancer and that being struck by lightning can transform a woman into a man.

They appeal to our most banal anxieties about birth, death and sex, they cater to our most xenophobic nightmares. Their humorous stories about roller-skating grannies and miracle babies surviving death plunges make the lackluster seem interesting. And whenever they expose the peccadillos of TV stars, they reassure us that they're just as human as we are.

In a 1984 Roper poll 20% of people used the word "accurate" to describe supermarket tabloids. The tabloids' own research indicates their readers

(Continued on next page)

are generally middle to lower class and white. They have blue and pink collar jobs. A little more than half of them own pulsating shower heads, their favorite meals are steak, chicken, and lobster (in that order) and the majority of them own outdoor grills.

In short, tabloid readers are everybody. But to listen to the mainstream press one would think only numbskulls read such rags, and that *nobody* believes them. Except to ridicule tabloids, journalism schools don't even talk about them — they're so low on their scale. This billion dollar publishing enterprise is dismissed and derided by illuminati who use "supermarket tabloid" as a kind of shorthand for anything frivolous, libelous, and dim-witted.

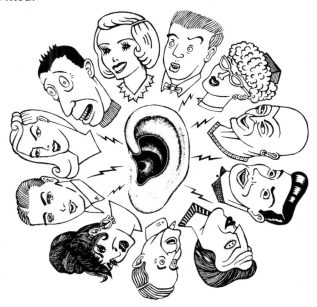

A look at the covers of *Time* and *Newsweek* makes one wonder what's so different about them and the tabloids. Perhaps *Time* gave up any pretense to seriousness last March when it devoted an issue to: Gossip.

Together, the six supermarket tabloids have a circulation of more than 10 million (compare this with 6.3 million of all Gannet papers combined). All six tabloids are owned by two private corporations, which concentrate editorial power into the hands of just two men — Globe Communications'

Mike Rosenbloom and *Enquirer* editor Iain Calder who carries out the will of McFadden Holdings.

Recent wheeling and dealing highlight the sheer market power of these newspapers. Last June, media tycoon Robert Maxwell reportedly offered between $200 and $300 million for Globe Communications' three tabloids (*The Globe, The Examiner,* and the *Sun*). It wasn't enough. The preceding March, when MacFadden Holdings Inc. (which already owns the *National Enquirer*) absorbed Rupert Murdoch's *Star* it paid $412.5 million — roughly the same price as a Japanese company paid to purchase the entire 7-11 convenience store chain from Southland Corporation.

Like it or not, tabloids are part of the American landscape. Their marketing methods have been copied by every newsmagazine elbowing its way into the supermarket checkout lines. Even the staid *Reader's Digest* has taken to supplying its single copy sales with a tear-off cover guaranteed to have the words "sex" or "diet" in 42 point type.

Tabloid celebrity coverage has forced newspapers and newsmagazines alike to include chatty "personalities" sections. A look at the covers of *Time* or *Newsweek* makes one wonder what's so different about them and the tabloids. Liquid diets, movie stars, Prozac, blurry photos of murder victims, executed Ceausescu, and Manuel Noriega mugshots have all graced their covers. Perhaps *Time* gave up any pretense to seriousness last March when it devoted an issue to: Gossip.

Time, too, was the newsmagazine that reported the findings of an Israeli graphologist that Saddam Hussein was mentally disturbed. *The National Examiner's* graphologist says the handwriting indicates he has AIDS, but then again the *National Examiner* also crudely doctored a photo of Saddam to make him a transvestite. The *New Republic* wasn't so crude. They hired the best retouching studio for their September 3 issue featuring a menacing-looking Saddam... with Hitler's mustache.

Nevertheless, tabloids are regarded by many as "unbelievable" compared to the mainstream media. There is little evidence to support this.

Leafing through any tabloid, the reader finds the very same phrases used by the *New York Times* to buttress its opinions. "Government sources say...," "Sources close to the President revealed...," or the ever-popular "In documents obtained by...". If

(Continued next page) **71**

"inside sources" are regarded as credible in the *Washington Post,* why not in *The Weekly World News?* And so what if the source is faked? The blurring between fact and fiction is essential in both mainstream and tabloid press. The only difference is the tabloids don't claim to be the Final Truth on anything. And, after all, it was the *New York Times* and not the *National Enquirer* that reported the Tawana Brawley case as gospel. It was the *Washington Post,* not the *Sun,* that gave us the Pulitzer prize-winning "Jimmy's World" by Janet Cooke. Bob Woodward, Cooke's editor and originator of that most famous anonymous source — Deep Throat — didn't bother to see if Jimmy was real or not, so why should we?

In a larger way the *New York Times* reflects the tabloids' influence by incoming editor Max Frankel's edicts to run larger front page photos and shorten stories from an average 800 to 1,000 words to 650 or 700. Frankel said readers just didn't "have time to absorb" articles that take so much of a page.

Obviously, *USA Today* has far more in common with the *National Enquirer* than the *Philadelphia Inquirer.* Splashy color photos, ridiculous snippets of useless information cast as essential facts (*USA Today's* perky little pie graphs on how much dental floss we're using) were all pioneered in the tabloids. Later this year the *New York Times,* too, will have color photos and who knows, maybe a horoscope column.

Little in the mainstream press conflicts with the contents of the tabloids. The Gulf War proved that. If *National Examiner* readers are told the story of how Saddam likes to wear a gunbelt while raping captive American girls, how can we not believe it? After all, the *Washington Post* has already reported that Saddam's wife is (gasp!) a bleached-blonde. After reading the *New York Times* stories of little Saddam's "tough streets of Baghdad" childhood, doesn't it follow that he really does strangle cocker spaniels as the *Examiner* claims?

The overnight switching of Iraq and Iran as friend and foe caused just as many problems for the tabloids as for the mainstream press, but they handled it in true Orwellian fashion. At the *Sun,* a story that was all ready to go about the diabolical Iranians sending AIDS-infected hookers to invade the United States had to be adjusted. By the time it was printed, the hookers were from Iraq. *Exam-*

iner readers may have been confused last April when reading the story of the kindly UFO that saved a hapless Iraqi jetliner from a cruel attack by Iranian fighters, since the demonization of Saddam had already begun. But the error was only because of our three-week lead time. The *Examiner* more than made up for it.

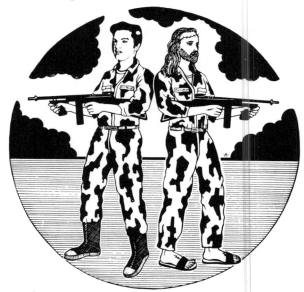

While the dailies merely passed on government lies about the war, the tabloids went one better. Suddenly, Jesus *and* Elvis appeared to our boys in the Gulf.

While the dailies merely passed on government lies about the war, the tabloids went one better. Suddenly, Jesus *and* Elvis appeared to our boys in the Gulf. Saddam's secret Rocky Mountain hideout was revealed and the Butcher of Baghdad's sexual kinks were made public from previously secret FBI files. The official *Globe* masthead, usually reserved for snide comments about television stars, began exhorting us to "Support America's Heroes." The effort did not go unappreciated.

"I am especially grateful for the support of all at Globe Communications for our efforts in the Persian Gulf," wrote George Bush to editorial director Phil Bunton. "It's important that our courageous troops face this historic challenge knowing that they have the support of millions of people around the world..."

(Continued on next page)

On the other hand, admitted Bunton, had Globe opposed the war, "we would have lost money hand over fist."

The war pointed up a critical fact about supermarket tabloids. Their content is essentially reactionary and has little to do with the actual politics of any editor. Tabs do not try to set the agenda for anything, but merely reinforce what they believe people are already thinking. This is normally perceived as right wing, which is just fine with the tabloids' publishers.

After all, it was to escape impending unionization that publisher Mike Rosenbloom moved Globe from its Montreal offices to Boca Raton, Florida in 1983. *Enquirer* founder Generoso Pope served at least one year in the CIA and his paper has been reputed to be a cover for U.S. spies all over the world. One of the editors at the *Examiner* used to write the "Cato" column for the *National Review.* Billy Graham, like George Bush, recognizes the power of the tabloids and has had a special relationship with the *Enquirer* for years. "My ministry is vitally concerned with reaching as many people as possible," explained the evangelist while visiting the *Enquirer's* Florida offices, "and the *Enquirer* is a powerful means of reaching millions of people every week."

"MUST THIS GIRL DIE..." screams a *Globe* headline, "while government money that could save her life is going to illegal aliens?" Just how the illegal aliens were depriving the girl of a liver transplant was never really explained but that hardly matters. In the tabloid world, non-white foreigners are presumptively disgusting. The Japanese are trying to buy the Statue of Liberty and install it on Mount Fuji, native tribesmen of Africa or South America are forever engaging in painful religious rites, third world girls keep having babies at age six — when they're not being raised by wild animals.

The *Examiner* called Arabs "Camel Jockeys" in one of its pre-war headlines. In December 1989 the *Sun* ran photos of hanged Arabs, supposedly executed for drinking alcohol (even though the signs in Arabic hanging around their necks accuse them of spying — minor detail).

American and European women are invariably "leggy" when under the age of 50 and "grannies" if they are older. Females who don't know their place are dealt with by being shut up in cages, basements or attics for years at a time. It is considered proper procedure for men to control women with any force necessary. But, if a woman just can't be made to obey, then it is possible to get rid of her by losing her in a card game or trading her in for a hunting dog. And just in case you think this is going too far don't forget, a recent *Sun* article has exposed a dastardly plan by women to take over the world by the year 2030.

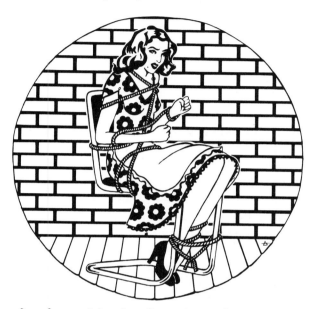

In the tabloids, females who don't know their place are dealt with by being shut up in cages, basements or attics for years at a time.

It seems a certain Professor Emil Carruthers of the University of London has revealed that women around the world are secretly buying guns, communicating world bulletins through soap operas and gearing up for a mass slaughter set to begin by the year 2000. Within forty years, the only men left "will be 'sensitive types' like Alan Alda and Phil Donahue who will be allowed to stay alive for breeding purposes."

And while drug users are invariably "sickos" and degenerates, drinking alcohol is looked upon with favor. Not only will drinking beer help you live longer, lose weight and remove wrinkles, but by saving the cans you can build such useful items as canoes or cottages. Or perhaps your beer can collection will win you your fifteen minutes of fame

(Continued next page) **73**

in a tabloid centerfold. Drunkeness normally produces hilarious situations especially if one of the drinkers is fat and passes out on top of someone else, pinning him until help can arrive. And alcohol is always a fine reward for winning any sort of physical contest.

So far the tabloids have done nothing to challenge the status quo. Their biggest power is in maintaining the misbeliefs and fears of the masses. The only detectable variance from the Establishment Line is the tabloids' ridicule of government waste, and even that normally centers on the "welfare queens" or an egghead scientist's study of the sex life of some obscure insect. Not exactly daring stuff.

But what if the tabloids were to become *pro-active* in their policies? What if these lobotomized giants formed editorial policies at odds with the status quo? What if they, for instance, advised their readers that instead of getting ripped off by all these illegal aliens and welfare cheats they simply stop paying taxes to the IRS? What if they began advising workers of just how often their numbers are killed at the workplace?

What would be the result if, instead of reporting on the progress of South America's killer bees, they reported on the hillocks of corpses piling up in El Salvador — at taxpayer expense? It's not because they don't know it's happening. Tabloid editors read dozens of newspapers a day and keep a sharp eye on the television.

All anyone has to do is read the mainstream press to see the "tabloidization" of all the media. One measure of this is how frightened they are of being compared to these "sleazy" and "inconsequential" rags. *Newsweek,* while trying to squirm away from the fact that its cover story, too, was generated by the *Globe* (sorry, "the seamy supermarket tabloid," the "bottom of the media food chain") credited William Woo, editor of the St. Louis Post-Dispatch with this snooty gem about the corruption of the *New York Times*:

"What we have," he said, "is a case where a supermarket tabloid edited the most influential paper in America."

It seems Mr. Woo is a little confused as to which newspaper is more influential, the one that does the leading or the one that does the following.

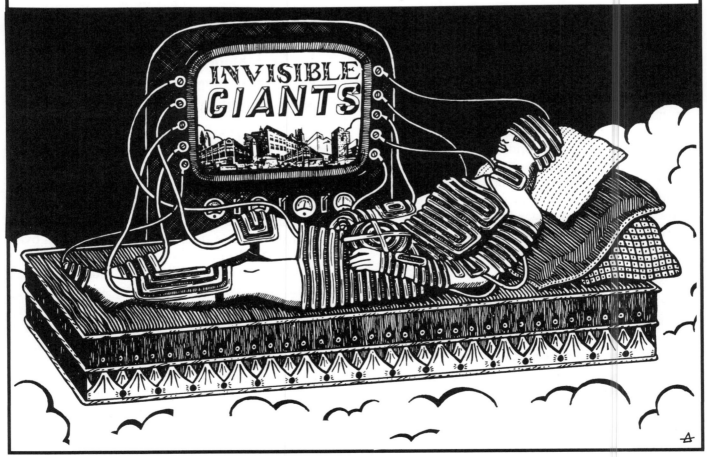

ENERGY FARMING IN AMERICA

A practical answer to America's farming, energy and environmental crises.

© 1989 by Lynn Osburn

On June 12, 1989, President Bush addressed his campaign promises to deal with the pollution problems long facing the United States.

He unveiled an ambitious plan to remove smog from California and the nation's most populous cities, as well as efforts to reduce acid rain pollution. Bush recommended auto makers be required to make methanol-powered cars for use in nine urban areas plagued by air pollution. Methanol is the simplest form of primary alcohol and is commonly called wood alcohol.

Bush called methanol "home-grown energy for America." He further proposed a 10 million ton reduction in sulfur dioxide emissions from coal-burning power plants; that's a 50% reduction over present standards. Sulfur dioxide is a major cause of acid rain, which kills 50,000 Americans and 5,000-10,000 Canadians yearly. (Brookhaven National Laboratory, 1986)

William Reilly, chief of the Environmental Protection Agency, at a briefing before Bush's speech, estimated the cost of the plan would be between $14 billion and $19 billion a year after its full implementation at the turn of the century.

Bush said, "Too many Americans continue to breathe dirty air, and political paralysis has plagued further progress against air pollution. We've seen enough of this stalemate. It's time to clear the air." Political paralysis seems to be a dominant trait in Washington in any given decade, but what did he mean by "stalemate?"

The root of this "stalemate" can be found in the concept of world energy resources. The industrial world currently runs on fossil fuel: natural gas, oil, and coal.

Fossil fuel resources are non-renewable, being the end product of eons of natural decomposition of Earth's ancient bio-mass. Fossil fuels contain sulfur, which is the source of many of the aggravating environmental pollution problems threatening America.

Removing sulfur compounds from fossil fuels is a major expense to the energy producers. Also, burning fossil fuels releases "ancient" carbon dioxide, produced by primeval plant life eons ago, into the atmosphere, causing the air we breathe to be over-burdened with CO^2, increasing the danger of global warming and the greenhouse effect.

In the late 1800s, the fledgling petroleum industry aggressively competed with the established biomass-based energy industry in an effort to gain control of world energy production and distribution. Fossil fuel producers succeeded in their campaign to dominate energy production by making fuels and chemical feedstocks at lower prices than could be produced from bio-mass conversion. Now the pendulum is swinging against them.

It is likely that peak oil and gas production in the coterminous United States has been reached. The bulk total production of roughly 80% will be reached by the year 2000. Peak world production will occur about the same year.

The situation for recoverable coal, world wide, is more favorable. Peak production is estimated to happen shortly after the year 2100. However, increasing numbers of Americans are unwilling to accept the escalating costs of environmental pollution and destruc-

tion associated with coal-fired power plant smokestack emissions and the land destruction resulting from coal mining.

If the pollution problems inherent with fossil fuel use are solved, the dollars and cents cost of this form of energy will continue to rise due to the dwindling availability of this non-renewable resource. On the other hand, the dollar cost of energy production from biomass conversion will remain relatively constant because the world biomass resource is renewable on a yearly basis.

The point where the cost of producing energy from fossil fuels exceeds the cost of biomass fuels has been reached. With a few exceptions, energy from fossil fuels will cost the American taxpayers more money than the same amount of energy supplied through biomass conversion.

Biomass is the term used to describe all biologically produced matter. World production of biomass is estimated at 146 billion metric tons a year, mostly wild plant growth. Some farm crops and trees can produce up to 20 metric tons per acre of biomass a year. Types of algae and grasses may produce 50 metric tons per year.

Dried biomass has a heating value of 5000-8000 Btu/lb. with virtually no ash or sulfur produced during combustion. About 6% of contiguous United States land area put into cultivation for biomass could supply all current demands for oil and gas. And this production would not add any net carbon dioxide to the atmosphere. (*Environmental Chemistry,* E. Manahan, Willard Grant Press, 1984)

For its Mission Analysis study conducted for the US Department of Energy in 1979, Stanford Research Institute (SRI) chose five types of biomass materials to investigate for energy conversion: woody plants, herbaceous plants (those that do not produce persistent woody material), aquatic plants, and manure. Herbaceous plants were divided into two categories: those with low moisture content and those with high moisture content.

Biomass conversion may be conducted on two broad pathways: chemical decomposition and biological digestion.

Thermochemical decomposition can be utilized for energy conversion of all five categories for biomass materials, but low moisture herbaceous (small grain field residues) and woody (wood industry wastes, and standing vegetation not suitable for lumber) are the most suitable.

Biological processes are essentially microbic digestion and fermentation. High moisture herbaceous plants (vegetables, sugar cane, sugar beet, corn, sorghum, cotton), marine crops and manure are most suitable for biological digestion.

Anaerobic digestion produces high and intermediate Btu gasses. High Btu is methane. Intermediate-Btu is methane mixed with carbon monoxide and carbon dioxide. Methane can be efficiently converted into methanol.

Fermentation produces ethyl and other alcohols, but this process is too costly in terms of cultivated land use and too inefficient in terms of alcohol production to feasibly supply enough fuel alcohol to power industrial society.

Pyrolysis is the thermochemical process that converts organic materials into usable fuels. Pyrolysis produces energy fuels with high fuel-to-feed ratios, making it the most efficient process for biomass conversion, and the method most capable of competing and eventually replacing non-renewable fossil fuel resources.

PYROLYTIC REACTOR

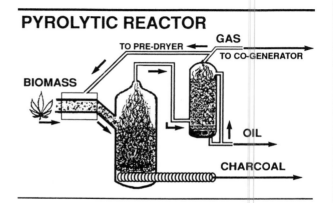

Pyrolysis is the technique of applying high heat to organic matter (lignocellulosic materials) in the absence of air or in reduced air. The process can produce charcoal, condensable organic liquids (pyrolytic fuel oil), non-condensable gasses, acetic acid, acetone, and methanol. The process can be adjusted to favor charcoal, pyrolytic oil, gas, or methanol production with a 95.5% fuel-to-feed efficiency.

Chemical pyrolysis is the same technology used to refine crude fossil fuel oil and coal. Biomass conversion by pyrolysis has many environmental and economic advantages over fossil fuels, but coal and oil production dominates because costs are kept lower by various means, including government protection.

Pyrolysis has been used since the dawn of civilization. If some means is applied to collect the off-gasses (smoke), the process is called wood distillation. The ancient Egyptians practiced wood distillation by collecting tars and pyroligneous acid for use in their embalming industry.

(Continued on next page)

Pyrolysis of wood to produce charcoal was a major industry in the 1800s, supplying the fuel for the industrial revolution, until it was replaced by coal.

In the late 19th Century and early 20th Century, wood distillation was still profitable for producing soluble tar, pitch, creosote oil, chemicals, and non-condensable gasses often used to heat boilers at the facility.

The wood distillation industry declined in the 1930s due to the advent of the petrochemical industry and its lower priced products. However, pyrolysis of wood to produce charcoal for the charcoal briquette market and activated carbon for purification systems is still practiced in the US.

The wood distillation industry used pyrolytic reactors in a process called destructive distillation. The operation was carried out in a fractionating column (a tall still) under high heat (from 1000-1700° F). Charcoal was the main fuel product and methanol production was about 1% to 2% of volume or 6 gallons per ton. This traditional method was replaced by the synthetic process developed in 1927.

The synthetic process utilizes a pyrolytic reactor operation as a gasifier by injecting air or pure oxygen into the reactor core to completely burn the biomass to ash. The energy contained in the biomass is released in the gasses formed. After purification, the synthesis, hydrogen and carbon monoxide in a 2 to 1 ratio, is altered by catalysts under high pressure and heat, to form methanol. This method will produce 100 gallons of methanol per ton of feed material.

Methanol-powered automobiles and reduced emission from coal-fired power plants can become a reality by using biomass derived fuels. The foundation upon which this will be achieved is the emerging concept of *energy farming,* wherein farmers grow and harvest crops that are converted into fuels. Energy farming can save American family farms and turn the American heartland into a prosperous source of clean renewable energy production.

Universities, government agencies, and private firms have conducted studies looking into the feasibility of growing biomass at low cost to make fuels at affordable prices, but the most promising plant species was never considered because it is prohibited. Instead emphasis has centered around utilizing waste products: agricultural residues after harvest, forestry wastes from the timber and pulp wood industry, and municipal wastes. All of these combined cannot produce enough fuel to satisfy the needs of industry or the American consumer's automobile. Yet biomass conversion to fuel has been proven economically feasible in laboratory tests and by continuous operation of pilot plants in field tests since 1973.

Farmers should be encouraged to grow energy crops capable of producing 10 tons per acre in 90-120 days. The crop has to be naturally high in cellulose. It must grow in all climatic zones in America. And it should not compete with food production for the most fertile land. It could be grown in rotation with food crops or on marginal land where other crop production isn't profitable.

At congressional hearings on alternative fuels held in 1978, Dr. George T. Tsao, professor of chemical engineering and food and agricultural engineering, director of laboratory of renewable resources, Purdue University, said $30 per ton for biomass delivered to the fuel conversion plant is an adequate base price for the energy farmer. The price of $30/ton has also been suggested by other researchers.

Both Dr. Serge Gratch, director chemical sciences laboratory, Ford Motor Co., and Dr. Joseph M. Colluci, director of fuels and lubricants, General Motors Research Laboratories, testified their companies were willing, especially Ford, to make cars that would run on methanol fuel. The scientists said it would take several years to tool up factories to make methanol powered autos. They said industry could solve the problems associated with methanol as fuel. And it would take about the same amount of time for the energy industry to build methanol production facilities.

So why don't we have methanol at the filling station? The scientists said the problem was government certification under the Clean Air Act required automobile manufacturers to meet standards set by the EPA based on fuels available on a national level. Since methanol fuel standards had not been set, the car makers couldn't make the new fleet until the methanol fuel was available at the pump. This Catch-22 situation continues today. Government is unwilling to subsidize pilot energy farms and biomass efficiency construction because fossil fuel producers control the energy industry.

The way to end this political stalemate is to start literally from the ground up. When farmers can grow hemp for biomass they will make a profit energy farming. Then it will not take long to get 6% of continental American land mass into cultivation for biomass fuels — enough to replace our economy's dependence on fossil fuels. And as the energy crop grows it takes in CO_2 from the air; when it is burned the CO_2 is returned to the air, creating a balanced system. We will no longer be increasing the CO_2 content in the atmosphere. The threat of global greenhouse warming and adverse climatic change will diminish.

The energy crop can be harvested with equipment readily available. It can be "cubed" by modifying hay cubing equipment. This method condenses the bulk, re-

(Continued on next page)

ducing trucking costs from the field to the pyrolysis facility.

Sixty-eight percent of the energy in the raw biomass is contained in the charcoal and fuel oils made at the facility. The charcoal has the same heating value in Btu as coal, with virtually no sulfur to pollute the atmosphere. The pyrolytic fuel oil has similar properties to no. 2 and no. 6 fuel oil. The remaining energy is in noncondensible gases that are used to co- generate steam and electricity.

To keep costs down pyrolysis reactors need to be located within a 50 mile radius from the energy farms. This necessity will bring life back to our small towns by providing jobs locally. The pyrolysis facilities will run three shifts a day.

Charcoal and fuel oil can be "exported" from the rural small town in the agricultural community to the large metropolitan areas to fuel the giant power plants generating electricity. When these utility companies use charcoal instead of coal, the problems of acid rain will begin to disappear.

The charcoal can be transported economically by rail to all urban area power plants. The fuel oil can be transported economically by truck, creating more jobs for Americans.

When this energy system is on line producing a steady supply of fuel for utility companies, it will have established itself in commerce. Then it will be more feasible to build the complex syngas systems to produce methanol from biomass, or make synthetic gasoline from methanol by adding the Mobil Co. process equipment to the gasifier.

To accomplish this goal of clean energy independence in America we must demand an end to hemp prohibition, so American farmers can grow this energy crop. Our government foolishly outlawed it in 1938.

Hemp is the world's most versatile crop. It can yield 10 tons per acre in four months. Hemp contains 80% cellulose; wood produces 60% cellulose. Hemp is drought resistant making it an ideal crop in the dry western regions of the country.

Hemp is the only biomass resource capable of making America energy independent. Remember that in 10 years, by the year 2000, America will have exhausted 80% of her petroleum reserves. Will we then go to war with the Arabs for the privilege of driving our cars; will we stripmine our land for coal and poison the air we breathe to drive our autos an additional 100 years; will we raze our forests for our energy needs?

During the Second World War, the federal government faced a real economic emergency when our supply of hemp was cut off by the Japanese. The federal government responded to the emergency by suspending marijuana prohibition. Patriotic American farmers were encouraged to apply for a license to grow hemp. They responded enthusiastically and grew 375,000 acres of hemp in 1943.

The argument against undertaking this massive hemp production effort today does not hold up to scrutiny.

Hemp grown for biomass makes very poor grade marijuana. The 20 to 40 million Americans who smoke marijuana would be loath to smoke hemp grown for biomass, so no one could make a dime selling a farmer's hemp biomass crop as marijuana.

It is time for the federal government to once again respond to our current economic emergency by utilizing the same procedure used in WWII to permit our farmers to grow American hemp, so this mighty nation can once again become energy independent and smog free.

References:

U.S. Energy Atlas, David J. Cuff & William J. Young, Free Press/McMillan Publishing Co., NY, 1980.

Progress in Biomass Conversion, Vol. 1, Kyosti V. Sarkanen & David Tillman, editors, Academic Press, NY, 1979.

Brown's Second Alcohol Fuel Cookbook, Michael H. Brown (Senate hearing transcripts)

Environmental Chemistry, (4th edition), Stanley E. Manahan, P.W.S. Publishers, Boston, MA, 1979.

Hemp for Victory, US government documentary film, USDA, 1942-43.

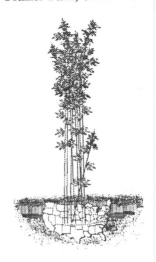

TOWARD A GREEN ECONOMY

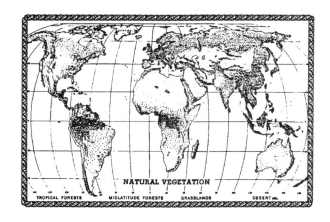

NATURAL VEGETATION

TROPICAL FORESTS   MIDLATITUDE FORESTS   GRASSLANDS   DESERT

© 1990 by Lynn Osburn

The nationwide popularity of Earth Week 1990 festivities seems to indicate the American people are concerned with the continuing degradation of the global environment. The twentieth anniversary celebration of the original Earth Day focused on ways the individual citizen can reduce waste and retard pollution.

The necessity of recycling used materials and lowering power consumption was demonstrated in a plethora of multi-media displays from coast to coast. It indicated a change in lifestyle is needed to halt the poisoning of earth.

An environmentally conscious population would prove to be a frugal one if those Earth Week programs were adopted.

Assuming Americans are willing to cut back on energy consumption and muster the effort to recycle their trash, are industrial corporations and energy producers willing to do the same?

Will corporate America drop the aggressive sales pitches wherein billions are spent encouraging people to buy impulsively? Will people be able to kick the mass consumption habit generations in the making? Will corporate America even entertain abstaining from the short term profit fix and consider what the consequences of quick return capitalism have done and will do to future generations of life on earth?

President George Bush's speech, given just days after Earth Week 1990 at the 178 nation conference dealing with global pollution problems held in Washington D.C., drew criticism from European participants. He emphasized scientific and economic uncertainties in what was seen as a White House foot dragging effort on the environmental issue.

A memo prepared by administration staffers for members of the US delegation read, under the heading "Debates to avoid:" It is "not beneficial to discuss whether there is or is not warming, or how much or how little warming. In the eyes of the public we will lose this debate. A better approach is to raise the many uncertainties that need to be better understood on this issue." Bush repeatedly stressed the need to find policies that do not limit economic growth: "Environmental policies that ignore the economic factor, the human factor, are destined to fail." (*Science News, April 28, 1990*)

President Bush is proud of the public image his career in the oil industry presents. He is, to say the least, an energy industry celebrity. And he has gone to great lengths to represent himself as the environmental president.

If the Bush administration believes, "in the eyes of the public," they will lose the debate questioning the scientific validity of the greenhouse effect, is it reasonable to conclude they don't believe the excessive accumulation of greenhouse gasses generated by burning fossil fuels is unbalancing the global carbon dioxide cycle? Or is it possible the corporate industrial energy complex that controls the trillion dollar per year energy industry fears profit loss, and unlike the American people, is in no way willing to make a sacrifice in corporate "lifestyle" to help heal the Earth.

President Bush is right about one thing: "Policies that ignore the economic factor, the human factor, are

destined to fail." In this case the economic factor and the human factor converge in the dire strait: if we do not convert from a fossil fueled economy to a biomass fueled economy, the human factor will become fossil history on planet earth.

The corporate industrial energy complex is collectively holding its breath on the topic of biomass resource conversion to replace fossil fuels. The industrial energy giants spend millions in public relations explaining how they are environmentally responsible energy producers. Yet it is the fossil fuel resources they peddle that are endangering the fragile ecosphere. The majority of scientists throughout the world agree: the single most effective way to halt the greenhouse effect is to stop burning fossil fuels.

It was proven in the 1970's that biomass, specifically plant mass, can be converted to fuels that will replace every type of fossil fuel currently produced by industry — and these biomass fuels are essentially non-polluting.

Fossil fuel materials: coal, oil and natural gas were made by nature from

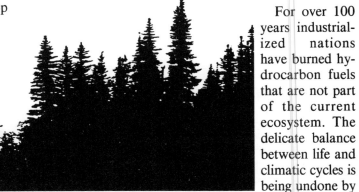

Burning fossil fuels is the major cause of the greenhouse effect. The forests of the world can reverse it, if the trees are allowed to grow.

earth biomass that lived over 160 million years ago. Crude fossil fuels contain hydrocarbon compounds that were made by plant life during the process of photosynthesis. Carbon dioxide and water were converted into hydrocarbon rich cellulose. Plants manufacture many other biochemicals in the complex and mysterious act of living, but cellulose and lignin are the compounds that give plants structure, body and strength. They are the main components of plant mass.

Nature took millions of years to concentrate the ancient plant mass into what we call fossil fuels. The eons long process that converted the once living biomass into hydrocarbon rich fossils also compressed sulfur into the fossil biomass. It is this sulfur that causes acid rain when belched out of power plant smoke stacks. According to Brookhaven National Laboratory, 50,000 Americans and 10,000 Canadians die each year from exposure to acid rain.

Mankind, through the science of chemical engineering, can transform modern biomass into hydrocarbon fuels that contain no sulfur because the fresh plant mass contains no sulfur. And the scientific method of biomass conversion into hydrocarbon fuels requires mere hours instead of eons to accomplish.

The inherent problem with burning fossil fuels to power industrial energy systems and economies is the mega-ton release of CO_2 into the air. However biomass derived fuels are part of the present day global CO_2 cycle.

The quantity of CO_2 released into the air from burning biomass fuels is equal to the amount of CO_2 the biomass energy crop absorbed while it grew. If the energy crop is an annual plant, then one year's biomass fuel when burned will supply the CO_2 needed for the next year's fuel biomass growth. There will be no net increase in atmospheric CO_2.

For over 100 years industrialized nations have burned hydrocarbon fuels that are not part of the current ecosystem. The delicate balance between life and climatic cycles is being undone by injecting ancestral CO_2 into the atmosphere.

The only way to reduce the ever-thickening blanket of CO_2 warming the earth is to grow more plants to absorb it. Yet the Bush administration's plan to plant one billion trees a year will only reduce by 15% the amount of CO_2 predicted for the end of the century. However, US CO_2 production (from burning fossil fuels) will rise by 35% during the same time period. (*Science News, April 28, 1990*)

The Bush administration's plan is futile as long as fossil fuels remain America's major energy resource. And at the rate forests are being cut down to make the paper our society is wrapped up in, a billion saplings a year will barely compensate for that loss in CO_2 absorption.

Wood happens to be the government's chief biomass candidate to replace the dwindling fossil fuel supply. Officials claim US yearly energy consumption can be met by harvesting one third of the trees in the National Forest on a rotating basis, coupled with more intensive silvaculture (tree farming) techniques. Estimated yearly biomass production in the National Forests is one ton per acre. (*Progress in Biomass Conversion Vol. 1*, Kyosti V. Sarkanen & David Tillman, editors)

(Continued on next page)

The US Forestry Service is the government bureaucracy promoting this ludicrous forests-for-fuel idea. However, private industry has been clear-cutting without conscience timber stands not protected by National Forests and Parks. And none of that wood goes into biomass fuel conversion.

The trees of the world are the biosphere's CO_2 cycle safety valve. Trees convert CO_2 into wood. Since a tree will live centuries, forests can gradually pull the excess CO_2 out of the air. Trees are not only aesthetically pleasing — they are the cure for our ailing atmosphere.

Is it realistic to halt construction to save trees, or ask people to stop using paper? If wood resources cannot hope to meet the demand for lumber, paper and biomass fuels, can any plant be cultivated to meet these needs?

This problem is not new. Civilizations have been exhausting vital resources and dooming themselves for many centuries. Versatility, cleverness and common sense are the hallmarks of the ones that survive.

About seventy-five years ago two dedicated USDA scientists projected that at the rate the US was using paper we would deplete the forests in our lifetimes. Those government scientists were endowed with common sense — something government officials are hopelessly lacking nowadays. So USDA scientists Dewey and Merrill looked for an alternative agricultural resource for paper products to prevent the disaster we now face.

They found the ideal candidate to be the waste material left in the fields after the hemp harvest. The left over pulp, called hemp hurds, was traditionally burned in the fields when the hemp fiber had been removed after the time consuming retting (partially rotting the hemp stalk to separate the fiber from the hurds) process was completed.

Hemp hurds are richer in cellulose and contain less lignin than wood pulp. Dewey and Merrill found after much experimentation that harsh sulfur acids used to break down the lignin in wood pulp were not necessary when making paper from hemp hurds. Sulfur acid wastes from paper mills are known to be a major source of waterway pollution. The coarse paper they made from hemp hurds was stronger and had greater folding durability than coarse wood pulp paper. Hemp hurd paper would make better cardboard and paper bag products than wood paper. They found the fine print quality hemp hurd paper to be equal to writing quality wood pulp paper. (*USDA bulletin no. 404*)

The only problem to implementing the paper industry resource change from wood to hemp hurds was machinery to separate hemp fiber from the hurds needed to be developed. Separation was still done by hand after the machine breaks had softened the hemp stalks. The "decorticating" machine that separated the fiber and hurds wasn't developed until the early 1930's. Even *Popular Mechanics* declared in 1937 that hemp would be a billion dollar a year crop because of this new machinery. And their predictions did not consider hemp's potential as a biomass fuel resource. Unfortunately, hemp was maligned. Its flower tops were condemned as marijuana and subsequently outlawed just when the fiber/hurd separating machinery was perfected.

If America had not been infected with marijuana hysteria, hemp could be solving our energy problems today. When marijuana was outlawed most people did not know "marijuana" was Mexican slang for cannabis hemp. The American people, including doctors who routinely prescribed cannabis extract medicines, thought hemp and marijuana were two different plants. Otherwise hemp prohibition would never have happened.

Hemp is a renewable natural resource capable of providing biomass alternatives to fossil fuels. Hemp cellulose and fibers can supply the demand for all products derived from wood

Eastern Europeans were not subjected to the hysterical anti-marijuana syndrome plaguing the West. Poland, Hungary, and Czechoslovakia, among others, continued to make clothing from hemp fibers and medicines from hemp flowers. They pressed the versatile and edible oil from the seeds and used the leftover high protein seed mash to make breakfast cereal and livestock feed. And they used surplus hemp for building insulation.

Currently in the USA, a private firm, Mansion Industries, has pioneered the use of agricultural fibers to make sturdy light weight construction paneling to replace plywood. Mansion Industries uses straw to make their Environcore panels. Based on Dewey and Merrill's test results, if hemp was a resource available, Environcore construction paneling would be even stronger.

(Continued next page)

It's not too late to save our environment, but it is absolutely essential that we start now. Restoring the balance to the biosphere's ecosystem will require courage and determination, but not self denial. We need not give up our comforts or quality of life.

America stands at the cross roads of greatness and decline. The might of weaponry will not sustain us anymore. Our chance to again lead the world will require the same kind of determination we once initiated to convert our peace time economy into war production during the 1940's. But now the "war mentality" won't help. This time we must be innovative and change the very way we produce our energy resources.

Hemp prohibition must end at once in order to inaugurate a nation-wide green economy. To save the world that gives us life, we must begin immediately to grow our own energy.

Hemp is the only plant capable of becoming the American biomass energy standard. Hemp grows well everywhere on earth except the polar regions. Hemp will out produce wood at a rate greater than four to one per acre in cellulose/pulp. And by analyzing pre-prohibition hemp crop reports from various states, ten tons per acre becomes a reasonable biomass production figure. Hemp will make ten times more biomass per acre than forest wood.

Wood is not a viable fuel resource. The forests are essential to scrub the excess CO_2 from the air. Soft wood forests should not be harvested for paper products or biomass — their only economic value. Hemp can supply that need. Hardwood trees should be harvested, utilizing sustainable yield ecology, for board and finishing lumber only. Hemp will make pressed boards lighter in weight and more durable than plywood.

Hemp can be grown for: crude biomass fuels on energy farms; fiber/hurds for textiles, pressed board and hurd cellulose products; seed for oil and high protein foods; flowers for pharmaceutical grade extract medicine and recreational herbal products for adults.

The Green Economy based on a hemp multi-industry complex will provide income for farmers in every state. Regions for each hemp agricultural industry application will be established through open free market competition. The historical and traditional hemp fiber growing areas in the eastern US will re-emerge, creating new jobs in an old industry. The economically devastated northern plains will see a boom as the nation's energy farming states. Medicinal and intoxicant grade hemp will be grown on less productive higher elevation lands. Mountainous areas have traditionally produced intoxicant quality hemp.

Ironically, the hemp medicine and intoxicant industry will generate the least amount of capital, though it is the target of prohibitionist "reefer" propaganda. The hemp seed oil and food resource industries, and the hemp textile and cellulose industries will develop thousands of new products generating tens of thousands of sustainable new jobs. Hemp energy farming will become the backbone of a trillion dollar a year non-polluting energy production industry. And the petroleum corporations need not fear this, for their expertise, hardware and manpower are vital to turn the farmer's raw biomass into refined fuels.

These projections represent a tremendous boon to our flagging economy that can be realized as a by-product of saving our world from human induced biocide. If we as a society have the courage and determination to set upon this bold path to planetary restoration, we can in our life times leave a healthier world to our children, and a lifestyle based on renewable resources in a balanced ecosystem that our children can leave to their children for generations to come. ●

**Reprinted by permission of Access Unlimited.
For further information, send $1.00 to:**

**∧ccess
∪nlimited**

**P.O. Box 1900
Frazier Park, CA 93225**

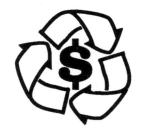

*Renewable resources
mean economic growth
and stability*

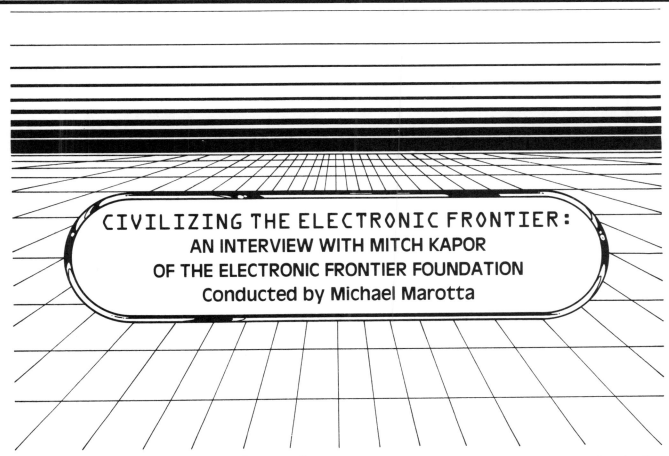

CIVILIZING THE ELECTRONIC FRONTIER:
AN INTERVIEW WITH MITCH KAPOR
OF THE ELECTRONIC FRONTIER FOUNDATION
Conducted by Michael Marotta

In 1982, Mitch Kapor founded Lotus Corp., marketers of the best-selling spreadsheet program, LOTUS 1-2-3. On July 10, 1990, together with Grateful Dead lyricist John Perry Barlow, and Apple co-founder Steve Wozniak, Kapor announced the creation of The Electronic Frontier Foundation. Their goal was to "bring law and order to cyberspace." They were responding to a series of Federal law enforcement actions publicized under the banner "Operation Sundevil." These raids showed a disturbing lack of understanding of computer technology and a cavalier attitude toward the First Amendment.

The EFF came to the defense of Steve Jackson and Craig Neidorf. (See "Did Thomas Jefferson Wear Mirrorshades, or: Why is the Secret Service Busting Publishers?" Loompanics Catalog, 1991.) They filed an amicus curiae brief in the case of Len Rose, a programmer who was swept up in the raids. The EFF has also spoken up on issues relating to the policies of Prodigy, a BBS run by Sears and IBM, because Prodigy has censored messages among its clients. (See, for instance, "When is Gardening a Subversive Act?", New York Times, Jan. 31, 1991.) In addition, the EFF helped the state of Massachusetts draft a computer crime law which can serve as a model in balancing property and free speech interests.

(This interview was conducted via e-mail in the Summer and Fall of 1991. Supporting Kapor was EFF legal counsel, Mike Godwin.)

MAROTTA: *The EFF engaged in three highly visible actions. You helped Craig Neidorf, Steve Jackson and Len Rose. How do you see the differences in the issues raised by each case? What attributes do these cases share?*

KAPOR: There are some common elements among these three cases, not the least of which is that they all arose from the same set of investigations: the E911 cases. These cases are all connected, in one way or another, with the purported theft of an online document concerning the Emergency 911 system. The government maintained that this information was both secret and dangerous in the wrong hands.

Craig Neidorf was prosecuted because he published the document in his online newsletter, *Phrack*. The government chose in that case to characterize Craig as a conspirator who received stolen property, but a better analogy would be to the *New York Times* editors who received the Pentagon Papers. First Amendment rights were directly implicated by the Neidorf case, which also raised issues of the propriety of the government's uncritically accepting the "victim's" valuation of the

First published in 1992 Main Catalog *(Continued on next page)* **83**

"stolen property." (Bell South initially valued the E911 document as worth nearly $80,000; it was discovered during preparation for trial that the information in the document was publicly available for less than $20.)

Steve Jackson Games, unlike Craig, was never charged with (or suspected of) wrongdoing. But the E911 investigations led the government to a BBS run at home by an SJG employee. Without any apparent probable cause to search the company, the government nevertheless did so, resulting in the company's near-bankruptcy and the months-long delay in publication of the company's latest game book, *GURPS Cyberpunk*. The government also seized and searched the company's bulletin-board system, which SJG used to maintain contact with its writers and customers, and which was also used for general discussions and electronic-mail correspondence. Thus, the case involves Steve Jackson Games' First Amendment and Fourth Amendment rights, and the users' rights of freedom of association and e-mail privacy.

Our formal involvement in the Len Rose case involved a narrower issue: whether the Computer Fraud and Abuse Act is unconstitutionally broad. Len Rose was prosecuted on the basis of e-mail seized in Craig Neidorf's student account at the University of Missouri. In that e-mail, Rose explained how a program called login.c could be modified to capture users' passwords. EFF was concerned that the federal statute in question seemed to forbid people even to talk about ways that computer security could be breached — we regard this as an unconscionable breach of First Amendment rights, and filed an amicus brief to raise that issue. The case was settled, however, before the issue could be resolved by the court.

The three cases differ on the particular facts, but they all arose out of the same set of investigations, and they all implicate First Amendment issues.

MAROTTA: You focus on the First and Fourth Amendments. The Ninth is the one that says you have more rights than are listed in the Bill of Rights. Wouldn't that include the right to privacy?

KAPOR: The Ninth Amendment seems to be less a guarantee of additional rights than a rule of interpretation for the other Amendments. But regardless of the source, the right to privacy is a right that's (still) recognized by the Supreme Court, and it's protected both in Constitutional law and in some federal and state statutes. And, if you'll recall, the reasoning behind the Court's recognition of the right to privacy in *Griswold v. Connecticut* is based in part on interpretations of the First and Fourth Amendments, so we can't focus on those Amendments without raising privacy issues. The First Amendment has been construed to guarantee freedom of association, and privacy is necessary for much of the exercise of that freedom.

MAROTTA: Well, if the police torture a confession out of someone who is "really" guilty, we let the accused go because that is better than living in a country where the police are allowed to use torture. So some people have said, "Yes, their rights may have been violated, but these hackers were still violating property rights." In truth, however, isn't it plain that the First Amendment would completely cover Craig Neidorf as the publisher of Phrack? *In other words, you have a right to receive mail? And that would apply to Steve Jackson and Len Rose as well?*

KAPOR: This is really two questions, it seems to me. The first question, about defendants' rights, points to one of the hard things we always have to deal with when we try to keep our criminal procedure within the bounds of the Constitution. Basically, we have to work to protect the rights of people who may turn out to be guilty in order to protect the rights of the innocent. The issues that are being raised in the prosecution of hackers now will affect everyone's understanding of our rights in the future, so it's important that we get recognition of those rights now.

> *"The issues that are being raised in the prosecution of hackers now will affect everyone's understanding of our rights in the future, so it's important that we get recognition of those rights now."*

The second question, about the First Amendment, deserves a qualified "yes." The First Amendment doesn't "completely cover" anything, but it seems certain that Neidorf would qualify as a publisher under any reasonable interpretation of the First Amendment. This does not squarely apply to what he was accused of, however — the government alleged that he had conspired in the theft of information from Bell South. Absent a conspiracy charge, it is certainly the case that a publisher is not breaking a law if someone gives him information. I'm not sure how you're connecting the Steve Jackson and Len Rose cases, which have different facts, to Neidorf's.

MAROTTA: Len Rose was indicted under the Computer Fraud and Abuse Act. This law specifically forbids communicating the methods of fraud. Wouldn't this apply to mystery stories, as well?

(Continued on next page)

> *"Absent a conspiracy charge, it is certainly the case that a publisher is not breaking a law if someone gives him information."*

KAPOR: The original provision of the Computer Fraud and Abuse Act, which seems to forbid "trafficking" in information that could be used to break into a computer, is certainly overbroad, and probably unconstitutional. Yes, it would seem to ban certain kinds of mystery stories or discussions of computer security. However, Len was originally indicted under the CFAA, but his superseding indictment focused on wire fraud. The Wire Fraud statute does not specifically forbid communicating the methods of fraud. Only the CFAA does that.

> *"The original provision of the Computer Fraud and Abuse Act, which seems to forbid 'trafficking' in information that could be used to break into a computer, is certainly overbroad, and probably unconstitutional. Yes, it would seem to ban certain kinds of mystery stories or discussions of computer security."*

MAROTTA: Well, then, to what do you attribute the zeal with which law enforcers are willing to ride roughshod over the Bill of Rights? They aren't busting Pocket Books for publishing Nancy Drew and the Hardy Boys. Why are they chasing computerists?

> *"It's important to remember that law enforcement doesn't see itself as opposed to the Bill of Rights. Their attitude tends to be 'If we haven't been told by the courts that we can't do this, we can do it.'"*

KAPOR: It's important to remember that law enforcement doesn't see itself as opposed to the Bill of Rights. Their attitude tends to be "If we haven't been told by the courts that we can't do this, we can do it." There's a certain amount of resistance to the notion that law enforcement should be respectful of First and Fourth Amendment rights in contexts that haven't been addressed by the courts. They expect the adversarial process to resolve any tricky rights issues over the long run, resulting in guidelines for them to follow.

The problem is that, while they usually try to be sticklers about the rules that already have been laid down, they tend to "push the envelope" in gray areas like computer-crime searches and seizures. Not until case law clearly establishes the rights of computer owners and users will this problem be resolved.

MAROTTA: What are the issues in the Prodigy case?

KAPOR: Although EFF is not involved at the moment in any activities directly relating to the Prodigy dispute, we believe that the dispute touches some basic issues with which we are very concerned, and that it illustrates the potential dangers of allowing private entities such as large corporations to control or even set the tone for the market for online electronic services.

Prodigy management has hired editors "with journalistic backgrounds" to review messages for suitability before they are allowed to be publicly posted. The member agreement allows the management to limit public discussions of topics and to edit postings of individual members for obscenity or illegal content... or for anything else, at Prodigy's discretion.

The result of this broad management prerogative? One member is reported to have had his posting about population problems in Catholic countries censored, presumably out of the editors' fear that Catholic users would be offended. More significantly, some whole discussion topics, including a debate between Christian fundamentalists and gay activists, have been removed without warning from the conferences.

The initial solution to the censorship problem was simple: Take the discussions to e-mail. Prodigy users began to rely on a mailing-list feature of the program to continue their (now-uncensored) discussions. But soon a crisis had brewed. The Prodigy users who had been told to take their no-longer-welcome public discussions to e-mail were now being told that they wouldn't be able to use the e-mail service at the flat rate any longer.

The result of this policy change was predictable: irate Prodigy users began to protest, complaining on Prodigy's public boards about the new usage fee and attempting to organize a write-in campaign notifying Prodigy's management and — when management turned a deaf ear to their protests — its advertisers of their disaffection. Prodigy management responded by

(Continued on next page) **85**

terminating the accounts of 12 of the protestors, claiming that the protestors had violated their membership agreements, which forbade "harassment."

> *"The Prodigy experience to date reveals a serious mismatch between the expectations of Prodigy's management and its customers."*

The Prodigy experience to date reveals a serious mismatch between the expectations of Prodigy's management and its customers. Here the market clearly seemed to want unrestricted public conferencing and electronic mail. But as demand for these features has mounted, the supplier, rather than trying to satisfy its customers, has cut back on the features' availability because it did not correspond to or fit with the company's view of the purpose of the service. To the extent to which this type of thinking is representative of the general way large commercial interests may offer on-line services, it clearly represents a turning away from the use of digital media as open forums of public communication. In the extreme case, in a situation in which Prodigy and its commercial competition all choose to censor and control communication on their services, the public interest will not be well served.

MAROTTA: How does Prodigy essentially differ from any other BBS?

KAPOR: With respect to the large degree of control it has chosen to exercise over its subscribers' postings, Prodigy is at the far end of the spectrum of BBSes. At the opposite end are those BBSes which are entirely free forums in which postings are never rejected or removed by the sysop. Most BBSes fall somewhere in the middle, with sysops foregoing prior review entirely, but reserving the right to remove messages (although this rarely needs to be done). Prodigy is different because it has chosen to employ a newspaper/magazine metaphor on its service. It is clear that Prodigy management was originally uncomfortable with the notion of a free forum; they chose to describe their service as a "publication" rather than as a forum precisely because they want to have an editor's prerogatives to dictate, absolutely, what the content of the "publication" will be. We hope that they will reconsider this posture and loosen up.

MAROTTA: What is EFF's interest?

KAPOR: We at EFF do not dispute that Prodigy is acting within its rights as a private concern when it dictates restrictions on how its system is used. We do think, however, that the Prodigy experience has a bearing on EFF interests in a couple of ways.

First, it demonstrates that there is a market—a perceived public need — for services that provide electronic mail and public conferencing.

Second, it illustrates the fallacy that "pure" market forces always can be relied upon to move manufacturers and service providers in the direction of open communications. A better solution, we believe, is a national network-access policy that, at the very least, encourages private providers to generate the kind of open and unrestricted network and mail services that the growing computer-literate public clearly wants. One way to implement such a policy would be to limit legal liability for service providers who merely store and forward their users' public and private messages. With such a policy in place, Prodigy management might be more comfortable with the risks of providing a relatively unregulated public forum.

> *"We at EFF do not dispute that Prodigy is acting within its rights as a private concern when it dictates restrictions on how its system is used. We do think, however, that the Prodigy experience... illustrates the fallacy that 'pure' market forces always can be relied upon to move manufacturers and service providers in the direction of open communications."*

MAROTTA: It is easy to agree that Prodigy has a narrow viewpoint of computing. They are not my service, that's for sure. In fact, I have been kicked off FidoNet Echoes. I was bounced from the Virus Echo for saying that self-reproducing programs have merit. I was excluded from the Stock Market Echo for saying that Ivan Boesky is a political prisoner. I have run afoul of the Communications Echo for posting about EFF. Are you going to identify FidoNet as a restrictive system? I think they'd say that I have a perfect right to buy a computer and start the Mike Marotta Echo. As long as I am a guest, do I not bear a responsibility to observe the rules of the house?

KAPOR: The mention of guests and houses is clearly a metaphor. Responsibility in the online world should be a function of the details of a particular situation, not a metaphor. I don't know what else to say about this.

(Continued on next page)

MAROTTA: In "Crime and Puzzlement" by John Perry Barlow, the ignorance of law enforcement people is noted. There was a case on the West Coast where a BBS closed and the number was given to a doctor's office. Then the police busted people who called the old BBS number, on the grounds that they were trying to break in to a medical computer system. The police pleaded ignorance of computing. One of the EFF's primary goals is to bring law and order to cyberspace. Have you been able to bring computer literacy to law enforcement?

KAPOR: There's no question that the law enforcement community itself is trying to increase its computer literacy — they hold frequent seminars about computer crime, for example, and there are a number of publications, available from the National Institute of Justice and elsewhere, that are designed to bring law-enforcement officials up to speed on computer crime. The problem has been that these education efforts are a bit one-sided — they focus on the means of committing and of investigating and prosecuting computer crime, but they tend to give little or no time to the civil-liberties issues that are raised by such crimes and by those investigations and prosecutions.

> *"Even when law enforcement knows how not to make mistakes in handling and examining software and hardware, they may still engage in overbroad seizures or overlook the First Amendment significance of bulletin-board systems or the statutory restrictions on searches of electronic mail."*

So, even when law enforcement knows how not to make mistakes in handling and examining software and hardware, they may still engage in overbroad seizures or overlook the First Amendment significance of bulletin-board systems or the statutory restrictions on searches of electronic mail.

At EFF we're trying to fill that gap by publishing articles about search-and-seizure law and policy, and by conducting speaking events in which these issues are raised. We also hope that the Steve Jackson case will settle some of the issues about what a computer crime investigator ought to be expected to know.

MAROTTA: NREN is the National Research and Education Network, a proposal that is likely to pass Congress and be approved by the President. You expressed reservations earlier because many decisions seem to be made by default on this. NREN will be built with public money and it will be administered by a private company. It seems that this contract will go to ANS, Advanced Networks and Services. ANS was founded by Merit, IBM and MCI and in turn, ANS subcontracts management of the National Science Foundation's NSFnet back to Merit. The president of ANS is Alan Weis, formerly of IBM. How is NREN in the 21st century essentially different from railroads of the 19th? More to the point, Western Union began with some government contracts and after the Civil War, Washington signed over to them thousands upon thousands of miles of line built with public funds. NREN seems like a tune we've heard before.

KAPOR: ANS has the contract for the NSFnet backbone, which expires in October 1992. NREN funds will go for many things, including gigabit networking. It's possible NREN funds may go to ANS, but this is not the ANS danger. The danger is of the government handing ANS an advantage over commercial competition. This would be unfair and must not be allowed. There has to be equal access for all commercial carriers to any government-supported network.

MAROTTA: Well, as long as there are people like EFF out there, I suppose the door is shut on cyber-fascism. For one thing, Bitnet and Usenet on the Internet already support fairly open communication. These people see FidoNet as "priestly," while FidoNet's moderators are restricted from inserting their own viewpoints the way Usenet moderators do. So we have varying degrees of openness. The folks at Merit are very proud of the fact that so much NSFnet and Bitnet traffic consists of file transfers, people getting and sending data from and to open systems with public accounts for what they call "Anonymous FTP." So, overall, then, do you see EFF as the focal point, as the expression, of a general tendency toward freedom in cyberspace?

KAPOR: It's not *the* focal point, but it's *a* focal point for freedom in cyberspace.

Electronic Frontier Foundation, Inc.
155 Second Street
Cambridge, MA 02141

Internet address eff@well.sf.ca.us

JOHNNY SOLD HIS GUN
The Untold Story of US Outlaw GIs in WWII Europe

by Chet Antonine

© 1992 by Chet Antonine

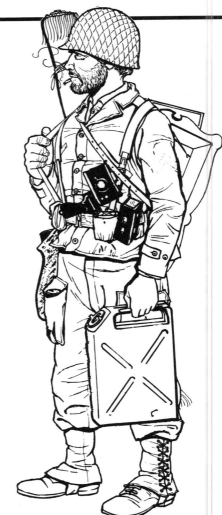

When Jack Benny was sent to visit "front line troops" toward the end of World War II, he was amazed at how high the morale was among the men — the scourge of total war didn't seem to have broken the pure American spirit of these GIs at all and their clean-shaven faces beamed back at him as he praised their bravery. They chuckled appreciatively at his one-liners and scrambled like puppies when he threw them his necktie.

One could hardly believe these were the same boys who had suffered and bled in the frozen forests at the Battle of the Bulge, picked their way through the rubble of firebombed cities to herd the dazed occupants into displaced persons camps.

Of course Benny's audience wasn't composed of front line troops at all. Combat troops were still being shot to pieces on the front lines where ill-trained emergency replacements were being killed days after they arrived at their shit-filled foxholes. Men who were previously classified 4-F were suddenly reclassified 1-A and drafted. After a ship ride to England, the greenhorn "dogfaces" were dumped off on the beaches of Europe and pointed toward Germany. Corporal guides brought them up to the front in small groups and told them to dig in. Thousands were killed without ever knowing just what they were supposed to do. Sergeants started asking command to stop sending them. Useless in battle, they only increased the carnage. Those who did survive got cynical, to say the least.

Although it was not reported at the time, thousands of American soldiers had gone AWOL and were wandering the European countryside in criminal bands hijacking trucks and trains and making their livings off the black market.

Although it was not reported at the time, thousands of American soldiers had gone AWOL and were wandering the European countryside in criminal bands hijacking trucks and trains and making their livings off the black market.

In his novel, *In the Spring the War Ended,* Steven Linakis tells the story of an American deserter in Belgium. Linakis, who served in the Army from 1943 to 1946, describes the breaking point that sent so many men "over the hump."

After describing a ferocious six months of front line duty ending in the Huertgen Forest, Linakis gives an account of mass desertion:

"Everything had gone wrong in the Huertgen and they were all dead in that splintered timber where eighty-eights were huge buzzsaws cutting down the trees. That was when you saw your infantry

First published in 1992 Main Catalog

(Continued on next page)

taking off, going AWOL by squads, yelling their heads off, 'Fuck the war! Fuck the lousy war!' and nobody tried to stop them."

Stories of heroism like the American defense of Bastogne, its hard-boiled commander responding "Nuts!" to a German demand for surrender are easy to find. Not so easy to find are reports of the panic, confusion, and pants-shitting fear the soldiers also felt that night German floodlights lit the sky and nine armored divisions from a supposedly defeated army attacked without warning.

"Out of the fog came German infantrymen camouflaged against the snow in white overalls," wrote correspondent Cyril Ray twenty four years after the war. "Some Americans stood firm — admirably firm. Some broke and ran. One colonel of an armored unit handed over to his number two and was last seen 'in a highly nervous state and hurrying to the rear "for ammunition." ' (Before the week was out, one major-general who had never before seen action had his division taken away from him, and died of heart failure.)"

As the battle of the Bulge took shape, many soldiers found their attitudes becoming more mercenary than patriotic and decided to go for the gusto.

As the battle of the Bulge took shape, many soldiers found their attitudes becoming more mercenary than patriotic and decided to go for the gusto. By the time Benny was bantering with Ingrid Bergman in front of wolf-whistling GIs at the rear, American troops were busy looting the German city of Jena where the famous Zeiss company made the best cameras in the world. While Patton's tanks ran out of gas fighting at the Siegfried line, US soldiers had clogged the entire Champs-Elysees in Paris, turning the famous boulevard into a veritable bazaar of stolen and looted clothing, food, cigarettes — and as much gasoline as you wanted. One thousand gallons of gasoline were stolen every day in Paris alone. A year after the war, $10,000 worth of army goods were still being stolen every day from a single Quartermaster's Depot in Ludwigsburg .

Even before the massive German counter offensive that began slaughtering American GIs in great swipes of artillery (companies in the Huertgen were taking 70% losses) there were already 15,000 soldiers who had gone over the hump. They had deserted in the face of the enemy and couldn't care less. To support themselves they lived off the fat of the land, ripping off the Army.

In France and Belgium, bands of American deserters hijacked trains and carted away boxcars of supplies. They posed as officers, gained access to airfields and stole silk parachutes (worth quite a lot as material for ladies' dresses) by the truckload. They stole and sold jeeps, tanks, halftracks... one group in France managed to steal a whole train full of soap and cigarettes. Another group of bandits in the French zone of Germany ripped off a train of 13 wagons and a locomotive, drove it to the American sector where it was loaded with potatoes before driving it back to the French sector. And in Naples, a U.S. Liberty ship and its cargo disappeared from the harbor only a few days after arriving from America.

By war's end a thick, tan-colored directory of "Continental AWOLs" listed as many as 50,000 men, each with a string of asterisks beside his name to show how many months he had been gone. These were not guys who had gotten drunk one night and lost their regiment; they weren't soldiers missing in action. These were guys who had decided to take their chances as fugitives in war-torn Europe. More than two divisions of soldiers were AWOL on the continent and supporting themselves by crime.

But the deserters represented something greater than two divisions — if one considers who did the deserting. Officers and rear echelon troops had little reason to run away — their life was pretty good. Even a hundred miles from the front officers were quaffing beer in Clervaux (a "recreation center" in Luxemburg) and enlisted men were chasing the local girls, going fishing, going to the movies. They had little reason to desert. It was the combat soldiers, the business end of a division, who went AWOL.

Out of a division of 15,000 men, only 6,000 actually cowered in foxholes and lobbed grenades at German pillboxes. The rest were support troops. Assuming there were 35 infantry divisions in the European Theater of Operations, then Paris alone would have been home to something around a fourth of the front line. Clearly the military could not allow their front line troops to run away and began vigorously hunting down these AWOLs, giving them a choice between prison and the front. When too many started opting for jail, they were given no choice at all. Although the Army could have theoretically imposed the death penalty, things weren't that desperate... at first.

Naturally, none of this was reported in the United States where only the Jack Benny view of things was presented. Nevertheless some enterprising reporters managed to hint at what was going on. In the April 7, 1945 *New Statesman and Nation*, V.S. Pritchett buried

a report of looting in a story describing the Army's entry into a bombed-out town.

"It occurs to you the street is yours," he wrote. "Any street, any house. You can have the lot. Climb over the wreckage, dig out a motor bicycle, 'Help me with this goddam door, I've seen a lot of tools I want, Boys! Wine glasses! What have you got? Anything in there? Books? Wine? Cameras? Some son of a bitch has been here before.' You go in your boots crunching the glass. You climb gingerly into a bedroom..."

Naturally, none of this was reported in the United States where only the Jack Benny view of things was presented. Nevertheless some enterprising reporters managed to hint at what was going on.

New York Herald Tribune reporter John Steinbeck managed to sneak in a story about three soldiers arrested for dealing in watches and once wrote about an infantryman's deserting to get back to see the World Series. But reports like this were rare. One of the reasons was that the war correspondents themselves — dressed up in Army fatigues, carrying machine guns — joined in on the feeding frenzy. Alan Moorehead of London's *Daily Express* could hardly contain himself when writing of the bounty the war provided.

"We looted parmesan cheeses as big as cartwheels," he wrote, "and tins of strawberries, barrels of wine and cases of chocolate, binoculars and typewriters, ceremonial swords and Italian money galore."

In fact there was so much money to be made on the black market a fellow might be considered a fool not to go into the business. Hundreds of thousands of dollars were sent home by black marketeers. In a ruined world where a pack of cigarettes sold for $100 American, GIs were millionaires. A candy bar bought sex from nearly any starving German girl. Two pounds of coffee could be traded for a diamond. Merely by selling his weekly ration of cigarettes, candy and whiskey, any GI could send home at least an extra $10,000 a year. That's if he didn't receive any packages from home for resale and never stole a thing.

Stories of soldiers sending home far more money than they earned as cannon fodder were common. In the first four months of the Occupation, American soldiers sent home $11,078,925 more than they were paid. In October of 1945 U.S. military personnel sent back $5,470,777 more than was earned. "Just like Chicago in the days of Capone," commented the provost marshall of the Seine base section. As an example he told of a major he had arrested who had just sent home $36,000 earned on the black market. When the Army forbade sending home more than a soldier's pay plus 10% (for gambling winnings) GIs simply began sending goods. Since no customs declarations were necessary for packages sent from Germany, millions of packages stuffed with saleable goods poured out of the country. One general may have set the record when he sent home a single shipment of 166 crates full of silver, tapestries, paintings and other valuables he'd presumably won in late-night card games.

Officers from the American and British armies where insatiable in their penchant for robbery. One British division, called upon to make a rapid advance in one of the last actions of the war, was slowed down when it was found to be twice its normal length as a result of all the cars stolen from Germans along the way. The stolen cars had to be driven off the road and set on fire to allow the column to advance.

And wherever the Germans surrendered it was really party time for Allied officers who routinely took over castles and villas in the countryside, staffed them with German labor and inspected their territories from lavish private railroad trains. One staff sergeant by the name of Henry Kissinger made good use of his authority to become the absolute lord of the town of Bensheim. After evicting the owners from their villa, Kissinger moved in with his German girlfriend, maid, housekeeper and secretary and began to throw fancy parties in a region where the average German had a daily food intake of fewer than 850 calories — less food than was given prisoners at Bergen-Belsen.

"What a set-up!" wrote one of his dinner guests on October 21, 1945. "Like a castle... (Kissinger) really enjoyed the trappings of authority."

President Truman's special advisor, Brigadier-General Harry Vaughan, sold his spare clothes on the Berlin black market for "a couple thousand dollars" while other officers went on sprees in palaces and libraries stealing millions of dollars in artwork, antiques and ancient books. Gold bullion, jewels and cash worth around two billion dollars in today's money was forcibly removed from the Reichbank first by soldiers of the German army and then by the Allies as the war ended. A cubic yard of gold bars was dug up in the Bavarian Alps near a town called Mittenwald and driven away by two American intelligence officers — who promptly disappeared. In 1946 Allied intelligence found cartels of American officers dealing in kilos of platinum, other precious metals and gems. Further investigations uncovered Americans involved in "mas-

(Continued on next page)

sive" blackmarketing of furs, carpets, opium, cocaine, penicillin ("white gold"), radium, titles to property, industrial chemicals, explosives, and millions of dollars worth of optical instruments. One ring even had an agency in New York! A million sewing needles stolen from the Singer factory in Darmstadt (under American control) mysteriously showed up in Italy while a Jewish survivor of the "death camps" emigrated to the U.S. to set up a sales office for the Necchi sewing machine company. He earned a million dollars in the next two years.

> **Further investigations uncovered Americans involved in "massive" blackmarketing of furs, carpets, opium, cocaine, penicillin ("white gold"), radium, titles to property, industrial chemicals, explosives, and millions of dollars worth of optical instruments. One ring even had an agency in New York!**

Officers could afford to do their black marketing without deserting. But without the protective privileges of rank, a dogface had to go over the hump, live like a fugitive and make the most of his freedom before the MPs caught him and sent him back to the front.

Once a GI went over the hump he entered a subterranean world where he could trust no one and yet had to trust almost anyone who would help him. Civilian life was out of the question — these guys could neither return to the Army nor pass as Europeans. Regular employment was impossible. They had to be constantly on the look-out for "snowballs" (MPs), they had to be wary of being betrayed by other soldiers, other deserters, or the locals who didn't take kindly to the shoot-'em-ups that sometimes erupted between the deserters and the MPs.

Yet these locals prized their relationships with American deserters and there developed a symbiosis between them. Protection from discovery was traded for access to booty. And there was no shortage of Europeans ready to improve their lifestyles even with bombs falling around them. As Linakis recounts in his novel, robbery had become commonplace:

"Seemed that every Belgique was involved in the *marche noir* or thievery of some sort or another. Belgiques had been very patriotic when they stole from the kraut. Now that the kraut had left, there were the Anglais and les Americains to steal from. Amerique,

after all, was a very rich country.' We all became thieves and smugglers, doing *beaucoup marche noir,* he said. 'Being AWOL was the most important thing to the army, but being AWOL was the very least of it.'"

Survival was the most important thing, and to that end deserters tended to congregate in certain "liberated" cities, such as Paris or Brussels. There they lived in rooms rented to them by local prostitutes or black marketeers, tried to blend into the background and earned their keep by stealing. They had plenty of company. There were even more British troops absent without leave, not to mention German AWOLs and other refugees from the fighting. There was very little thought of the future — only to avoid getting picked up by the MPs and sent back to the front. Liberated zones also offered more opportunity to raid supplies from the States with the complicity of U.S. soldiers stationed at the various supply depots. In Italy (home to at least 10,000 American deserters) a soldier himself could become a commodity in what was known as the "flying market."

> **Survival was the most important thing, and to that end deserters tended to congregate in certain "liberated" cities, such as Paris or Brussels. There they lived in rooms rented to them by local prostitutes or black marketeers, tried to blend into the background and earned their keep by stealing.**

Curzio Malaparte, who covered the Russian Front for the Italian newspaper *Corriere della Sera,* describes in his book *The Skin* how liberated Neapolitans sought out mainly black soldiers to con into believing they were being treated like royalty when in fact they were being exploited for their access to the PX. Paying each other for the right to "own" a soldier, Italian children befriended the black soldiers and brought them home with them.

"The price of a Negro on the flying market is based on the lavishness and recklessness of his expenditure," wrote Malaparte. "If the cost of hiring a Negro on the flying market for a few hours was only twenty or thirty dollars, the cost of hiring him for one or two months was high, ranging from three hundred to a thousand dollars or even more. An American Negro was a gold mine.

(Continued next page) **91**

"A Negro's master treated his slave as a honored guest. He offered him food and drink... let him dance with his own daughters... And the Negro would come home every evening with gifts of sugar, cigarettes, spam, bacon, bread, white flour, vests, stockings, shoes, uniforms, bedspreads, overcoats, and vast quantities of caramels... cases of corned beef... treasures of every kind, which he filched from the military stores..."

Especially valuable, writes Malaparte, were colored drivers who could haul away goods by the truckload or the trucks themselves and even the occasional tank.

The family then turned around and sold the booty, or perhaps they sold the Negro himself, who was oblivious to the whole process.

Avoiding military duty and going AWOL have been American traditions since Civil War days, when tired soldiers managed to lose their front teeth... so necessary for the crimping of cartridges used in those days.

Avoiding military duty and going AWOL have been American traditions since Civil War days, when tired soldiers managed to lose their front teeth... so necessary for the crimping of cartridges used in those days. And deserting in search of a better life happened often enough in the First World War. In 1920 the Paris police submitted complaints to the U.S. government about the estimated 1,500 doughboy deserters still hanging around the city running guns and making a living "chiefly from the illicit sale of drugs."

Things were no different in World War II, as thousands of soldiers deliberately wounded themselves or faked insanity to get out of combat. A 1947 *Harper's Magazine* article estimated as many as 20% of those who "hit the sick book" did so in a desperate attempt to go home. For them, the war was literally without end, since their only hope of survival was to endure combat until the enemy surrendered (and after the battles in the Huertgen and Ardennes that did not seem imminent), to get wounded or desert. The mental stress was incredible. Medical evacuations due to mental breakdowns ran at 23%. In Vietnam, by contrast, they accounted for just two out of every 1,000.

Here at home, a million men managed to get thrown out of the Army in the first two years of the war. Bedwetting at one Texas training camp went up 1200 percent when the Army declared that condition a psychological reason for discharge. But this phenomenon disappeared quickly when the Army removed this as sufficient grounds for rejection. As manpower became scarcer, so did the requirements to defend democracy become less stringent. Within a year a soldier was considered fit for duty if his fever was less than 103 degrees. And the Army's reputation for neglect and violence toward its own men didn't exactly engender loyalty.

Bedwetting at one Texas training camp went up 1200 percent when the Army declared that condition a psychological reason for discharge.

Yanked from the civilian world to the military one of KP, endless saluting and physical pain, GI grunts were also segregated according to rank. That system treated an infantryman with approximately the same respect that the infantryman gave the black. But it could get worse. In Lichfield, England two sergeants from Harlan County, Kentucky became notorious for the sadistic delight they took in beating the daylights out of the draftees for the slightest infraction of base rules. Beatings and torture were so savage there that it was a real relief to these men when they were sent to Omaha Beach on D-Day.

It was this combination of circumstances that drastically altered the way the Army treated AWOLs. Already down to the dregs of their conscript forces and faced with stiff German resistance, the Army began to treat captured deserters to a little re-education.

First, the AWOL would be carted off to the disciplinary center in France, perhaps at Reims or Loire. There the men were put on half rations while being forced marched at double time from sunrise to sunset. Any infractions were punished with the "solarium," an eight foot deep pit with barbed wire over it. On Saturdays the men were made to watch a hanging or two. Executions on portable gibbets were so frequent in Reims that GIs referred to it as "Hangtown." Although these men were being executed for crimes other than desertion, the AWOLs were led to believe that this is what awaited them if they deserted again.

In the end this kind of treatment resulted in more violence toward the MPs, who began to be gunned down by deserters who saw no choice. This in turn upped the ante for the Army, which started court-martialing deserters, handing out sentences of thirty, forty, fifty years. As things progressed, death sentences for desertion were handed down — although only one was carried out, on

(Continued on next page)

private Eddie Slovik, a Detroit boy whose death order was signed by General Eisenhower himself.

> **As things progressed, death sentences for desertion were handed down — although only one was carried out, on private Eddie Slovik, whose death order was signed by General Eisenhower himself.**

There were more than seventy U.S. witnesses to Slovik's execution and word spread quickly. Once again the Army miscalculated the effect and was unprepared for the outrage that followed. Although 49 soldiers had received the death sentence, there were no more executions and Ike quickly rescinded the order on two other soldiers he had condemned to die. At war's end the Army had prosecuted and sentenced 2,864 deserters, but seems to have abandoned the crusade against deserters as angry GIs demanded to be sent home.

> **Allied propagandists tried to direct GI discontent toward the Germans by hanging large photographs of the "death camps" in mess halls or other areas where soldiers might congregate. It was disbelieved.**

Allied propagandists tried to direct GI discontent toward the Germans by hanging large photographs of the "death camps" in mess halls or other areas where soldiers might congregate. It was disbelieved. One regiment surveyed found forty percent thought it was "only propaganda." A British P.O.W. refused an interview to a correspondent from the *Daily Telegraph* who had written an article about Belsen a few days after it was liberated. He did not want to speak to a reporter who would spread such lies about the Germans. All in all, the U.S. propaganda must have been as convincing as the heavy-handed German radio programs telling soldiers their wives were home fucking Negroes. Nobody cared about whom they were supposed to hate, they just wanted to go home. There were even two GI insurrections at bases in the Pacific *before* the atom bomb was dropped. Within days after the war ended, the government was instituting a point system to rotate the soldiers home as quickly as possible. The hunt for deserters was off.

> **There were even two GI insurrections at bases in the Pacific *before* the atom bomb was dropped.**

What happened to them? Many of them probably came home by simply climbing aboard ships departing from France, or England. Once back home there was little to do but dodge ticker tape and look for a job. A goodly number of them undoubtedly stayed on in Europe as they had in World War One. Perhaps some of them got bogged down in ordinary life, marrying and having children. Others may have continued their lives of crime and ended up in prison. Only nine thousand of them had been found by 1948.●

Sources

"Close Up of Democracy," Paul Dreher, *Virgina Quarterly Review* (Winter 1947)

In The Spring The War Ended, Steven Linakis, (Putnam 1965)

The Execution of Private Slovik, William Bradford Huie (Signet 1954)

"The Second Aftermath," John McPartland, *Harper's,* February 1947

New Era in the Pacific, John Hohenberg (Simon & Schuster, 1972)

"A 'Good War' it Wasn't," James J. Martin, *Journal of Historical Review,* Spring 1990

"How the Censors Rigged the News," Fletcher Pratt, *Harper's, February 1946*

"The Bitter Battle in the Snow," *Cyril Ray, Observer Magazine,* December 21, 1969

The First Casualty, Phillip Knightley (Andre Deutsch, 1975)

Interview with G.A. Rollins, an MP in Europe at the end of the war.

The Skin, Curzio Malaparte, 1952, English edition (Marlboro Press, 1988)

Wartime, Paul Fussel (Oxford Press, 1989)

From the Ruins of the Reich, Douglass Botting (Crown Publishers, 1985)

NIGGER JACK

A Short Story

by G.J. Schaefer

Illustrations by Deb Calabria

The warden of the Florida State Prison at Starke strapped John Spinkelink into the electric chair and fried his ass on May 25, 1979 and right away convicts began scheming for the job of death chamber orderly; that was because of a hooker named Sonia.

Sonia was the whore who'd murdered two cops down in Broward County: Trooper Black of the Highway Patrol and Constable Irwin from Canada. She'd shot them dead at a rest area off I-95 hard by Pompano Beach. A stinking scum-sucking rat by the name of Walter Rhodes had turned state's evidence and put Sonia's pretty young tail in line to fry on Old Sparky. She'd burn with her convict boyfriend, Jesse Tafero. It would be an event to see.

It all added up that Sonia would be riding the lightning. Spinkelink had murdered an ex-con rapo-faggot and the State had burned him, so there was no doubt that Sonia would be coming along to pay us a visit by and by. Everybody in the joint believed it would happen and almost everybody wanted to be on hand to watch — not because Sonia was disliked, but because she was prime pussy. She'd been a high-priced hooker on the streets, she'd blown away a pair of law dogs, she had great teats, and was the reigning Queen of Death Row.

The State would burn Sonia and some lucky convict would be assigned the job of mopping up her pee and emptying her knickers after the execution. The prison guards always have someone handy to dump the executed person's drawers before turning the smoking corpse over to the free-world undertaker, so we all knew someone would luck into the job of dumping Sonia's. It was a job to covet, and there was more to it than the chance to see real pussy. The job carried a guarantee of an endless income of coffee and cigarettes tendered by anyone wanting to hear the true story of Queen Sonia on her electric throne. Look at it as a form of chain gang Social Security.

We knew this to be a fact because of Curly Bill. Curly had personally watched a cunt sizzle in the Alabama electric chair in 1957. This unusual event occurred while Curly was pulling a stretch at the Holman Penitentiary, and for a small gratuity he'd sit down and tell anyone the whole story. I'd heard he told it well, so being of a curious nature I went down to the prison canteen, picked up a jar of Maxwell House Coffee and a bag of Oreos, and moseyed on down to Curly Bill's cell. I found him sitting on his bunk rolling a smoke.

I poked my mug in his door and said, "Curly Bill, if you're in a yarning mood I'd like to hear the story of the fried cunt." I took the jar of coffee out of the paper sack and tossed it on his bed. "Talking can dry a man out. I brought you a little something to wet your whistle while you talk." A flagrant bribe.

Curly Bill eyed the coffee. His tongue ran out and dampened the rolling paper for his cigarette. "Whole damn jar, all for me?" he inquired.

First published in 1992 Main Catalog

(Continued on next page)

I shrugged. "Sure, why not? I heard you tell quite a story."

He lit his cig and took a drag. "What sort of story are you wanting to hear?"

"What kinds you got, Curly?"

He pursed his lips in thought. "Well, there's the kind I tell the Man when he comes snooping around. And there's the kind I tell the social science girlies from the university day trip every month. And then there's the true fact of what really happened the night the Captain strapped a Tutweiler cunt to Old Sparky and she rode the lightning down to the flaming pit of Hell." He cocked an eyebrow at me and said, "That pussy was so hot steam rose from between her legs. Now... what sort of yarn did you fancy, Jerry?"

"The one with the smoking hole."

Curly Bill grinned. "That's the one the free people don't want to hear."

"I ain't been free for awhile, Old Man."

He nodded the truth of that statement. He'd been seeing me on the yard for over ten years. He told me to come on into his cell and set my tail on a Number Ten can. I hunkered down while Curly cracked the seal on the jar of fresh mud and put a stinger in his cup to heat water. Steaming coal-black coffee, roll-your-own smokes, and all the time in the world. No place to go, nothing to do. Pulling a life hitch. May as well listen to an Oldcock tell a tale of the way things were in the Alabama chain gang, not so long ago, not so far away.

Curly Bill was one of the slimiest human slugs ever to crawl out from between a whore's legs, but he was a good storyteller. He perched himself on the edge of his rack, took a sip of the smoking Joe and began his story.

"Her name was Rhonda Belle Martin and they'd drove her up from the Julia Tutweiler Penitentiary for Women earlier that day. She rode the prison death train north, a chained bitch in an unmarked van with a one-way ticket to the State Electric Chair. She was con-demned meat, the kind the prison screws burn at Holman Penitentiary. They kept her in a cell right by the electric chair for a few hours, then Warden Hobbs got him a call from the Governor's Office at the State Capitol. The message was plain and simple: 'Fry the Bitch.'"

"Were they burning women regular back then, Curly?"

"More than these days, but not a passel. Now, a bitch figures she can get away with murder, but back then it wasn't such a sure thing."

"So they brought her up from Tutweiler, and then what?"

"It was a little bit secret actually. The first sign we men on the cellblocks had that she'd burn was when a death house screw come up into our living area to fetch Billy Mumford out'n his cell. Billy had the job to shave the condemned. Head and leg."

"What kind of job is that?" I wondered.

"That's Special Barber assignment. Before they take you and set you in the chair you got to have a body shave so the electricity runs all around you nice and smooth. Billy does the leg where the electrode fits on, and he does the head. They let a man shave around his own peter..."

I gave Curly Bill a snort of disbelief. "I have my doubts anyone has to shave the hair around his peter for a ride on Sparky. What's the sense in it?"

"It's a rule, Boy. And if you don't care to believe my true tale you can march your dumb ass down to L-Wing and ask that nigger Jim Richardson about the body shave he got when they was making a practice run on him back in 1970. Body shave means they take every single hair off, even the ones on your nuts, Boy."

"And a woman?"

"They skin her beaver."

"Hard to believe."

"I ain't asking you to believe. I'm telling you how it was and what I saw up to Holman when Rhonda Belle sat on Sparky." Curly Bill slurped some coffee and continued.

"So Billy went off to the Death House with the screw and later Billy comes back and tells us we won't believe it but there's a cunt from Tutweiler down in the Death Cell and they are fixing to fry her bottom real soon. He damn sure had our undivided attention when we heard it was a real female. Then we wanted to hear about the body shave. You know, did he shave her or what?"

"Well? Did he?"

"Billy told us he did shave her. He gave us the entire story. And it was his claim that when he was shaving her leg, her skirt was raised and he could see all the way up to where some brown pussy hair was sticking out from underneath the elastic around the leg hole. We were all asking him, 'Did she just set there and let you look?' and Billy swore that she didn't seem to mind his admiration of her charms at all. Now ain't that a treat?"

I bobbed my head acknowledging that it was indeed extraordinary and Curly Bill continued, "Billy told us she wore a white panty. Nothing fancy, just the plain

(Continued on next page)

kind the State issues to the gals at Tutweiler, but he could see a pelt of dark brown hair under the crotch part. And he truly believed that he could make out her crack right there in the center part, because there was like a little furrow where the panty indented and running along this groove was a wet spot dead in the center, right where her hole would be underneath the cloth."

"I'd have been looking my own self. Bet on it!"

Curly Bill hooted and slapped his knee. "And remember now in those days a gal didn't show her leg all the way up to her asshole like they do now." It was a real unusual sight for Billy to behold, especially her being alive and setting in a chair right smack dab in front of his face. We all wanted to hear more and Billy told us everything two and three times, and each telling got better as he recollected little details and related them to us.

"What sort of details do you mean?"

"Her name for one: it was Rhonda Belle Martin. Ain't that a lovely name — Rhonda Belle? Her eyes: she had these big brown sad eyes with long eyelashes. Her voice: it was a lady's voice. Southern and polite, and sexy when she answered a question. He told us about her bosom: a real nice big one, and when she breathed it moved. Billy was taken with her hair... long, clean, pretty brown hair halfway down her back, almost to her waist. And then to prove it to us, Billy reached into his jacket and pulled out a swatch of thick brown hair held together by a rubber band around one end. It reminded me of one of those Red Indian movies where they scalp a pioneer lady then run off with her hair and hook it onto a pole."

"They let this guy Billy walk off with her hair?"

"He's the Special Barber, ain't he? He cuts the hair and hauls it off to the trash bin. Only this time he took him a little souvenir to show us in the cellblocks." Curly smiled a little, remembering her hair.

"We all smelled that long hank of hair. Put it right up to our noses and inhaled; it smelt real nice. Billy couldn't get enough of it. For a long time he would lay on his bunk, spread that spill of curly locks over his face, and jack his dick. For Billy, it was love at first sight between him and the cunt. He told us how he walked into her cell and right away saw she was no sweat hog. She was a sweet, pretty little woman. He had to tell her what to do. Take off your shoes. Peel down the nylon stocking. Put your foot in the bucket. She was shaking like a virgin and he had to calm her. Be gentle with her.

"There he is, soaping her leg and it's trembling in his hands. Billy knows where she's going, so he tries to go slow to give her a few extra minutes. She's about to die, but he's making love to her with his eyes. Maybe she loved him back. He said she did. She cried when he cut her hair."

"Sounds like Billy was gone."

"Billy was speculating about that wet spot in the center of her crotch. He claimed it was love dew seeping, due to the way he was rubbing his hands up and down her leg. I reckoned it was plain old pee. I told Billy not even the horniest nympho at Tutweiler would be oozing love dew while sitting in the Holman Penitentiary Death House, even if Frank Sinatra was rubbing her leg."

"He took it pretty serious."

"Billy went all moony. We respected that. Didn't mention a word about the meat wagon from Bates Funeral Parlor that rolled in the back gate while he was down in the Death Cell sparking Rhonda Belle. Freddy, down by the gate, he saw it roll in and put it on the grapevine. I reckoned that gal from Tutweiler was thinking about something other'n Billy Mumford's passionate love while she was shaving the hair offen her own snatch. But I didn't tell Billy that."

"What did you tell Special Barber Billy?"

"We told him she'd get a stay from the courts. They'd send her back to Tutweiler and she'd write him fuck letters about what she'd do to him when he got out. What else?"

"Wishful thinking."

"Sure. And we were joshing Billy about it when Captain Scotty Crowe came walking up to the cellblock door. Captain Crowe ran the Death House. Enjoyed his work too. Got his name in the papers the time they burned that preacher's daughter from Anniston. Cute little blonde with big tits, killed her mama and her daddy. Told everyone the Devil made her do it. Maybe so. Then she come up to Holman and starts up that the Captain made an indecent proposal to her, so Warden Hobbs let him strap her cunt to the Chair. He did such a fine job they let him supervise every time a bitch burned. For all I know he's still up there frying those girlies."

"Do you think he made an indecent proposal to that preacher's daughter?"

"Bet your hairy ass he did. Told me so hisself. Said that little blonde was so fine it would give a man a hard-on just to look at her. One night he goes down by her cell and suggests he could fix it so's she'd die with a smile on her lips. She wanted to know how. He told her. She went off like a firecracker. Preacher's daughter.

(Continued on next page)

She was no screamer. It makes for a better story if I tell it with Rhonda Belle screaming and begging but you said you wanted the *true* story." He blew on his coffee. "What actually happened was that Warden Hobbs marched off into that room where the condemned wait for the call to the Chair and told her pure and simple it was her time. He gave her the usual choice; she could come strolling in like a lady or he could have her drug in by a couple of big screws on the execution detail. It didn't matter a lick to him one way or the other. Miss Rhonda chose to go peaceful."

"So much for the cat fight."

"Maybe. Maybe not. With a woman you never know. Captain Crowe used to say it was because a gal is a high-strung, emotional type of creature. Women can get hysterical fast. He told me he'd seen it happen."

"So she said she'd go peaceful. Then what'd she do?"

"Nothing much. The door from the holding cell opened and there she was. Two big bulldagger matrons from the Tutweiler Women's Penitentiary were with her. Big mean looking bitches in black uniforms. Rhonda Belle weren't no young gal, thirty years old if she was a day. Her big brown eyes were roaming around the room, flickering here and there taking everything in. She seemed a little shaky but not too much. I'd seen men worse."

"What was she wearing?"

Curly Bill thought on that one for a few beats. "She had a flowered scarf over her head. Covered up her being bald. She was dressed nice. Ladylike. A black dress. Sunday-go-to-meetin' clothes. Maybe like she'd wear to a funeral, come to think of it. Nylon stockings. Black patent leather high-heeled pumps that made a clickety-clack sound on the cement when she walked. There was make-up on her face: shiny red lipstick, rouged cheeks, powdered nose. She was wearing nice perfume. Back then a woman wore what she pleased to her own execution. Rhonda Belle fancied heels and hose, plenty of Chanel perfume. You could see how Billy had fallen for her. She was pretty. She smelt real sweet." Curly Bill licked his lips at the memory.

"The two matrons had her by the elbows and steered her straight to the Chair. Warden Hobbs asked her to take a seat, so she turned herself around and sat down. She did it quick and smooth. She made a little squeak of alarm, like maybe she figured she'd get a shock from the Chair. But when nothing happened she scooched herself around and settled her nerves. She looked at Warden Hobbs and grinned sheepishly. He asked her if she was comfortable, and she bobbed her head."

"Then Warden Hobbs turned to Captain Crowe and ordered him to strap her in for the ride. She was looking a bit dazed, like maybe she really had been thinking she'd be going back on down to Tutweiler where she'd sit in her cell and write steamy letters to Billy Mumford at Holman and all of a sudden it dawned on her that a stay wasn't coming after all. She was in for a big shock, compliments of the State of Alabama. I asked the Nigger, 'Who'd she kill?'

" 'Captain say her husband ate poison. Rat poison.'

" 'Cold bitch to do that to a man.'

" 'Fixin' to warm her right up, Curly Bill.'

"That was a fact. The pretty flowered scarf was gone and the Captain was taping a strip of metal to the egg-smooth skin of her head. The Nigger explained that was the primary electrode; he told me that at the pull of a switch, 4500 volts of electricity would boil her brain. Rhonda Belle sat in the Chair and quivered. The fat matron with the dishwater blonde hair unceremoniously pulled up Rhonda Belle's skirt and unfastened her nylon stocking and peeled it down her left leg, impatient as a lover. The skirt was so high we could see the rubber strap holding up her other stocking, and the white fabric of her panty rucked up in her crotch. Me and the Nigger looked hard but didn't see the pussy hair curling out. I reckoned maybe that body shave rule applied to Tutweiler gals after all.

" 'Oh my God!' the Nigger sighed.

" 'Amen, Brother!' I added.

"We could see everything between the top of her stocking and the white panty. Meat the color of chicken breast at Sunday dinner. The tender, sweet kind. *Rhonda Belle* was tender, and she was sweet. I couldn't believe they were about to kill her. I had an impulse to step forward and tell them to leave her alone."

"Bullshit," I said. I just couldn't see old Curly Bill going sentimental on a condemned piece of ass. Curly cocked his eyebrow at me. It wiggled like a caterpillar crawling across his brow.

"God's truth. I'd never seen a woman put to death. It stirred me, way down inside somewhere." His eyes clouded and he looked away. The bastard seemed to have feelings of some kind and I waited for them to subside.

"Anyway. They fastened another metal electrode on her leg just below her knee. Clamped it on real tight with a butterfly nut. Her stocking was in a little heap around her ankle. Then they took her ankles and set them in the wooden stocks and locked them in."

(Continued on next page)

"Stocks? Why'd they do that, Curly? I mean she ain't going nowhere."

"Holds 'em steady so they get an even burn."

"Oh." That shut me up.

"Yeah, and when they fix the ankles that way it spreads the woman's legs. Opens them right wide, and when that happened we could see all the way up." Curly Bill clearly relished this part.

"What did you see, the famous wet spot?"

"Nope. Looked like a nice fat jellyroll wrapped in white cotton cloth. The Nigger gave me a little elbow and we were both straining our eyes looking up her skirt, but we couldn't see no wet spot atall."

"So you really didn't see that much, did you?"

A smug look spread over Curly Bill's wide face. "We saw plenty, Sonny. *Plenty*. You ever seen a woman sit on Sparky?"

"Sure."

"You have! Where?"

"Right here on Q-Wing. Girls from the college tours sit on Sparky every month... used to anyway. They'd sit up there and some of 'em would show their panties. It ain't that much to see, unless you see one that ain't wearing no panty. Then it's worth a real hard look."

Curly Bill rubbed his crotch and eyed me like he wasn't too sure he was going to give up any more story. I'd have to prompt him.

"Well? What was Rhonda Belle doing in the Chair, Curly?"

"She weren't doing a damn thing but sitting there warming the seat — legs spread like some honkytonk tramp looking for a boner. Her forearms and wrists were strapped down to the armrests on the Chair. There was a black rubber belt drawn across her belly and another one that ran under her arms just beneath her big ole bazooms; made it so they were pouched up like a movie star's titties. She was sticking them out like she was Jayne Fucking Mansfield on a casting couch. Bet you never seen no college girl wearing a set of death straps!"

"Well..." I shrugged.

"Damn right you ain't seen no woman's ass *strapped* to no goddamned 'lectric chair. When they lay that belly strap acrost her gut and snap it tight, the gal lets out a grunt like some stud just ran a ten-inch hardhead up her box."

"No shit! Why so tight?"

"Because, Idgit, when she rides the lightning, she arches her back just like she does when she comes. They got to hold that stuff down in the Chair, Boy, or it would be an *obscenity*. Decent folk don't want to see no whore with her cunt raised." He caught my look and quickly amended, "Not at an official proceeding at any rate."

"What were you and the Nigger doing all this time?"

"Sheeeeit. We was standing right there looking at her snatch with our tongues hanging out!" Curly stuck his tongue out and panted to give me the idea. I punched his arm.

"Go on, Man!"

"OK, once they got her body restrained, then they ran another rubber strap acrost her forehead. So she was pretty well immobilized. Warden Hobbs stepped up right in front of Rhonda so she could see him and read off the Execution Order from the Governor's Office. He read it slow and clear, so she wouldn't miss a word. When he was done Chaplain Curtis came in and read a few words from the Good Book over her."

"I wonder what she was thinking."

"I never found out. She had a chance to tell us but she was a quiet one. Warden Hobbs approached her and asked her real nice if there was something she'd like to say because if so she was welcome to speak up. She seemed to be contemplating an answer. I was thinking she might crack wise and ask Hobbs to hold her hand, or sit on her lap or something. But she just said she didn't have nothing to say about nothing. Very polite. Nice soft South'ren voice. The Nigger was real disappointed. He'd been expecting a speech, he said. Captain Crowe had told him some ladies get downright chatty at the last moment. Captain said the Preacher's daughter ran on for more than twenty minutes about how hard liquor and sex was the cause of her trouble. She'd finished up her story by giving everyone a charming smile and going '...and here I am.' "

"Wow. What happened to the Preacher's daughter?"

"Same as what happened to Rhonda Belle Martin. Warden Hobbs gave a nod to one of those big bull daggers that rode up from the Women's Pen and she walked right up to the Chair and commenced to pushing wads of cotton up Rhonda Belle's pretty nose.

"The fat matron went right to work at it. She'd take a wad of cotton out of a blue box and work it into Rhonda Belle's nostril, then jam it on up there as far as she could with her finger. Didn't wear no rubber glove or nothing. Stuffed that cotton way to hell up there too. Me and the Nigger couldn't hardly believe it when we saw it happening."

(Continued on next page) **99**

"What the hell was the reason for the cotton?"

Curly Bill gave me a look of disgust. "So her fucking brains wouldn't leak out of her nose, Bozo. When they throw that switch and four or five thousand volts zap her in the head, the brain *boils*. And then it plain runs out your nose and down the front of your shirt. Or in this case, you'd see her sweetmeats dribbling down between her tits onto her lap." He leered at me. His eyes had the evil glint of a jackal.

"That's disgusting!"

"Happens all the time. You want to hear the story? Or maybe we'd better quit while we're ahead." He stood and hitched up his pants. "I don't want you puking up your Oreos, Kid. Think you're up to it? It ain't no pretty tale."

"Naw, naw, Curly, I ain't no pussy. I came here to hear a yarn and I'm a-gonna set this one out. That is, if you're still pouring coffee."

"Oh you finished already? Well I guess you been drinking while I been yapping..." he was teasing me. "I reckon I could fix another cup, if you're gonna stick around."

"Yeah Curly, come on and run the story. I want to hear it."

Curly settled the stinger for another round and continued. "The other fat dyke had an ass on her like a John Deere tractor. She was cramming cotton into Rhonda Belle's ears with the eraser end of a Number Two lead pencil. Sometimes the brains squirt out the ears too, you know?"

My mouth twisted with disgust. "How'd the girl react to all that poking into her head?"

"Howled like a fucking maniac is what she did. She was having a regular damn fit and shrieking 'What are you doing? What are you *doing*?' over and over like a busted Victrola record. The two matrons didn't pay her no mind. They were as busy as a son-of-a-bitch pulling cotton from the blue boxes and making it disappear into Rhonda Belle.

"While they were packing her, the two matrons were clucking and crooning, 'Be still now! Act like a lady! This don't hurt! This is for your own good! Behave yourself!' and happy horseshit like that. And I'll tell you something else what happened just then."

"What?"

"The Nigger leaned forward and lowered his voice. Muttered, 'Curly Bill' toward the floor. I leaned toward him to catch it. 'You reckon they'll pack her hole?' he whispered."

"The Nigger said that right there in the execution chamber?"

"Sure, he was a sex freak, remember?"

"Yeah, I see what you mean."

"I said I'd never heard of no such thing, but I kinda hoped they would, now that I got to thinking about it." Curly slurped his java. "What the Nigger said next was even more interesting."

"I'm on the edge of my can."

"Nigger said, 'If they put something in her hole, I'll be obliged to take it out later.' And I looked over at him and saw that he was serious. I could see it in his bugged-out eyes. His mouth was wet with spit because he kept licking his lips."

"Pure freak for that hot pussy, huh?"

"Hell yeah. By then Rhonda Belle was screaming and trying to wriggle out of the Chair. She wasn't getting nowhere, just howling like a bitch. Her nose was swole up with the cotton. She was crying. Tears running down her cheeks making wet trails through her make-up. She was a pitiful sight. We were watching it close, taking it all in. The Nigger whispered to me, 'That there be a *real* cunt, Man.' I gave him a look, trying to make out where he was coming from, and he came back real quick. 'Curly Bill, in here you can get a boy to suck your dick; you can bend him over and get you some shithole, but where you gonna get you some real pussy at Holman Penitentiary? Where else but right here?' "

Curly Bill paused and looked straight at me, waiting for me to say something.

"He had a point, I suppose."

"Bet your cracker ass he had a point. I told him I wasn't too sure about what he was getting at. I said Rhonda was wired for the electric enema, and that put me off my feed, so to speak."

"Did I miss something? They give her an enema?"

"That's what they call it when they hit you with 4000 volts and it blows the shit right out your ass and down your leg. I had heard of it. There was a good chance I was about to see it. That is, unless the bull daggers put cotton up Rhonda's asshole. Now don't get me wrong. I like a boy to suck me off same as anyone in the joint. But I told the Nigger that dipping my wick in some whore's shit wasn't my idea of an afternoon delight. But the Nigger had an answer for that." Curly smirked and sat back.

"What was the Nigger's remedy?" I prodded, intrigued.

(Continued on next page)

"The black son-of-a-bitch said the electric enema weren't nothing at all. He said, 'I've got me a water hose back there and I'll just spray some over her hole, wash it off real nice, and she'll be ready to ride. That juicy thing is gonna be as hot as a two-dollar pistol on a Saturday night.'"

"That makes sense," I commented judiciously.

"Damn right it makes sense. So I told that slimy fucker that maybe I'd go on back there and give it a closer look after he'd rinsed her off. Maybe hit a stroke or two. You should have seen those rubber lips smile. That boy was grinning like a weasel in a hen house."

"He knew he was gonna get him some white pussy now."

"Yup, sure as hell did," Curly Bill snorted.

"Did the prison matrons put cotton up her butt?"

"Nope, those bulldaggers didn't fool around with that. I figured they'd dive right into her panties and straight up her hole. But they never messed with her."

"Too bad, that would've been a sight to see."

"Yeah. There was nothing to look at but the panties, so I looked up at her eyes and they were like Billy had said: large and brown and wet with tears. And miserable. She knew she was on her way to wherever fried cunt goes, and she wasn't too anxious to take that ride. Those eyes. They were desolate. Then Captain Crowe covered her face with the rubber death mask and she started going, 'Oh. Oh. Oh,' behind the mask. The strangest sound you ever heard a woman make."

"Sounds like it took a long time to get her ready."

"Well, not really. The event moved right along. Everyone seemed to know just what to do. They'd had plenty of practice. They burned men regular at Holman. Women only came in once in a while but it went down smooth enough. When the fat matrons were done, Warden Hobbs walked around the Chair giving Rhonda Belle a close inspection. He checked the straps and apparently he liked what he saw. He thanked the two dykes from the Women's Penitentiary for their assistance and asked Captain Crowe to show them to the door.

"Back then the only woman allowed to see an execution was the guest of honor, and she didn't really see it. The two matrons took one last fond look at Rhonda Belle and waddled on off with the Captain. Warden Hobbs waited until the dykes were clear of the room, then he turned and looked thoughtfully at Rhonda Belle sitting there on the Chair making her funny little noises. It was so weird. She kept going, 'Oh. Oh. Oh,' over and over, and making a noise like a hiccup. She'd twitch, and she was sort of trying to wriggle around. She had the Warden's attention. He watched her for a minute like he was memorizing her reactions.

"He pursed his lips and scratched behind his ear. Then he turned and gave a nod toward the black drape hanging off to one side."

"What's that for?" I asked.

"The executioner stands behind it, and when he gets the nod he pulls the switch."

"And he got the nod..."

"He damn sure did. One moment Rhonda Belle was wriggling around making squeaky noises, and a second later she was slammed forward into the straps so hard it made the leather creak. She came up off that Chair like a gymnastical gal trying to arch her body toward the roof." Curly Bill was checking me out, to see if I got the picture.

"She came right up off the Chair?"

"Damn right! They gave her a straight shot of 4500 volts and when the power took her, it lifted her up and tried to fling her right out of the Chair."

I could just see it. Curly Bill was smacking his lips, warming to his topic. "When those straps bit into her, she gave a grunt like someone hit her a punch in the belly, and at the same time she let go a fart. A real ripper, lewd and unladylike. And listen to this: a jet of pee squirted right through the white crotch of her panty like it was coming from a pressure hose."

"You mean it shot out in front of her? How far would you say?"

"A coupla feet at least. Came jetting right out. Made a little pool in front of the Chair and between her legs. Her butt was maybe six inches off the Chair. The pee wet her pants and dribbled. There was only that first jet that came through, when they put the juice to her. She didn't pee a whole lot, just that little puddle for her behind to sit in when it came down. Course, when the panty got wet we saw the crack. The McCoy. I recollect it perfect to this very day." Curly Bill was licking his lips, and I imagined that the bright look in his eyes was not too different from the one he had seen in Nigger Jack's.

"Is it true what you heard about the electric enema?"

Curly Bill sucked in his breath. "Oh, it's true all right. All the shit up inside Rhonda leaped right out her asshole and slithered around inside her drawers like a damn snake. The turd came out and coiled up in her pants. Made 'em sag with the load until they drooped

(Continued on next page) **101**

down and touched the seat under her. The stink was vile. It rose up from under her and radiated around the room. There is no smell like it on this earth. Smoke was coming off her head. Her flesh was sizzling like bacon at the electrodes and her drawers were full of shit. The stench would gag a maggot.

"The Nigger's eyes were popped wide. He said, 'Curly Bill, that's what they call the electric enema.' I didn't know what to say. Then he said, 'Don't let it put you off none. All that washes off. I'll take care of that.' You see, he was coming on strong. He wanted that white pussy, and he'd do just about anything to get her. He knew I was standing between him and her, and he was working on me the only way he knew how."

"He was trying to work you up so you'd want a little piece yourself."

"Right. And he could see I was about to go a little green around the gills from smelling her frying flesh, so right away he started in on that."

"The smell?"

"Yeah. He said, 'Curly Bill, did you smell her perfume when they brought her in?' I gave him a nod while drilling my eyes on her body. It was changing color from white to deep pink. She was turning colors like one of them lizards that can go from brown to green when they take a notion. Only she was going from white to red. Her leg where the electrode was around it was as red as a lobster in a pot above the electrode and white as a catfish belly beneath."

"She was changing colors while you were watching her?"

He nodded. "She was cooking between the electrodes is why. A big ole burn blister rose up on her leg just above the electrode cuff. It swole up with liquid and then it popped and smoke rose up from it. The watery stuff soaked down into the cuff and hissed like a snake. Steam came up in a white cloud. Smelled so awful I could feel my dinner coming up on me."

I stared at him. He was really into the story. His lips were curled up in a grimace as if recoiling from the stench of frying flesh.

"Curly Bill. Didn't the Nigger say something about her perfume?"

"Oh yeah," he sniffed unconsciously. Maybe that cleared out the memory of the deathstench, because his face relaxed. "Nigger Jack told me she put perfume on her tits and in the crack of her behind."

"How'd he know?"

"He watched her through the security mirror."

"What's that?"

"It's where the prison officials watch a woman when she's naked. They watch her when she takes off her prison uniform and puts on her execution clothes."

"The *men* watch her?"

"Sure they do. That's security. Suppose she jumps on those matrons? Anything could happen in that room. She could kill them two matrons in there and who'd know? They *got* to watch."

"Makes sense. But it must really embarrass the woman."

"Well they do it in a polite way, so she don't feel embarrassed."

"Who watches?"

"Oh, the Captain and whoever else he lets come in to see the strip show," Curly Bill chuckled. "He would have killed the Nigger if he knew he was watching the white woman, but Nigger Jack slipped his sneaky black ass into the room while Captain Crowe was off checking on the death straps and had himself a nice long look. That Nigger, he got him an eyeful, and he was giving me an earful."

"Wanted to get your cock up for Rhonda."

"That's it. He said he'd watched the white lady shave the hair off her cunt. She squatted on the toilet and soaped it, then she shaved it, washed it by pouring water from a plastic cup over it, and patted it dry with a paper towel. Then when she was done she stood up and the fat matron handed her a little bottle of perfume and Rhonda Belle put some on her finger and went up behind her ears with it. She dabbed a bit on her neck, then ran her finger down smack between her teats. Lifted up each titty and put a dab under each one. Finally she rubbed some between her legs and reached around and drew her finger up the crack of her ass. The Nigger told me he took out his cock and jacked off into his bandana just from the sight of her."

"Think he was lying?"

"Nope. I saw the look on his face." Curly Bill took out a cigarette paper and sprinkled some Kite tobacco onto it. He rolled it, licked it and fired it up. He puffed away at it, recollecting Rhonda's perfume.

"Nigger tell you anything else he saw?"

"They took away her brassiere. Made her go to the Chair without it."

"That's weird," I remarked. "Why?"

"No metal is supposed to be between the electrodes. None at all. The brassiere she had been wearing had

(Continued on next page)

metal fasteners and stuff on it, so they confiscated it from her. They made her wear special underpants too."

That got my interest. "Special in what way?"

"The Nigger knew all about it. He told me the panties the State issues convict women have elastic at the waist and leg. The elastic melts when they cook the gal, so before she comes up here, they sew up a special panty for her, one with no elastic. It's got drawstrings like one of them bikini suits Brigitte Bardot wears.

"So after Rhonda Belle was shaved and perfumed, the matron tied the bikini on her ass. They knotted that sucker up tight too. We had to slice it with a razor to get it off."

"So you *did* get to see her pussy!"

"Saw it? Damn right I did. I saw it snuggled up in her panty when she was alive. I saw it squirt pee when they ran the lightning through her. I saw her raise that pussy up off the Chair like a woman ready to fuck. And I saw it bleed — "

"What do you mean, *bleed?*"

"What I mean is ... she was arched up in the straps and turning red as a cooked beet. Her hands were curled into grotesque claws with her fingers angling out in every whichway. She was shaking so hard her shoes fell off and her toes were curled up like she was coming hard. She was sizzling like a pan of fried meat. Up inside her belly some female part of her must have burst, because the blood rushed out from her. It gushed from her hole, it soaked her panties dark red. Made a pool on the Chair and dripped onto the floor."

I took a deep breath. I was trying to think of some reasonable explanation. "It must have been her time of month, Curly Bill."

"Nope. For that they put the woman on the rag. She wasn't on her period. She just busted up inside and the blood ran out her cunt, that's all."

"That is totally fucking *gross*." Curly Bill's story was starting to get to me. I started to tell him to stop, but I figured it couldn't get any worse. Curly Bill looked like he was in another world, like he was actually seeing the whole disgusting spectacle and couldn't tear his eyes away. "Now you know why they don't let ladies come in and see the executions. Even a girl reporter might be upset by a sight like that."

"You can bet the women will be here to watch Sonia Jacobs when she cooks."

"Yeah, and you can bet Sonia will have more cotton stuffed in her than a teddy bear. This ain't like the old days. Sonia won't get no 4500 volts neither."

"What will she get?"

"Not more than 2800 volts, about enough to just knock out her eyeballs. Damnedest thing you ever saw, eyeballs popping out of the head and hanging on the cheeks by the optic nerve. Happens every time. Why do you think they make them wear a mask?"

"I guess I never thought about it, Curly Bill. Or at least, not enough."

"Sonia will have it easy compared to girls in the old days. They'll stick cotton up her cunt, up her butt, let her wear a ministration rag to pee on, and give her plastic pants to boot. Then they'll tickle her to death with a measly couple thousand volts." Curly Bill spat out a shred of tobacco on the floor.

"1800 volts will kill you."

"Sure. After awhile, so will these RIP's." He blew smoke at me. "But Rhonda Belle, they ran the power through her for three minutes, then quit. Rhonda Belle went limp in the straps, sat down in her own fucking pile of slop as dead as anyone you ever did see. Doctor Garcia, the prison sawbones, was called in to examine her. He told everyone she was dead. Captain Crowe said, 'No shit, Sherlock?' and the sawbones scuttled on out of there. The stench was so thick you could almost see it; and it wasn't Rhonda Belle's Chanel we were smelling. That smell is really something. They ought to bottle it and make juvenile delinquents take a whiff every time they get to feeling ambitious." Curly chuckled at his own little joke, and I urged him on.

"So the fried lady was sitting there..."

"Oh yeah. Well, Warden Hobbs yelled to Nigger Jack, 'Git this damned mess out of my 'Lectric Chair!' and the Nigger comes back, 'Yes Sir, Mister Warden, Sir!' He unfastened all the straps and buckles, then loaded her onto a metal gurney and wheeled her away to the back room."

"Where were the screws?"

"The screws were fucking gone — *long* gone. The show was over and the audience cleared out fast. Like I said, the place was stinking so bad, people were ready to puke. It's a *real bad* smell."

"So nobody was around but you and Nigger Jack?"

"Me and Nigger Jack — and Rhonda Belle." Curly Bill grinned like the very Devil himself. "We took that cutie into the back room and the Nigger got to work cleaning her up. He pulled down those nasty panties, cut the knots with his razor, and slid them off her ass. It was like he promised, exactly. He had his hose and he played it all around her hindparts. Steam rising off that hot ass, swear to God. Got after her with the lye soap. The mess

came off her and went down the drain. He stuffed her soiled clothes into a bag. He poked her eyeballs back into their sockets and stuck a piece of adhesive tape over them to hold them in."

"Why was he going to all that bother?"

"That part was his *job*. He has to fix her up for the free-world undertaker. But soon as he was done with his *job*, he took her and draped her over a nail keg. He put the garter belt back on her and attached the stockings. Her head was down and her bottom was up. There was a big smile on those nether lips. Smooth as a baby's behind, and bright pink. The Nigger ran his hand over the full round ass end of her. His hands real black against the bright pink of her behind. He took his fingers and dropped them down to the center of her pussy and spread the petals. It was a gentle gesture. Nigger Jack was very tender with Rhonda. He asked me, 'When do you figure she last had a man, Curly Bill?' "

"You stood there let that Nigger handle her that way?"

He shrugged. "Hell, I had my eyes on that pussy. You would too. That stuff looked real good — pink and soft. And there was no more nasty smell at all. She was nice and clean from the soap job the Nigger gave her. I got up a little closer to her, and I caught a whiff of her perfume too."

"She was dead."

"Fresh off the Chair, Sonny. And still hot — about 106 degrees and cooling fast."

"But she was dead, Curly Bill, *dead*!"

He paused a beat. "More like dead *drunk*, actually. She weren't stiff, and she didn't smell bad at all. That Chanel on her neck..."

I licked my lips. Puffed out my cheeks. Held my peace while I waited for him to come back.

"It was the Nigger that did it. Had him a hard-on from sticking his hands in Rhonda's privates to clean her. He started to rub on it, then opened his pants and took it out. He spit in his hand and rubbed it on his dick. Then he just turned around and stuck his johnson right up her poop chute."

"Cornholed her?"

"As I live and breathe. I watched him."

"What did you say to the black bastard?"

"I told him I had first dibs on her cunt," he answered with a straight face.

"First dibs," I repeated. "Then you fucked a woman who just got off the Electric Chair?"

"I never said that," Curly Bill disclaimed.

"Was it good?"

A look at Curly Bill's long yellow teeth was my only answer.

I got up off the buttcan and stretched. "I think I'll get moving, Curly Bill."

"Oh? What's the big rush, Sonny?"

I looked him in the eye and said, "I'm going down to see the Death House Captain about an orderly job."

"Figuring you might get that job?"

I nodded. "Sonia. I've seen her picture. I'm in love. Hearing what you say, I'm ready to give it a try my own self. I know I'll never get me no more live pussy. So what the fuck."

"You can forget Sonia," Curly Bill said, a little smile curling one side of his mouth.

"Oh? Why is that?"

His curious smile became an outright leer. "Because the job's been took already. They gave it to the only convict in this joint with experience handling a burnt woman."

"*You*!" I whispered.

"Yup. Me. And when it's done, come on down and I'll tell you how she was." Curly Bill gave me a big wolfish smile as I turned on my heel and went back to my own cell.

Nigger Jack

by G. J. Schaefer

Copyright 1990, 1991 Media Queen Ltd. Inc. All Rights Reserved.

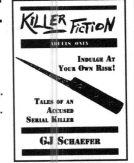

Houses, Houses, Everywhere, Yet Not A Place To Sleep: The War Against Affordable Housing

by James B. DeKorne

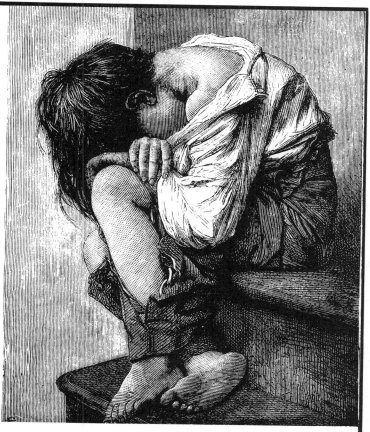

I think that the law is really a "humbug," and a benefit principally to the lawyers.

Thoreau — *Journal*: Oct. 12, 1858

The Massachusetts state constitution contains the phrase: "a government of laws and not of men..." Although most of us can guess the *intent* of that clause (somebody's fantasy about "impartial" justice), the fact is that law enforcers usually find it expedient to follow the *letter* of any law, rather than its *intent*, and the literal or *letter* meaning of the above phrase has appalling implications. The point becomes a bit clearer if we rephrase it: "a government of laws and not of humans" or (since humans make and interpret the laws) "a government of lawmakers and not of the people," or "of governors and not of the governed." Such whims eventually endorse "legal gridlock" as an ideal condition. To eliminate individual discretion from the governmental process is the universal goal of the totalitarian mentality. Legal gridlock is attained when we permit our lawmakers to contrive a network of laws so convoluted that almost everything is illegal.

If our cultural beliefs deem it *essential* to have a profession of full-time "lawmakers" (which is basically giving lawyer-types *carte blanche* to impose their mind-set upon everyone else), a relatively parasitic class of people is created which is *unemployed* unless it is constantly tinkering with our liberties. Since, by definition, all power is usurped by these lawmakers, it is safe to assume that this is one profession which will never go out of business. With such a system in effect, it is inevitable that every area of human endeavor must eventually be subjected to some kind of regulation. Nowhere is this more obvious than in the relationship of building codes and allied ordinances to our nation's current crisis in homelessness and housing.

> **If our cultural beliefs deem it *essential* to have a profession of full-time "lawmakers" (which is basically giving lawyer-types *carte blanche* to impose their mind-set upon everyone else), a relatively parasitic class of people is created which is *unemployed* unless it is constantly tinkering with our liberties.**

In their original *intent*, building codes were just common-sense rules for the protection of people living in close proximity. If Joe Doaks in the apartment next door wants to repair his fireplace chimney with 2 X 4 lumber, that decision will have a potentially dangerous effect on him and anyone living in his vicinity. A defined set of rules is not unreasonable in such circumstances; it falls within the basic *intent* of the social contract — an agreement among individuals in which each agrees to abide by a minimum criterion of group security in return for the benefits of being a member of the community.

In the beginning, building codes were meant to be a compilation of rational standards for the erection of

human dwelling-places and were largely created to protect the public from jerry-built housing. Construction techniques, the kinds and qualities of materials used and reasonable safety considerations were all taken into account in these codes, and they were generally intelligent documents. No discerning individual would *want* to live in a house that didn't meet such minimum standards.

In time, however, because of the accelerating juggernaut of full-time lawmaking, building codes began to evolve into tomes thicker than the Los Angeles Yellow Pages, documents in which every conceivable (and inconceivable) aspect of home construction was spelled out in the minutest detail. The codes long ago transcended their original intent of common-sense health and safety rules, but it wasn't until the seventies that the situation began to assume surrealistic proportions. The following quotation was written almost a decade ago — since then the predicament has worsened:

> Housing prices rose faster than incomes from 1970 to 1980. In the same period mortgage interest rates doubled from 8 percent to 16 percent. We have reached a point where only 15 percent of first-time home buyers can afford to purchase the median priced new house — a sharp drop from the 50 percent who could do so 10 years ago. Today, housing prices and interest rates are so high that a majority (60 percent) of existing homeowners could not afford to purchase their present homes without the benefit of accrued equity.
>
> — *Affordable Housing — What States Can Do*, International City Management Association, 1983

This is clear evidence that something is egregiously wrong. When a majority of the citizens of any nation are theoretically blocked from attaining affordable housing — along with food and clothing, one of the basic necessities of life — we know that somewhere the system is approaching terminal dysfunction. Although the sharp rise in housing costs since 1970 isn't *entirely* due to constipated building codes, much of the problem can be traced to exactly this kind of over-regulation. Gone are the days when an individual could build a simple and intelligent house — something that anyone would have been more than satisfied to live in back in 1940. Even though thousands of living American adults grew up in comparable homes, nowadays these structures would be considered sub-standard and a contemporary builder would be liable for a fine or imprisonment or both if he constructed such a dwelling.

Everyone — professional contractor, owner-builder, indeed, anyone who wants to live in a house — must now cope with a vast interlocking network of lawmakers, bureaucrats and vested interests of all sorts who are engaged in the continuous definition and redefinition of what constitutes "acceptable" building and housing standards. Today there are no less than *three* different versions of "model" building codes in America — one each for the Northeastern, the Midwest/Western and the Southern states. (It would seem that the bureaucrats themselves are unable to agree among themselves what constitutes an "acceptable" standard.) Since each of these codes is actually updated every year to be re-published every three years, it doesn't take very long to accumulate regulations so nit-picky as to defy the comprehension and common sense of anyone condemned to live under their control. According to an article in the January, 1989 *Journal of Light Construction*, "in any given year, each of the model codes generally makes between 80 and 200 changes."[1]

When a majority of the citizens of any nation are theoretically blocked from attaining affordable housing — along with food and clothing, one of the basic necessities of life — we know that somewhere the system is approaching terminal dysfunction.

It isn't difficult to imagine the effect this has on the construction trades, particularly the small independent contractor. To keep current with a continuously proliferating canon of mandatory fine-print gobbledy-gook is almost a full-time job — equivalent, perhaps, to memorizing all of the instructions we get each year from the IRS on how to fill out our income tax forms. In Itasca, Illinois, for example, a group of builders has found it expedient to meet with code officials *once a month* so that they can stay on top of the endless code changes and environmental regulations they face in their professions.[2] You don't need a Ph.D. in economics to understand how this can only escalate construction costs to ever higher levels. Not only does a contractor have to include the building and materials cost of complying with each new regulation, but he must also factor in the time he spends on studying and memorizing them.

What kind of regulations are these? They range from the sublime to the ridiculous, and as if the situation wasn't already insufferable, they don't always necessarily fall into the strict category of building codes. Which is to say: *in addition* to familiarizing himself with the recently adopted code which requires him to install complex fire sprinkler systems in all new apartment

(Continued on next page)

buildings, the contractor must also abide by a constantly proliferating set of surrealistic "safety" rules. These are "building" codes of another kind, in which a bureaucrat dictates to a professional how he must practice his craft.

Here's a recent example from OSHA: It is now a federal offense, punishable by "fine or imprisonment, or both," not to have guard rails, safety nets and body belts/harnesses in place before all construction requiring the use of ladders or stairways begins — and a ladder or stairway is mandatory in all locations where there is a drop of 19 inches or more.[3] Can you conceive of any building construction that doesn't require the use of at least a step-ladder? Can you imagine the hassle involved in setting up safety nets, harnesses, etc. every time you must move your ladder during construction? It isn't necessary to be familiar with building techniques to anticipate situations in which these "safety precautions" could create situations more dangerous than those they were designed to abolish.

> **It is now a federal offense, punishable by "fine or imprisonment, or both," not to have guard rails, safety nets and body belts/harnesses in place before all construction requiring the use of ladders or stairways begins — and a ladder or stairway is mandatory in all locations where there is a drop of 19 inches or more.**

Here's another new rule: "As of January 1994, any products and systems specified for federally funded construction projects must be sized using metric standards."[4] This one boggles the mind. To force builders into using an unfamiliar and arbitrary new standard for no particular purpose other than that it pleases some bureaucrat's sense of universal proportion is insane. It may sound absurd now, but how many years will pass before buildings are condemned as unfit for human occupancy because they're made of 2 X 4s instead of some metric equivalent? Do you wonder why construction costs are so high? Do you wonder why free-born American citizens are dying of exposure on the streets surrounded by empty buildings which could house them?

If the following statistic is accurate, the situation is getting steadily worse:

> The number of homeless persons continues to increase at a rate of 25 percent per year, according to a recent study by the National

Coalition for the Homeless, creating further strain on existing housing units. The dream of home ownership has become more and more elusive as housing prices continue to rise dramatically.

> — *Affordable Housing in Older Neighborhoods: Multiple Strategies*, National Trust for Historic Preservation, Philadelphia, 1989

Indeed, the system is now approaching full legal gridlock, which is another way of saying: "We're all hog-tied — we can't get there from here." In terms of housing for the homeless, we have probably already reached this ideal. If it weren't for the specter of fellow human souls compelled to dwell like stray dogs and cats in sleazy urban jungles, the situation would actually have humorous overtones.

Out in California, that economic Disneyland where real estate and construction costs have utterly transcended any semblance of human reason, a group in Marin County (the Yuppie enclave bordering San Francisco) has proposed the construction of a sixty-bed shelter for the homeless budgeted at two-million dollars![5] According to current estimates, there are between 650,000 and three million homeless people now "not-dying" (one can hardly call it "living"), in the gutters and dumpsters of America. At over $33,000.00 per bed per street-person, one can only imagine the financial consequences if this Marin County standard were applied nationally.

Based on any criterion of common sense, the solution to current problems of homelessness assuredly does not lie in the creation and consequent enforcement of more laws. In a 1988 publication by the National Housing Task Force, entitled *A Decent Place to Live*, no fewer than forty-five recommendations were made with the laudatory objective of rectifying America's housing dilemma. This is a wonderful example of how the road to hell is paved with good intentions. Note the mind-set in the wording of these prescriptions (the emphasis is mine): "The federal government SHOULD create and invest in a Housing Opportunity Program..." "The federal government SHOULD provide favorable tax treatment for low-income housing." "The federal government SHOULD..." in effect create *at least* forty-five more openings for bureaucratic meddling in the lives of its citizens.

Any adult with six months worth of life-experience in this culture can imagine the Byzantine officialdom inherent in the creation and implementation of a new "Housing Opportunity Program." First, lawyers will define the parameters of the "program" to feed their interests and those of the upper levels of the administrative hierarchy; the next layer of cream will go to the

(Continued on next page) **107**

developers, contractors and influence peddlers who siphon as much as they can for themselves; last comes that ubiquitous "pettiness which plays so rough" endemic to the psyches of the low-echelon administrators and "enforcers" who can always be relied upon to value the letter of any law over its intent. ("I'm sorry, that's not my department — you'll have to see Mrs. Sanchez on the eighth floor.") By the time the process is complete, the nation will be burdened with yet another closed-loop parasitic clique, structured primarily for its own perpetuation and protection.

> **...potential housing is currently unable to be utilized because the constant "up-dating" of fire codes has elevated the concept of Catch-22 to new levels of absurdity. In this Brave New World, homeless American citizens are "protected" from the threat of *potential* fire so that they can for-sure freeze to death on the streets!**

Whether the homeless will ever get their needs met is more than questionable, however. To take just one example: From Atlantic to Pacific there exist hundreds of thousands of perfectly adequate empty buildings, most of which have withstood two or three human generations of "not burning down." This potential housing is currently unable to be utilized because the constant "up-dating" of fire codes has elevated the concept of Catch-22 to new levels of absurdity. In this Brave New World, homeless American citizens are "protected" from the threat of *potential* fire so that they can for-sure freeze to death on the streets! That is, a man of sixty is not even allowed to sleep (let alone live) in a building that met all the fire codes when he was born, but is currently deemed unfit for human habitation because of some arbitrary new standard dreamed up by another man who sleeps every night in a heated waterbed.

The answer to the problems of our homeless fellow humans does not lie in the creation of more laws, but in pruning the existing codes drastically so that we can all have the freedom to pursue common-sense lives again. This includes our god-given right to screw-up, if that's in the cards for us. It's the absurd pursuit of the "perfectly safe environment," enforced by law of course, that makes the environment not only unsafe (it's *safe* to sleep in a cardboard box on the streets of a slum?), but dreary and life-negating as well.

Will these ordinances and codes ever be edited to conform to real world problems? Probably not without some form of civil disobedience. But when the laws of the land actually prevent citizens from fulfilling their fundamental human need to live under half-way tolerable conditions, then surely we have as much right as our Founding Fathers to revolt against such restrictions.

> The Ninth Amendment reserves for the people certain intrinsic rights. I would argue that the right to shelter is a fundamental right. No matter how wise or sophisticated we think we are, we are all under an immediate compulsion to protect ourselves from the elements. We have to shelter ourselves. It's really synonymous with the right to life.[6]

Ideally, laws should create a *reasonable* space for us to thrive, being neither too loose nor too restrictive, a dialectic between expansion and contraction, throttle and brakes. Laws must only be created when there is a clear and rational need for them — never at the whim of bureaucrats who are paid to do nothing but hallucinate new concepts of social constraint. The human brain is capable of differentiating any given subject into infinity, and that seems to be the level which our lawmakers have reached. The Soviet Union finally hit the wall with this kind of reality construction and the people said: "Enough!"

It's not too much to say that we are overdue for a similar sort of rebellion. ∎

NOTES

1. "Model Code Primer," Steve Carlson, *The Journal of Light Construction*, January, 1989, p. 41.

2. "Breakfast, Better Communication Benefit Homebuilders," *The Journal of Light Construction*, July, 1991, p. 7.

3. "OSHA Wants More Attention to Ladder and Stair Safety," *The Journal of Light Construction*, July, 1991, p. 7.

4. "From What We Gather," *The Journal of Light Construction*, July, 1991, p. 8.

5. "From What We Gather," *The Journal of Light Construction*, September, 1991, p. 7.

6. Monte Marshall, quoted in *The Owner-Builder and the Code*, Ken Kern, et. al., Owner-Builder Publications, Oakhurst, CA, 1976, p. 111.

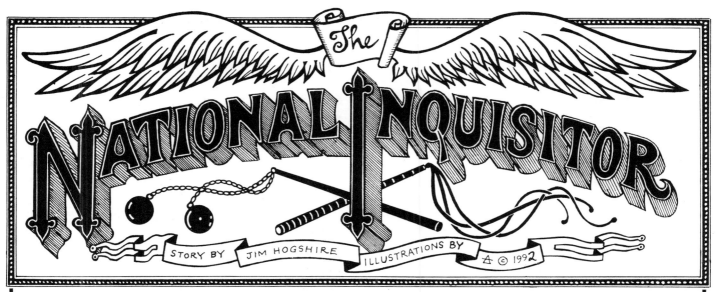

STORY BY JIM HOGSHIRE   ILLUSTRATIONS BY   A © 1992

A Day in the Life of a Tabloid Editor

Boynton Beach, Florida 10:00 am

95° outside, 65° inside

Coffee: bitter

There was a time when people cared about the news. When reporters didn't satisfy themselves with press releases and writing down the cops' version of what happened while they were sleeping. Readers wanted to feel the heat of a tenement fire, hear the gurgles of drowning sailors.

And when we wrote news, we didn't water it down with any "on the one hand this, on the other hand that" gibberish. We made a stand and if some movin' & shakin' jerk wouldn't come out and fight, we'd make him come out and fight. Ask him hard questions if he showed up in public, corner him in an elevator and press up against him blowing bad breath in his nose — break into his house and rifle his desk. I don't care if he was a fuckin' millionaire or a trillionaire, the public has a need to know. Maybe not a right, but for sure we have a need.

And libel? I'll tell you what libel is... libel is anything you print that is not true and that you knew wasn't true when you printed it and — on top of all that — gets adjudicated libel after a long-ass court battle. And anything, but anything a cop puts in his report is libel-proof. Use that as-is, Mister, because there's nothing they can do about it. So any situation involving human beings is going to have an element of tension — even the most boring stuff can be news.

If a guy gets the cops called out to his house because his weeds are growing too high, they have to write that down and then you can start spreadin' the news. Interview the perpetrator, let him know he's getting dragged through the shit because his neighbors hate his

guts so much they called the cops on his weeds. Get a picture of him shaking his fist. Listen to every word he screams and then quote him to the best of your recollection. Check out the vindictive neighbors and give them the same treatment.

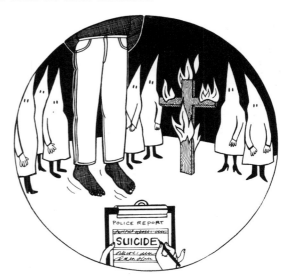

And don't wait for the news to come to you. Go out and find it. You want to do a story on the plight of the homeless? Don't go asking the Salvation Army lady, don't even ask the homeless people. Instead, go spend a few nights in the streets without your press badge and without any money. After you're good and stinky, you can talk to the Salvation Army and the bums. At least then the story you tell will be true.

And none of this "alleged" shit. Is the guy a fag or not? If you're not too sure, at least call him "swishy." Use your language. What's the difference between a "frown" and "a mask of outrage?" One is boring, the other is interesting. But you don't have to make anything

up. I swear to God, everybody's got dirt on him. You might have to spend time looking through county records till your eyes are crossed, you might have to stake out his house, living in a bush and pissing in a milk carton, but you will find something, probably something you weren't even looking for. Everybody gets hungry and everybody gets horny. Eventually something happens.

Find some drama. Dog bites man is news. Especially if it was a big snarling dog with fangs that attacked for no reason right in front of the guy's house. There was blood, there was a struggle, there was a prayer going through the guy's head, his daughter screamed, the monstrous beast seemed possessed. You can't have a big carnivore try to eat a person and not have news. Think about it.

Take what people say at face value. If the lady says she saw a tattoo on the mayor's dick, you can report that, and if the mayor says it's not true, you can report that, too. Let the readers decide what to believe. If the spokesman says it was a surgical strike and you got pictures of old people on fire, then publish both those things. Don't keep secrets and don't let anyone else keep secrets. If the dude says "No comment," he's really saying "Shake me down."

You and I both know Jesus Christ could walk across Lake Michigan, stand on Lakeshore Drive and start healing the lame, and the only thing you'd get is a "disturbance" at the beach involving "a number of people" and an "alleged" man who "claims"....

But not at my paper, not at the *National Inquisitor*. At the *National Inquisitor* we report Jesus each and every time he appears. And anytime somebody narrowly escapes death in the jaws of a vicious animal, we report that, too. And no advertiser tells us what to do. Go ahead, flip through our pages and see who advertises with us. See that? There's thousands of people working with us, there's vitamin people and backache people and lose-weight people and stuff-envelopes people. We got full page ads for things you don't see anywhere else — pudgy ceramic dolls, commemorative Desert Storm coins. We got millions of teeny tiny ads for fortune tellers, anti-fungus cream, and lonely hearts. And the smallest, ittiest bittiest ad is 200 bucks. We do not kiss ass.

We report the news.

This morning I am doing as I always do — drinking my coffee out of a mug that says "Sexy Grandpa" on it, chewing up little handfuls of baby aspirin and poring through the wires for news. I'm scanning 30 different newspapers from around the world, scissoring-out anything that seems like a lead. I got a stack of lead sheets

a half a foot thick, turned in by my reporters, who think they know everything.

In the *Times of India* I got a 7-year-old girl who was found in a trap along with a howling wolf. The little girl was howling too. Nobody in the village had seen her before and when they shot the wolf, she cried out, "Mama!" Now the kid is scurrying around on all fours at the local mission, biting anyone who comes near her. This is a good, basic, gee whiz story. I assign it to a reporter to rewrite.

He rewrites it, puts his byline on it and waits for another assignment.

On the wire, I see a teen-aged girl was arrested for strangling another girl outside a bowling alley in Mawlik, Wisconsin. According to the article, they were both students at the same high school. One of the shocked friends says she can't understand how this could happen, since the two were best pals. Hmmmm. A fight over a boyfriend? It says here the dead girl was last year's Fall Festival Queen. Jealous rivalry maybe? Maybe she didn't even do it. But surely a call to the local cops will net us comments like "repeated blows to the head" and "smelled alcohol" — the kind of thing we can work with. Surely the victim's parents will give us possible motives and the accused girl's family will yield anguished pleas for her innocence. I only hope a little kid answers the phone. Kids are the best, they'll say anything. Highly quotable. I assign this to another writer. He knows how to find the neighbors.

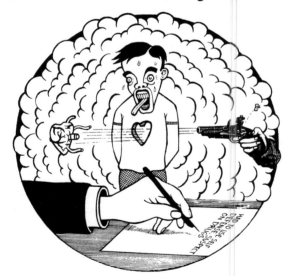

Out of the reporter's leads I get a lot of old news they cut out of hometown newspapers and try to jazz up for me. The young ones give me a lot of kooks who say they can run their car on urine or got video tape that can cure AIDS. Some of it's useful, some of it isn't. There's a lead here for a "Human Crock Pot" — some guy who saves

(Continued on next page)

energy by putting meat and rice and vegetables in a plastic bag with a string tied around it. Then he swallows the bag and holds it there all day till he comes home from work. Then he pulls up the bag and he says he's got perfectly cooked stew.

That reporter has put this lead on my desk three times now, but I always reject it. He's got no pictures. You've got to have a picture for a story like that. And even if there was a picture, it would be no good because the human crock pot's black. Nobody wants to see a black guy with a string hanging out of his mouth. I've tried explaining this to him.

The fax spews out a few feet of news from our Hollywood Bureau (actually a small office in L.A.). Not bad. Buddy Ebsen was busted for soliciting a prostitute, Liz Taylor bounced a check at a department store, a trainer from Sea World says they use electric shocks to tame the dolphins, and a new drug called "Choke" has arrived on the scene and is ten times more powerful than crack at half the price.

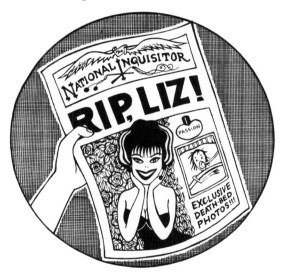

The Ebsen thing is good — a headline is forming in my head with "clamp it" in there somewhere. We'll need to double check Liz. We love Liz. We've got a standing special-issue salute to Liz ready to go the moment she kicks. That's one of the best things about dead people. They cannot be libeled. But right now, she's still alive, and besides that, she's a symbol of hope for millions. If I trash Liz too much, the *Inquisitor's* sales might dip a point or two. That's my only nightmare.

It was risky enough breaking all those stories about Jim Bakker's homo lovers in prison. A lot of our readers looked up to him, but that's what made the stories so tempting. I sweated bullets over those, even got a call from the publisher up in Montreal over it. He threatened to fire me if we dropped a single percentage point in

sales. Well, that would have been the fourth time he would have fired me in the last ten years and....

Did I tell you about the publisher? Alexander Folger's his name. He's a real bastard. Doesn't know shit about newspapers. Not shit. But the fucker's sharp with money and he's worth hundreds of millions. He almost never comes down here to Florida, and when he does, it's usually to cut some real estate deal and fire a bunch of people. One day he walked in here and fired 60 people. We had to set up a triage center in the Holiday Inn over in Boca just to process all of them. Us I should say. I got fired that day, too. So what? They gave me two months severance pay, a thousand dollars cash and kept our insurance paid for the next six months while we all went to the beach and collected unemployment. Then we all got jobs with the six other tabs located here in beautiful Palm Beach County, home of "right-to-work" laws and tax breaks. Alcoholism and shuffle-board.

Anyway. Let's hold Liz and look into the dolphin. Animal cruelty is always good, but we need him to say this on tape. The lawyer will insist on that. That's for next week.

So far the issue's shaping up pretty well. What I really need is a Hey Martha!

In tabloids this is the gold ring — a Hey Martha! It's better than a Pulitzer, it's the story that compels a reader to buy the paper. An irresistible headline. No one can know for sure what's going to be a Hey Martha! The *Enquirer* sold six million copies of its Dead Elvis issue — but that wasn't a Hey Martha! That was old news. The picture of the King in his coffin was spectacular, but it was also expected.

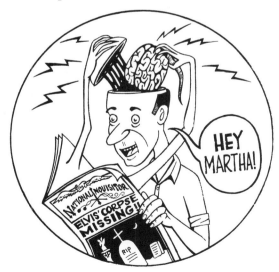

A real Hey Martha! is a story that grabs you by the brain stem and yanks you into the paper. If you're

(Continued on next page)

standing in line at the supermarket, you will buy the paper because this story is too unbelievable to not be absolutely true. A story that hooks something in your darkest fears. Or maybe something that promises you an edge over reality.

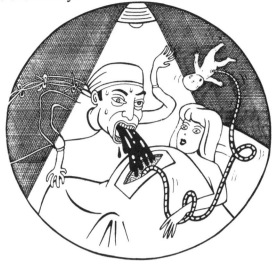

"Grossed-Out Surgeon Vomits Inside Patient" was our all-time best. Every copy sold out. No one could resist it. How disgusting! How possible! How horrible that nobody thought to prevent such a thing! Hey Martha! Look at this!

"Scientists discover Secret Day of the Week" was another. Imagine, a three-day weekend, every weekend! And doesn't it just make sense that the government would slap regulations on it the very first thing? Now the only people allowed to use that day are specially licensed researchers. And they're saying maybe we should leave the extra day alone and leave it as nature intended it.

So, unfortunately, I got no Hey Martha! at the moment. The girl raised by wolves is not good enough. Wolves have done that so many times, those kids ought to start a support group. Now if she were born half wolf, half girl, that might be better. There's so much anxiety surrounding birth, so much fear involving wombs and blood, it's a surefire winner — like a predictions issue or like an Elvis sighting (I always thought the *Enquirer* made a mistake by making such a big deal out of Elvis' death. Now they can't use him anymore.) It's not like you can haul out a goat-boy story every week, but you can use it a good four times a year. Same goes for reincarnating Elvis.

Maybe the dolphin. Maybe I can get the guy to say he shocked Flipper so many times the poor fish started crying out "Please stop!" in English. That's a long shot.

Well that can't be helped. Right now I've got to deal with these jackass reporters who all they want to do is chase down Demi Moore or waste the expense account trying to catch Tony Danza in bed with another man. Right now I got to deal with this stupid garlic and mayo diet Folger's forcing me to put in. And what a time for my herpes to start flaring up! I decide to head for the restroom and put some cream on it. Got this special cream with ginseng in it.

In the restroom, I run into the reporter who turned in the human crock pot. He's all hopeful, standing by the urinal going, "Didja see my lead? Didja see my lead?" I just smack him upside the head.

On the way back from the can, I pass by the little vending area where I spot Harold Luce drinking his tea. He's this pompous Brit who came over here during the 70's while Gene Pope was staffing the *Enquirer*. Pope would go over to Fleet Street and get these ruthless fuckin' reporters, pay their way over to Florida, give 'em huge salaries, treat 'em like shit for six months, then fire 'em and use 'em for stringers. He'd make those guys crank out hit stories week after week, and the instant they flagged, they were fired.

Harold was one of those guys. He was real good at getting tit shots of the stars drinking up in Palm Beach. He'd sit in a corner of a dark bar swilling Scotch and fingering his infra-red camera. As soon as one of those babes started reeling on her stool and leaning forward, Harold knew that was his chance. He'd hunch up in his seat like a panther waiting in a tree, and then as soon as her tit popped out, he start snapping away.

He'd get compromising shots of all the drunk celebs hanging all over each other. Perfect for bolstering any claims that a certain star was having an affair. Photographs are libel-proof, you know. Li-bel-proof.

But then Harold started milking the expense account so much, even Pope couldn't take it. Harold took off on a ten-week tour of Europe and scammed the whole time, stayed in cheap hotels but got receipts from the most expensive ones — that sort of thing. Down in the Riviera he got a picture of Helen Reddy deep-kissing John Travolta with her right hand on his crotch. It was beautiful. But when he got back, he got nailed on the expense account thing. At the time, he was getting $98,000 in salary, never mind all the free lunches and overseas sprees.

Palm Beach County is full of Brits who once worked for the *Enquirer*. Some of them made it in other tabloids, some wormed their way back into the *Enquirer*. Harold and I are about even. He's fired me once and I fired him once. Right now, he's one of my editors and he hasn't done a thing in 14 years. I think the Pope firing broke his spirit. He just sits at his desk and sleeps sitting up. We put "kick me" signs on his

(Continued on next page)

back. Sometimes he goes for tea. The rest of the time he badgers reporters, telling them about the old days when he walked 50 miles through snow to get his infrared pictures.

Right now he's haranguing the crock pot reporter, who's listening to him with rapt attention. I still got work to do.

Two hours later, and I'm getting a little harried. Turns out Liz not only bounced the check, she shoplifted a few things, too. This could be big, so I'm keeping all the lines open for Hollywood to call me back and confirm. Buddy Ebsen's people already tried to get us to squash the prostitute story, but we couldn't deal. His agent's the same one who handles Katy Segal and I told them I'd be willing to trade Ebsen for an exclusive about her miscarriage, but he hung up the phone. He also handles Tom Jones, who I've been wanting to label a queer for a long time. Maybe he'll call back. Still no Hey Martha! and I could really use one if Liz's crime spree doesn't pan out.

All this stress is doing nothing for my herpes. They're not even festering anymore, now they're boiling. Feels like I got shot with a **BB** gun down there. I gotta put more cream on these things.

As soon as I hit the restroom door, I gasp. For a second, I think I walked into the wrong room. Then I think I walked into the wrong universe.

The floor is covered with what looks like Beef-A-Roni and right in the middle of it Harold Luce is squatting down with his big ass towards me. Against the wall, facing Harold, is the crock pot reporter holding his shirt up to his chest. For a second, I think Harold's giving him a blow-job, but they're not close enough. Harold tells him to smile and the reporter does — even though he's got a piece of twine hanging out of his mouth and he's so pale he looks like he's about to barf. His stomach is bulging out like he swallowed a helmet.

"Hold it, young man," Harold bellows, "Steady," and then a flashbulb goes off. "Now to the side," he commands and the reporter shows him his profile. The sight is riveting, his belly is so big he looks pregnant. There's another flash and Harold stands up and starts dancing around in the Beef-A-Roni, waving his camera in the air.

"Hey Martha!" he yells, "It's perfect!"

The reporter's eyes start bugging out while he gags and pulls out the baggie. As soon as it's cleared his mouth he throws the thing on the floor where another blob of Beef-A-Roni splashes on the tiles.

The reporter looks at me all hopeful. "Didja see that? Didja see that?" he asks.

I feel a lump of pride in my throat.

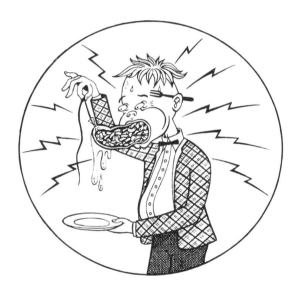

Fuck Liz Taylor. We got the Human Crock Pot.

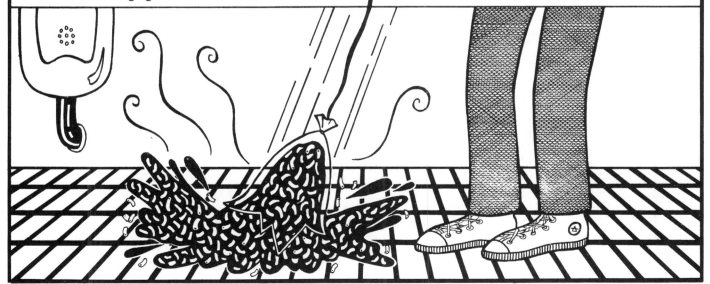

TWISTED IMAGE by Ace Backwords ©1991

Panel 1: JOE RADICAL IS HAVING MANY PROFOUND REALIZATIONS!!

TELEVISION IS **BRAINWASHING** THE MASSES INTO WASTING HOURS AND HOURS OF THEIR LIVES EVERYDAY, **STARING AT A BOX, MAN!!**

Panel 2: THE FLASHING LITTLE DOTS OF **LIGHT** BLINK OFF AND ON AT SUCH BLINDING **SPEED** THAT THEY **HYPNOTIZE** OUR MINDS AND PARALYZE OUR REASONING ABILITIES!!

Panel 3: ALL THESE MONOLITHIC **MULTINATIONAL** CORPORATIONS COULDN'T EXIST WITHOUT TV'S ABILITY TO MASS-TRANSMIT THEIR INSIDIOUS MESSAGES TO THE **LOBOTOMIZED MASSES!!**

Panel 4: TUNE IN TOMORROW — **SAME** TIME, **SAME** COUCH — AS JOE HAS EVEN **FURTHER** PROFOUND REALIZATIONS!!

TV...uh...CREATES A **STUPOR**-LIKE PASSIVITY... ...uh...mumble, mumble... **SHEEP**-LIKE...uh.....etc..

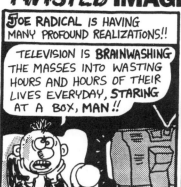
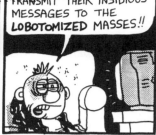

TWISTED IMAGE by Ace Backwords ©1991

Panel 1: CHUCK!! HAVE I GOT A BRILLIANT IDEA FOR A NEW CHUCK RAMBONEGGER FLICK!! "RAGING VET IV"!!

Panel 2: DIG!! YOU FIND OUT THAT THERE MAY BE 3 AMERICAN M.I.A.'s ROTTING AWAY IN A VIETAMESE PRISON!! HMM...

Panel 3: BECAUSE OF YOUR **DEEP CONCERN** FOR THESE 3 PATRIOTIC **P.O.W.S**, YOU RISK LIFE AND LIMB GOING BEHIND ENEMY LINES, KILLING HUNDREDS OF VIETNAMESE AND BLOWING UP HALF OF THE COUNTRY TO **SAVE** THESE FORGOTTEN VETS!! I LIKE!

Panel 4: THAT'S GREAT, BUT WHAT ABOUT THE **THOUSANDS** OF VIETNAM VETS WHO WERE SO SCREWED UP BY THAT WAR THAT THEY'RE PRESENTLY ROTTING AWAY IN OUR **OWN U.S.** PRISONS?!!

Panel 5: ARE YOU **KIDDING**?? THAT WOULDN'T EVEN MAKE A HALF-WAY DECENT MADE-FOR-TV FLICK!! SHEESH!

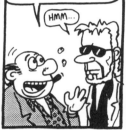
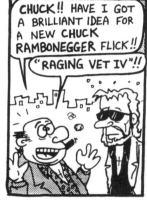
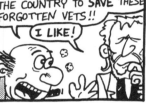
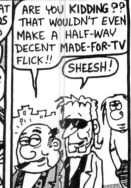

TWISTED IMAGE by Ace Backwords ©1991

Panel 1: WELCOME TO ANOTHER CONSCIOUSNESS-EXPANDING INSTALLMENT OF "DONAHOOEY"!! TODAY'S TOPIC: "WHY DO PSYCHO-PATHIC, MASS-MURDERING, SERIAL-KILLERS SADISTICALLY CHOP PEOPLE UP AND EAT THEM? AND WHAT CAN WE DO ABOUT IT?"

CATCHY THEME MUSIC

LET'S FIND OUT, SHALL WE....

Panel 2: PHIL, I THINK **PARENTS** NEED TO **STRESS** TO THEIR CHILDREN THAT CHOPPING UP AND EATING PEOPLE IS **WRONG!!**

HMM..... GOOD POINT!!

CLAP! CLAP! CLAP!

Panel 3: WHAT DO THE **EXPERTS** THINK?

PHIL, I **FIRMLY** RECOMMEND THAT **ALL** INDIVIDUALS WHO CHOP UP AND EAT PEOPLE SHOULD SEEK PROFESSIONAL COUNSELING!!

CLAP! CLAP! CLAP!

Panel 4: I COVER THIS SYNDROME EXTENSIVELY IN MY NEW BOOK: "WHEN **GOOD** PEOPLE ARE CHOPPED UP AND EATEN BY **BAD** PEOPLE AND THE **SMART** PEOPLE WHO WRITE BOOKS ABOUT THIS"

CLAP! CLAP! CLAP!

Panel 5: **SYLVESTER STALLONE** — WHAT IS YOUR OPINION AS A CELEBRITY?

PHIL, IN ALL MY MOVIES WHERE I PORTRAY PEOPLE BEING CHOPPED UP AND EATEN I ALWAYS MAKE A POINT OF STATING I DON'T **CONDONE** THIS BEHAVIOR!!

CLAP! CLAP! CLAP!

Panel 6: AND WHAT HAS OUR **SERIAL KILLER** LEARNED FROM ALL THIS?

PHIL, I NOW REALIZE THAT CHOPPING PEOPLE UP AND EATING THEM IS **WRONG!!**

CLAP! CLAP! CL

Panel 7: WELL, THAT'S ALL FOR TODAY...TOMORROW'S TOPIC: "SO YOUR HEAD'S BEEN CHOPPED OFF — PAINFUL STIGMA OR ALTERNATIVE LIFESTYLE?"

HMM?

CATCHY THEME MUSIC

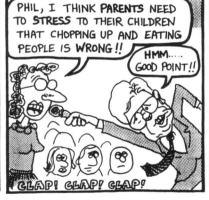
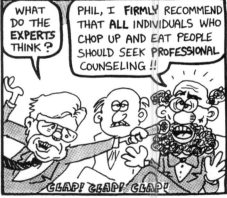
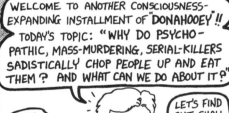
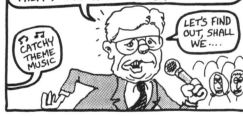
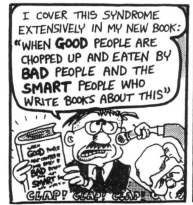
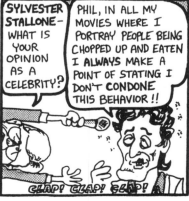
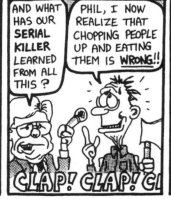
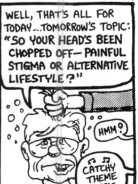

First published in 1992 Main Catalog

TWISTED IMAGE by Ace Backwords ©1991

Panel 1: MAN!! WHAT CRAP!! IT REALLY INFURIATES ME HOW ALL THESE TV PROGRAMMERS ASSUME WE'RE ALL A BUNCH OF IDIOTS!!
YEAH!

Panel 4: IT'S EVEN MORE INFURIATING HOW WE ALL **ARE** A BUNCH OF IDIOTS!!
YEAH!

TWISTED IMAGE by Ace Backwords ©1991

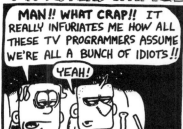

Panel 1: AND NOW THE SHOCKING SEQUEL TO THE RED-HOT PUBLISHING EXPOSÉ OF THE DECADE
MORE DIRT ON NANCY by Kitty Kelly
PUNK! EAT MY DIRT!

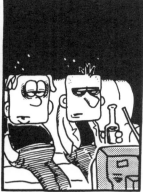

Panel 2: CHAPTER 427.... AIDES COULDN'T HELP BUT NOTICE THE GOO-GOO EYES **NANCY** MADE WHENEVER ORVILLE REDDENBACHER WAS NEAR !!! NOR THOSE LONG, PRIVATE SESSIONS OF ALLEGED "POPCORN EATING"!!!
MORE POPCORN, TOOTS? HAW.

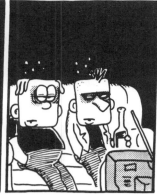

Panel 3: CHAPTER 842.... AND WHILE PUBLICLY FOSTERING AN ANTI-DRUG IMAGE, WHAT OF THOSE MARATHON PEYOTE-AND-SMACK PARTIES WITH HUNTER S. THOMPSON AND KEITH RICHARDS? (THOUGH I CAN'T PROVE THIS, SOMEBODY TOLD ME THIS, SO IT MUST BE TRUE)
OH **HUNTER!!** JUST SAY YES!! YES!

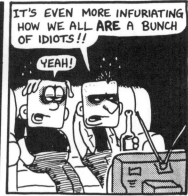

Panel 4: CHAPTER 941.... MEANWHILE, **NANCY** WOULD GO TO **ELABORATE** LENGTHS TO KEEP HER **DOUBLE-LIFE** SECRET FROM HER INQUISITIVE HUSBAND !!!
um... I'M GOING DOWN TO 7-11 TO PICK UP A SLURPIE.... BE BACK IN ABOUT SIX HOURS...
SURE THING, HON'

TWISTED IMAGE by Ace Backwords ©1991

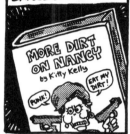

Panel 1: FUNNY HOW THE MEDIA RARELY MENTIONS THE **REAL** ROOT CAUSE OF THE GULF WAR — NAMELY, THE BRITISH ARBITRARILY CARVING UP THE BORDERS BETWEEN IRAQ, KUWAIT, AND SAUDI ARABIA AFTER WW I, WHICH DENIED IRAQ ACCESS TO THE GULF (AND KEPT ALL THAT OIL IN THE HANDS OF BRITIAN/U.S. ALLIES, NATCH).
HEY! WE NEED THAT WATER!! IRAQ IRAN KUWAIT SAUDIA PERSIAN GULF
DON'T WORRY. THE BRITISH KNOWS WHAT'S BEST FOR THE BRITISH.

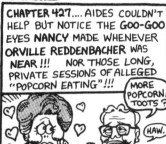

Panel 2: FUNNY HOW THE MEDIA RARELY MENTIONS THAT THE U.S., FRANCE, GERMANY, AND THE SOVIET UNION ALL MADE **BIG BUCKS** SELLING HUSSEIN SOPHISTICATED CONVENTIAL AND CHEMICAL WEAPONS (INCLUDING NERVE GAS!) FROM 1982 RIGHT UP UNTIL THE DAY HE INVADED KUWAIT.
I CAN TELL FROM THE COLOR OF YOUR MONEY THAT YOU'RE TRUSTWORTHY!!

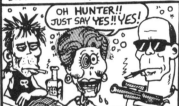

Panel 3: FUNNY HOW THE MEDIA RARELY MENTIONS THAT THE U.S. **HAS** SUPPORTED "NAKED CRIMINAL AGGRESSION" WHEN ① THE ISRAELIS INVADED LEBANON IN 1982, KILLING 20,000, ② THE INDONESIANS INVADED EAST TIMOR IN 1975, KILLING 200,000, AND ③ THE U.S. FINANCED AND BACKED THE DEATH SQUAD GOVERMENT OF EL SALVADOR, KILLING 200,000
YES, BUT HUSSEIN IS KILLING PEOPLE WE DON'T WANT KILLED!!
IT'S A MORAL OUTRAGE!!

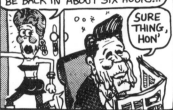

Panel 4: I GUESS THEY'RE JUST TOO PREOCCUPIED WITH MORE IMPORTANT ISSUES...
...AND THE LATEST POLLS REVEAL THAT 82% OF THE AMERICAN PUBLIC BELIEVES THAT HUSSEIN IS MORE EVIL THAN HITLER, WHEREAS 16.4% BELIEVE HE'S ONLY AS EVIL AS CHARLES MANSON...

TWISTED IMAGE by Ace Backwords ©1991

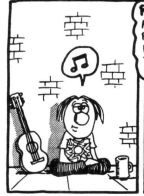

Panel 2: **RUN!! FLEE!!** IT'S DANNY PARTRIDGE AND THE GANG FROM "DIFF'RENT STROKES" RUNNING RAMPANT ON A CRIME SPREE IN A DESPERATE ATTEMPT TO REGAIN THE NOTORIETY THEY ENJOYED DURING YOUTHFUL SUPERSTARDOM !!!

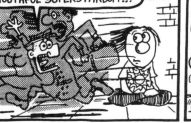

Panel 3: FORK OVER THE DOUGH, PUNK!!
YOUR MONEY OR YOUR LIFE, MAN!!
C'MON, MAN!! LET'S GO BEAT UP SOME TRANSVESTITES!
Bonk! Bonk! GUH! Bok! Bok!

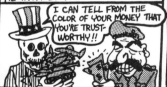
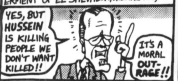

Panel 4: YA KNOW... IF IT WASN'T FOR THE MASSIVE AMOUNTS OF MIND-ALTERING CHEMICALS THAT I CONSUME ON A DAILY BASIS, I WOULD FIND THIS TO BE A RATHER **DISTURBING** COMMENTARY ON MODERN SOCIETY...

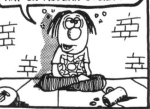
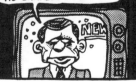
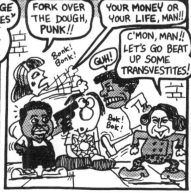

TWISTED IMAGE

by Ace Backwords ©1991

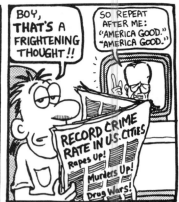

Panel 1: WE CANNOT STAND BY WHILE **SADDAM HUSSEIN** BRUTALLY RAPES AND PILLAGES A DEFENSELESS NATION!!

Panel 2: ALL **PEACE**-LOVING COUNTRIES MUST STAND UP TO THIS NAKED, **CRIMINAL** AGGRESSION!!

Panel 3: IT'S OUR **PATRIOTIC** DUTY TO IMPOSE AMERICA'S **MORAL STANDARDS** ON THE REST OF THE WORLD!!

Panel 4: BOY, **THAT'S** A FRIGHTENING THOUGHT!! — SO REPEAT AFTER ME: "AMERICA GOOD." "AMERICA GOOD." / RECORD CRIME RATE IN U.S. CITIES / Rapes Up! / Murders Up! / Drug Wars!

TWISTED IMAGE

by Ace Backwords ©1991

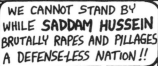
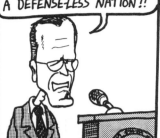

DEJA VU PRODUCTIONS PRESENTS "THIS IS NOT ANOTHER VIETNAM!"

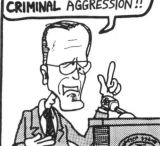

Panel 1: THE SAME COUNTRY THAT BRUTALLY INVADED VIETNAM JUST TWENTY YEARS AGO IS NOW CONDEMNING IRAQ FOR BRUTALLY INVADING KUWAIT. — YES, BUT WHEN **WE** SLAUGHTERED THE VIETNAMESE WE DID IT IN THE NAME OF RIGHTEOUSNESS AND DOMINO THEORIES!

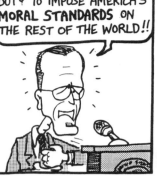

Panel 2: THE SAME RICH, WHITE POLITICIANS WHO DODGED MILITARY SERVICE IN VIETNAM ARE NOW GIVING INSPIRATIONAL SPEECHES TO THE TROOPS IN THE GULF. — SO LET'S YOU AND HIM FIGHT AND DIE FOR ME!! O.K.?

Panel 3: THE SAME BRAINS WHO ORCHESTRATED THE COMPLETE MILITARY DISASTER IN VIETNAM ARE NOW REGURGITATED TO GIVE THEIR "EXPERT" ADVICE ON THE GULF. — AND MY BRILLIANT ADVICE IS THAT WE MUST AVOID DOING WHAT I BRILLIANTLY ADVICED YOU TO DO IN VIETNAM!!

Panel 4: AND THE SAME PENTAGON "SPOKESMEN" WHO LIED THROUGH THEIR TEETH ABOUT VIET NAM ARE NOW TELLING US WE SHOULD TRUST THE "SANITIZED", CENSORED, INFORMATION THEY'RE DOLING OUT ON THE GULF. — MASSACRED CIVILIANS? WE **DIDN'T** KILL 'EM!! NOBODY SAW US KILL 'EM!! YOU CAN'T PROVE WE KILLED 'EM... / MY LAI-ER, MY LAI-ER, YOUR PANTS ARE ON FIRE!!

TWISTED IMAGE

by Ace Backwords ©1991

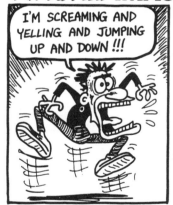

Panel 1: I'M SCREAMING AND YELLING AND JUMPING UP AND DOWN!!!

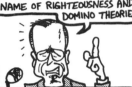 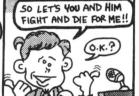

Panel 2: I'M SMASHING UP PROPERTY AND SETTING FIRE TO POLICE CARS!!! — WHACKA! WHACKA! WHACKA!

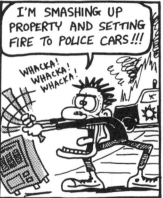

Panel 3: I'M BANGING MY HEAD AGAINST THE GROUND AND HOLDING MY BREATH UNTIL MY FACE TURNS RED AND— / Bonk Bonk Bonk — EXCUSE ME, SIR... WHY ARE YOU DOING THAT?

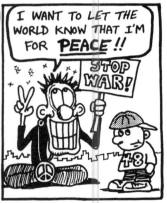

Panel 4: I WANT TO LET THE WORLD KNOW THAT I'M FOR **PEACE**!! / STOP WAR!

TWISTED IMAGE

by Ace Backwords ©1991

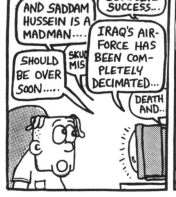

Panel 1: AND SADDAM HUSSEIN IS A MADMAN.... COMPLETE SUCCESS... IRAQ'S AIR FORCE HAS BEEN COMPLETELY DECIMATED... SHOULD BE OVER SOON..... SKUD MIS DEATH AND..

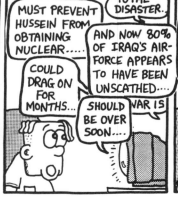

Panel 2: MUST PREVENT HUSSEIN FROM OBTAINING NUCLEAR..... TOTAL DISASTER... AND NOW 80% OF IRAQ'S AIR-FORCE APPEARS TO HAVE BEEN UNSCATHED.... COULD DRAG ON FOR MONTHS... SHOULD BE OVER SOON.... WAR IS

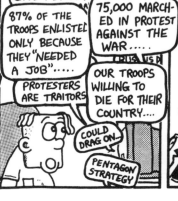

Panel 3: GIVE PEACE A.. 87% OF THE TROOPS ENLISTED ONLY BECAUSE THEY "NEEDED A JOB"..... 75,000 MARCHED IN PROTEST AGAINST THE WAR..... PROTESTERS ARE TRAITORS OUR TROOPS WILLING TO DIE FOR THEIR COUNTRY.... COULD DRAG ON... PENTAGON STRATEGY

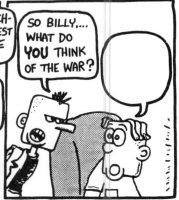

Panel 4: SO BILLY.... WHAT DO **YOU** THINK OF THE WAR?

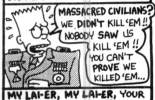
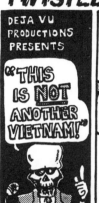

116

TWISTED IMAGE by Ace Backwords ©1991

Panel 1: WELCOME TO "THE WAR SHOW" — THE FIRST WAR BROUGHT TO YOU LIVE WITH SNAZZY LOGOS AND REALLY REALLY COOL THEME MUSIC!!

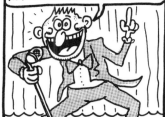

Panel 2: FIRST WE HAVE SOME REAL COOL, "PENTAGON-APPROVED" FOOTAGE TO GET YOU IN THE MOOD FOR WAR!! NO MESSY, AGONIZING SHOTS OF PEOPLE BEING BLOWN TO BITS — JUST NICE, CLEAN SHOTS OF AMERICAN PLANES AND HEROIC PILOTS!

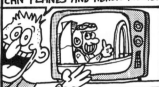

Panel 3: WAIT!! WE INTERRUPT THIS WAR SO WE CAN SHOW YOU A GUY IN A NICE, CLEAN SUIT SAYING MANY IMPORTANT THINGS

SCUD MISSLES!
SURGICAL BOMBING!
ANTI-SCUD SURGICAL BOMBING MISSLES!
ETC.!

Brainy-Type Expert

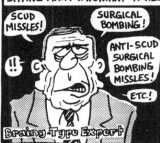

Panel 4: YES!! WE HAVE A REALLY BIG WAR FOR YOU!! WE'LL BE RIGHT BACK WITH MORE CARNAGE RIGHT AFTER THIS IMPORTANT MESSAGE ...HIT IT BOYS!!

REALLY REALLY DRAMATIC, OMINOUS THEME MUSIC!!

the WAR SHOW

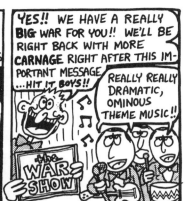

TWISTED IMAGE by Ace Backwords ©1991

Panel 1: WELCOME BACK TO THE WAR SHOW NETWORK!! WE'VE JUST RECIEVED A DRAMATIC UPDATE FROM WSN CORRESPONDENT BERNARD SHLAW

the WAR SHOW DATELINE TO A REALLY BIG MESS

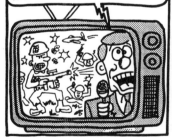

Panel 2: GO AHEAD, BERNIE.... JIM, I DISTINCTLY HEARD SEVERAL EXPLOSIONS FROM MY BAGHDAD HOTEL ROOM!! THEY SOUNDED NOT UNLIKE THIS: "KaCHONK!" "KaCHONK!" "KaPEWWY!"

□ Baghdad

VOICE OF BERNARD SHLAW WSN Correspondent

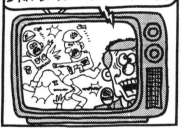

Panel 3: JIM, I'M SO AWE-STRUCK BY THE AWESOMENESS OF THIS OCCASION THAT I FEEL THE NEED TO MAKE UP SOME PROFOUND QUOTE THAT WILL PERHAPS REVERBERATE DOWN THROUGH THE PAGES OF HISTORY..... "WAR IS LIKE LOTS OF FIREWORKS, EXCEPT PEOPLE GET BLOWN UP AND STUFF!!"

VOICE OF BERNARD SHLAW WSN Correspondent

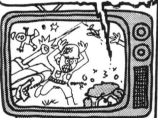

Panel 4: BERNIE, WE JUST RECIEVED REPORTS THAT THE EXPLOSIONS ACTUALLY SOUNDED MORE LIKE THIS: "KaBLAM!" "KaBLAM!" "KaBLORKO!".... CAN YOU CONFIRM OR DENY??

DAMN!! I COULD WIN A PULITZER FOR THIS STUFF!!

THOUGHTS OF BERNARD SHLAW WSN Correspondent

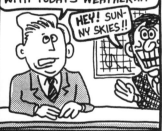

TWISTED IMAGE by Ace Backwords ©1991

Panel 1: BOB, THIS JUST IN!! I'VE GOT A CONFIRMED REPORT THAT I HAVE, IN FACT, BEEN HIT WITH IN-COMING FIRE!!

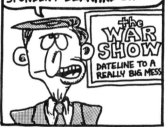

Panel 2: I'VE BEEN UNABLE TO IDENTIFY THE SPECIFIC ARTILLERY USED IN THIS ASSAULT, BUT I CAN REPORT THAT AT THIS JUNCTURE I AM BLEEDING ACTUAL BLOOD!!

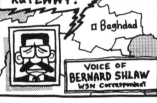

Panel 3: THOUGH I CAN'T BE 100% CERTAIN, THE EARLY INDICATIONS ARE THAT I AM LOSING CONSCIOUSNESS AND FADING OFF INTO OBLIV.......

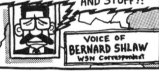

Panel 4: THAT WAS THE LATE ROBERT CLARKE, REPORTING DEAD FROM THE PERSIAN GULF... NOW HERE'S JOE WITH TODAY'S WEATHER....

HEY! SUNNY SKIES!!

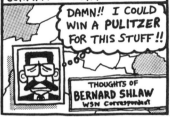

TWISTED IMAGE by Ace Backwords ©1991

Panel 1: THE MIDDLE EAST EXPERT EXPLAINS: THIS COUNTRY HATES THAT COUNTRY!! AND THAT COUNTRY HATES THIS COUNTRY!!

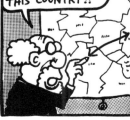

Panel 2: THIS COUNTRY HERE HATES THAT COUNTRY THERE....BUT THEY WILL BAND TOGETHER BECAUSE THEY HATE THAT COUNTRY EVEN MORE THAN THEY HATE EACH OTHER!!

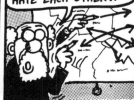

Panel 3: BUT IF THIS COUNTRY HATES THAT COUNTRY, THAN THE OTHER COUNTRIES WILL HATE THEM EVEN MORE THAN THEY WERE PREVIOUSLY HATED!!

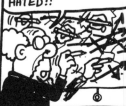

Panel 4: FURTHERMORE.. ALL THESE COUNTRIES HAVE HATED EACH OTHER SINCE BIBLICAL TIMES AND EVEN CENTURIES BEFORE THAT!!

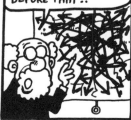

Panel 5: BUT BUSH IS CONFIDENT HE CAN GET IT ALL SORTED OUT IN A COUPLE OF WEEKS....

ZIP!

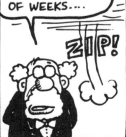

IF YOU LIKE SOCIAL SECURITY, YOU'RE GOING TO LOVE NATIONAL HEALTH CARE

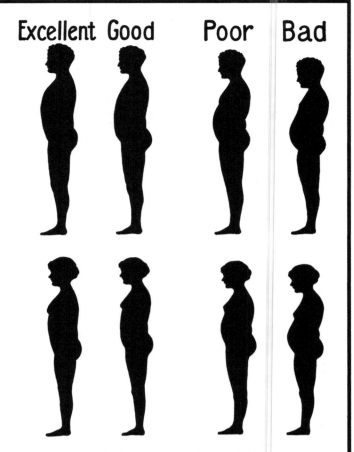

Excellent Good Poor Bad

© 1992 by Edwin Krampitz, Jr.

You don't have to be running for office to see that the United States is in the midst of a serious crisis in health care.

You don't have to be running for office to see that the United States is in the midst of a serious crisis in health care. More than $650 billion was spent on health care in the U.S. last year, nearly triple the 1980 amount. Health care expenses accounted for 12% of 1990 gross national product, up from 9% in 1980. Over the last decade, the cost of medical care has grown at several times the rate of inflation, with devastating consequences for health insurers, employers and individuals. Today, some 35 million Americans have no health insurance.

The solution being touted by presidential candidates and media pundits is national health insurance, formerly known as socialized medicine. The government will provide for the health care needs of all Americans. Joe Citizen can pop into any clinic or hospital anywhere in the U.S. and Uncle Sam will pick up the tab. The costs will be distributed fairly and evenly through taxes on businesses, individuals, or both.

This is such bullshit that it would be laughable if so many people who should know better weren't taking it seriously. All we have to do is look at the Soviet Union's old system of socialized health care: characterized by shoddy work, riddled with corruption, it provided excellent treatment for the *nomenklatura* — the privileged few — with little or no care for the masses. The British track record with socialized medicine is not much better. One reform under consideration in England is to ensure that non-emergency conditions are treated within *two years.* That means it currently takes *more than two years* to get non-emergencies treated. Older people and those with terminal illnesses are routinely triaged out of the system. In Britain, barring unusual circumstances, no one over 55 years of age can get kidney dialysis through the public system. For an example of how well socialized medicine will work in the United States, simply ask any retired military person what they

(Continued on next page)

think about government-provided health care, and be prepared to hear a colorful string of obscenities.

> *Ask any retired military person what they think about government-provided health care, and be prepared to hear a colorful string of obscenities.*

Along with a dramatic decline in the quality of health care, we can expect a sharp increase in costs. There are those who say that only the government can get health care costs under control, but when have you ever seen a government control its spending of *your* money? As taxpayers, we spend hundreds of dollars for a Defense Department hammer or a NASA ballpoint pen. How much do you think a Health Department band aid is going to cost us? As for the quality of service, as one observer recently put it, care givers under socialized medicine usually have all the compassion of tax collectors. No one who has studied socialized medicine would give it a second thought here.

> *Government reports come out on a weekly basis showing how awful our current health care system is.*

Yet we move closer and closer to national health insurance the closer we get to national elections. Why? Government reports come out on a weekly basis showing how awful our current health care system is. According to a 1991 report, American doctors are paid on average double what their Canadian counterparts make, and many U.S. doctors also profit on the side from diagnostic tests performed in facilities in which they own a stake. In June of 1991, the General Accounting Office (GAO) went so far as to give a ringing endorsement of the Canadian national health care system. Despite the fact that Canadians are migrating south of the border for medical procedures that are unavailable on a timely basis in their home country,

many bureaucrats and politicians are pointing to our northern neighbors as a model of universal health care access.

> *It's true, the U.S. health care system has problems. There seems to be no limit to the amount of money doctors and hospitals will spend to treat a patient, no matter how slim the possibilities for success.*

It's true, the U.S. health care system has problems. There seems to be no limit to the amount of money doctors and hospitals will spend to treat a patient, no matter how slim the possibilities for success. And as long as the cost is passed on to someone else through insurance, no one seems to object to the outrageous sums spent on treatments that are marginal at best. So, yes, health insurance is becoming too expensive for businesses to provide, and more Americans are going without it. There's no such thing as a free lunch, and so health care is now moving away from group insurance to a pay-as-you-go system. But at least in America you can get treatment if you can scrape up the bucks. Compare this to Canada, where everyone is entitled to equal health care — equally *bad* health care and those who want to pay for something a cut above are unable to get it.

Despite the fact that the Canadian health care system fails in ways that Americans wouldn't tolerate (if they knew what was coming), the government keeps pushing. Report after report criticizes U.S. health care, and it's not just the Medicaid and Medicare bureaucrats trying to give all Americans what has been available to only a select few. One of the most obvious features of the Canadian system of socialized medicine is a "health access" card, issued to every citizen, which must be presented at doctors' offices and hospitals to demonstrate coverage. There are many in the U.S. government who've been trying to give us a universal identity card for years. For such people, national health insurance is one more opportunity

(Continued next page) **119**

to introduce a national identity card. Consider the track record of the national identifiers:

• In the early 1970s the head of the U.S. Passport Office stated that Americans should be issued and required to carry a national identification card, according to Scott French in *The Big Brother Game*, on the ground that the government "owes each citizen a true national identity." Luckily, because of the post-Watergate mood, the Department of Health, Education, and Welfare issued this response: "The bureaucratic apparatus needed to assign and administer a standard universal identifier (SUI) would represent another imposition of government control on an already heavily burdened citizenry."

• In 1982 the Senate approved a bill to combat the illegal immigration "problem" that would have mandated a national identification system — consisting of a card that every U.S. Citizen would have to carry. Columnist William Safire railed against the bill on libertarian grounds, and the legislation got no further at the time.

> *During the 1980s, despite the Reagan administration's official anti-big government stance, new regulations increased the use of the Social Security (SS) number as a universal identifier.*

• During the 1980s, despite the Reagan administration's official anti-big government stance, new regulations *increased* the use of the Social Security (SS) number as a universal identifier, despite the statements of the Social Security Administration originally that the number was only meant for SS use, and despite the passage of the Privacy Act in 1974 forbidding most other uses of the SS number. (When President Franklin D. Roosevelt campaigned for a second term in 1936 using SS as a campaign issue, some observers had the foresight to see where it would lead. The Hearst newspapers asked: "Do You Want a Tag and a Number in the Name of False Security?")

• By the late 1980s, as Robert Anton Wilson pointed out in the pages of the 1989 *Loompanics Main Catalog*, California required that all passengers — not just the driver — in a vehicle stopped by the police carry identification, I guess once again to combat the illegal alien "problem." Today's trends in California often become tomorrow's mandates nationwide.

• In July 1989, after a two-year study, a federal task force mandated by Congress to study the problem of "criminals and the deranged" getting firearms came up with one option that should now be familiar to readers: a national identification card that every adult citizen would have to carry. The twist is that this would be a "smart card," a card with an electronic chip the size of a fingernail embedded in it instead of the more familiar magnetic strip on the back. The card's chip would contain encoded identifying information — fingerprints, genetic data, a retinal scan, etc. — as well as one's criminal conviction record and, presumably, medical record. When a gun is bought, the dealer would use a decoder to read the purchaser's smart card and then electronically tie in the gun's serial number to the purchaser (presumably in some central government data bank).

• The U.S. Army is considering adopting a smart card being developed by Syscon Corporation to replace soldiers' traditional dog tags. During the 1991 Persian Gulf War, a Syscon representative indicated that "The Saudi Arabian government could certainly use the system today to keep tabs on who is inside their country. They'd be able to distinguish terrorist from refugee." Smart cards have been in use in Europe for a few years already and are also used by a number of private companies.

> *With smart card technology, the government will want some sort of genetic sampling or DNA typing embedded in the card.*

One of the main advantages the U.S. government sees in Canadian-style national health insurance is the issuance of a national "health access" card.

(Continued on next page)

Under the guise of protecting the taxpayer from fraud, the government will require that everyone sign up for a health card. And, with smart card technology, the government will want some sort of genetic sampling or DNA typing embedded in the card. After all, in addition to being an identifier, the card will help medical professionals provide treatment by revealing important biological information.

> *The smart card will update your medical history every time you use it. Any illness you have — broken bones, syphilis, AIDS, mental abnormalities, etc. — will be noted on the card.*

Perhaps you are beginning to see where this new health card is leading? Did you know that every time you use a cash machine, the machine updates the magnetic stripe on your access card, so the bank can keep track of how often you use the card and what you use it for? Well, you can imagine what a health access smart card will be like. It will update your medical history every time you use it. Any illness you have — broken bones, syphilis, AIDS, mental abnormalities, etc. — will be noted on the card. Your entire medical history will be available to anyone who has your card and the technology to read it. And that technology has to be cheap and widely available in order for the system to work: you'll see card readers in every drug store, every doctor's office and clinic, every hospital and every government office that deals with the bureaucracy of health care.

So now they have a smart card with your medical history on it — what's next? Well, you never know when you're going to be in an accident, so everyone should have to carry their health cards with them at all times. And since everyone has to carry one at all times, isn't it convenient to check for health cards if you're looking for illegal aliens? And wouldn't it be a good idea to require that convicted drunk drivers have that information embedded in their health cards? In fact, shouldn't anyone convicted of *any* crime have that noted on their health card? Why should people be burdened with having to carry a Social Security card and a drivers license and all those other cards, when all that stuff can be included on their health card?

> *Your entire medical history will be available to anyone who has your card and the technology to read it.*

Eventually, your health card is going to be required for any major transaction: check writing, check cashing, cash machine use, car rental, hotel reservations, airline reservations, prior to accepting employment, to register for school, to sign up for garbage removal, etc. When that day comes, even your library rentals will be shown on your smart card. And everyone will go along. Because, with the government spending billions of dollars on health care, the health card will be an essential weapon in the battle against fraud. And it will be a convenient way to keep track of criminals. And it will make it easy for the IRS to catch tax cheats. So, if you have nothing to hide, you have nothing to fear from a smart health access card, right? Everyone will go along.

> *Eventually, your health card is going to be required for any major transaction: check writing, check cashing, cash machine use, car rental, hotel reservations, airline reservations — etc.*

And maybe ten years from now or so, you're going to be in line at the hospital waiting for some bureaucrat to decide whether or not, given your genetic make-up, you should be allowed to go on living, and maybe you'll be thinking back to the 1992 elections when Joe Politician said, "We need a national health care system like Canada's," and maybe you'll be wishing people had thought it through a little more? ●

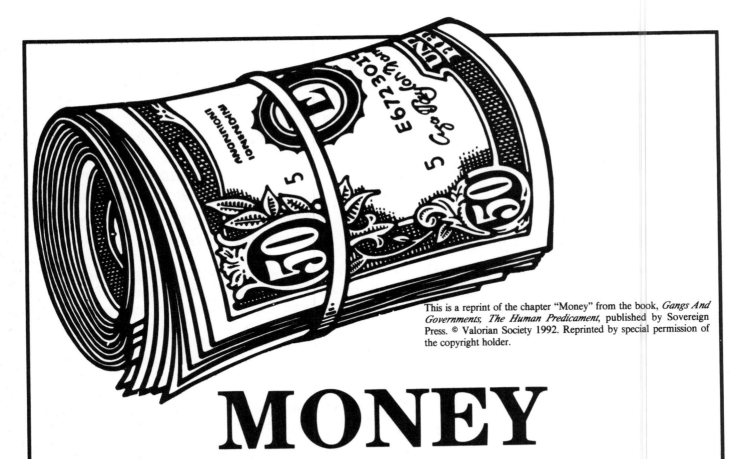

This is a reprint of the chapter "Money" from the book, *Gangs And Governments, The Human Predicament,* published by Sovereign Press. © Valorian Society 1992. Reprinted by special permission of the copyright holder.

MONEY

Values change when there are changes in the frame of reference.

Money, that is simply used as a medium of exchange, is a unit measure of value.

Money, that is simply used as a medium of exchange, is a unit measure of value. A container of a specific size can readily turn edible grain into the medium-of-exchange type of money. For instance, one container of grain is exchanged for one chicken. Fifty containers of grain are exchanged for one cow. The frame of reference is a group of individuals who value grain and chickens and cows for food.

Karl Marx, in his book, *Capital*, that became the bible of communism, focused on a specific use made of money. He looked at money, not as a medium of exchange, but as a manipulative force. Marx did not want to remove the manipulative power of money. He wanted to enter the game of creating and controlling group-entities. He wanted to create a group-entity by inciting one group within an existing group-entity to fight another group over how the manipulative power of money, that had become the lifeblood of group-entities, should be used. By word definitions, he verbally divided employers and employees into homogenous groups called capitalists and laborers. He wanted to manipulate the laborers to take the manipulative power of money away from the capitalists. He had joined the group of manipulators. His frame of reference was manipulators that value group-entities as extensions of their own power.

We want to preserve human sexually based values by moving toward a recapture of individual sovereignty, which is essential to full development of sexually based values.

In this paper, our frame of reference is organic life. We look at human group-entities as moving toward a complete return to asexual organic life, and as already being over nine tenths of the way there. We want to preserve human sexually based values by moving toward a recapture of individual sovereignty, which is essential to full development of sexually based values. We are in mortal opposition to asexually oriented group-entities. In our frame of reference, money, as an instrument for perpetuating group-entity values, operates in diametrical opposition to our values.

Money, itself, did not create group-entities. Before money could be transformed into a means of perpetuating group-entity values, human group-entities and their asexual values had to be created.

Money, itself, did not create group-entities. Before money could be transformed into a means of perpetuating group-entity values, human group-entities and their asexual values had to be created.

But money, as it has been used during its known history, is a wordless frame of reference for promoting the asexually based values that were created by group-entities.

Coined money, made of metal that had intrinsic value, began to function as the lifeblood of group-entities about 4500 years ago.

Coined money, made of metal that had intrinsic value, began to function as the lifeblood of group-entities about 4500 years ago.

Coined money was rapidly accepted by individuals as simply "a medium of exchange." Since coins were made by pouring liquid metal into various sizes, it was easy to put the symbol of the group-entity on the coins. At first that was taken as an indication of the metal's purity, and individual moneychangers began dealing in coins between various group-entities.

It was not long before the stamp of a specific group-entity on the coin became more important than the metal's intrinsic value.

It was not long before the stamp of a specific group-entity on the coin became more important than the metal's intrinsic value. Instead of collecting all the foodstuffs, group-entities required that taxes must be paid in money issued by their own group-entity. In order to get money to pay taxes, everyone had to participate in activities approved by the group-entity. The use of a coin with a particular stamp came to be tacit acknowledgement of the indicated group-entity's ruling power.

Coined money thus became much more than a medium of exchange. A group-entity's money became a unit of the group-entity's power. But, being in anonymous form, the group-entity's power could be used, and gradually came to be used more and more, by anonymous persons for purposes of their own.

About seventeen hundred years ago, the Roman Empire decided it could use the Judaeo-"Christian" church, created by Paul, as a weapon to promote meekness and submission among its subjects. It made Paul's church the official church of the Roman Empire. But the Church, itself a group-entity, collected enough money from its members, so that, together with its verbal control over its members' actions, it took over the power that the Roman Empire had amassed. It extended its power over all Europe. The takeover was so complete that a king held power only because a pope placed a crown on his head.

(Continued next page) **123**

> *When the church's power began to disintegrate, a private group of international moneychangers and banks came to virtually control many governments throughout the world.*

When the church's power began to disintegrate, a private group of international moneychangers and banks came to virtually control many governments throughout the world.

Looking at such enormous power that *apparently* exists in money, itself, many individuals are tricked into believing that enough money will restore their individual sovereignty. They fail to realize that the power with which money has been endowed is limited to the power to create and operate group-entities. An individual can only pile up "wealth" that is under control of some group-entity. It can be used to put on a braggadocio display of false power, or it can be used to create a "gang" — an embryonic group-entity. But no amount of money can restore an individual's innate individual sovereignty. Life on the plateaus of sexual being is dependent on individual sovereignty.

> *Orientation on money as a weapon of power is unequivocal commitment to the asexual values promoted by group-entities.*

Orientation on money as a weapon of power is unequivocal commitment to the asexual values promoted by group-entities.

There is now a strong push throughout the world toward "free international trade." A big privately owned corporation is an embryonic group-entity. Its controllers take a hand in the contest between governments. Most are simply willing, unofficial agents of the government that claims them as its component part. Some actively oppose the government that claims them. Some play governments against each other.

All are contributing to the destruction of individual sovereignty, because all are promoting orientation on the asexual values that have been imposed on money. A biologically sexual human whose values are oriented on money has already become asexual in his thinking processes.

> *Money has now been totally removed from dependence on anything of intrinsic value. It represents the economic and military power of the group-entity whose stamp is on it — and nothing else.*

Money has now been totally removed from dependence on anything of intrinsic value. It represents the economic and military power of the group-entity whose stamp is on it — and nothing else.

Present day money is nothing but an anonymous delegation of power. The anonymous players cause confusion in the game. This creates the "mystery" that surrounds the popular concept of money.

An exhibition of the power of its money by a group-entity is mere braggadocio. It is as lacking in solid substance when done by a group-entity as when done by an individual. An individual can impress other individuals. A group-entity can impress brainwashed *individuals*, including *individuals* of a rival group-entity. But in the relationship between group-entity and group-entity, braggadocio carries little weight. Group-entities are asexual. The ultimate interrelationship between them is always eat-or-be-eaten.●

My Kids Don't Go To School

An Interview with Kathleen Richman about "Homeschooling"

by Steve O'Keefe

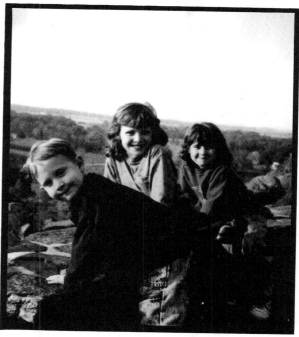

Kathleen Richman has joined a growing number of parents who are yanking their kids out of school and teaching them at home. Some parents are motivated by the violence of urban schools: in Detroit, New York and other U.S. cities, bullet-proof vests are quickly becoming part of the school dress code. For other parents, the problem isn't where the kids are learning, but *what* they're learning (or *not* learning). Many Christian fundamentalists object to sex education classes; libertarians and anarchists object to both the regimented style and blatantly statist bias of most classroom instruction. Most homeschoolers simply recognize that their kids don't learn anything of value in the public school system.

For the pioneers of homeschooling, the road has been difficult. Imagine you're upset with the public school system, but can't find an affordable or acceptable alternative. The thought of just withdrawing your children and keeping them home is quite intimidating. Will you be able to teach them what they need to know? Will you have to re-learn all the worthless crap you forgot — diagraming sentences, the binomial theorem, how a bill becomes a law — in order to pass this wisdom along to your children? Will your kids make friends and grow up normal? Will they drive you insane?

As more people have gone the homeschooling route, they've figured out some of the thornier problems and smoothed the ground for those who follow. Now there are books, newsletters, videos and other instructional materials to help. There are also a growing number of homeschooling networks — perhaps even several of them right in your community. Formed by homeschooling parents, these networks share resources and talents while providing group activities for the kids. Some of these networks have become political forces, lobbying school districts to make tax-supported resources such as classroom space, library access and textbooks available to homeschoolers.

Kathleen and Sheldon Richman live in Woodbridge, Virginia, a suburb of Washington D.C. They have three children: Jennifer (age 8), Emily (age 6) and Ben (age 4). They are both atheists and libertarians, and have problems with state schooling that features authoritarian values and historical dishonesty. They also found the quality of instruction dismal. Like many parents, their first approach was to try to get the most from public schooling by shopping school districts and taking advantage of special programs. But school is school. Rather than give in, they took their kids out of school and are teaching them at home.

Our interview is with Kathleen Richman because she has assumed the role of primary "instructor." Obviously, both she and Sheldon participate in the kids' education, but it's Kathleen who gave up working to homeschool, and she's the one who's with them all day, every day.

How long have you been homeschooling?

Since the conclusion of the 1990-91 school year.

What sort of bureaucratic hoops did you have to jump through to get started?

In Virginia, parents are required to let their local school superintendent know by August 1 that they intend to homeschool. The parent must be a certified teacher OR a college graduate OR submit a curriculum that meets the superintendent's approval. I've had to deal with one office (the Department of Pupil Personnel, whatever that means). I requested a form, they sent it, I returned it, they sent back their approval. They seem to be cooperative, but not in a supportive way; it's more like they're just doing their jobs. I have a sense that the more structure there is to your program, the easier it is to get it approved.

How does the state evaluate your children's progress? Do they watch over you?

The state requires that you submit "evidence of academic progress" by August 1 of the following year. Right now, that means homeschoolers must submit standardized test scores showing the 40th percentile or better OR an evaluation by an acceptable educator OR a portfolio of the student's work.

For the first year, we've chosen to submit an evaluation. Our evaluator is a longtime homeschooler with a master's degree in education, teaching credentials, experience as an evaluator and administrator of standardized tests, etc. She bases her evaluation on a review of each child's portfolio of work and interviews with the children and parents. We sent a letter she provided to our local school superintendent explaining the evaluation process, and we received approval in advance for this arrangement.

Please describe a more-or-less typical day or week of homeschooling?

We sleep until 8:30-9:00 a.m., have a leisurely breakfast, do the dishes, get cleaned and dressed, make the beds, straighten the house. By this time it's going on 11:00 a.m. We then take care of any outside errands — going to the store, the library, the bank, etc. — before sitting down to lunch. Most of the "schooling" takes place after lunch. Our activities vary by day.

Monday: We'll probably do something to prepare for a field trip: reading aloud, plotting our route on a map, watching a video tape (*Johnny Tremain* before visiting Boston, for example), perhaps discussing something related to the trip. We might also watch *Muzzy*, a French language course on video tape, and go through a few pages of the activity book that accompanies the tape. The kids probably watch *Muzzy* a couple times a week.

Tuesday: Tuesday is field trip day. Our field trips are built around whatever segment of history we are studying. We combine reading material, videos and field trips to better understand history. During the six weeks we studied the Civil War, we went to Gettysburg, Frederick Douglass's house, Robert E. Lee's house, the Manassas battlefields. During the month of December we studied Christmas customs in other cultures and other times. We made wreaths to celebrate St. Lucia Day, the girls made costumes and we prepared a special breakfast to mark the opening of the Swedish holiday season. We went to Williamsburg to participate in some of the colonial festivities there.

On those Tuesdays without field trips, we catch-up on other subjects, usually math. Because of the state's watchful eye, I get concerned about "keeping up" in subjects such as math. Of course, they get math in the daily routine: cooking, piano, figuring out how many subscribers are needed for their magazine to break even, and earning and spending their earnings from household jobs. Left on my own, I would be confident that they would eventually get the math they need, even if they ran "below grade level" during some years.

Wednesday: Housecleaning day! And free time — the *real* learning time. The kids might play with dolls, write a play, make scenery, build a town with blocks, draw pictures, play piano, whatever. Jennifer is editor of a magazine called *It's Kids!* which is by and for kids, mostly homeschoolers. Emily and Ben contribute to the zine, and I help with some of the production. Jennifer is learning to use the computer and is learning to run the Pagemaker program. Emily takes a ballet lesson for one hour Wednesday afternoon. All the kids are into drama. We put on a five-act play for family friends recently, and Jennifer and Emily both won parts in a community theatre production of *Cat on a Hot Tin Roof*.

Thursday: Our piano teacher comes Thursday mornings and gives each one of the girls a half-hour lesson. I get a half-hour lesson, too. Jennifer has an hour of ballet in the afternoon. The rest of the day is free time. Thursday is also laundry day, which everyone helps with at one stage or another.

Friday: We spend Friday afternoons at a Sports Activity Group at a community center, sponsored by a local homeschooling group. It's an unstructured,

(Continued on next page)

"bring-your-own roller skates, jump rope, basketball, whatever" kind of thing, and the kids seem to enjoy it. This has proved to be a good place for the kids to make friends.

Weekends: We might make preparations for a field trip. We plot the people we studied that week on our timeline. The kids spend a lot of time playing with friends. Everything else is "free play."

Other: A few days each week, the girls and sometimes Ben go to a friend's house to play or have a friend over. After dinner, we try to get something done on work-in-progress: play writing, finishing a story, cleaning up a basement that looks like a toy tornado hit it, etc. We rarely watch TV. The kids occupy their time with writing, coloring, playing piano, playing with toys, playing with each other, reading. Bedtime has gotten later than when they were in school. They are all usually in bed by 10:00 p.m.

How do your kids like homeschooling?

They like it a lot. They like it that we only do fun things, that if we're doing something they're not interested in, they can almost always get up and find something else to do that does interest them. That is really what homeschooling is all about.

How do your children meet other kids and make friends?

They meet other kids through neighborhood play, mutual friends, sports teams, the Friday Sports Activity Group, ballet, children's theater, etc. In addition, because homeschooled kids are not socialized to relate to adults entirely as authority figures, my kids have genuine friendships with adults. They certainly consider our piano teacher a friend. They relate to several of Sheldon's and my friends as their friends as well. I think opening up friendship opportunities with people in a wider age range makes some homeschooled children's lives much richer than those children who associate only with kids their own age.

Do you think your children might develop a distorted view of human nature and contemporary culture by not being exposed to both the good and bad aspects of a typical schooling experience?

I believe kids *in* school develop a distorted view of life, and for good reason — they're not exposed to it. They are intentionally removed from everyday life and put in a very artificial environment where education comes through authority figures and instructional

materials rather than hands-on, real-life problem solving experiences.

I suppose a parent could shelter a child from outside influences, though that is not a natural outcome of homeschooling. We discuss ideas that deviate from our own, and we explain as best we can why we think some people believe certain things and why we do not believe them. Of course, "our side" has a big advantage in such discussions, but I think that's only proper. We want to share our values with our kids. We want them to make their own decisions about whether to adopt our viewpoints as their own. We don't want them challenged daily by outside authority figures, as young children are very susceptible to peer pressure and want to fit in.

Do you think that anyone should be able to withdraw their children from the educational system and school them — or NOT school them — as they see fit?

I believe anyone should be able to withdraw from the system. I don't believe any standards are necessary. Even parents who do nothing at all that could be considered schooling would be allowing their kids a better education than they would be getting otherwise. About the only way it could be worse than public schools would be if the kids sat in front of the TV all day long — but I think that would be very unusual.

What kind of changes has home schooling meant for you personally and for your family's economic situation?

The time-consuming nature of homeschooling and of having three young children around all day long has convinced me to give up most business activities. With the resulting lower income, we have to sell our house and move into smaller quarters. I really love our home, and it was very hard for me to accept the conclusion that we need to move. But it's not the end of the world.

Outside of lost income, homeschooling has certain other costs: materials (which can run up), extra-curricular classes, field trips, etc. I'm considering taking the kids on a cross-country train trip, stopping at towns of interest along the way. I'd also like to plan a trip to Europe some year soon, especially as our French improves. These are both expensive propositions. Of course, if the state would just return our school taxes...

Don't you long for time away from your family?

Sometimes — but I don't need a lot of time. I'd like to get into a regular routine where Sheldon takes the

(Continued next page) **127**

kids for a four-hour outing every Saturday or something. I get most of my free time by staying up very late. I normally go to bed at about 1:30 a.m., which gives me three hours with the house to myself. This does cut into my sleep a bit.

What advice would you give to others who are dissatisfied with the school system but don't know how to get started homeschooling?

The way to get started with homeschooling is simply to stop sending your kids to school. The rest happens naturally.

A lot of parents I talk to say they don't feel qualified to teach their kids. Who do they think their kid is going to get for his third grade teacher, Albert Einstein? The average parent considering homeschooling has great advantages over any teacher. They love their children and they care whether the children learn. Pre-school children learn rapidly at home. They learn their parent's language, they learn to walk, they learn a great deal about cause and effect, they come to understand numerous scientific principles, and more. This learning is accomplished by letting the child explore his world, with a minor degree of guidance and assistance, in an atmosphere of love and encouragement.

I think most adults would agree that they learned a lot more in the first five years out of school than they learned throughout schooling. There's a good reason for this: *school restricts people from being able to interact with, and learn from, the real world.* Who believes they learned their profession in school as opposed to their initial job? One exception may be the medical profession, where much of the training is more like an apprenticeship than most schooling. School kids think in terms of "what do I want to be when I grow up," whereas homeschoolers think, "what do I want to do now?"

Are there any books, videos or related materials you would recommend to someone considering homeschooling?

The Big Book of Home Learning by Mary Pride lists lots and lots of educational materials (books, games, audio and videotapes, etc.). She evaluates them, and provides supplier addresses/phone numbers. Another helpful publication is *Growing Without Schooling*, a bi-monthly newsletter founded by the late John Holt and published by Holt Associates. A set of encyclopedias is also a very handy thing to have.

Specific curriculum materials I would recommend include the "Muzzy" language courses; Scrabble (the game); Cuisinaire Rods for learning math concepts; Math-It for easy techniques for remembering math facts; and SomeBody, a game of Colorform pieces of body parts that you put together to build a whole body while learning about what each part does.

The most successful tool I've found for teaching basic math is letting the kids earn and spend money. It's amazing how quickly those math concepts are learned!

Is there anything else you'd like to add?

When people think of "homeschooling," they get this picture of kids sitting in little school desks in their living room with Mom standing in front of them with a blackboard and pointer. It's not like that at all. The parents' job is more that of a guide than an instructor: you answer questions, you help them find resources, you help them to see the many opportunities, lifestyles, occupations, hobbies, etc., they have to choose from. In short, you expose them to the world so they can figure out how they would best like to fit into it.

A friend of mine was recently explaining to her seven-year-old daughter that I homeschool my children. "So you see, Jennifer's mom is like her teacher." I had to interrupt and say, "No, it's really like I'm just her mom and she doesn't have a teacher." I use the term "homeschooling" because people at least sort of know what you're talking about. It would take a lot more explaining — though it would be more accurate — if I just said, "My kids don't go to school." ●

FOR MORE INFORMATION:

Muzzy **tapes:**   Early Advantage
47 Richards Ave.
PO Box 5708
Norwalk, CT 06856-9929
1-800-367-4534

Holt Newsletter: *Growing Without Schooling*
Holt Associates
2269 Massachusetts Ave.
Cambridge, MA 02140
617-864-3100

Mary Pride Book: *The Big Book of Home Learning*
Available from:
Liberty Tree Catalog
Independent Institute
134 98th Ave.
Oakland, CA 94603
1-800-927-8733

SHOW US YOUR

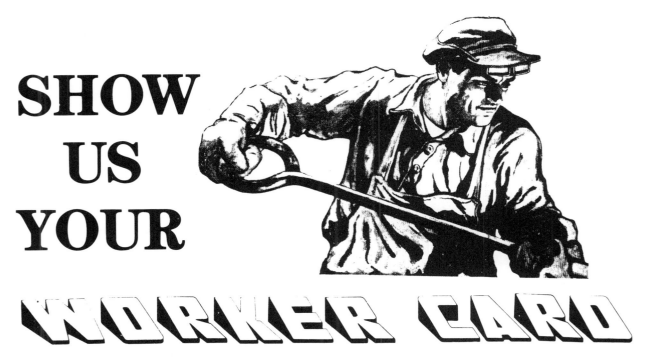

WORKER CARD

by John Q. Newman

Some day soon, when you're pulled over for a traffic violation, don't be surprised to hear the officer say, "I need to see your license, registration and worker card." Excuse me. Worker card? What's a worker card?

> *Some day soon, when you're pulled over for a traffic violation, don't be surprised to hear the officer say, "I need to see your license, registration and worker card." Excuse me. Worker card? What's a worker card?*

A worker card, or something like it, will be a national identity card, issued by the Immigration and Naturalization Service, and required for all Americans who seek work. Eventually, it will be required for all identification purposes. While there is still a great deal of resistance in the United States to a national identity card, there is growing pressure from Washington D.C. to adopt such a system. Whether it will fully come to pass remains to be seen. However, the bureaucrats aren't waiting for a referendum to start the national identity ball rolling.

There are many people in the federal government and in law enforcement who would like to see the United States adopt a national identity document. To be effective, this document would be required for all citizens, and it would be mandatory to carry it on one's person at all times. The refrain, "May I see your papers?" is not yet a reality in the United States, but it may be soon. Certain steps are being taken right now to allow for the creation of such a national identity system.

If this sounds chilling, it should. In the United States, only those who were convicted of serious crimes must register with the police, and we can still get a passport even if we owe the IRS a little money. But changes are coming, surely and slowly, one step at a time. The first big step occurred in 1986 when the Immigration Reform and Control Act was passed by Congress. Although it was sold as a way to control illegal immigration and the employment of illegal aliens, it contains record keeping provisions that will allow for the creation of a similar type of national identity database that exists in most European countries.

The Immigration Act of 1986

The Immigration Reform and Control Act of 1986 has three key provisions: an illegal immigrant natural-

ization program, 1000 new border patrol agents, and new record keeping requirements for employers. The record keeping requirements have set the stage for a new national identity program.

Under the provisions of the Act, all employers must have proof of any worker's identity and eligibility to work in the United States. A prospective employer must, under penalty of law, fill out a form that requests at least two types of identification from the new employee. One piece of ID can be a drivers license or state identity card, or something similar. The second piece must be either a birth certificate or Social Security card. The employer is required to maintain these forms on all workers and make them available to immigration inspectors upon request. The employer is not under any obligation to verify the accuracy of the documents presented, only to maintain a record of them.

Currently, a demonstration project is going on in Texas that allows employers to verify Social Security numbers over the telephone.

Currently, a demonstration project is going on in Texas that allows employers to verify Social Security numbers over the telephone. The project is being implemented in a few Texas cities that have large numbers of illegal immigrants who work in seasonal jobs, such as construction. Many of these illegal immigrants have purchased phony Social Security cards and use them to get work. Under this pilot project, a special Social Security office was set up to handle requests for verification from employers. This special Social Security office is generally able to provide an answer within a day on whether a Social Security number is valid.

This is a major shift in U.S. identification for two reasons. First, the huge Social Security Administration database is being accessed directly by outside groups for identity verification purposes. Second, it brings us a step closer to turning the information that employers must now collect into an active database run by the Immigration and Naturalization Service (INS). How would this database function? When a new employee is hired, the employer completes two copies of the INS form. The original goes into the employer's files and the copy is mailed to a regional INS office where the data is entered into INS computers.

For the first time, almost all Americans would have a file with a law enforcement agency.

The INS would then offer an on-line computer match of Social Security numbers against the Social Security Administration's database. For the first time, almost all Americans would have a file with a law enforcement agency. After all, the INS is an enforcement agency within the U.S. Justice Department. The database that will be created out of this process will be enormous because almost all people eventually enter the labor force. While this database is not a full-fledged national identity system, one key requirement has been met: a single, nationwide, detailed and up-to-date database that includes most people in the country.

The Role of The States

The United States is unique among nations because of our highly decentralized identification bureaucracy. Almost all identification comes from state governments and not the federal government. A check of the average American's wallet will usually reveal no federal identity documents. The only federally issued identity document most Americans will have is a Social Security card, and most people do not carry it on their person. A passport is another piece of federally issued identification, but only 25% of all Americans will ever have a passport.

From this it is clear that for any future U.S. national identity system to work, it will require cooperation from the states. This will be accomplished in two ways: data sharing with the federal government, and standardization of the format of state-issued identity documents. Let's look at data sharing first.

The focal point of the national identity system to come will be the database the INS builds as employers provide information on employees. As this data is received by the INS, "John Doe's" file will be updated with his new employer and home address. This allows the database to develop a sequential history of everyone in it. People tend to keep updated records of themselves with their employers to insure that paychecks and benefits are received without delay. The INS database will be updated each time a person changes jobs, so it will be a very current file indeed.

Data sharing allows the federal government to expand the database even further. With access to state

(Continued on next page)

drivers license records, motor vehicle records, and the Social Security Administration's files, the INS would be capable of creating an ominous database. Presto! Gone are all the barriers between state and federal databases. The states will go along with it because the feds will tell them that it will allow them to catch fugitives from justice more easily. For the first time, a federal law enforcement agency will be in routine custody of massive personal datafiles on nearly every American.

The second critical element the federal government will push is standardization of state identity documents. The feds will encourage the states to use coding and numbering patterned off the Social Security number. For example, many states currently use an individual's Social Security number as their drivers license number. The federal government wants all states to do this. Although the physical appearance of the license may differ from state to state, the coding will be identical. This brings us closer to a national drivers license and a national identity card. As you can see, the Social Security Administration will play a key role in allowing the federal government to pull all of these sources together. Let's see how.

Social Security's Vital Role

The closest equivalent in the United States to a person-number is the Social Security number. This is because your Social Security number is the only truly unique identifier you have. In a country the size of the United States, there may be other people with the same first, middle and last names as you. Certainly, there are many other people with your same date of birth. But your Social Security number is a unique identifier. That's why the federal government urged the states to use this number on state-issued identity documents until the Privacy Act of 1974 prohibited this requirement. This act says that states can ask for your number, but they cannot refuse you a service if you fail to provide it.

The federal government has gradually tried to punch holes in the Privacy Act's protection of Social Security numbers. When draft registration became mandatory again in 1980, the Selective Service board was given access to birth data in the Social Security Administration's files. Using information from these files, the Selective Service generates lists of 18-year-old males who have failed to register for the draft.

Social Security numbers allow numerous databases to be pulled together quickly and to be indexed by a unique numerical sequence. But to make a Social Security number into a genuine person-number requires

a few more steps. First, everyone must be required to have a number. The Internal Revenue Service (IRS) has taken a step that provides a big boost in that direction. The IRS now requires that all children over five years of age must have a Social Security number in order to be claimed as deductions on income tax returns. This policy has resulted in millions of young Americans getting Social Security numbers.

The IRS now requires that all children over five years of age must have a Social Security number in order to be claimed as deductions on income tax returns. This policy has resulted in millions of young Americans getting Social Security numbers.

The next requirement is to be able to "retire" Social Security numbers once someone has died. All countries that use a person-number system permanently retire a number when its holder dies. In the United States, the Social Security Administration is making progress toward just such a system.

When a person who has been collecting Social Security benefits dies, the Social Security Administration (SSA) places his or her number into a special database. The SSA has been trying to get states to report the death of anyone receiving state benefits so the information can be recorded in the federal database. The SSA would like it to become routine practice to be notified by states of any deaths. Over time, the SSA will build up a repository of retired numbers. Coupled with most Americans receiving numbers early in life, a close approximation of a person-number system is being created around the Social Security number.

Another essential step is to be able to distinguish between numbers issued to U.S. citizens and those issued to non-citizens. This is now being done. Non-Americans who do not have the right to work in the United States are given Social Security cards that have the legend NOT VALID FOR EMPLOYMENT printed across them. Also, the Social Security Administration forwards information on all foreign nationals to the INS.

Another feature of a true person-number system is the ability to track the foreign travel of citizens. The United States has already set such a tracking system in motion.

(Continued on next page) **131**

As of January, 1989, it became mandatory to provide one's Social Security number to get a passport. The number is included in the machine-readable coding on modern passports. Whenever a person returns from a trip overseas, the first agency they deal with is the Immigration and Naturalization Service. When your passport is presented to the immigration officer upon arrival, a record of your return is added to the INS database. The link between this and your other data files is the Social Security number.

How Will It Be Sold To The Public?

The necessary steps to create a national identification system are in their nascent stage. The INS will probably run the system. A final step will be the issuance of a "United States Authorized Worker Card," or some similarly named document. The issuing agency would, of course, be the INS. Being a law enforcement agency, the INS would likely have access to the FBI's central records system. Without question, these records would then be integrated into the INS database.

The FBI has two primary databases. One is the National Crime Information Center, or "NCIC." This is the computer system that your name is run through any time you are pulled over for a traffic violation. The NCIC contains the names of fugitives and information on stolen property, as well as the names of certain missing persons. The FBI also maintains a criminal records index containing information on anyone convicted of a federal offense. The INS will have access to these files, and will no doubt check each new piece of information against the FBI's files.

The federal government will proclaim that illegal immigration is out of control and foreigners are taking jobs that rightfully belong to Americans... and that these immigrants are a major source of crime.

Now you can see how this system will be sold to the public. The federal government will proclaim that illegal immigration is out of control and foreigners are taking jobs that rightfully belong to Americans. We will also be told that these immigrants are a major source of crime, and that the only way to stop the flow of illegal

immigrants is to issue an identity card that only U.S. citizens or lawfully-admitted aliens are allowed to carry. We will be told that this is not a "national identity card," but simply a card that shows that the holder is entitled to work in the United States. The reality, as we have seen here, is completely different.

National Identity And Privacy

As should be obvious to knowledgeable privacy seekers, a national identity system does not mean the end of our privacy. The classic methods of identity changing would still allow you to penetrate the new national identity system on your own terms. Using a mail drop, your home address can remain unknown to the data hounds. Using a fake birth certificate and supporting documents, you can still create a completely fictitious legal identity for day to day use, thus leaving your natural legal identity untouched — a blank slate to be used when needed.

Using a fake birth certificate and supporting documents, you can still create a completely fictitious legal identity for day to day use, thus leaving your natural legal identity untouched — a blank slate to be used when needed.

The coming national identity system will not alter any of the traditional methods of identity creation. You still build up a paper person's background as you do now. The only difference is, once you have obtained all your state-issued identity documents — your birth certificate, drivers license, voter registration card, etc. — you make a final stop at the Immigration and Naturalization Service to pick up your "Worker Card." All identity systems rely on paper and numbers; learn to manipulate the paper and numbers, and you can manipulate your official identity and the corresponding benefits and penalties.●

John Q. Newman is the author of *The Heavy Duty New Identity, Understanding U.S. Identity Documents* and *Be Your Own Dick: Private Investigating Made Easy.* All three books are available from Loompanics Unlimited.

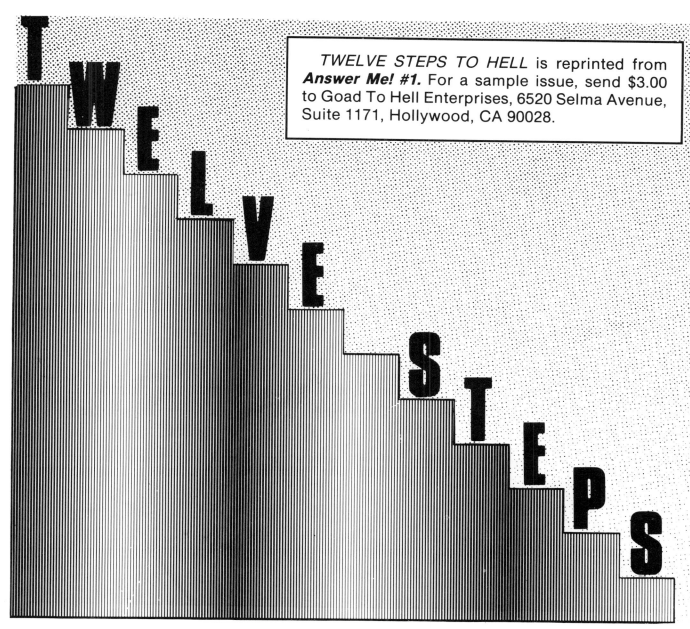

TWELVE STEPS TO HELL is reprinted from **Answer Me! #1.** For a sample issue, send $3.00 to Goad To Hell Enterprises, 6520 Selma Avenue, Suite 1171, Hollywood, CA 90028.

A re you an alcoholic, coke fiend, codependent, pothead, dope shooter, gambler, debtor, child abuser, agoraphobic, savings and loan victim, prostitute, survivor of suicide attempts or incest, tobacco junkie, overeater, or just an everyday obsessive-compulsive?

Well, your troubles have just begun. No matter what your affliction, there's a Twelve-Step group somewhere waiting to support you, stroke you, validate your feelings, and hug the shit out of you. All of the disorders listed above have engendered Twelve-Step programs and may herald the day when society has sympathy for victims of excessive tire wear, survivors of weak orgasms, and adult children of Rotary Club members.

Alcoholics Anonymous, the original Twelve-Step program, started with three sobered businessmen in 1935 Ohio. That nucleus has exploded, according to A.A. estimates, into eighty-eight thousand groups with two million adherents throughout a hundred and thirty-four countries. That's impressive, but not necessarily a validation: Both the bubonic plague and communism spread similarly. As with chemotherapy, the cure is often as bad as the disease. Twelve-Step programs are widely held as near-sacred and untouchable, so of course

I'm gonna wipe my greasy, bony fingers all over 'em.

I'll admit that I loathe the lingo of pop psychology. If I run across another codependent from a dysfunctional family who's in recovery and is learning to process their issues and nurture the child within, I'll spit in their face. Get your nose out of your ass! Grow the fuck up! Grab a knife and stab the child within! But I feel this way because I'm in denial, right?

Twelve-Step programs have all the earmarks of an organized religion: an inspired group of founders which begat legions of uninspired followers, a main text (the ominously titled "Big Book"), a sacrament (checker-sized plastic chips), and liturgies which are read aloud at each meeting.

The Big Book tells the story of A.A.'s founders and hammers home the program's basic tenets. Paraphrased, the first three steps are: 1) Say that you have no power over your drinking; 2) Place your faith in some ethereal power; and 3) Submit your will to this power. The Big Book systematically debases any notion of individual empowerment and self-control:

> Any life run on self-will can hardly be a success. . . . The alcoholic is an extreme example of self-will run riot. . . . The fact is that most

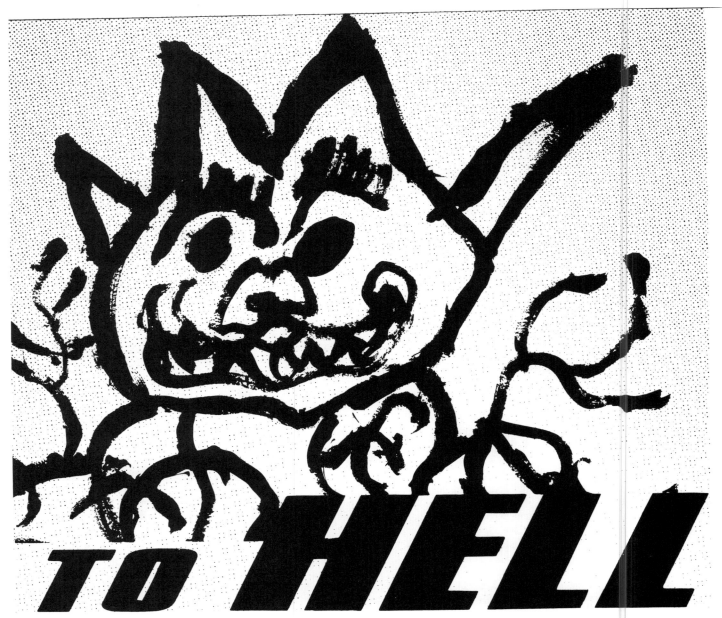

TO HELL

ANSWER Me!
REFUSES TO GET WITH THE PROGRAM

alcoholics, for reasons yet obscure, have lost the power of choice in drink.... The actual or potential alcoholic, with hardly an exception, will be absolutely unable to stop drinking on the basis of self-knowledge.... They were drinking to overcome a craving beyond their mental control.... You can't win unless you try God's way.... Many alcoholics have concluded that in order to recover they must acquire an immediate and overwhelming "God-consciousness." ... Our ideas did not work. But the God idea did.

In place of communion wafers or the blood of a slain virgin, Twelve-Steppers celebrate their faith with "sobriety chips," which are given to those who've been on the wagon for specified intervals. In the film *Clean and Sober,* Michael Keaton reminisces about his first coke-free month after receiving a thirty-day chip:

I've been to a funeral. I've been to about nine million job interviews. I'm fifty-two thousand dollars in debt. And I got this

chip. I got this chip *[eyes become misty]*, and I've got the startling belief that I'm an alcoholic and a drug addict.

Hmm—in exchange for morbidity, repeated rejection, and fifty-two thousand bucks, I get a lil' plastic chip? How do I sign up?

MEETING #1:
REEFER REMORSE

You'll find two things at almost every Twelve-Step meeting: unquestioning acceptance and steel vats of piping-hot coffee. The brown bean's aromatic nectar floats down a dusty church corridor. A cheerfully plump guy hands us styrofoam cups, and my wife and I tap into the dark liquid stimulant.

Slurping the free, legal addiction, we enter a sleepy Sunday-school room. Thick planks of sunshine illuminate dust particles and weather-beaten wooden floors. We sit on steel folding chairs which are

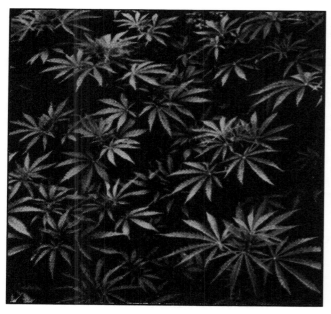

painted the standard dull beige. People mill around, hugging each other, nodding understandingly. It's a mix of sensitive guys and women on the edge of breakdown. Blacks in kufi hats share kind words with generic Caucasoids. It's the only place in L.A. where I've seen something approaching racial harmony, however forced. People who wouldn't make eye contact with me on the street look at me with twinkling expressions that say, "Hi! How ya doin'? Glad ya could make it!" We notice that one woman is staring at us with an open smile. "Are you guys first-timers?" she asks.

Uh, yep. She walks over to where we're sitting and hugs both of us. Yuck. "Keep coming back," she instructs us, skipping back to her seat. FLASH! Déjà vu. These folks remind me of the Jesus freaks from the seventies: hardcore ex-sleazeballs who've found a program of undiluted niceness. I half-expect them to roll their eyes back in their heads and start babbling in tongues. Collective brainwashing predates biblical times.

"Shhh!" whispers the group leader, a pepper-haired graduate of the Phil Donahue school of male submissiveness. "Ready? Welcome to the ———— meeting of Marijuana Anonymous. My name is Sarkis." (*ANSWER Me!* will substitute Arabic first names throughout the article.)

"HI, SARKIS!" shouts the group in unison.

"Hi. . . . Are there any newcomers in the group with less than thirty days of sobriety?" We raise our hands. "If so," Sarkis continues, "will you please stand up and give your names so that we can get to know you better?"

Trembling, my wife stands up. "Hi, my name is Debbie, and I've been free from marijuana for two weeks." (It was actually more like two hours.)

"HI, DEBBIE!" screams the crowd, which

explodes into deafening hysteria, with several solo yelps of joy rising above the din. You'd think Debbie had discovered a cure for cancer.

I stand and kiss her forehead. "My name's Jim, and I'm a marijuana addict."

"HI, JIM!" More shrill applause.

Sarkis resumes reading from a handbook. "The only requirement for membership is the desire to stop using marijuana. There are no dues, no fees for membership. We are fully self-supporting through our own contributions. We are not aligned with any sect, denomination, or political organization. We do not wish to engage in any controversy with the media. *[OOPS!]* We choose twelve steps to recovery because it has been proven that the Twelve-Step program works."

A woman is summoned to read from chapter five of the Big Book. "Hi, my name is Suad, and I'm a marijuana addict."

"HI, SUAD!" Clap, clap, clap. After she finishes reading, they clap again.

"Would anyone like to receive a welcome chip?" asks Sarkis, looking directly at us. What the hell? We accept more hugs and two lavender chips. On one side of the key chain-type device is the pyramidical, pseudo-Satanic M.A. logo. On the other side is the frightening command, KEEP COMING BACK. We realize that the crowd is quietly staring at us. Sarkis motions for us to stand and re-introduce ourselves.

"Hi, I'm Jim, and I'm a marijuana addict."

"HI, JIM!" The sound of forty hands clapping.

"Hi, I'm Debbie, and I'm an addict."

"HI, DEBBIE!" More palms slapping together.

"Thirty days?" asks Sarkis. Someone lifts his arm, the crowd applauds, and the thirty-day suckling is given a thirty-day chip. "Hi, my name is Zoroaster, and I'm an addict."

"HI, ZOROASTER!" Applause.

Another guy walks up and takes a chip. "I'm Khalil, and I'm a marijuana addict."

"HI, KHALIL!" Guess what? More applause.

"Uh, sixty days?" asks Sarkis. Someone raises his hand to more hoots and hollers, then walks up to receive the chip.

"I'm Telal, and I'm a marijuana addict, and, uh . . ."

"HI, TELAL! WHEE!"

The leader gives a small inspirational speech, which brings more applause. "Uh, ninety days?"

he asks. Nothing. "Nine months?" A woman raises her hand to awestricken gasps and more clapping. Sarkis bestows upon her the special nine-month chip.

"Hi, I'm Nefertiti, and I'm a pot addict."

"HI, NEFERTITI!"

"I know that I still have a real problem," she says. The crowd loves this statement and gives her a special nine-month round of applause. Sarkis then turns the meeting over to the main speaker.

With gnarled locks of grey hair and bugged-out, worried eyes, the speaker introduces himself. "Hi, my name is Yacub, and I'm an addict."

"HI, YACUB!"

Like almost everyone else in the group, he says he was born in Brooklyn and claims he was an addict from birth. He discovered "grass" in his teens while listening to Hendrix. Is that a cliché or *what*? If you weren't a smoker, he didn't want to know you. He got married, but his wife left him, claiming that he resembled a "walrus with one tusk." (He always had a joint in his mouth.) He spent his vacation every year in Jamaica, mon.

"I was just going further and further into my addiction," he says, "not wanting to believe that I'd fallen into a trap. . . . I always thought I'd be smoking dope on a rocking chair when I was ninety years old." He says his brother had been shooting smack for twelve years but kicked it with the help of a recovery program. "Some

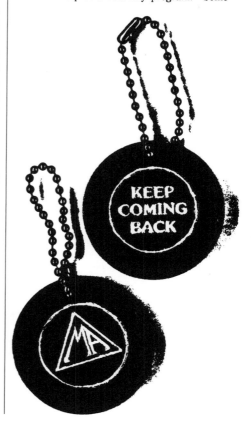

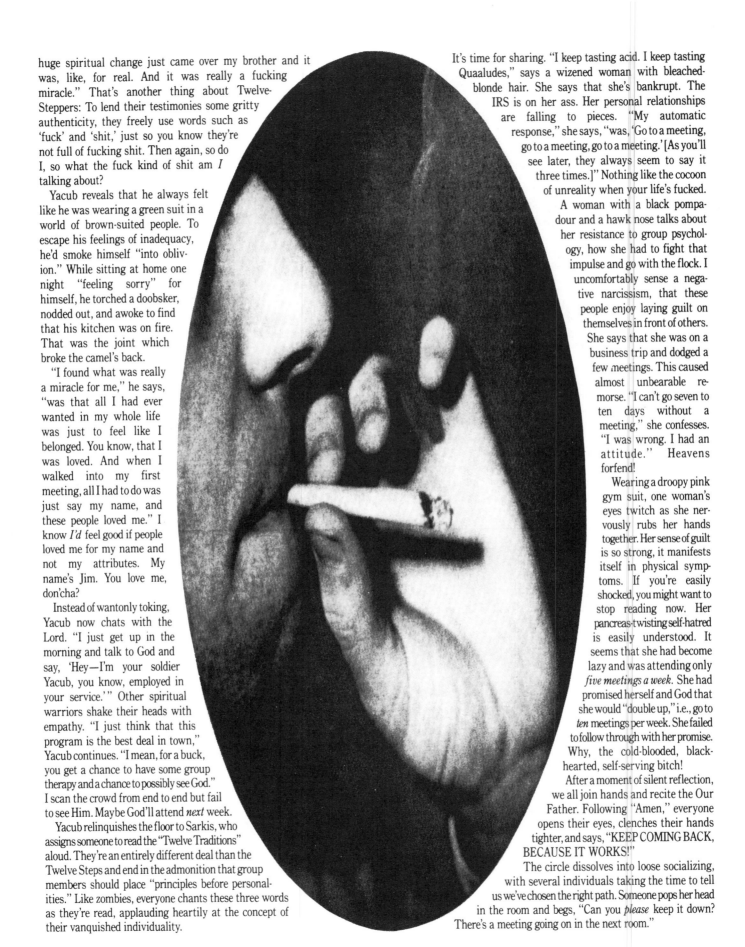

huge spiritual change just came over my brother and it was, like, for real. And it was really a fucking miracle." That's another thing about Twelve-Steppers: To lend their testimonies some gritty authenticity, they freely use words such as 'fuck' and 'shit,' just so you know they're not full of fucking shit. Then again, so do I, so what the fuck kind of shit am *I* talking about?

Yacub reveals that he always felt like he was wearing a green suit in a world of brown-suited people. To escape his feelings of inadequacy, he'd smoke himself "into oblivion." While sitting at home one night "feeling sorry" for himself, he torched a doobsker, nodded out, and awoke to find that his kitchen was on fire. That was the joint which broke the camel's back.

"I found what was really a miracle for me," he says, "was that all I had ever wanted in my whole life was just to feel like I belonged. You know, that I was loved. And when I walked into my first meeting, all I had to do was just say my name, and these people loved me." I know *I'd* feel good if people loved me for my name and not my attributes. My name's Jim. You love me, don'cha?

Instead of wantonly toking, Yacub now chats with the Lord. "I just get up in the morning and talk to God and say, 'Hey—I'm your soldier Yacub, you know, employed in your service.'" Other spiritual warriors shake their heads with empathy. "I just think that this program is the best deal in town," Yacub continues. "I mean, for a buck, you get a chance to have some group therapy and a chance to possibly see God." I scan the crowd from end to end but fail to see Him. Maybe God'll attend *next* week.

Yacub relinquishes the floor to Sarkis, who assigns someone to read the "Twelve Traditions" aloud. They're an entirely different deal than the Twelve Steps and end in the admonition that group members should place "principles before personalities." Like zombies, everyone chants these three words as they're read, applauding heartily at the concept of their vanquished individuality.

It's time for sharing. "I keep tasting acid. I keep tasting Quaaludes," says a wizened woman with bleached-blonde hair. She says that she's bankrupt. The IRS is on her ass. Her personal relationships are falling to pieces. "My automatic response," she says, "was, 'Go to a meeting, go to a meeting, go to a meeting.' [As you'll see later, they always seem to say it three times.]" Nothing like the cocoon of unreality when your life's fucked.

A woman with a black pompadour and a hawk nose talks about her resistance to group psychology, how she had to fight that impulse and go with the flock. I uncomfortably sense a negative narcissism, that these people enjoy laying guilt on themselves in front of others. She says that she was on a business trip and dodged a few meetings. This caused almost unbearable remorse. "I can't go seven to ten days without a meeting," she confesses. "I was wrong. I had an attitude." Heavens forfend!

Wearing a droopy pink gym suit, one woman's eyes twitch as she nervously rubs her hands together. Her sense of guilt is so strong, it manifests itself in physical symptoms. If you're easily shocked, you might want to stop reading now. Her pancreas-twisting self-hatred is easily understood. It seems that she had become lazy and was attending only *five meetings a week.* She had promised herself and God that she would "double up," i.e., go to *ten* meetings per week. She failed to follow through with her promise. Why, the cold-blooded, black-hearted, self-serving bitch!

After a moment of silent reflection, we all join hands and recite the Our Father. Following "Amen," everyone opens their eyes, clenches their hands tighter, and says, "KEEP COMING BACK, BECAUSE IT WORKS!"

The circle dissolves into loose socializing, with several individuals taking the time to tell us we've chosen the right path. Someone pops her head in the room and begs, "Can you *please* keep it down? There's a meeting going on in the next room."

MEETING #2: SNOW JOB

Another day, another church, another twelve steps to descend. Of all the addicts our wonderful world has to offer, I probably have the least sympathy for coke freaks. I call cocaine the "emperor's new drug," perfect for conformist achievers who can't trust themselves to achieve. Why people would blow their life's savings on a hyperinflated coffee buzz that doesn't alter their minds is beyond me. I don't quite *enjoy* heart murmurs and having my dick drained down to raisinlike proportions.

There are only four others besides us, and they're a tangled mess of frazzled ganglia, tapping their feet, blinking uncontrollably, and squirming in tiny chairs designed for kindergarteners. Their raging neurons are giving me a headache. I feel like strapping everyone down and pouring cold water on them.

Even though there are so few of us, the group leader keeps fucking up everyone's names. A hairy grizzly of a man, he uses the ultimate Twelve-Stepper's excuse: "I guess I haven't had my coffee yet....Do you feel like leading a meeting?"

He's talking to me. I decline, so he hands me a laminated card and asks that I read from the Big Book's passage on the Twelve Steps, modified to replace 'alcohol' with 'cocaine.'

"Hi, my name is Jim, and I'm an addict."
"HI, JIM!"

HOW IT WORKS

Rarely have we seen a person fail who has thoroughly followed our path. Those who do not recover are people who cannot or will not completely give themselves to this simple program, usually men and women who are constitutionally incapable of being honest with themselves. There are such unfortunates....Here are the steps we took, which are suggested as a program of recovery:

1. We admitted we were powerless over cocaine—that our lives had become unmanageable.
2. Came to believe that a Power greater than ourselves could restore us to sanity.
3. Made a decision to turn our will and our lives over to the care of God *as we understood Him.*
4. Made a searching and fearless moral inventory of ourselves.
5. Admitted to God, to ourselves, and to another human being the exact nature of our wrongs.
6. Were entirely ready to have God remove all these defects of character.
7. Humbly asked Him to remove our shortcomings.
8. Made a list of all persons we had harmed, and became willing to make amends to them all.
9. Made direct amends to such people wherever possible, except when to do so would injure them or others.
10. Continued to take personal inventory and when we were wrong promptly admitted it.
11. Sought through prayer and meditation to improve our conscious contact with God *as we understood Him,* praying only for His will for us and the power to carry that out.
12. Having had a spiritual awakening as the result of these steps, we tried to carry this message to cocaine addicts, and to practice these principles in all our affairs.

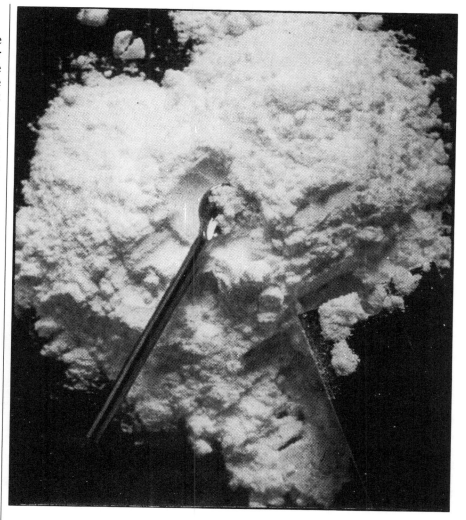

Our leader begins to share a lil' bit of himself with us, his voice assuming the soft, muted tone that people of the psychotherapeutic ilk use to assure you they're not *really* a seething vessel of wretched hostility. He says he's in his mid-thirties, coming out of twenty-one years of addiction. "I'm just a fifteen-year-old scared little kid who needs love," he says. Well, don't look at *me.*

"Ya wake up and ya find yourself doing something fundamentally different than ya've ever done it before," he coos, "and it's all a result of just hanging around here, ya know, and letting recovery happen at the slow pace that it happens." He says he lost his job and is recently divorced, but he remains upbeat. "I went on an interview yesterday, and I didn't give the interviewer the power to hire me, because I had heard a recovery tape that if God is all-knowing and all-loving and all-present, then He has the power. And the only way ya can give somebody else the power is to *give* it to them. If ya know that they don't have the power and that God has the power for all these decisions, then ya just go in there and turn it over. And I did." I wouldn't have hired him just because he listens to recovery tapes.

The next guy to share wears shorts, sandals, and the look of the hunted that comes from prolonged stimulant abuse. He says he's back from a weekend vacation where he drove eleven hours up to California redwood country. "It was kinda nice," he says. "I was all wired up on

coffee....I went back to the truck and it was hard for me to sleep, because I was just so sober. I went to some meetings up there. People are very open, and they're very into being sober. They're working their steps."

He's working them, too, stepping all over his ego, kicking it until it's bruised and nearly dead. Everyone in the program seems willing to talk about how horrible they used to be. "I'd smoke pot and do coke, smoke pot and do coke," he recalls, "just switchin' one addiction for another. First it's sex, then it's pot, then it's sex, then it's eating, then it's sex, then it's pot, then it's eating, and all these addictions just keep coming back. Why not just, 'Don't worry, be happy,' and just go on with life?" Sounds good, O thou one of damaged nerves, but why trade your previous addictions for enslavement to coffee and the program?

I'll tell you why. Because people like being slaves. The program demands that you smother your natural individualistic impulses and become a single cell within a free-floating, unthinking group jellyfish. The Big Book even quotes a neurologist who congratulates A.A. for encouraging the "herd instinct." *ANSWER Me!* believes that creativity never comes from collective thought, whether it be the establishment's consensus or that of the vaunted "counterculture." But most others aren't like us. They gather like lemmings and leap off cliffs in the name of the newest mass deception.

"Being sober is a great thing to be," continues the unwitting Nazi of positivity. "Do the steps, go over the program, come to the meetings. That's the way to be. You wanna control your attitude? Come to the meetings. You wanna learn something about life? Come to meetings. That's what the whole thing's about. You think meetings are stupid? I was two weeks sober before I came into meetings, and that's the whole

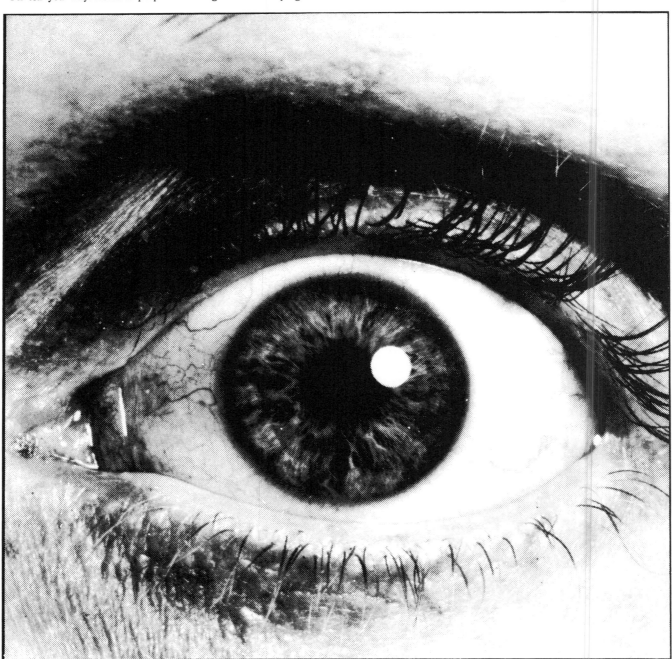

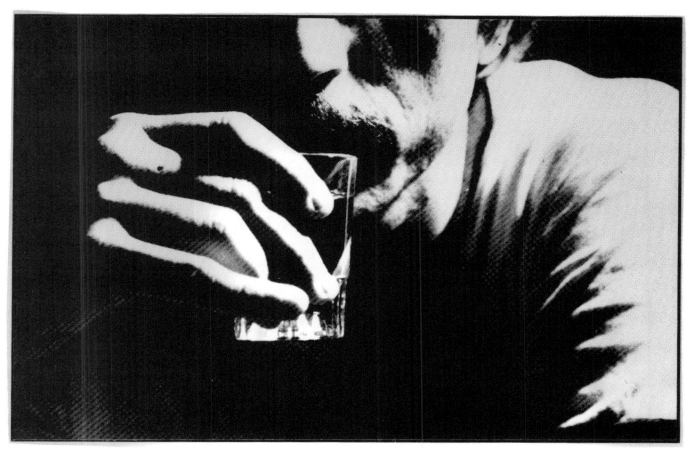

thing—I wanted sobriety, and I didn't want my attitude anymore. To control my attitude, I had to come to meetings. The guy I went with on this trip, he's a kid, he's like twenty years old, and he's got sixty days of sobriety. That's all we did—we just sat and talked about sobriety, and we read out of the Big Book. And it was kind of like a Bible study. But the thing is, the Bible tells you how to *work* on life, but the Big Book tells you how to deal with life on life's terms. And if you can relate to dealing with life's terms, that's the best way to be." Touché, but if you want to face life head-on, why the FUCK do you need a program, a Big Book, and a higher power?

I don't have time to ask, because the leader enjoins us to form a circle and recite the Our Father, which again ends with the "KEEP COMING BACK!" hand squeeze. The leader waddles up and hugs us with his sweaty bear's body. "People are really loving and open here," he tells us. "You can just go into any meeting anywhere and just be comfortable with it. It's real warm, real magical." *Magical?* I think to myself. *The more a person strains to be sincere, the more full of shit they become.*

Another ex-cokehead hugs us and says he's been to twenty-six meetings in the last fourteen days. He's planning to attend yet another one in a few hours. "I gotta keep going to meetings, going to meetings, going to meetings," he insists. "The meetings are all we have. The program is all we have."

MEETING #3: OF ALCOHOL AND GUYANESE KOOL-AID

This meeting's a giant alcoholic carnival of nearly two hundred persons. It's midday, but the women are in full makeup and boho club gear, fawning over stubbly guys with Christ-length hair. Buff biker dudes with ponytails charge across the room to hug women in rhinestone glasses and leopard jackets. I smell a meat market, as if all of Melrose Avenue had suddenly entered recovery.

We sit in the back row. Watching the hug-in, I consider how fragile such a conspiracy of belief is—in an instant it could fall apart or congeal into something far more dangerous. I'm sure that back in the seventies, most of those who joined up with Jim Jones and his People's Temple did so for what they thought were positive reasons. After a few years and more than a few lies, they were willfully sipping poisoned Kool-Aid and dropping like bird shit.

"I got to the program because somebody Twelve-Stepped me," says the female speaker, making her spiritual awakening sound oddly like a physical assault. "I think that's really important, because I would've never gotten here on my own. I didn't have the guts to stop. I would've died before I reached out my hand for someone." She delivers her words in an unwavering pitch reminiscent of the disembodied teacher's voice from Charlie Brown's classroom in *Peanuts.* "I got here," she says, "because there was no place for me to go anywhere else." The crowd chuckles knowingly. "I got out of bed and came to a meeting. It's a spiritual program. It was really important for me to learn that I was gonna have to find something bigger than you guys in this room to take my ass out of booze and drugs. And I decided to turn my life over to Him. I spent a lot of time lying to myself. A lot of time trying to be, you know, what my mom and dad wanted me to be, what my boyfriends wanted me to do, and what society wanted me to do."

Now she's got her shit straight—she's doing what a *higher power she never met* wants her to do. She says she wanted to be a rock star, but those weren't "God's plans" for her. In her drunken days of yore, she had been raped, mugged, and beaten, but now God's teaching her to "take responsibility." This is another thing I find annoying about the Twelve-Steppers: They're eager to guilt-trip about their

malodorous past deeds, even going so far as to blame themselves for things that couldn't have been their fault, such as being raped. But when it comes time to take credit for any *positive* action in their lives—POOF!—they had nuttin' to do with it. Blame the higher power for that one. It seems that their spiritual awakening consists of the realization that they can do nothing but wrong. People are usually so devoid of self-knowledge that when they get a little, they blow it out of proportion and lend it some cosmic significance.

The chip-giving ritual begins, and people respond to the tiny "APPLAUSE" and "HI, ——!" signs flashing in their heads. Speeches follow in rapid succession, each a radical thematic departure from the previous one. Consider the diversity of opinion evidenced in the following spiels:

A) I just want everyone out there to keep coming to meetings. I like it a lot. I'm keeping with the pro-gram, and every day is one more. I keep coming back to A.A. meetings.

B) I keep going, going, going to meetings.

Isn't it great? The first keeps *coming* to meetings, while the second keeps *going* to meetings, and yet A.A. finds room for *both* of them!

We finally sniff the rarefied air which lies above the many levels of chipdom. A wedding-sized cake is carried out to honor those whose sobriety transcends mere days and months. A list of names is read, accompanied by the number of years it's been since each of them last boozed it up. The crowd joins together in song:

> Happy birthday to you/
> Happy birthday to you/
> Happy birthday, dear A.A./
> Happy birthday to you./
> Keep com-ing baaaaaaack!

Teetotaling celebrants approach the cake one by one. As each is introduced, an organizer lights an appropriate number of candles. The crowd applauds at each introduction, then again after the candles are blown out, and yet again after each person delivers their speech. The birthday boys and girls spout the shopworn slogans about God being in charge and loving the child within, but one statement stands out as an existential nightmare:

"What I did was work within the Twelve Steps. In any situation, we only have twelve choices."

MEETING #4: NARCOLEPSY

I guess heroin's cool if you want to look like Keith Richards or an extra in *Dawn of the Dead*. But in the AIDS era, anyone who bangs dope is a formaldehyde-preserved moron. *ANSWER Me!* believes in doing nothing halfway. Either live your life or end it. Don't stumble around using your wrist for an ashtray or scratching zits off your ass. People actually think that shit's romantic? Plenty of L.A. metalheads do, but it just makes them easier to beat up.

At a stifling, unventilated Narcotics Anonymous meeting, I sense that most of

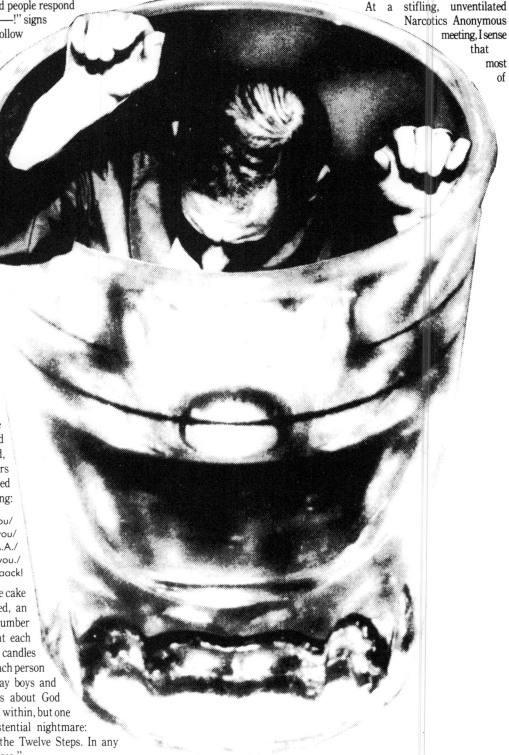

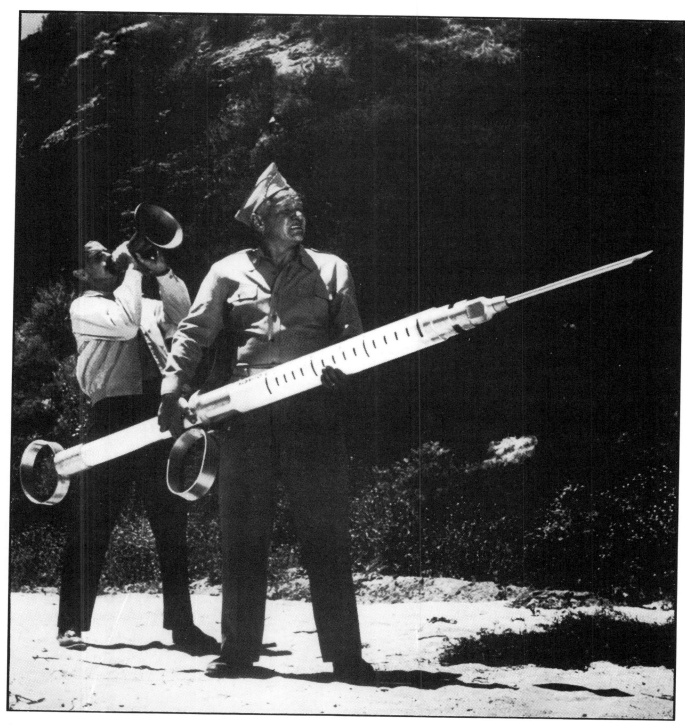

these folks' brains are still swimming in a narco syrup. They're either stupid or brain-damaged, but it's the only group where people have trouble reading the literature aloud. One simian-faced oaf (let's call him "Anwar") reads an agonizing syllable at a time, stalling on complex words such as 'their,' 'terms,' 'enemy,' and 'methods.' He can't even *pronounce* 'significant' after repeated phoneticization by his cohorts. Another junk casualty reads a section from the Big Book, tripping over the words 'acceptable,' 'protective,' and 'substitute.' I vow that I'll never, *ever* take narcotics.

A ruddy, Kris Kringlish man is the guest speaker. He calls himself an "ex-drunk" who's been sober for thirty years—as long as I've been alive.

I don't know why an alkie is at Narcotics Anonymous, but for some reason I trust him. That is, until he really starts talking.

"We have a common enemy," he says, "one great common enemy, and I'll tell you who it is—the name is 'You.' You are your own worst enemy. Remember—everything that has happened to you in your life, you caused it. Understand it—you cannot blame anybody for using or drinking. You made that decision. Nobody put a goddamned gun to your head and said, 'If you don't shoot this needle in you, we're gonna blow your brains out.' No. You did it because you wanted to. Understand that. You are the one that started your addiction. Nobody else. So don't blame your mother, your father, your wife—no human power made you what

you are today. You did it. Now, how do we solve that problem of 'You?' You have a choice—you can stop at any time you want. Most people have to go through a lot of living hell, all kinds of shit, before we realize and come to a point, 'Either I stop, or I don't stop and I'm gonna kill myself.' All alcoholics at one time or another, or addicts at one time or another, wanted to do away with themselves, because that's the other enemy—you. You hate you. You can't get along with you. Nobody understands you. That's why you fight with you.... Ego will kill you." Silly me—here I was, thinking it was the main component of my survival.

The meeting unravels into a discussion of the Twelve Steps that perhaps only a numerologist would find worthwhile. "The only time another human being comes into your existence is step five, and that's the only time," says the sober Santa Claus. "Six and seven—you wanna know something? Three and four is your whole goddamned program. Follow me, if you know this program. After you pass five, five goes back to three. Eight goes back to four. Nine goes back to four. Ten goes back to four. Eleven goes back to three, and twelve goes back to three. There's your program." Yeah, but what if six was nine? Wouldn't you mind?

A woman speaks up. "The Big Book tells me that if the third step is not immediately followed up at once by steps four and five, it has little or no permanent effect. How do you feel about that?"

"Well," answers the overweight cherub, "number three is, once you have found a power greater than yourself, then you have to make a decision to turn your power over. Now, that's strictly you and God. The fourth step then becomes you and you and you. And the fifth one is, like, you and somebody else *and* God. Does that make sense to you?"

Amazingly, it does. "How do you Twelve-Step?" asks another.

"Well, Twelve-Stepping's entirely different to me. I still Twelve-Step," he says. I still do the Mashed Potato, but that's between me and God.

Instead of joining hands and saying the Our Father, we lock arms in a circular hug and recite the Serenity Prayer:

> God grant me the serenity to accept the things I cannot change, the courage to change the things I can, and the wisdom to know the difference. Amen. KEEP COMING BACK! IT WORKS IF YOU WORK IT! YEAH!!!

There's a final announcement from Anwar, the *Sesame Street*-level reader, as the group disperses. "Hi, I'm Anwar, and I'm your secretary."

"HI, ANWAR!"

He grimaces. "I mean, I'm your *treasurer!*" This guy fucks up *everything.* The group laughs forgivingly as he pops himself in the head with an "I coulda had a V-8" move. Anwar finally laughs, too. "I'm in recovery, alright?"

ANSWER Me!'s TWELVE STEPS

It's not my intention to make fun of people's pain, just their seeming inability to get their shit together without social or spiritual crutches. I consider all of these people better off now than when they were guzzling, snorting, or slamming spikes into their arms. I know firsthand that alcohol is a MOTHERFUCKER. It causes people to lose their inhibitions, and from my experience, I prefer them with their hang-ups. There's nothing I hate more than a grinning drunk leaning in my face. These slobs are said to be responsible for more than half of the fifty thousand or so yearly auto fatalities in the U.S. If one of you stewed creeps ever rams into *my* car, you'd better take me out entirely, because I won't wait for the cops to get there. I'll bash your brains in with a crowbar.

Whew! You know, I feel better. Why don't we all stand up, take a deep breath, and stretch? I'll wait....

OK? This is my main beef: In its wholesale degradation of individuality, the placement of "principles before personalities," the program decapitates the ego when it should be repairing it. A sense of powerlessness and avoiding responsibility is why most of these people became addicts in the first place. Instead of attacking the problem at its source, the program merely substitutes one addiction for another. Call it "positive powerlessness."

There's a distinction between healthy self-reliance and plain bull-headedness which the Twelve-Steppers fail to make. They view the human personality in extremes, both of them lousy. For them, it's either blind defiance or total submission. That's what *ANSWER Me!* calls a "fecal duality"—two shitty choices.

Twelve-Steppers make much of total honesty. If they were truly honest with themselves, they'd admit that when they pray to their "higher power," they're only talking to a mental projection. Their prayers never rise above the ceiling. If anyone wants to tell me with inalienable certainty that they've actually spoken with God, let me point the way to the nearest mental hospital.

The second problem, the need for group support, hinges on the first. The program gives an artificial structure (complete with slogans, communal meetings, and Twelve Commandments) to people who are too weak to structure their own lives. If you form a dependence on others,

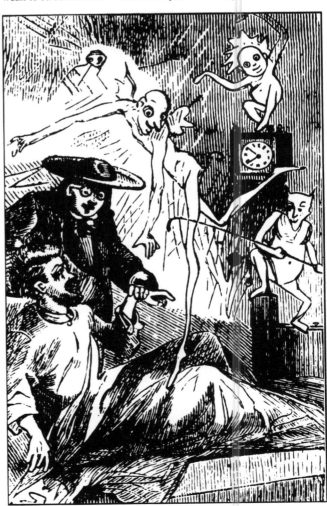

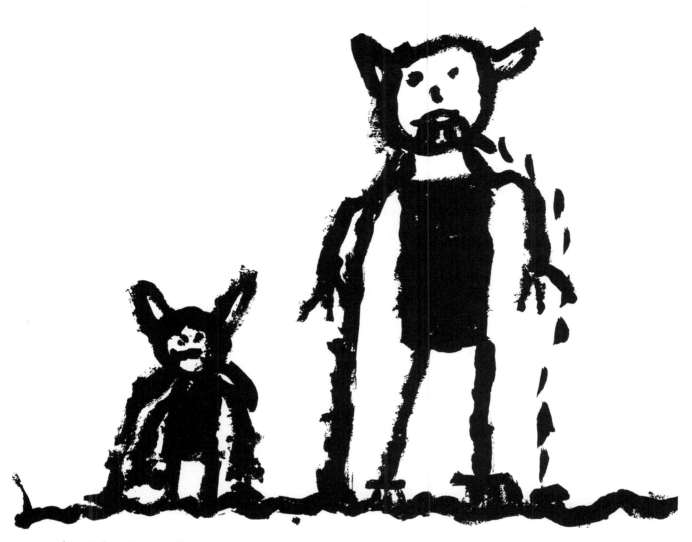

you never learn to depend on yourself.

The group is also an unrealistic setting: Unconditional love and acceptance may feel good, but you'll never find it outside of the group's womb. There's a nascent movement called Rational Recovery. It's basically A.A. without the God angle. It doesn't eliminate the need for the group, but at least it gets rid of the higher power. That's a step in the right direction. Only eleven more to go.

"Yeah, Jimbo," you scoff, "you talk that talk, but can you walk that walk? It's easy to criticize, but have *you* ever kicked an addiction? If *you* ever had to go cold turkey, maybe your nuts wouldn't be swinging so low." Alright, asshole, you've twisted my arm. Since I wrote in the Statement of Intent that a journalist who doesn't reveal his background is a liar, you'll have to permit me some psychodrama.

My old man was a brutal alcoholic, the nastiest person I've ever known. His father, whom I never met, was said to be the town drunk of a small backwoods community in Vermont. I tasted the family's legacy of violence early on—my brother tells me that dear ol' dad punched mom in the stomach while she was pregnant with me. My sister says that only days after my newborn body was brought home from the delivery room, dad and one of my brothers got into a fight. An ashtray got smashed into someone's head, and the glass fragments fell into my crib. One of my earliest memories is of watching my sister hunched over the toilet, her mouth drip-drip-dripping blood into the bowl, each drop dissolved by the clear water. "You see this?" she cried at me. "This is what your father's all about."

I don't know how many times I came home to find the old bastard unconscious, sprawled out like a homicide victim on the living-room floor, in the basement, or in the back alley. When I was five, I watched him trembling as he read a newspaper. "Why are you shaking like that?" I asked, and it blew his mind. Embarrassed that his problem was obvious to a preschooler, he quit drinking.

Three years later, my deaf brother (dad's oldest son of three) was murdered while vacationing in Paris. The old man, perhaps ashamed that his genes had produced an imperfect son, had been especially cruel to him. I suppose dad's guilt was too much to handle. After returning from the funeral for a small gathering at our house, I remember walking into the kitchen to find my father at the table, a half-empty bottle of whisky in front of him.

He started boozing again full-tilt, and since my remaining siblings were married and gone, I became the whipping boy. On one Saturday afternoon when I was nine or ten, I had the misfortune of being home alone with him. Something random enraged him, and he chased me up and down the stairs, through every room in the house, until he caught me. He whacked me several times in the face, finally drawing blood. In my little litigious way, I spit red saliva onto a piece of loose-leaf paper, writing down the date and time of occurrence. I was ready to testify,

because I was certain that my mother would divorce him.

She never did. To this day, she denies that he ever mistreated any of her kids. In fact, when I was about twelve, she egged him on as he lashed at me with his belt for coming home late from school. That beating left zucchini-sized welts up and down my thighs, bruises so extensive that my legs were more purple than pink. The abuse didn't stop until I reached my late teens and decided to hit him back, knocking his ass on the floor and cracking his dentures in half.

He finally kicked his drinking habit on a detox farm, but it was too late. A lifetime of red meat and alcohol had given him colon cancer, and he died within his first year of sobriety. He was a hateful mofo even when sober, but the booze fueled his rage like gasoline on a stove top. Unless you've experienced full-blown alcoholism firsthand, trust me: It's a drunk thing—you wouldn't understand.

Statistics suggest that most alcoholics come from alcoholic families. By the time the old man croaked, I had discovered the fruit of the grape myself, and I was a mean drunk, too. I took to brawling with friends, enemies, strangers, and cops. After downing a fifth of cheap tequila and a quart of Colt 45, I fought with two policemen in suburban Philly. At least that's what *they* told me—I woke up in jail eight hours after the arrest, remembering nothing. I saw myself turning into my father and promptly quit. That was almost ten years ago, and I haven't had so much as a bite of rum cake since.

I continued using drugs, though, mainly weed and acid. The acid experience is redundant and too intense to be addictive, but my weed habit progressed from a weekly to a daily to a five-times-a-day ritual. I toked with zeal throughout most of *ANSWER Me!*'s production phase. (Check out *24 Hours on Sunset* or *Swallowed by Jersey.*) I was spending almost as much on weed as I was on rent. Besides being alarmed that I was smoking all of my discretionary income, I tired of hacking up tarlike gobs of resin and losing my train of thought in mid-sentence. Suffering from an abundance of self-esteem, I quit. At press time I've been completely sober for two months, and I'll never look back. So *there!*

No one taught me to respect myself. I grew up without role models. I reached inside and found that the higher power was me. Therefore, here are *ANSWER Me!*'s Twelve Steps:

1. We admitted that our addictions were fucking us up.
2. Came to believe that since we started them, only we could stop them.
3. Made a decision to follow our gut instincts *as we understood them.*
4. Didn't bullshit ourselves about our many flaws.
5. Having admitted our flaws, we kept them to ourselves—they're nobody else's business.
6. Were entirely ready to argue with anyone who disagreed.
7. Filled with self-respect, we did nothing humbly.
8. Made a list of all persons we had harmed and realized that most of them deserved it.
9. Paid all our police fines, then burned all our bridges.
10. Continued to be ruthlessly honest with ourselves and admitted all our wrongs—to ourselves.
11. Trusted ourselves and only ourselves with what's best for us.
12. Having assumed full responsibility for our lives, we weren't foolish enough to try to change anyone else—first, it's a losing proposition, and second, we couldn't care less.

What saved me (besides practical considerations) was the act of banishing from my mind the idea that I needed my addictions. That's all. I don't need alcohol, I don't need dope, I don't need others' support, and I sure as fuck don't need a goddamned chip! ■

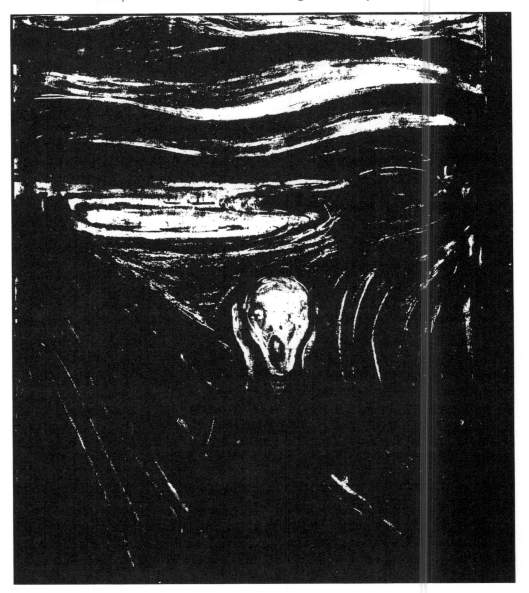

VIRTUAL REALITY

by Len Bracken

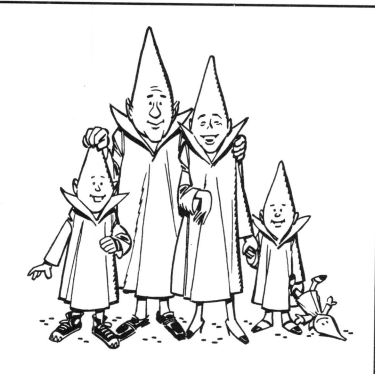

"It's as large as life, and twice as natural!" This quote — often attributed to Lewis Carroll — was written by anonymous. Just as Carroll saw fit to put this simile in the context of Wonderland, I think it can be inserted in the debate on VR (virtual reality) — the obvious connotations being superrealist stylistics or Baudrillardian hyperreality, wherein simulation becomes more real than material reality; less obvious, the socially interactive nature of speech and its role in consciousness.

In choosing this point of departure, I've raced ahead of myself.

Over the past few years I've followed with amusement the expositions of VR in the mainstream press and the hysterical manifestos of its proponents in specialized magazines and exhibition catalogues. Now what I see is an equally hysterical groping for an ideology, which recalls the stupefied reception Pop art justly received before the words of critics invested it with meaning. (That the artists themselves are unable to articulate their project is glaringly apparent in Warhol's *Popism.*)

In the catalogue of Art Futura 1990 — a virtual reality exhibit in Barcelona, Spain — Rebecca Allen writes "...computer generated characters realistically commenting on her piece "Steady State" on *Buzz MTV*, Allen referred to her characters as objects. She is right insofar as the creator and viewer are concerned (for them the characters always remain objects).

Yet, in the obscure reality of art, characters are imbued with the subjectivity of the creator, and in their interactions become subjects in their own right. How realistically human — in terms of logic and behavior — can objects (characters) generated by an object (a computer) be? What is vital to art is the interaction of subjects, be it the characters within the work, or in the dialogue between the viewer and the creator that continually reverses the poles of subject and object — such as when the viewer sees the subject (the creator) through the work, as a subject.

Allen forsees a day in the near future, once our perceptions of reality have been properly expanded by VR, when our interaction with computer characters will be indistinguishable from reality. This, she says, will be putting her "technical capabilities to use to improve the human condition." Isn't this a hiatus from reality and substitution of the human condition for an inhuman condition? Within the VR interface objects interact — there is no dialogue of subjects from positions of autonomy.

First published in 1992 Winter Supplement (Continued next page)

In another Art Futura essay, Luis Racionero evokes Judeo-Christian millenarianism and states that VR displays this quest to escape reality. This charitable admission prepares the simulated ground for more exasperating nonsense. According to Racionero, the traditional arts and our senses have reached their limits. What is needed is "a different program for the brain" based on chemistry and computers. The apparent goal is to short circuit the brain so that it mistakes data from a program for data from reality, as part of a "religion of science" founded on quantum physics!

> **Luis Racionero evokes Judeo-Christian millenarianism and states that VR displays this quest to escape reality. This charitable admission prepares the simulated ground for more exasperating nonsense.**

In his Art Futura essay Timothy Leary states that "new vehicles and information devices" are linked with human evolution. To my less than transhuman mind, these mean-oriented engineering advances with no clear objective are unrelated to human evolution. I'm leery of efforts to improve man by technological means. The former drug guru sounds like a zoo keeper who wants to tame the animal in us by putting us behind bars of a screen.

Is the "assumed, if not obvious goal" of making representation indistinguishable from reality, as Scott Fisher of NASA wrote in the Art Futura catalogue, a worthwhile objective? The traditional arts make no pretense to being anything other than representation, yet they bring us closer to reality. Through distortions and exaggerations the viewer enjoys a certain distance — paradoxically, distance encourages forms that are suited to expressing and illuminating human experience.

To paraphrase a venerable ancient: what appears real to me is real for me, and what appears real to you is real for you.

In her article "Art and Activism in VR" (*Verbum 5.2*) Brenda Laurel writes that realism and photorealism will be overshadowed by postrealism. She illustrates this style with Karl Sims' work *Panspermia*, which is, "filled with lush, fantastic plants growing from seeds on an alien planet." According to Laurel, this and other works that are, "based on incredibly intricate models of objects, physics and natural processes [...] initiate a post realistic style, a kind of neuromanticism in computer art."(?)

Sims' creation of a computer gene pool that grows plants somehow, "goes beyond mere modeling into a region of worship." These "deep simulations" are merely reification of the scientistic mythology of molecular biology minus the pretense of objectivity. Laural states that, "the techniques that derive from this style feed back to the medium and transform it," whereas postrealist techniques and style — as she uses the terms — are one and the same.

If technique is what is important, Sims' values are obviously similar to those of a genetic engineer. If content is of greater importance, then there are the images of irreal plants growing on a distant planet, geese flying, reflections in water... which could be perceived as beautiful. According to Schiller, the cognitive perfection of perception is the prerequisite of artistic beauty. What has Sims done, other than borrow his understanding of the internal dynamics of an object from science and use that to program a computer?

Whereas Pop was primarily concerned with form (low culture, comics, ad graphics, serial production — forms suitable to mass marketing), the VR crowd has internalized the artistically purposeless forms of Pop and turned their whole attention to the material aspect of form. What is important about form is its correlation with content. In the hands of a master, the material vanishes in the forms that express the will of their creator.

While this material aspect of form is the most obvious place to begin to look at a work of art, it is a secondary importance. Its value exists in its ability to express and order the emotional-volitional aspects of form. In this sense, the material is essentially extra-artistic — a question of technique or craftsmanship.

(Continued on next page)

Those who argue that the manipulation of material is essentially artistic — that the material aspect of form is on the artistic plane — are the proponents of a vacuous aesthetic creed: stimulate pleasant, but incomprehensible or irrelevant, sensations. My tastes run toward value-related works, works directed toward the world, toward reality, works concerned with human beings in social relations — directed toward something apart from material.

In *Art and Answerability* (1919), M. M. Bakhtin describes the dilemma faced by all artists, but especially by the VR artist: "A whole is called 'mechanical' when its constituent elements are united only in space and time by some external connection and are not imbued with the internal unity of meaning. The parts of such a whole are contiguous and touch each other, but in themselves they remain alien to each other."

Art is outside of life, but life can be in art if the art answers to the ethical problems of daily existence. Art creates its own reality in which thought and action take place — it places humans in nature, humanizing nature and naturalizing man — it contextualizes in much the same way life does.

A new form is created when a new axiological relation to a given context comes into being, or when humans — such as Gibson's cyberpunks — are placed in a new context. (What makes his novels work for me is the slum naturalism of the near future that uses many of the forms of the 19th century dirty realism, not life in the net.) The material of VR may be of cultural importance (in the broad sense of the term), but it is extracultural in the artistic sense of regroup-ing social values (due to its technological focus, it is particularly poor at this — even in the hands of skilled artists it tends to bolster dominant values).

> **Instead of overcoming the material, VR artists seem overcome by it. Granted, technique is needed for creation, but isn't part of the aesthetic whole because it has little relation to aesthetic contemplation.**

Instead of overcoming the material, VR artists seem overcome by it. Granted, technique is needed for creation, but isn't part of the aesthetic whole because it has little relation to aesthetic contemplation. In these terms, content reigns — form merely embodies content. Ethics are the essence of content.

When contemplating a work of art or creating, one must somehow treat the ethical component of a work through content. Creation is a question of will and value. In short, creator and viewer ask: "What is the purpose of the work?" Without a purpose, one is left with the naive esthetic of the ancients: the greater the technical perfection, the better the art, which has lead to absurd art for art's sake that regularly falls back on the tired neo-dada one sees on shopping bags.

The blind preoccupation with the material aspect of form is seen throughout the VR literature, but nowhere is it more apparent than the USNET's VR network. To their credit, some of the participants have begun to ask themselves serious questions about the nature of their business. When Bruce Cohen asks his colleagues to respond to the "metaphysical" question: "What is 'virtual reality'?" — one knows one is witnessing a crisis in the ranks.

In the material expression of letters or sounds, the words "virtual reality" are a sign, a sign that represents the now familiar goggle-glove, etc., apparatus, which is outside that sign. While continuing to exist on the material plane, the apparatus of VR generates signs, signs that reflect another reality. I mention this to keep in mind the distinction between technology and the world of signs, both of which are equally real.

VR technology is the material that gives the expression to forms. Given its early association with the military and toy manufacturers, VR tecnology seems suited to expressing the forms of guns and adversaries. In this philosophical void, several partisans (Leary, Laurel, and Barlow in *Verbum 5.2)* have issued a call for artists to exploit their medium for some, seemingly any, socioartistic purpose.

They make many arguments for their medium, the primary ones being immersion, interaction, and multi-media stimulus. Because all signs have ma-

(Continued next page) **147**

terial embodiment (sound, mass, color, movement) they are an outer experience regardless of how immersed in the medium one is. There always exists a border between signs and the psyche, even though the psyche is composed of signs.

The key interaction in perception is between a new sign and the psyche — if a reference is made between the new sign and a pre-existing sign, there is understanding. Without conscious understanding, all there is, is the physical object, like an amorphous lump of clay in a museum. Greater understanding can be attained through knowledge of the culture in which the work was created. For example, we know more about the art of antiquity than pre-historic art because we can place the former in a specific cultural context via texts. And through theory, we have a way of understanding even the most objectless Modern art.

Pictures, music, ritual, human conduct, etc. can only be understood with inner speech. These non-verbal mediums can't be replaced by words, but they can't be separated from them either — they are supported by words. Words, not images, are the primary medium of individual consciousness, the semiotic material of inner life. If non-verbal signs are given meaning, it is always, in part, from verbally constituted consciousness (consciousness is a social act, as an individual can only be conscious of his or herself in relation to others).

The prospect of a telepuppet party in VR presents the possibility of great carnivals with animated masks and promiscuity without peril. The sad fact is that this is no dimming of the footlights and bringing art to the streets, merely subject to object, and object to object, communication. What you have is a private puppet party, closed off from history and true social realization — the subjective empty sensations of psychophysiological apparatuses for perception.

The interactive aspect of VR was touted by Leary as the technology that will liberate humans from television dictatorships. The participants can create environments and scenarios, albeit within the confines of the program and available data. So instead of TV networks — it remains to be seen if they will be supplanted — we would be encumbered by programmers who are run by computers.

The VR process is one of interchange — the exchange of reality for abstraction, the commutation of one's unique and sovereign body into a telepuppet that can be shared by one and all, and the interchange of being able to do what one wants to do, with what the machine allows one to do. Interchange displaces intercourse.

> **Each field of creativity has its own orientation toward reality, that of the partisans of VR being technological (it could be argued that their orientation with reality is a simulation of it, which prompts the charge that they are merely simulating creativity).**

Each field of creativity has its own orientation toward reality, that of the partisans of VR being technological (it could be argued that their orientation with reality is a simulation of it, which prompts the charge that they are merely simulating creativity). Like many others before them, they feel that their particular distortion of reality, their special point of view, is the best. To my mind, the more persuasive argument is that words are the best medium of social intercourse.

Words have no existence outside their function as signs — they signify something. One learns the signifying process from one's parents and society, internalizing society's speech as inner speech. In this sense, words are irreducibly social, the key building blocks in the social formation of mind.

One is most immersed in the medium of words because words are the most meaning-saturated form of expression: they resonate with one's inner speech, with one's way of understanding. While there are acute differences between the language of daily life and narration, fiction highlights the social role of consciousness: the apperceptive background of the reader co-creates the work — without the reader, there is no creation. The mute form of perception, reading, is more actively creative than any other medium.

(Continued on next page)

In a way this is my response to another of Cohen's questions: "How does VR compare and contrast in the quality of experience to other kinds of interaction (art, ceremony, intellectual discourse, etc.)?" The partisans argue that language can't keep up with the technological advancaes, but they do so with language. Far from lagging behind technology, words are a much more sensitive indicator of social change than an image-based device. The word can be created by the indivdual with the material of the body, without any outside device.

In a laughable statement, John Barlow of Greatful Dead fame spoke of "postsymbolic communication." No form can be understood until it is transformed into a symbol. In their Zen quest for an always elusive techno-nirvana, the partisans of VR confuse paradox with oxymorons, and are engaged in the proliferation of nonsensical terms (postrealism, virtual reality, neuormanticism, Barlovian cyberspace, etc.). Barlow is particularly egregious in his surfing analogy, comparing VR technology to being in heavy white water (strange to see references to surfing swell up in USENET's VR net — what is awesome about surfing is man in peril with nature, something hackers will never have behind their screens).

If virtual images, music and telepresence were better means of communicating than words, the partisans of VR would use them among themselves. It is amusing for me to see so much energy go into gimmicks such as stereoscopic goggles, when we already always see stereoscopically with perception of dimension. Perhaps it is not eyes, but ears that should be given the attention.

To quote Brenda Laurel: "You can fall asleep with the television blaring, but when you're driving along absorbed in a really good radio show, you don't even see the road — the visual part of your mind is elsewhere, partying down with your imagination." ("Art Activism in VR," *Verbum 5.2,* fall/winter 91.) Laurel writes that "sensory incompleteness" is essential to deep participation" with art. There you have it from one of the partisans — words.

If deep participation is the goal, one need look no further than the novel — the reader performs the work, either out loud or mutely. Even with mute per-ception, the words become those of the reader, the reader becomes the author through the inter-orientation of the text and the reader's psyche. Subtle shifts in contexts, foregrounding and emphasis of certain phrases, events, and characters necessarily occur when one reads, and no one reads exactly the same way, as we all bring our unique psyches to the reading.

Laurel's remarks argue against a multimedia approach, an approach which is not new. Chinese watercolors accompanied by a poem come to mind, as do Chinese scrolls — accordion books — that fold in on themselves so that epics can dance backwards and forwards through the panels: these books are also an excellent medium for anthologies, each artist making original art on two seamless pages.

I recently had the good fortune to see the paintings of Naruo, an artist from China's Yunnan Province who works in the medium of his Naxi language, an iconographic writing system still in use. Theoretically, this would be the most united form of communication, the sound and picture corresponding to the same object: complete unity of verbal and visual symbols.

Naxi is one of the few remaining icongraphic languages, which leads me to surmise that it is one of the best. It may, on the other hand, have continued to exist because of the isolation of the Naxi people within China. Why is it that so many iconographic languages have died out? They can be beautiful, but they are not powerful or flexible enough to cope with social change and contamination from syllabic or logographic languages.

VR's technical virtuosity could make it fast enough to change with social wind, but less so than words. My guess is that once the novelty wears off, this technology will be as banal as the telephone. We will be left with the empty sensation of a thing, a technical experiment lacking any artistic importance. What will remain interesting is what is said, because content is the most social aspect of a work. How that message is perceived by the individuals who make up society and the social context of a work can only be partially understood through socio-historic knowledge, which is verbally attained more than any other way.

Those who argue that "visual input" is far better than "the tyranny of word categories" remind me of Artaud, a very sick man, who lamented the "numbing dislocation of my language in relation to my thought." We all experience moments when a word is on the tip of our tongue, when we have an impression of a sign or object that we can't fully differentiate. This nuisance is a far cry from the problems inherent in trying to convey thoughts with pictures — a round of Pictionary should be enough to convince anyone.

This player's hunch is that games like Virtuality will be big money winners, but devoid of anything of real value. It's amazing to see multimedia and VR enthusiast Howard Rheingold now write about "the potential effects of blurring the line between war and video games" (*Whole Earth Review,* Winter 1991) following the Gulf War, or to hear him say on National Public Radio that VR will make the ultimate couch potatoes.

Many partisans, most of all the manufactures, are quick to point to the educational value of VR. We now have kids playing Nintendo with Mattel's version of the data glove. One man who stands to make a fortune on this device, Jaron Lanier, said in an interview in *Mondo 2000,* "If the technology makes people more powerful or more smart, then it's an evil technology." This statement begs to be restated in the affirmative: good technology makes the user weak and stupid.

> **Would NASA be interested in VR if it didn't give users the power to manipulate an environment? VR promises to put more power in the hands of the technocrats.**

Personally, I don't believe Lanier was being altogether honest. Later in the interview he jokingly admitted, "But my nose is three miles long." Would NASA be interested in VR is it didn't give users the power to manipulate an environment? VR promises to put more power in the hands of the technocrats.

Cyberpunk novelist William Gibson understated another danger, "Virtual Reality will be another way to get even further into the consumer than we already have" (*Exposure,* October 1990). The Power Glove toy certainly does its part to socialize rich children to consume themselves in the material of VR, to make spectacles of themselves. It gives them the illusion of power, and alienates them from their bodies at an early age by hypnotizing them before the screen for hours on end, rendering them more and more sedentary.

Instead of the interactive, multi-media education some children are already receiving, they should be encouraged to work with low-tech media, such as books, that focus on content, that will bring them into society via words. I was struck by the Apple Computer advertisement that promoted computer education with a personalized variation of Duchamp's Mona Lisa transformation (the teacher scanned the photo of a student and the latter penned in a moustache). We no longer have denigration of the bourgeois stuffiness in Renaissance art, but Pop commercialization of a Dada gesture.

> **At the end of the film *The End of the World,*which featured some VR horror, the novelist character said it fairly well: "...the disease of images and the healing power of words."**

It is very telling that Gibson's Mona Lisa (*Mona Lisa Overdrive*) is completely illiterate. In my opinion, users of VR will soon become specimens of the reflexologized Freudians one finds at the corner of Madison and Pennsylvania Avenues. At the end of the film, *The End of the World,* which featured some VR horror, the novelist character said it fairly well: "...the disease of images and the healing power of words."

● ● ● ● ● ● ●

PRIVACY ACT & FREEDOM OF INFORMATION ACT REQUEST

_____   _____

_____   (date)

_____

(requester's name and address)

Federal Bureau of Investigation
Records Management Division - FOIA/PA Office
9th & Pennsylvania Avenue NW
Washington, DC 20535

Gentlemen:

This is a request for records under the provisions of both the Privacy Act (5 USC 552b) and the Freedom of Information Act (5 USC 522). This request is being made under both Acts.

I hereby request one copy of any and all records about me or referencing me maintained at the FBI. This includes (but should not be limited to) documents, reports, memoranda, letters, electronic files, database references, "do not file" files, photographs, audiotapes, videotapes, electronic or photographic surveillance, "june mail", mail covers, and other miscellaneous files, and index citations relating to me or referencing me in other files.

My full name is: _____. My date of birth was _____.

My place of birth was: _____. My social security #: _____.

I have lived in these places: _____

_____

Other names, places, events, organizations or other references under which you may find applicable records:

_____ .

As you know, FOIA/PA regulations provide that even if some requested material is properly exempt from mandatory disclosure, all segregable portions must be released. **If the requested material is released with deletions, I ask that each deletion be marked to indicate the exemption(s) being claimed to authorize each particlar withholding.** In addition, I ask that your agency exercise its discretion to release any records which may be technically exempt, but where withholding serves no important public interest.

I hereby agree to pay reasonable costs associated with this request up to a maximum of $25 without my additional approval,. However, I strongly request a fee waiver because this is, in part, a Privacy Act request.

This letter and my signature have been certified by a notary public as marked below.

Sincerely,

_____

requester's signature

_____   _____

requester's printed name   notary stamp and signature

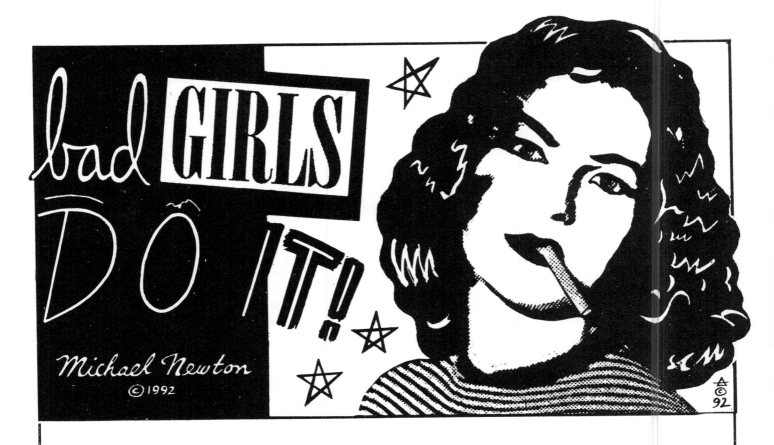

bad GIRLS DO IT!

Michael Newton ©1992

*Oh woman, woman! when to ill thy mind
Is bent, all hell contains no fouler fiend.*
                    Homer, *Odyssey*

Feminists complain, and rightly so, that women's contributions have been largely overlooked and undervalued in the annals of American history. It is high time, they insist, that members of America's statistical majority receive full credit for their numerous achievements in such varied fields as politics and education, medicine and social activism, science and the arts. Ironically, a venue typically ignored by feminists is also one where modern girls and women demonstrate a strong determination to succeed.

That field is crime.

According to the FBI, in 1991 female offenders accounted for 18.4% of America's total arrests. It comes as no surprise, perhaps, to learn that 64% of all arrested prostitutes and 56% of runaways were female, but what of 44% locked up for fraud, 41% for embezzlement, 34.6% for forgery and counterfeiting,

or 32% for larceny and theft? Last year, American women also accounted for 19% of disorderly conduct arrests, 17.8% of crimes against family or children, 16.8% of all drug violations, 13.8% of gambling arrests, 13% of arrests for arson and aggravated assault, 10.4% for homicide, 10% of all reported auto thefts, and 8.3% of robbery arrests. Reversing the traditional view of women as victims, they further logged 7.7% of all arrests for sex offenses and 1.1% of arrests for forcible rape.

From all appearances, the ladies are no shrinking violets anymore.

In fact, if we roll back the clock a thousand years or so, we find that America's first mass murder was plotted and executed by a woman. Freydis was Leif Erickson's illegitimate half-sister and, as luck would have it, also his sister-in-law, married to Leif's brother Thorwald. When Thorwald led a party to the New World, following Leif's tracks, Freydis went along for the ride. The Norsemen were barely ashore when Freydis began making waves, forbidding brothers Helgi and

152

First published in 1992 Holiday Supplement

(Continued on next page)

Finnbogi, along with their shipmates, from living in Leif's house. The outcasts were forced to build their own dwelling, and matters went downhill from there, with Freydis stirring the pot at every opportunity. By spring, the two groups were barely speaking, and Freydis had her own Final Solution in mind.

Visiting Finnbogi in the pre-dawn hours, she proposed an exchange of ships, and Finnbogi agreed. Returning home, she woke her husband with a different story. "I have been to see the brothers, to try to buy their ship," Freydis said, "but they received my overtures so ill that they struck me and handled me very roughly."

> *America's first mass murder was plotted and executed by a woman.*

America's first false accusation of male-female assault left Thorwald no options. Viking machismo demanded blood, and he promptly roused his shipmates, marching on their neighbors at the crack of dawn. Taken by surprise, the members of Finnbogi's crew were bound, led from the hut one by one, and hacked to death on orders from Freydis. Even so, Thorwald's men balked at killing five women in the party, whereupon Freydis shouted, "Hand me an ax!" When she was finished, smeared with blood from head to foot, she managed to persuade the men that they should keep the incident a secret. Sailing home a short time later in Finnbogi's ship, Thorwald reported having left the others safe and sound in Vinland.

Another Norse immigrant, Belle Paulsdatter Storset, followed an elder sister to America in 1881. Married in Chicago three years later, she soon lost patience with her role as wife and mother, plotting some changes on the domestic front. Arson came first, with insurance payoffs resulting from destruction of her husband's business and the family home. Next, her children started dying of "acute colitis," followed by Belle's husband — all displaying symptoms which, in retrospect, were very similar to those of strychnine poisoning. A move to Indiana followed, where the widow Sorenson used her latest insurance bonanza to purchase a farm near La Porte. In April 1902 she married Peter Gunness, a Norwegian farmer, but he lasted only eight months before an "accidental" skull fracture left Belle alone with three children and one on the way. She began hiring drifters to help work the farm, but transients are a fickle lot, prone to vanishing without a trace. Searching for a better class of help-mate, Belle began to advertise in the "lonely-hearts" columns of Norwegian-language newspapers throughout the Midwest, entertaining a series of prospective suitors at her farm. Somehow, none of them measured up to her standards... and none of them were ever seen again.

In April 1908, the Gunness homestead was leveled by fire. Searchers, digging through the rubble, found four charred bodies in the basement, including three children and a headless woman thought to be Belle Gunness. By early May, more bodies had begun to surface at the ranch. Dismembered, wrapped in gunny sacks and doused with lye, the corpses told a graphic tale of wholesale slaughter spanning years. The final body-count is still uncertain, but a coroner's report lists ten male victims, plus two females and an unspecified quantity of human bone fragments, for a minimum total sixteen dead. Belle's suitors were buried together, in the muck of a hog pen, while her female victims had been planted in a nearby garden patch. More to the point, authorities decided that the headless woman in the basement was a ringer. Belle had slipped away, presumably well-heeled with money stolen from her "guests," and she was never seen again.

Another "lonely-hearts" killer, 280-pound Martha Beck, was working as a nurse in Florida when she met bigamist Raymond Fernandez, in 1947. A professional gigolo and swindler, Fernandez had Martha pegged as his next victim, but the hefty nurse swept Raymond off his feet, delighting him with her approval of his larcenous life-style. Together, they devised a scheme where Beck would pose as Raymond's sister, standing by to help while he bilked other

(Continued on next page)

women of their savings, joining him for kinky sex between engagements. It was Martha's brainstorm, prosecutors later claimed, to guard against arrest by killing off the love-sick victims once their bank accounts were drained. Over two years time, the deadly duo killed at least a dozen women — some say twenty — in a string of crimes that ranged from Illinois to New York state. Finally arrested in January 1949, Beck and Fernandez horrified police with their smirking confessions to multiple murders. A Chicago victim, Myrtle Young, reportedly "croaked from over-exertion" after a weekend of nonstop sex with Fernandez. When their targets were encumbered with children, Martha killed the little ones as well. Despite Raymond's boast that "I'm no average killer," the guiding hand in every case apparently belonged to Martha Beck. It was finally too much, and New York jurors rejected the couple's insanity plea in August 1949. Both defendants were executed at Sing Sing prison in March 1951.

California's Carol Bundy was also a nurse, but she lacked Martha Beck's self-esteem. Bundy was struggling to support her two children in January 1980, when she met Douglas Clark in a Los Angeles country-western bar. It was lust at first sight, Clark devoting his nights to a crash course in ecstasy that made Carol his virtual slave. She swallowed her pride when Clark brought younger women home for sex, dutifully snapping photographs on command. One of Doug's conquests was an 11-year-old girl, picked up while roller skating in a nearby park, but Carol made no complaint as kinky sex gave way to pedophilia, increasingly spiced with discussions of death and mutilation. By June, Clark had begun to act out his morbid fantasies, hiring prostitutes or snatching teenagers at gunpoint, shooting his victims in the head while they sucked his penis. Clark enjoyed Exxie Wilson enough to lop off her head and carry it home for more fun and games. "We had

a lot of fun with her," Carol later told police. "I was making her up like a Barbie with makeup." Nor was Bundy a mere passive bystander in the L.A. murder spree. That August, when a male acquaintance grew suspicious of her strange relationship with Clark, Carol shot him, stabbed the corpse nine times and slashed its buttocks, finally removing the head to prevent ballistics tests. Driven by her conscience to confess a few days later, Bundy turned state's evidence against Clark, earning a life sentence when her testimony sent Doug to death row.

When a male acquaintance grew suspicious of her, Carol Bundy shot him, stabbed the corpse nine times and slashed its buttocks.

At that, Clark was not deprived of feminine companionship for long. Pen pal Veronica Compton was serving time for attempted murder in Washington state, but she still had a soft spot in her heart for California killers. A self-styled poet and aspiring actress, Compton was twenty-three years old when she attached herself to "Hillside Strangler" Kenneth Bianchi, then serving time for a double murder in Bellingham, Washington. Always a shrewd judge of character, Bianchi noted Veronica's passion for murder and mayhem, proposing a bizarre defense strategy. Compton would visit Bellingham, strangle a woman there, and leave traces of Bianchi's semen on the body to persuade detectives that the "real killer" was still at large. Obtaining the requisite sperm sample in a jailhouse visit, passed to Compton in the cut-off finger of a rubber glove, Veronica chose a Bellingham victim at random, but she bungled the murder, allowing her prey to escape. Convicted and sentenced to prison in 1981, Compton soon tired of Bianchi, repulsed by his weeping in court, and turned her attention to Doug Clark. "Our humor is unusual," she wrote in one letter, voicing a classic understatement. "I wonder why others don't see the necrophilic aspects of existence as we do?"

One who might have shared the joke was Indiana's Gertrude Baniszewski, though in

(Continued on next page)

retrospect, the grim-faced housewife rarely laughed at all. Raising three children on a meager income in the early 1960s, Gertrude scraped by with one spoon in the house, sharing it out when her brood dined on frozen dinners or ate leftovers straight from the can. In 1965, to supplement her earnings, Gertrude struck a deal to board the Likens sisters, Sylvia and Jennie, while their parents traveled with the circus. There was nothing to account for what came next: starvation, beatings, torture, and confinement in the musty basement of the Baniszewski home. Gertrude herself could not explain the sadistic delight she found in tormenting 16-year-old Sylvia Likens, burning the girl with matches, encouraging her own children and neighboring youths to stretch their imaginations in devising new forms of torture. Paula Baniszewski broke a hand punching Sylvia and returned from the doctor's office wielding her cast as a new weapon. Some evenings, Sylvia was stripped and forced to dance naked for neighborhood boys, with Gertrude serving as the choreographer, snapping commands in a sharp, shrewish voice. Later, Gertrude directed a dim-witted hoodlum, Ricky Hobbs, to heat needles and brand Sylvia's stomach with the legend: "I am a prostitute and proud of it." When Sylvia finally died from a beating that August, Gertrude called police and tried to blame a non-existent street gang for the murder. Jennie Likens overcame her terror to confide in homicide detectives and the truth was thus revealed, but Gertrude's motives remained obscure. At her trial in Indianapolis, awaiting a life sentence, she could only repeat, "I had to teach her a lesson."

Teaching was also the vocation of New Jersey's Margaret Kelly Michaels, but she liked her students younger, in the pre-school range.

> *Gertrude Baniszewski herself could not explain the sadistic delight she found in tormenting 16-year-old Sylvia Likens, burning the girl with matches, encouraging her own children and neighboring youths to stretch their imaginations in devising new forms of torture.*

A bright, attractive 23-year-old, Michaels was hired by Maplewood's Wee Care Day Nursery in September 1984, soon promoted from the rank of part-time aide to full-time teacher of her own class. When her students began to exhibit strange behavior at home, some weeping hysterically at nap time, most parents dismissed the symptoms out of hand. It would be April 1985 before one concerned mother took her son to a pediatrician and thereby opened Pandora's box. By that time, Michaels had moved on to another nursery in East Orange, New Jersey, but she could not escape the charges that followed. First one child and then another described the "games" they had been forced to play at Wee Care, sometimes in the classroom, sometimes in a choir loft of the church that housed the day-care center. Kelly Michaels liked to play at "taking temperatures," inserting plastic spoons and other objects in the rectums of her tiny charges. There was also fondling and oral sex, some of it interspersed with slaps and pummeling. Some children were compelled to snack on Kelly's feces, nicknamed "peanut butter," or to lick the menstrual blood from her vagina. On less intense occasions, Michaels would content herself with stripping down and playing nude piano numbers for her captive audience. At trial, in 1987, Kelly Michaels struck a pose of injured innocence, taxpayers shelling out $54,000 for defense "expert" Ralph Underwager's testimony that the Wee Care victims had been brainwashed by malicious counselors. A jury disagreed, convicting Michaels on 115 counts of child abuse, with a resultant prison term of forty-seven years.

If Kelly Michaels loved the little ones too much and in a twisted way, Oregon's Jeannace Freeman had a very different view of children. Raped by a stranger at age four, Freeman grew up hating men, a self-described "butch" who

(Continued on next page) **155**

told her lesbian cronies, "I'd vomit if a man touched me." Settling in Eugene, Oregon, after a brief prison term, Freeman met Gertrude Jackson in early 1961, embarking on a love affair that cast Jackson, a divorced mother of two, in the role of Freeman's love slave. Jackson was compelled to walk around her home stark naked for Freeman's amusement, dressing only in the presence of her children, and even those interruptions were soon too much for Freeman to bear. On May 10, 1961, the women drove Jackson's children to a picnic site overlooking Crooked River Canyon. Gertrude obediently went for a stroll while Jeannace strangled her six-year-old son, hacked off his genitals, and tossed his body over a cliff. Returning moments later, Jackson helped strip her five-year-old daughter before Freeman strangled, slashed, and discarded the girl in like fashion. Back in the car, Jeannace licked the blood from her hands before the two women made love. Discovery and identification of the small corpses led to swift arrests, but psychiatric tests postponed the killer couple's trial for three more years. Convicted of murder and sentenced to death in 1964, both women later saw their sentences commuted to life imprisonment.

Another pair of deadly dykes hailed from Walker, Michigan, plying their trade at the Alpine Manor Nursing Home. Gwendolyn Graham and Catherine Wood were nurse's aides at Alpine Manor when they met and fell in love, in 1986. They swore eternal devotion to one another, sealing their pact with a lethal game designed to "ease tension" when one or the other would have a "bad day" at work. Simply put, the sport involved Graham smothering elderly patients while Wood served as lookout, sometimes eavesdropping on the murders from her intercom at the nurse's station. Clever to a fault, Graham chose her victims alphabetically, attempting to spell M-U-R-D-E-R with the first initial of their surnames.

> *Clever to a fault, Gwendolyn Graham chose her victims alphabetically, attempting to spell M-U-R-D-E-R with the first initial of their surnames.*

On the side, she also boasted of her crimes to other lesbians, who laughed the statements off as "jokes." Graham also enjoyed bathing her lifeless victims, and simple discussion of the crimes was so stimulating that Wood and Graham were often moved to have sex on the spot. Even so, "forever" ran out in the summer of 1987, when Graham found herself a younger girl and moved to Texas. Cathy Wood was jealous for a while, then sickened by a call from Graham that included hints about a plan to murder babies on her new job, at a hospital in Tyler, south of Dallas. Wood confessed the local slayings to her former husband, and arrests were made in December 1988. Eleven months later, Gwen Graham was convicted of multiple murder and sentenced to six life terms without parole. Cathy Wood got off easy, swapping her testimony for a single count of second-degree murder and a sentence of 20 to 40 years in prison.

Marybeth Tinning also dabbled on the fringes of the medical profession, working as a part-time ambulance driver, but most of her attention focused on her husband, home, and children in Schenectady, New York. For a devoted mother, Tinning seemed to have no luck at all in raising children, losing nine of them in thirteen years. The first to go was daughter Jennifer, just eight days old when meningitis took her life in January 1972. Less than three weeks later, little Joseph Tinning, Jr., turned up DOA at the emergency receiving ward, his death ascribed to viral infection and "seizure disorder." Six weeks later, autopsy surgeons blamed the death of four-year-old Barbara Tinning on "cardiac arrest." Sudden Infant Death Syndrome was blamed for the demise of Timothy and Mary Tinning, four years apart, while "pulmonary edema" allegedly killed five-month-old Nathan. No cause of death was ever determined for Jonathan Tinning, in 1980, but physicians who diagnosed bronchial pneu-

(Continued on next page)

monia in brother Michael's death, a year later, also noted a "high level of suspicion" surrounding the case. Tami Lynne was the last to go, with another SIDS diagnosis in December 1985, but detectives finally pressed their investigation, arresting Marybeth Tinning after she confessed, "I smothered them with a pillow because I'm not a good mother." In retrospect, psychiatrists diagnosed Tinning as suffering from a curious condition called "Munchausen's syndrome by proxy," wherein persons craving sympathy pursue it by deliberately harming members of their families. A less than sympathetic jury convicted Tinning of Tami Lynne's murder in July 1987, and she was sentenced to prison.

If Marybeth Tinning had trouble keeping her children alive, New Mexico's Darci Pierce had a rather different problem. Obsessed with motherhood and yet unable to conceive, she fabricated tales of pregnancy and donned maternity clothes, somehow deceiving her husband and family even when gestation dragged on from the customary nine months to an incredible fourteen. Compelled to find a baby or admit her lie, Pierce loitered outside an Albuquerque maternity clinic in July 1987, abducting Cindy Lynn Ray when the mother-to-be emerged from a meeting with her physician. A short drive brought them to the nearby mountains, where Darci Pierce choked her victim unconscious and performed a crude Cesarean section, using her car keys in place of a scalpel. The result was a premature infant and one dead mother, but Darci was pleased with her work. Smearing her body with Cindy Ray's blood, Pierce raced to the nearest hospital and spilled out a wild tale of giving birth alone, by the roadside. Physicians were confused by Darci's vehement rejection of their efforts to examine her, and the police were finally summoned to investigate. Confronted with detectives, Darci broke down and confessed, directing searchers to the corpse of Cindy Ray.

Some eighty years ago, arch-chauvinist Rudyard Kipling warned us that the female of the species is more deadly than the male.

Statistically, he may have been mistaken, but the gals are definitely catching up. Nurse Jane Toppan poisoned an estimated 100 patients around the turn of the century, three generations before Donald Harvey bagged 87 in Ohio and Kentucky. The old boy's club of organized crime has yet to produce an Alice Capone, but the shift is probably inevitable, with the likes of Griselda Blanco — self-styled "god-mother" of Miami's cocaine trade and architect of the 1979 Dadeland shopping mall massacre — as a working example. In crime, the sky's the limit.

If our modern feminists possess a single, overriding weakness, it is probably their bent toward viewing sexual equality through rose-colored glasses. Aileen Wuornos isn't *really* a serial killer, we're told, simply a misunderstood rape victim, forced to "defend" herself by flagging down male motorists and blowing their brains out before she rifled their pockets and stole their cars. Female gang members are products of a racist/sexist environment, while their male counterparts are simply... well... a bunch of macho little shits. A sadist like Charlene Gallego, who assists her man in raping, torturing, and killing teenage girls for sport *must* be victim of abuse, since women are incapable of vicious crimes. Case closed.

Or, maybe not.

Before equality becomes reality, we must learn how to take the bitter with the sweet. On any given day in the United States, blacks *do* commit more violent crimes than whites, per capita. Female offenders *are* committing more crimes — and more *violent* crimes — than in years past. Perhaps, at last, equality means kicking back and learning to appreciate the brand-new crop of misfits, much as men have done throughout recorded history. Ma Barker was a sister, after all, and sisterhood is powerful.

Sometimes, in fact, it's powerful enough to blow your head clean off. ●

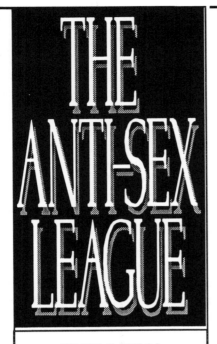

THE ANTI-SEX LEAGUE

THE NEW RULING CLASS
© by Butler Schaffer

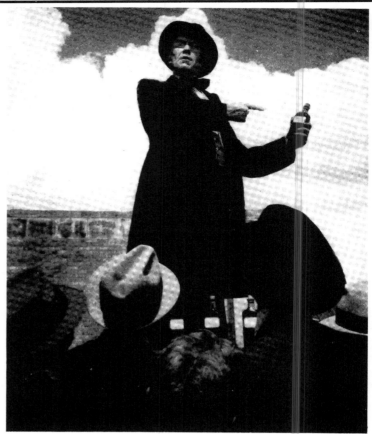

Suppose there has been a major hotel fire, and during the police investigation that occurs afterwards, an unidentified person tells a police officer that he saw you leaving the building with a gasoline can just before the fire began. Because this individual cannot be found, the State — in its prosecution of you for the crime of arson — puts the police officer on the witness stand to testify not to what he saw, but to what this unknown person told him he had seen. Suppose, further, that the court allows this police officer to so testify and, on the strength of his testimony, you are convicted. You appeal your conviction all the way to the United States Supreme Court, and your conviction is upheld, with the court rationalizing the use of such hearsay testimony against you as not being a denial of due process of law. You might find such a decision beyond the realm of what even *this* court might find acceptable in its mission to create a full-blown police state, and yet this is precisely what the Supreme Court held just a short time ago.

You might not have heard much about this decision. Had it arisen out of a criminal trial for arson, or burglary, or murder, the court's opinion might even have shocked the conscience of the *L.A. Times* or the *Orange County Register,* and even engendered a spate of television talk shows or news specials to ponder the course of American justice. But this case involved the crime of child abuse, a sexually defined offense, and, as a consequence, little, if any, criticism was offered. Had a child been kidnapped, and her alleged kidnappers brought to trial and, at the trial, instead of having the kidnap victim testifying against the defendants, a police officer or a social worker was permitted to testify — *in place of the child* — as to what the child told them, there would likely have been a good deal of reaction to such a wholesale attack on the principle that hearsay testimony, the testimony of non-witnesses to the criminal event, ought not be the basis of a criminal conviction. But when a child has allegedly been sexually fondled, the Supreme Court declares that it is prepared to suspend this centuries-old prohibition against hearsay. How "conservative" can a court be when it is willing to throw over such long-standing common law traditions?

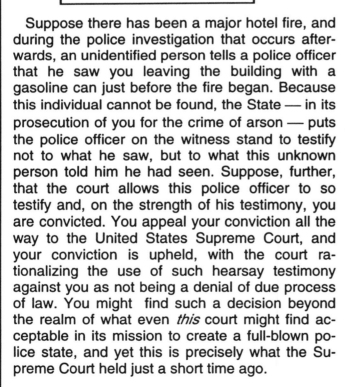

158

First published in 1993 Main Catalog

(Continued next page)

My point is this: had this case involved any crime *other* than a sex crime — murder, burglary, arson, embezzlement, assault — the Supreme Court would not have dared such an assault on the hearsay doctrine. It felt perfectly safe, by contrast, in doing so where the alleged crime involved sex. The Court has apparently sensed the emergence of what Charles Mackay might have defined as the current generation's contribution to the *Extraordinary Popular Delusions and the Madness of Crowds*, that is, the modern "*Anti-Sex League.*" The Anti-Sex League is one of the many phalanxes of the institutional order's continuing war against individual autonomy and non-institutional forms of social organization.

> **The Anti-Sex League is one of the many phalanxes of the institutional order's continuing war against individual autonomy and non-institutional forms of social organization.**

Those who have heard me before are aware of my views regarding institutions. Unlike most Libertarians, I regard institutions, generally, to be incompatible with the self-directed, self-interested nature of human beings. Institutions are those forms of social organization that have become their own reasons for being and, as a consequence, have trained us to accept, in our own thinking, a division between our purposes and institutional purposes. Whether we are considering those more violent institutions known as the state, or the institutions that manipulate our behavior in less coercive ways, they share a common interest in subjecting each of us to their control. Their methods may differ, but the desired result is the same. Thus, schools and churches have helped us condition our minds to be obedient to the state, to be respectful of authority, and to suppress our individual ("selfish") wants for the "greater good" of others! The institutional order in our society has a common enemy: *you* and *me.* If you doubt that this is so, please inform me of any fundamental conflict that has arisen in recent years between the state

and the corporate community, or organized religions, or educational institutions, regarding the role of the individual in an institutionalized world. Please let me know of any instances in which the public schools, or the "Fortune 500," or major church organizations have come to the defense of individual autonomy and a sense of self-purpose in the face of State demands for obedience. The record, I am sorry to report, is in the other direction: when the State announced its "War on Drugs," the schools immediately undertook campaigns to condition the minds of children against drugs, and to subject children to arbitrary searches for any evidence of drugs. At the same time, the parents of these children were being subjected to random drug-testing at their places of employment, and were told that any drug use on their part would be grounds for dismissal. The churches, fearful of any influences (chemical or intellectual) that might alter the thinking of their clientele, began offering moralistic arguments against drug use. And, of course, the news and entertainment industry, those public relations flacks for the institutional order, began grinding out their "news stories" and motion pictures and police shows about the evil nature of drug users, and the selfless, heroic nature of the police officers who battle such forces.

> **In order to get us to overcome our otherwise natural dispositions for personal autonomy, institutions have had to introduce into our thinking the rather pernicious idea that there is a fundamental division between "Good" and "Bad" behavior, between "goodness" and "evil."**

In order to get us to overcome our otherwise natural dispositions for personal autonomy, institutions have had to introduce into our thinking the rather pernicious idea that there is a fundamental division between "Good" and "Bad" behavior, between "goodness" and "evil." Such notions, which go back at least as far as the teachings of Zoroaster, implicitly contain, as a corollary proposition, the idea that there is a fundamental

"goodness" and "evil" within ourselves, and that the inner struggle between these competing forces must, if the "good" side of our selves is to prevail, be undertaken under the direction and control of such external agencies as the Church and State (although, in recent years, the role of *schools* has largely taken over the function of churches in conditioning us into acceptance of such external authority). In order to get us to play this game, we have had to be conditioned to accept our individual sense of purpose, direction, and pleasure as expressions of the "evil" side of our natures. Thus, our individual sense of purpose became equated with selfishness and greed; our personal sense of control became characterized as disobedience (or, in today's more clinical language, hyperactivity); while our sense of individualized pleasure came to be treated as the *self-indulgent* expressions of a "Me Generation."

> **The practitioners of puritanical Pecksniffery have as their underlying motives not so much the betterment of human society, as the improvement of their own sense of self.**

There has been surprisingly little work done, by students of liberty, on the role that guilt plays in the maintenance of systems of social control. To the degree we accept the idea that we have an evil side to our character that must be repressed or controlled, we set ourselves up to be intimidated and manipulated by those anxious to remind us, as well as others, of our short-comings. The more legal and moral restrictions we accept in our lives, the greater the likelihood that we will transgress one standard or another. Not wanting to be held up to either moral or legal condemnation, we have a tendency to restrain the pursuit of our interests. Furthermore, not being comfortable with the constant reminder of our flawed characters, we try to rid ourselves of such feelings by projecting such undesired qualities onto others. Fearful of our own moral shortcomings, we project onto our neighbors those transgressive tendencies we fear within our neighbors' characters and, in so doing,

reduce — for at least a short period of time — our inner discomposure. This is why morally and religiously structured people become such enthusiasts for the reform of *others.* The practitioners of puritanical Pecksniffery have as their underlying motives not so much the betterment of human society, as the improvement of their own sense of self. Self-styled altruists have always been the most dangerous practitioners of self-centered greed! This is also why the quest for individual freedom must always be undertaken within the mind of each individual.

In furtherance of their campaigns to suppress our own sense of individuality, in other words, institutions have had to wage a continuing war against pleasure. What young man — or woman, in this day in which feminists insist on their equal right to die for the glory of the State! — is likely to accept going off to the deserts of Iraq to get his or her head blown off, when more personally pleasurable and self-serving activities are not only available but acceptable alternatives? Thus, the refusal to die for the glory of one's political leaders gets characterized as "cowardice," or "disloyalty," or even "treason," while those who *accept* their State-serving conditioning are labeled as "heroic."

Institutions have had to continually maintain their campaigns against individual autonomy, of course, but there have been times when fundamental transformations in human consciousness have threatened to upset the patterns of thinking upon which their control over us has been based. (This is why, for instance, television newscasters have played such an important part in keeping our minds calmed during critical periods: you will recall when Ronald Reagan was shot, or George Bush became ill in Japan, the TV networks brought out medical doctors with jovial bedside manners to inform us all that "Oh, this is nothing to worry about; why, he'll be up and around in no time." This also helps to explain the attacks leveled against Peter Arnett, one of the few journalists who, during the war with Iraq, did more than simply attend government press briefings. He was offering Americans an alternative to the official State propaganda that the other news people were dutifully reporting as "fact.") When significant threats arise to the consensus definitions of reality — as defined by the institutions, of course — these institutions

(Continued next page)

often respond with frenzied campaigns that intensify violence and human suffering. When the early Christian church was endeavoring to solidify its power under Emperor Constantine, it began destroying competing religions — including what had been one of the more decent and intelligently-based Christian groups, the Gnostics — actions that included the burning of heretical texts. (The same tactics were, of course, used in the early days of both the Soviet Union, against Trotskyites and anarchists, and the United States, against the Tories.) We should also recall how the Bolshevik Revolution was accompanied by some of the most rigid, puritanical restraints on sexual expression. The Marxists have understood what military and church organizations have long known, namely, that the more repressive the institution, the more such institutions must resort to the suppression of any sense of individual identity or purpose in their conscripts.

During the *Age of Science,* when the doctrines of the Catholic Church were called into question by such men as Copernicus, Galileo, and others, the Church began persecuting free-thinking individuals as heretics. And when the Catholic Church was faced with the decentralist influences of the reformation movement, it responded with the bloody, vicious, and depraved practices of the Inquisition to crush, or burn at the stake, those who dared to have an opinion that deviated from that of the institutionalized priesthood. Of course, when these Protestant churches managed to get established, they, too, responded with terrorizing campaigns to root out "witches" and "sorcerers."

American history is also represented in this exercise of tyranny over the human mind and spirit. The institutional order of Massachusetts — left in a state of uncertainty by the restoration of the English monarchy of 1660 (replacing Cromwell's Puritan Commonwealth), as well as the Court of Chancery's 1684 annulment of the Massachusetts Charter (which left land titles in doubt) and restoration of 1689 — responded by trying and hanging "witches." It should be noted, however, that while we are justifiably inclined to regard the Salem witch trials as a dreary episode in American jurisprudence, their persecution of witches did not result in the suspension of hearsay rules of evidence. Current child abuse

cases — which are remarkably parallel to the early witch trial cases — may (according to the U.S. Supreme Court) justify excusing children as witnesses and allowing police officers to testify on their behalf, but the Salem judiciary required child witnesses to testify. Thus, in its own way, Salem jurisprudence was much to be preferred to that now extant in "modern-day" America!

More recently, when the depression and consequences of World War I befell Germany in the 1930s, Adolph Hitler and his Nazi party were able to persuade many, perhaps most, Germans that Jews, gypsies, communists, and homosexuals were to blame, and that only by purifying the Aryan race could Germany reclaim her "greatness" in the world. And when the post-World War II American nation-State was left without any viable "enemies" around which to organize the American public, Senator Joseph McCarthy and the House Un-American Activities Committee helped to identify a threat in the "international communist conspiracy."

Within the past few years, new threats to the rationale for State rule have emerged. With the collapse of the Iron Curtain, Marxism is now perceived as a dead system, its only signs of life remaining in American universities and a few affluent neighborhoods. With its demise, the "International Communist Conspiracy" has also disappeared as a threat around which to justify American State power. Even Keynesianism is dead! Thus, American statists have been engaged in a search for new "enemies." Those on the political left have responded with what I call *Surrogate Socialism:* the environmental, feminist, civil rights, animal rights, consumer rights, and other one-barreled causes (including the newly-emerging "health rights" cause) designed to carry on the same coercive methodologies on which State Socialism has been founded, namely, State direction and control of the lives and property of individuals.

Other "enemies" have been offered up for public consumption, to see which we would find a plausible substitute to rationalize State power: illegal aliens, drugs, and international terrorism being just a few. Of course, some of these "threats" have been elaborated into various police-State programs, including the *"war on drugs,"* that have been used to excuse all kinds

of State viciousness. The manufactured "threat" I wish to focus on here, however, is that which has been found in our *sexual* experiences.

The American culture has long had major hang-ups regarding sex. It is commonplace to blame such attitudes on the Puritan period of American history, but this is grossly unfair. In their own way, the Puritans were far less "puritanical" than many contemporary Americans. Currently, there is no subject that exceeds "sex" as the most frequent topic of radio and television talk shows. From "incest," to "abortion," to "gay and lesbian" issues, to "sexual harassment," to "date rape," to "pornography," and untold variations on the sex theme, such topics are far and away the most popular to be discussed. In Los Angeles alone, there are two radio talk show hosts who focus at least half of their time on the topics of (a) abortion rights and (b) the sex habits of listeners. A good deal of the debate over "politically correct" speech is directed toward sexually based issues and identities. Furthermore, such issues as pornography, child abuse, access to 976 numbers on telephones, even the threat of AIDS — a sexually transmitted disease — have their foundations in sexual behavior and attitudes. Would Magic Johnson have become such an instant folk and media hero had he announced that, instead of having the HIV virus, he was suffering from *emphysema* — an equally life-threatening ailment — and would have to retire from basketball? Johnson has become the latest recruit in the war against pleasure. Gay groups are anxious to have Johnson as an example of how AIDS can be transmitted through heterosexual means, while some moral traditionalists, desirous of having AIDS identified as the product of sexual deviancy and "perversion," have been hinting that Johnson has engaged in homosexual sex. It should be noted that AIDS makes a very potent threat to our ways of thinking, because it combines two of our biggest hang-ups: *sex* and the fear of *death*. The idea that one could contract a life-threatening illness from the enjoyment of behavior that many of us have been conditioned to think of as a "sin," is bound to drive some of us a little crazy! Should the schools be teaching sex education, or handing out condoms... or should they be teaching "traditional American and family values" — whatever on earth *that* may mean, other than

the kinds of sexual attitudes and practices favored by religiously and politically conservative groups? And what about all those X-rated movies, and the behavior of Madonna? And did Governor Clinton, Senator Gary Hart, Jimmy Swaggart, and Jim Bakker *really* engage in sex with the women named in the newspapers? Would Teddy Kennedy's political future have been damaged if there had been no allegation that he had sex with Mary Jo Kopechne just prior to that fateful turn at the bridge?

Other examples of the politicization of sex in our culture are found in laws against prostitution and sodomy, as well as recent campaigns to regulate or prohibit surrogate parenting. Just as laws prohibiting suicide are designed *not* to save lives, but to deny to individuals the sense of self-ownership implicit in having the final decision-making power over the question of taking one's life, legal restraints on reproduction deny yet another basic premise of self-ownership: the decision as to whether to continue one's own genes into yet another generation. In this regard, at least, many feminists have correctly understood the abortion issue as involving this question of self-ownership. On the other hand, the feminists who have opposed the right of women to engage in surrogate parenting (or to pose for *Playboy* or *Hustler* magazines, or to perform in X-rated movies) have denied the only viable philosophic ground on which to base a woman's right to choose to have an abortion, namely, the ownership of one's self.

Along these same lines, any discussion of the Anti-Sex League would be incomplete without reference to such absurd feminist babblers as Andrea Dworkin, who would have us believe that all sex between men and women is *rape*. Such attitudes reflect the depth of the irrationality that attends the war on sex and pleasure. In the interests of time, suffice it to say, in words borrowed from Ayn Rand, that any woman (or man, for that matter) who cannot tell the difference between a *violent* and a *voluntary* act, deserves to find out!

Still, this idea of consensual sex as an offense underlies a number of other issues, including "date rape." When women come forth — months or even years after having engaged in what they had thought was consensual sex — to announce

162

(Continued next page)

that, after having attended a feminist conference, they realized they had been *raped,* there is a rather fundamental flaw in existential thinking being expressed. Perhaps decades of unfocused political babbling, including references to such contradictory notions as "freedom under the law," and "free political systems," have all but obliterated any distinction between *voluntary* and *coercive* practices. "Freedom is Slavery," intoned George Orwell, to which Andrea Dworkin would doubtless add her *"amens"* (or, *"apersons"*).

> **When women come forth — months or even years later after having engaged in what they thought was consensual sex — to announce that, after having attended a feminist conference, they realized they had been *raped,* there is a rather fundamental flaw in existential thinking being expressed.**

The practice of some doctors, lawyers, professors, or employers engaging in consensual sex with their clientele has become a target for State action. That such activities might rise to the level of a breach of contract — or, where children are involved, constitute an *assault* that could be as easily handled as one would any other physical attack — does not seem to be taking care of the problem for anti-sexers. If a doctor, lawyer, professor, or employer had engaged in a joint business venture, or taken a pleasure trip, or gone out to dinner with one of their clients, little objection would probably be raised. But when the equally voluntary, consensual activity has to do with *sex,* no further analysis seems necessary to members of the Anti-Sex League. (As an aside, it is amusing to observe the feminists insisting upon the "right" of women to engage in military combat — whether as fighter pilots, tank commanders, or footsoldiers — on the grounds that women are as capable of fighting and defending themselves as are men. But when these same women are

transported into a classroom or the workplace and are confronted with a seduction proposition or a dirty joke, they suddenly become existential jello, incapable of looking after themselves.)

Just how preoccupied we are with sex has been no better illustrated than in the recent Clarence Thomas and William Kennedy Smith television circuses. Once it was alleged that Clarence Thomas had directed some vulgar sexual remarks to Anita Hill, nothing less than a full-scale televised hearing — one which even resulted in surpassing Saturday morning cartoon shows for audience share! — could assuage the public appetite. Did Clarence really talk to Anita about "Long Dong Silver," and, if he did, would we really want a man like that on the Supreme Court? Did any of you hear the question asked: "If we are going to have a Supreme Court, would we want it composed of people who are so rigid in their sense of propriety that they would never have told a dirty joke, or tried to seduce a sex partner? Do we really want this to be a Rhenquist Court in every sense of the word?"

> **So deeply entrenched are the hangups of so many over sex that... we seem prepared to scuttle notions of due process, as well as our epistemological standards, in service to the eradication of undesirable sexual practices.**

So deeply entrenched are the hang-ups of so many over sex that, as the aforementioned Supreme Court decision reflects, we seem prepared to scuttle notions of due process, as well as our epistemological standards, in service to the eradication of undesirable sexual practices. You may recall that, during the McMartin case, a modern-day travesty of justice, the absence of any evidence (other than confused and contradictory testimony of children that had been induced by interviewing psychologists) to support the charges against the defendants was *not* a cause for concern among the parents who were cheerleading this fiasco: quite the contrary! Their

(Continued next page) **163**

response was "Why would the children lie about something like this?" So utterly irrational, so mindless in the manner of their thinking were so many otherwise intelligent men and women that they accepted this evidentiary evasion as a standard for determining the truthfulness of a proposition. This same irrational practice was engaged in during the Clarence Thomas and the William Kennedy Smith episodes: "Why would Anita Hill, or the alleged victims in the Smith trial, lie about something like this? What do they have to gain? Look how it would damage their reputation to come forth as they did." Suppose I were to say to you that I had been taken aboard a space ship and flown, at the speed of light, to the planet Krypton where I spent a number of days and was returned to Earth. You ask for any evidence of my claim. What if I were to reply: "Why would I lie about something like that? What would I have to gain? Look how it would damage my reputation to come forth with my statement." Would you consider yourself obliged, epistemologically, to accept my allegations?

An intelligently educated man or woman learns more than just assorted facts: he or she learns how to learn, how to distinguish fact from fantasy, a sound idea from an unsound one; how to identify nonsense. What are we to say of the learning of men and women who are prepared to suspend their standards of separating fact and falsehood — if, indeed, they ever had such standards to begin with! — and to accept the complete absence of evidence as a justification for shifting the burden of proof to the listener to refute the unfounded allegation? Would you want to employ a *surgeon* who operated on such premises? If not, why would you want to obtain your "news" from a newscaster who did?

Let me add that, while I do not regard myself duty bound to explain the motives of the women who have made charges against Clarence Thomas or William Kennedy Smith, the idea that there could be no other explanation for such charges than a desire for "Justice" or truth-telling runs counter to yet another manifestation of the anti-sex craze: the eagerness of so many women to identify themselves, publicly, as victims of "incest" or "child abuse" in their pasts. We live in an age in which it is fashionable to be an *injustice collector*, to be seen as a *victim* —

particularly of some *male* wrongdoing. The grocery store tabloids have been replete with stories of entertainers revealing, in some cases for an attractive fee, their own alleged victimization. While I cannot speak for the specific motives of Anita Hill, or the complaining party in the William Kennedy Smith trial, any suggestion that the revelation of such charges is inherently harmful to the women making them simply does not hold up. Anita Hill has since become a quite well-known folk heroine among liberals and feminists. One organization named her its "Person of the Year." Any suggestion that her career has been harmed by making charges against Clarence Thomas is palpably absurd.

> **While I cannot speak for the specific motives of Anita Hill,... any suggestion that the revelation of such charges is inherently harmful to the women making them simply does not hold up. Anita Hill has since become a quite well-known folk heroine among liberals and feminists. One organization named her its "Person of the Year."**

Other intrusions on traditional notions of due process find their origins in reactions to sex. Modern courts take seriously claims to the denial of a "quick and speedy trial" when police officers, charged in the brutal beating of Rodney King, must wait 10 months (while out on bail, of course) for a trial. By contrast, Ray Buckey spent some *5 years* in jail awaiting his trial on child abuse charges (because the court had set bail at such an outrageously high level — in spite of what the Constitution demands — that it could not be met). When he was later found "not guilty" of the preposterous charges against him, the Anti-Sex League offered no remorse for the injustice done to this man, as well as to the rest of the family. "Our system of justice sometimes permits the guilty to go free in order to protect the innocent," was the kind of blame-the-victim

(Continued next page)

rationalizing engaged in by defenders of statist tyranny.

Nor should we overlook the Washington State statute that provides for incarceration of *previously* convicted sex offenders — who had already served their sentences — for "crimes" they might commit in the future. When South Africa, Israel, and the erstwhile Iron Curtain countries engage in such fascist practices known as "preventive detention," there is at least an occasional rumble of philosophic revulsion. I have heard very little opposition to this Washington statute, due, I suspect, to its sex-related application. If previously convicted muggers were rounded up and jailed, for indefinite periods, for crimes they might otherwise commit, I suspect there would be an appropriate reaction from various sectors of society. Should the Washington statute ever be reviewed by the U.S. Supreme Court, I strongly suspect that the thinking of the Rhenquists and Scalias will do nothing to impede its enforcement. After all, the United States Constitution poses a threat to our system of government!

> **The point I wish to get across is not simply that we are allowing standards for intelligent thinking — as well as procedural due process — to be corrupted in such an effortless manner, but that our preoccupation with matters of sex has made it much easier for us to do these things to ourselves.**

The point I wish to get across is not simply that we are allowing standards for intelligent thinking — as well as procedural due process — to be corrupted in such an effortless manner, but that our preoccupation with matters of sex has made it much easier for us to do these things to ourselves. What if Pee Wee Herman had been driving 90 miles per hour down a highway, and caused an accident that killed some people, instead of (as it has been alleged) exposing himself in an adult theater: do you think he would have been summarily dismissed from his television show? One could imagine voices rising to protest such an act of punishment-before-conviction, or even to suggest that there was no connection between the act of driving and how he performed on television. But throw in a charge that he was enjoying himself, physically, in an environment designed for that purpose, and no argument will be advanced on his behalf.

Why should all of this be so? Why should we have such hang-ups over sex that we are prepared to dismiss our standards of justice, of determining truth, as well as presidential and Supreme Court candidates and other entertainers, simply over allegations of sexual enthusiasm? Why do we insist on our being protected from becoming aware that other people are enjoying sex?

> **Much of the current reaction against sex stems, I believe, from an institutional hostility to the pleasure-seeking attitudes of the 1960s.**

Much of the reason, as I suggested earlier, can be traced to the fundamental conflict between institutional and individual needs. If we are to sacrifice ourselves to the purposes of institutions, we need to be continually reminded of the "evil" nature of those practices that are particularly individualistic in nature. Sex is, so I have been told, one of the most intensely enjoyable acts known to human beings. Indeed, what *physical* pleasures can surpass those derived from sex? Furthermore, what acts are more privately engaged in and experienced than acts of sex? Sex is not only the high-water mark of individual pleasure but, as with any kind of pleasure, is something only *individuals* can experience. Pleasure in general, and sex in particular, remind us of our individual natures, and of the fact that only the individual is the carrier and the experiencer of life. *Pleasure,* in other words, is the most personal reminder we have of the fallacy of regarding the *collective* as a thinking or experiencing being.

Much of the current reaction against sex stems, I believe, from an institutional hostility to the pleasure-seeking attitudes of the 1960s. If one needs further evidence of how the pursuit of personal pleasure diminishes one's commitment to institutional causes, one need only look at the interface between men and women of the "60s" generation and the failure of the Vietnam War to sustain the collective enthusiasm of Americans. It is no idle coincidence that the current war on pleasure, including the "war on drugs" and the "anti-sex league" crusades, comes at the same time that the American State has orchestrated a "popular" war in Iraq, including government-run "welcome the returning heroes" parades. The war with Iraq was pure Madison Avenue hype, designed to return the thinking of the American people to the pre-1960s mindset.

I am one who thinks the 1960s were, for the most part, the most significant cultural period of the 20th century America, not so much because of any coherent set of attitudes or ideas that emerged — indeed, I share with George Smith the feeling that this time period was too steeped in reaction against institutions to ever develop a truly alternative culture — but because they reflected the beginnings of a wider skepticism about the institutional order. I have long considered Lenny Bruce to have been the most radical political influence in my time, again, not because of any coherent set of ideas he developed, but because he helped us learn to think and to speak of politicians in four-letter terms. The State, and the rest of the institutional order, depends upon our sanction for its existence, and that sanction depends, in turn, upon our having a sense of reverence and awe for authorities. Indeed, that is what it means to *have* authorities in one's life. When Lenny Bruce stood up in public and referred to presidents and governors and senators in scatological terms, he was performing the 20th century role of the boy who saw that the emperor was naked.

If the spirit of the 1960s was one of the celebration of *pleasure*, that of the 1990s has become one of the celebration of *duty*, *obedience*, and *subservience*. The drug use of the '60s has been replaced by the Draconian "war on drugs;" the "free speech" movement of the '60s has given way to anti-pornography campaigns, as well as attacks upon those few members of the news media who are perceived as being less than enthusiastic tub-thumpers for the established order; the "anti-war" sentiments of the '60s have been replaced by the swinish super-patriotism that oozed forth in the Iraqi slaughter; in place of Lenny Bruce, we have Mark Russell; and of course, that ultimate expression of both individualized and shared pleasure, sex, has been under constant attack from crusaders marching under the banner of the "Anti-Sex League."

Still, I must admit to a sense of optimism for the future. Mankind has suffered through numerous belief systems that put us in conflict with our biological natures, but we have managed to prevail. After all, when *ideology* confronts *biology*, it is always wise to put your money on *biology*.●

166

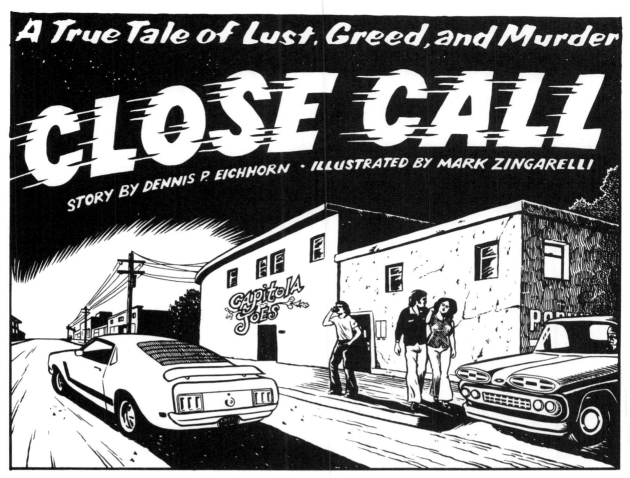

A True Tale of Lust, Greed, and Murder
CLOSE CALL
STORY BY DENNIS P. EICHHORN · ILLUSTRATED BY MARK ZINGARELLI

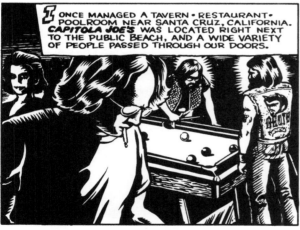

I ONCE MANAGED A TAVERN·RESTAURANT· POOLROOM NEAR SANTA CRUZ, CALIFORNIA. *CAPITOLA JOE'S* WAS LOCATED RIGHT NEXT TO THE PUBLIC BEACH, AND A WIDE VARIETY OF PEOPLE PASSED THROUGH OUR DOORS.

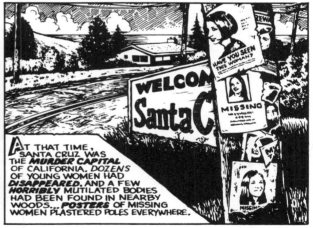

AT THAT TIME, SANTA CRUZ WAS THE *MURDER CAPITAL* OF CALIFORNIA. *DOZENS* OF YOUNG WOMEN HAD *DISAPPEARED*, AND A FEW *HORRIBLY* MUTILATED BODIES HAD BEEN FOUND IN NEARBY WOODS... *POSTERS* OF MISSING WOMEN PLASTERED POLES EVERYWHERE.

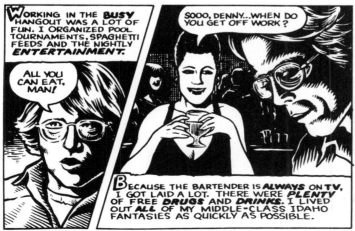

WORKING IN THE *BUSY* HANGOUT WAS A LOT OF FUN. I ORGANIZED POOL TOURNAMENTS, SPAGHETTI FEEDS AND THE NIGHTLY *ENTERTAINMENT*.

ALL YOU CAN EAT, MAN!

SOOO, DENNY...WHEN DO YOU GET OFF WORK?

BECAUSE THE BARTENDER IS *ALWAYS* ON TV, I GOT LAID A LOT. THERE WERE *PLENTY* OF FREE *DRUGS* AND *DRINKS*. I LIVED OUT *ALL* OF MY MIDDLE-CLASS IDAHO FANTASIES AS QUICKLY AS POSSIBLE.

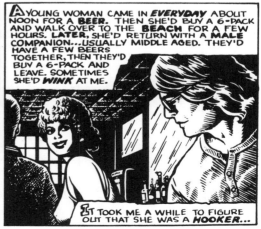

A YOUNG WOMAN CAME IN *EVERYDAY* ABOUT NOON FOR A *BEER*. THEN SHE'D BUY A 6-PACK AND WALK OVER TO THE *BEACH* FOR A FEW HOURS. *LATER*, SHE'D RETURN WITH A *MALE* COMPANION...USUALLY MIDDLE AGED. THEY'D HAVE A FEW BEERS TOGETHER, THEN THEY'D BUY A 6-PACK AND LEAVE. SOMETIMES SHE'D *WINK* AT ME.

IT TOOK ME A WHILE TO FIGURE OUT THAT SHE WAS A *HOOKER*...

First published in 1993 Main Catalog

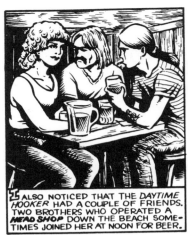

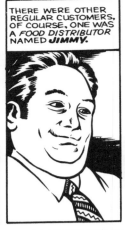
THERE WERE OTHER REGULAR CUSTOMERS, OF COURSE. ONE WAS A *FOOD DISTRIBUTOR* NAMED *JIMMY.*

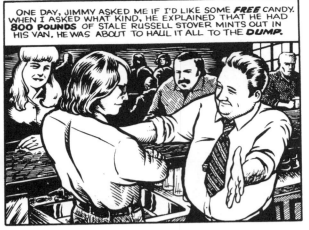
ONE DAY, JIMMY ASKED ME IF I'D LIKE SOME *FREE* CANDY. WHEN I ASKED WHAT KIND, HE EXPLAINED THAT HE HAD *800 POUNDS* OF STALE RUSSELL STOVER MINTS OUT IN HIS VAN. HE WAS ABOUT TO HAUL IT ALL TO THE *DUMP.*

I ALSO NOTICED THAT THE *DAYTIME HOOKER* HAD A COUPLE OF FRIENDS. TWO BROTHERS WHO OPERATED A *HEAD SHOP* DOWN THE BEACH SOMETIMES JOINED HER AT NOON FOR BEER.

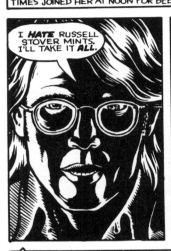
I *HATE* RUSSELL STOVER MINTS. I'LL TAKE IT *ALL.*

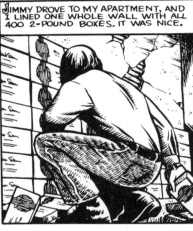
JIMMY DROVE TO MY APARTMENT, AND I LINED ONE WHOLE WALL WITH ALL 400 2-POUND BOXES. IT WAS NICE.

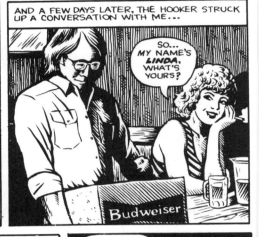
AND A FEW DAYS LATER, THE HOOKER STRUCK UP A CONVERSATION WITH ME...

SO... MY NAME'S *LINDA,* WHAT'S YOURS?

Budweiser

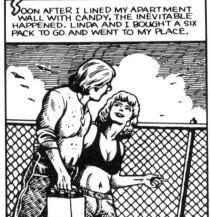
SOON AFTER I LINED MY APARTMENT WALL WITH CANDY, THE INEVITABLE HAPPENED. LINDA AND I BOUGHT A SIX PACK TO GO AND WENT TO MY PLACE.

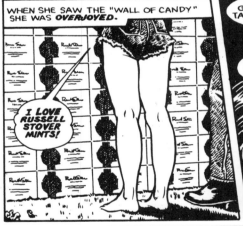
WHEN SHE SAW THE "WALL OF CANDY" SHE WAS *OVERJOYED.*

I LOVE RUSSELL STOVER MINTS!

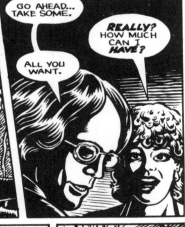
GO AHEAD... TAKE SOME.

ALL YOU WANT.

REALLY? HOW MUCH CAN I *HAVE?*

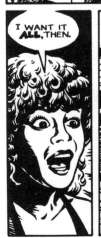
I WANT IT *ALL,* THEN.

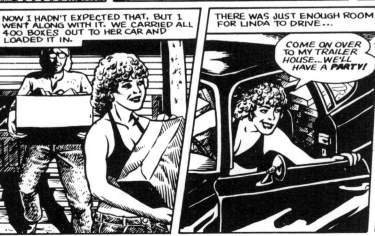
NOW I HADN'T EXPECTED THAT, BUT I WENT ALONG WITH IT. WE CARRIED ALL 400 BOXES OUT TO HER CAR AND LOADED IT IN.

THERE WAS JUST ENOUGH ROOM FOR LINDA TO DRIVE...

COME ON OVER TO MY TRAILER HOUSE...WE'LL HAVE A *PARTY!*

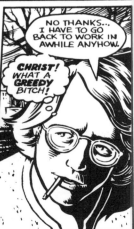
NO THANKS... I HAVE TO GO BACK TO WORK IN AWHILE ANYHOW.

CHRIST! WHAT A *GREEDY* BITCH!

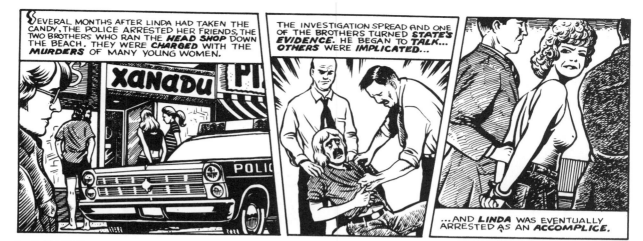

SEVERAL MONTHS AFTER LINDA HAD TAKEN THE CANDY, THE POLICE ARRESTED HER FRIENDS. THE TWO BROTHERS WHO RAN THE **HEAD SHOP** DOWN THE BEACH. THEY WERE **CHARGED** WITH THE **MURDERS** OF MANY YOUNG WOMEN.

THE INVESTIGATION SPREAD AND ONE OF THE BROTHERS TURNED **STATE'S EVIDENCE.** HE BEGAN TO **TALK...** OTHERS WERE **IMPLICATED...**

...AND **LINDA** WAS EVENTUALLY ARRESTED AS AN **ACCOMPLICE.**

THE POLICE SEARCHED LINDA'S TRAILER HOUSE. THEY FOUND **MONEY, DRUGS,** AND SOME **PERSONAL EFFECTS** OF THE **VICTIMS.**

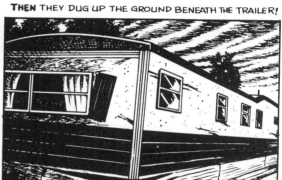

THEN THEY DUG UP THE GROUND BENEATH THE TRAILER!

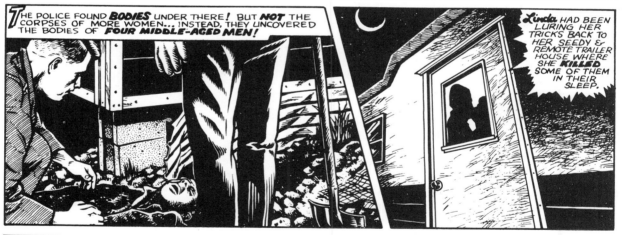

THE POLICE FOUND **BODIES** UNDER THERE! BUT **NOT** THE CORPSES OF MORE WOMEN... INSTEAD, THEY UNCOVERED THE BODIES OF **FOUR MIDDLE-AGED MEN!**

Linda HAD BEEN LURING HER TRICKS BACK TO HER SEEDY & REMOTE TRAILER HOUSE WHERE SHE **KILLED** SOME OF THEM IN THEIR SLEEP.

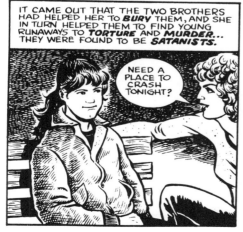

IT CAME OUT THAT THE TWO BROTHERS HAD HELPED HER TO **BURY** THEM, AND SHE IN TURN HELPED THEM TO FIND YOUNG RUNAWAYS TO **TORTURE** AND **MURDER**... THEY WERE FOUND TO BE **SATANISTS.**

NEED A PLACE TO CRASH TONIGHT?

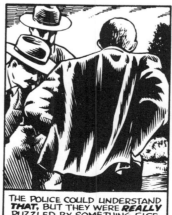

THE POLICE COULD UNDERSTAND **THAT,** BUT THEY WERE **REALLY** PUZZLED BY SOMETHING ELSE.

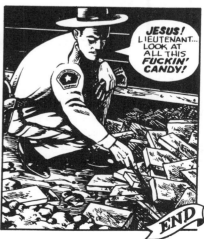

JESUS! LIEUTENANT... LOOK AT ALL THIS **FUCKIN'** CANDY!

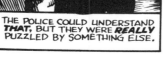

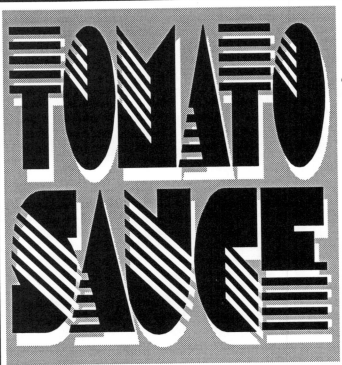

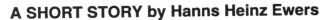

A SHORT STORY by Hanns Heinz Ewers

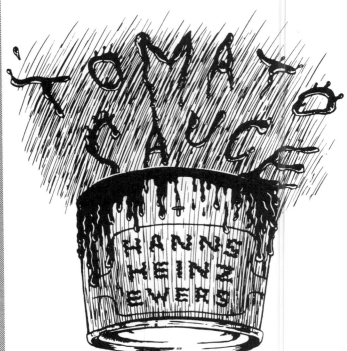

Illustration © 1993 by Brad Johnson

The first time: at the *corrida* five weeks ago, when the black bull of Miura gored little Quitino through the arm —

And again the following Sunday and the Sunday after — I met him at each bullfight. I used to sit in front in order to take a few snapshots; his subscription seat was next to mine. A little man with a round hat and the black smock of an English clergyman. Pale, smooth shaven, with a pair of gold-rimmed spectacles on his nose. And something else, too: he had no eyelashes.

I became aware of him immediately. At the moment when the first bull took the horse upon his horns and the tall *picador* fell clumsily off. The nag jumped up painfully again and cantered away, its body torn open, and its legs entangled in its own entrails, which hung down and dragged in the sand. At the same instant I heard a sigh at my side — a deep sigh of content.

We sat together the entire afternoon, never speaking a word. The pretty play of the *bandilleros* interested him very little. But when the *espada* thrust his blade into the bull's neck, so that the handle rose like a cross above the mighty horns, then he gripped the barrier with both hands and and leaned far over. And the *garocha* — that was the thing he prized most. When the blood squirted from the chest of the horse in a stream as thick as an arm, or when a *chulo* put the

mortally wounded animal out of misery by driving his short dagger into its brain, or when the maddened bull tore a horse's carcass to shreds in the arena, burying his horns in the lifeless mass — then this man softly rubbed his palms together. Once I asked him: "You are a bullfight fan — an *aficionado?*"

He nodded but said no word; he did not want to be disturbed in his enjoyment.

Granada is not a big place, so I soon learned his name. He was the chaplain of the small English colony; his countrymen always called him the "Pope." Apparently he was not held in high regard; nobody had anything to do with him socially.

On Wednesday I visited the cock-fight.

A small amphitheatre, perfectly round, with raised benches. In the center, the arena, directly under the skylight. The reek of the rabble, shouting and spitting — it takes some nerve to enter. Two cocks are brought in, looking like hens, with their combs and tails cut off. They are weighed, then taken from their cages. And they go for each other without a moment's hesitation. The air is full of flying feathers: again and again the two birds fly at each other, mutilating each other with beaks and spurs — without a sound. Only the human beasts around them cry and shout, curse and bet. Ha, the yellow cock has hacked out one of the white one's eyes, snapped it up from the floor and

swallowed it! The heads and necks of the birds, long since plucked bare, sway like snakes above the bodies. Not for a moment do they let go of each other. Their feathers are crimsoned. You hardly recognize their forms any more, as they hack each other to bloody chunks. Now the yellow one has lost both his eyes; he hacks blindly in the air while every second the beak of his rival beats down on his head. At last he sinks down; without resistance, without a sound, he permits the foe to finish his task. Nor is this quickly done; five to six minutes are still needed by the white cock, himself exhausted unto death by a hundred spur-thrusts and bites.

There they sit around, my fellowmen, human beings, all; they laugh at the impotent beak-thrusts of the victor, urging him on and counting each new bite — for the sake of the bets.

At last! Thirty minutes, the allotted time, are spent; the battle is over. One fellow, the owner of the victorious cock, rises; with derisive laughter he slays his opponent's bird with a club: this is his privilege. Now they wash the cocks at the pump and count the wounds in order to settle the bets.

I felt a hand on my shoulder.

"How do you do?" the Pope asked. His watery eyes, without lashes, smiled contentedly behind his large glasses. "You like that, don't you?" he proceeded.

For a moment I did not know whether he was in earnest. His question seemed so utterly and stupidly offensive that I stared at him without answering.

But he misunderstood my silence, took it for consent; so certain was he.

"Yes," he said quietly and very slowly. "This is real satisfaction."

We were pushed apart; they brought new cocks into the arena.

A few days later I was invited to tea by the English Consul. I was punctual, the first guest to arrive. As I greeted him and his old mother, he said:

"I am glad you are early. I want to have a few words with you in private."

"I am entirely at your disposal," I smiled.

The Consul drew his rocking-chair closer and, with strange earnestness, proceeded:

"Far be it from me to dictate to you, my dear sir! But, if it is your intention to remain here longer and to move about generally in society, — as well as in the English colony — I should like to give you some friendly advice."

I was quite curious to hear what he was driving at.

"And your advice?" I asked.

"You have been seen several times in the company of our clergyman — " he continued.

"I beg your pardon!" I interrupted. "I know very little about him. The day before yesterday we exchanged a few words for the first time."

"So much the better!" the Consul replied. "Then I should advise you to shun association with him, at least in public."

"Thank you, Consul," I said. "Would it be indiscreet to ask the reason for this?"

"Of course, I owe you an explanation," he answered, "although I am not so sure that it will satisfy you. The Pope — you know that they have given him this nickname ?"

I nodded.

"Well, then," he proceeded, "the Pope is taboo in society. He attends the bull-fights regularly, — that isn't so bad — he also never misses a single cock-fight; in short, he has tastes which render him impossible among Europeans."

"But, Consul, if, you condemn him so much for this, why do you permit him to retain his unquestionably honorable office?"

"Well, after all, he has been ordained," the old lady volunteered.

"And, besides that," the Consul confirmed, "in all his twenty years here he has never given the slightest tangible reason for complaint. Moreover, the position of clergyman in our tiny community is the worst paid on the entire continent — it would hardly be possible to replace him."

"Then you are satisfied with his sermons, nevertheless," I said, turning to the Consul's mother, making an effort to suppress a malicious smile.

The old lady straightened up in her chair.

"I would never permit him to speak a word of his own in the church," she answered very definitely. "Every Sunday he reads his sermons from Dean Harley's collection."

The answer flustered me somewhat, and I was silent.

"Incidentally," the Consul began once more, "it would be unjust not to mention one of the Pope's good traits. He owns a considerable fortune, and uses his income solely for charitable purposes, while he himself, apart from his passions, lives an extraordinarily modest, even poor, life."

"Nice kind of charity!" His mother interrupted him. "Whom does he assist? Wounded *toreadores* and their families, or even the victim of a *salsa.*"

"A — what?" I asked.

"My mother means a *salsa de tomates,*" the Consul explained.

"Tomato sauce?" I repeated. "The Pope assists the victims of — tomato sauce?"

The Consul laughed briefly. Then he said very seriously:

"Have you never heard of a *salsa?* It is an ancient, horrible custom of Andalusia, which still exists in spite of every punishment by civic and church authorities. Since I have been Consul here, there is proof that a *salsa* has twice taken place. But even in these cases no definite facts were established, in as much as the participants, in spite of the floggings habitual in Spanish prisons, would rather bite off their tongues than reveal even a syllable. Therefore, I could only give you a vague, possibly false, report; make the Pope tell you, if the horrible secret interests you. For he — in spite of the fact that nobody can prove it — is said to be an adherent of this awful custom, and it is particularly this suspicion which causes us to shun him."

A few guests entered; our conversation was interrupted.

When I went to the bull-fights the following Sunday, I brought along a few particularly good snapshots of the last *corrida* for the Pope. I wanted to make him a present of them, but he hardly looked at them.

"Forgive me," he said, "but they do not interest me at all."

I looked puzzled.

"Oh, I did not mean to offend you!" he proceeded. "You see, it is only the redness, the redness of blood which I care for."

It sounded almost poetic the way this pale ascetic said: "The redness of blood!"

At any rate, we entered into a discussion. And, in the midst of it, I said without warning: "I would like to see a *salsa*. Won't you take me with you some time?"

He was silent. The pale, cracked lips trembled.

Then he asked: "A *salsa?* — Do you know what that is?"

I lied. "Of course!"

Again he stared at me. Then his eyes fell on the old scars of student duels on my cheek and forehead.

And, as if these signs of childish blood-shedding were a secret passport, he stroked them softly with his finger and said solemnly:

"I will take you with me."

A few weeks later, one evening about nine o'clock, there was a knock at my door. Before I could say: "Come in!" the Pope entered.

"I have come to fetch you," he said.

"What for?" I asked.

"You know," he answered. "Are you ready?"

I rose.

"In a minute!" I cried. "Will you have a cigar?"

"Thank you. I don't smoke."

"A glass of wine?"

"No, thanks. I do not drink either. Please hurry."

I took my hat and followed him down the stairs into the moonlit night. Silently we walked through the streets, along the Genil, under pyrrhus-trees in red bloom. We turned to the left, ascended the Moor mountain and crossed the Field of the Martyrs. In front of us glowed, in warm silver, the snow-capped mountains of the Sierra; round about on the hills, fires shone from the caves where the gypsies and other vagabonds live. We circled the deep valley of the Alhambra, filled almost to the brim with a sea of green elms; then through the avenue of age-old cypresses towards the Generalife; and still higher up the mountain, from the top of which the last prince of the Moors, the fair-haired Boabdil, sent his farewell sighs down to lost Granada.

I looked at my strange companion. His glance, turned inward, saw nothing of the glory of this night. As the moonlight played over those small, bloodless lips, upon those sunken cheeks and the deep hollows in the temples, a feeling as if I had known this gruesome ascetic for ages overcame me. And

(Continued next page)

suddenly, like a flash, the solution came: this was the face which the fearful Zurbaran gave to his ecstatic monks!

Now the way led through broad-leaved agaves, which lifted the wooden stems of their blossoms the height of three men into the air. We heard the Darro roar as it leaped down the cliffs beyond the mountain.

Three men in brown, tattered coats approached us; already from afar they saluted my companion.

"Guards," the Pope said. "Wait here. I shall talk to them!"

He approached the men, who apparently had been expecting him. I could not understand what they said, but obviously it was about me. One of the men gesticulated vehemently, looked suspiciously at me, threw his arms in the air and shouted again and again: *"Ojo el caballero!"* But the Pope quieted him. Finally he motioned me to come closer.

"Sea Usted bienvenido, caballero!" He saluted me and doffed his hat. The two other guards remained at their post; the third one accompanied us.

"He is the patron; the manager, so to speak, of the affair," the Pope explained.

A few paces ahead we reached one of the cave dwellings, distinguished in no way from the hundreds of others along the slopes of Granada. In front of the door-hole, as usual, there was a small, leveled spot, surrounded by dense cactus hedges. There about twenty ruffians stood around, but there was no gypsy among them. In one corner burned a small fire between two stones; above it hung a kettle.

The Pope reached into his pocket and took out one *duro* after the other, which he turned over to our companion.

"These people are so suspicious," he said, "they take nothing but silver."

The Andalusian crouched down by the fire and examined each single coin. He rang them on a stone and bit them with his teeth. Then he counted them — one hundred *pesetas* in all.

"Shall I give him some money as well?" I asked.

"No," said, the Pope. "You'd better do some betting; that will give you a safer standing with these people."

I did not understand him.

"Safer standing?" I repeated. "How so?"

The Pope smiled.

"Oh — by betting you come down nearer to their level and make yourself more equally guilty with them."

"Tell me, Reverend," I exclaimed, "how is it, then, that you do not bet?"

He met my glance firmly and replied carelessly:

"I? I never bet! Betting detracts from the pure joy of watching."

In the meantime, another half dozen suspicious-looking individuals had arrived, all of them shrouded in the inevitable brown cloth which serves the Andalusians for a cloak.

"What are we waiting for?" I asked one of the men.

"For the moon, *caballero,"* he replied. "It must set first."

Then he ordered me a big glass of *aguardiente.* I declined, but the Englishman pressed the glass into my hand.

"Drink! Drink!" he insisted. "It is the first time for you — you may need it."

The others, too, partook of the liquor. However, they made no noise; only hasty whispers and hoarse murmurs penetrated the night. As the moon sank in the northwest behind the Cortadura, they fetched long pitch torches from the cave and lit them. Then they built a small stone circle in the middle; this was the arena. Around this circle they dug holes in the ground and affixed the torches. And, in the red gleam of the flames, two men began to undress; they kept only their leather breeches on. Then they sat down opposite each other and crossed their legs in Oriental fashion. It was only now that I noticed two strong horizontal beams sunk into the ground, each one of which carried two solid iron rings.

Between these two rings the two men had taken their places. Somebody ran into the cave and brought out a few lengths of heavy rope which they wound around the bodies and legs of the two, binding each one to the rings. They were fixed as in a vise; only the upper parts of their bodies could they move freely.

They sat without a word, sucking at their cigarettes and emptying the liquor glasses which were filled for them again and again. Clearly they were both quite drunk by this time, their eyes fixed stupidly on the ground. And all around them, in the circle of smoking torches, the other men settled down.

Suddenly I heard an ugly screeching behind my back which almost burst my eardrums. I turned around; somebody was carefully sharpening a small

navajo on a round grinding stone. He tested the knife with the nail of his thumb, put it aside and took another one.

I turned to the Pope.

"This *salsa* is a kind of — duel?"

"Duel?" he replied. "Oh no. It is a kind of cock-fight."

"What?" I exclaimed. "And why do these men engage in this cock-fight? Have they offended each other or is it jealousy?"

"Not at all," the Englishman answered quietly. "They have no reason at all. Perhaps they are the best of friends; perhaps they don't even know each other. They only want to prove their — courage. They want to show that they are no worse than the bulls and cocks."

His ugly lips essayed a wry smile as he proceeded:

"Something like your German student duels."

Abroad, I am always a patriot. That much I have learned from the English: right or wrong — my country!

Therefore I answered him rather sharply:

"Reverend, the comparison is ludicrous! That is something which you cannot judge."

"Perhaps," said the Pope. "But I have seen many a fine duel in Goettingen. Lots of blood; lots of blood —"

In the meantime the manager had selected a seat next to us. He pulled a dirty notebook and a small pencil from his pocket.

"Who bets on Bombita?" he cried.

"I!" — "One *peseta!*" — "Two *duros!*" — "No, I'm going to back Lagartijillo!" The drunken voices intermingled.

The Pope grabbed my arm.

"Arrange your bets so that you lose either way," he said. "Give them long odds; you cannot be too careful with this crowd."

So I took quite a number of the bets offered, and always at odds of three to one. Since I bet on both of them, I had to lose necessarily. While the manager was noting down all the bets in clumsy symbols, the sharpened *navajos* were handed round. The blades were about two inches long. Then they were shut, and passed to the two combatants.

"Which one do you want, Bombita Chico, my little cock?" The sharpener laughed.

"Let me have it! No matter which!" grunted the drunkard.

"I want my own knife!" shouted Lagartijillo.

"Then give me mine! It's better anyway!" croaked the other.

All bets were entered. The manager saw that each man was given another huge glass of *aguardiente,* which he emptied in one gulp. Both threw their cigarettes away. Then each one was given a long red woolen scarf, a hip girdle, which he tied around the lower left arm and hand.

"You may start, boys!" the manager shouted. "Open the knives."

The blades of the *navajos* snapped open with a click and remained fixed. A shrill, unpleasant sound. But the two men remained absolutely quiet; neither one made a movement.

"Begin, my little cocks!" repeated the manager.

But the battlers sat motionless; they did not stir. The Andalusians became impatient.

"Get him, Bombita, my young bull! Push your little horns into his body!"

"Ah — you want to be cocks? You are hens! Hens!"

And the chorus howled: "Hens! Hens! Why don't you lay eggs? You hens, you!"

Bombita Chico stretched himself and made a thrust at his adversary. The other lifted his left arm and caught the lazy thrust in his scarf. The two men were apparently so drunk that they could hardly control their movements.

"Wait! Wait!" the Pope whispered. "Wait until they see blood!"

The Andalusians never stopped baiting the two; first with good-natured raillery and then with biting scorn. And again and again they hissed in their ears.

"You are hens! Go lay eggs! Hens! Hens!"

Now they both thrust at each other, almost blindly. The next minute one of them received a small wound in his left shoulder.

(Continued next page)

"Bravo, darling! Bravo, Bombita! Show him, my little cock, that you have spurs!"

They paused a moment, and with their left arms wiped the dirty sweat from their faces.

"Water!" shouted Lagartijillo.

A large decanter was handed over and they drank thirstily. One could see how they sobered up. The dull glances became sharp, piercing. Hatefully they stared at each other.

"Are you ready, you hen?" asked the little one.

Instead of answering the other lunged forward and cut his cheek open for its entire length. The blood streamed down over the naked body.

"Ah, it begins — it begins," the Pope murmured.

The Andalusians were silent. Greedily they followed the movements of the one whom they had backed with their money. And the two human beings lunged and thrust —

The shining blades flashed like silver sparks through the red gleam of the torches and bit into the woolen guards on the left arms. A big drop of boiling pitch from one of the torches fell upon the chest of one of the men. He did not even notice it.

So rapidly did they flail their arms about in the air that it was impossible to see when one had struck home. Only the bloody rivulets all over the bodies testified to the growing number of cuts and gashes.

"Halt! Halt!" cried the patron. The men refused to stop. "Halt!" he cried once more. "Bombita's blade is broken!"

Two Andalusians rushed up, took an old door on which they had been sitting and ruthlessly threw it between the battlers, standing it on end so that the two could no longer see each other.

"Give me your knives, little beasts!" the patron shouted. The two obeyed willingly. His sharp eye had seen correctly; Bombita's knife was broken in half. He had sliced his opponent's ear and against the hard bone of the skull the blade had broken off.

Each one was given another glass of liquor, a new knife, and the door was taken away.

And this time they went for each other like two cocks, without thinking; blind with rage, stab for stab —

The brown bodies became crimson; the blood gushed from dozens of wounds. From the forehead of little Bombita a brown strip of skin hung down; moist wisps of hair licked the wound. While his knife caught in the enemy's bandage, the latter dug his knife twice, three times, deep into his neck.

"Take off your bandage, if you have the courage!" the little one shrieked, as he bore off his own with his teeth.

Lagartijillo hesitated for a moment, then followed suit. Automatically they still parried as before with their left arms, which were soon cut to shreds.

Again one of the blades snapped. Again the old door separated them. Again they got liquor and new knives.

"Stab him, Lagartijillo, my strong bull. Stab him!" one of the men shouted. "Tear the bowels out of the old horse!"

Unexpectedly Lagartijillo, at the very moment when the door was whisked away, gave his adversary a fearful thrust in the belly from below, and drew the blade sharply upward and sideways. A horrible mess of entrails crawled from the huge wound. And then, he stabbed once more from above, quick as lightning, and severed the big vein that nourishes the arm.

Bombita shrieked and doubled up while a stream of blood as thick as an arm gushed from the wound right into the other's face. It seemed as if he must topple over, utterly exhausted; but suddenly he rose once more, expanding his broad chest, raised his arm and lunged at his enemy who was blinded by blood. And he struck him, between two ribs, right in the heart.

Lagartijillo beat the air with both arms; the knife fell from his hand. Lifeless, the huge body fell forward over its own legs.

And, as if this sight gave new strength to the dying Bombita, whose blood squirted in a horrible stream over his enemy, he stabbed like a madman time and again, thrusting the lusty steel into the blood-soaked back.

"Stop! Bombita, my little brave, you have conquered!" the patron said quietly.

Then came the most horrible thing of all. Bombita Chico, whose life-blood already covered the beaten man in a shroud of red, leaned with both hands upon the ground and lifted himself high; so high that from the wide gash in his body the yellow entrails crawled like a brood of loathsome snakes. He stretched his neck, lifted his head and, through the deep silence of the night, sounded his triumphant:

"Cock-a-doodle-doo!"

Then he sank down. This was his dying salute to life.

It was as if a red mist of blood had suddenly enveloped my senses. I saw and heard no more. I sank into a purple, fathomless sea. Blood gushed into my ears and nose. I wanted to shout, but, when I opened my mouth, it filled with thick warm blood. I almost suffocated — but worse, much worse, was this sweet, obnoxious taste of blood upon my tongue. Then I felt a stabbing pain somewhere; but it took an eternity till I recognized the cause of the pain. I was biting on something, and it was the thing which I was biting that hurt me so. With an immense effort I wrenched my teeth apart.

When I took my finger from my mouth, I awoke. During the battle I had gnawed off my fingernail down to the root, and now I had bitten into the quick.

The Andalusian touched my knee. "Do you want to settle your bets, Caballero?" he asked. I nodded. Then he figured out in many words what I had lost and won. All the spectators pressed around us; no one bothered about the corpses.

First, the money! The money!

I gave the fellow a handful of coins and asked him to settle for me. He figured it out, and in a hoarse voice arranged matters with everyone.

"Not enough, caballero!" he said at last. I realized that he was cheating me, but I only asked how much more I had to pay and gave him the money.

When he saw that I still had some in my pocket, he asked: "Caballero, don't you want to buy Bombita's knife? It brings luck — much luck!"

I bought the navajo for a ridiculous price. The Andalusian shoved it into my pocket.

Now nobody paid attention to me any longer. I rose, and staggered out into the night. My forefinger hurt; I wound my handkerchief around it. In long, deep draughts I drank in the fresh night air.

"Caballero!" somebody shouted. "Caballero!" I turned. One of the men came towards me. "The patron sends me, caballero," he said. "Don't you want to take your friend home with you ?"

Oh, yes — the Pope, the Pope! During all this time I hadn't seen anything, hadn't thought of anything.

I turned back again, passed through the cactus hedge. The shackled, bloody corpses were still on the ground. And over them bent the Pope, stroking with caressing hands the pitifully torn bodies. But I saw clearly that he did not touch the blood. Oh no! only in the air his hands moved to and fro.

And I saw that they were the delicate, fine hands of a woman.

His lips moved. "Beautiful salsa," he whispered, "beautiful red tomato sauce!"

They had to tear him away by force; he did not want to give up the sight. He stammered and tottered uncertainly around on his thin legs.

"Too much booze!" one of the men said. But I knew: he had not touched one drop.

The patron took off his hat and the others followed his example.

"Vayan Ustedes con dios, caballeros!" they said.

When we reached the main road, the Pope followed me obediently. He took my arm and murmured:

"Oh, so much blood! So much beautiful blood!"

He clung to me like so much lead. Painfully I dragged the drunken man towards the Alhambra. Under the Tower of the Princesses we stopped and sat down on a stone.

After a long while he said slowly:

"Oh, life! What wonderful things life gives us! It is a joy to live!"

An icy night wind wetted our temples. I shuddered. I could hear the Pope's teeth chattering; slowly his blood-intoxication evaporated.

"Shall we go, Reverend?" I asked.

Again I offered my arm.

He declined.

Silently we descended towards sleeping Granada.

About the Author:

Hanns Heinz Ewers (1871-1943) was a strange figure mostly known for weird short stories of the ultra-cruel. "Tomato Sauce" was originally published in the 1920s. It is reprinted here from the Valcour & Krueger collection BLOOD, which was privately printed in 1977. ●●●

The WAR ON DRUGS is Perfectly NORML

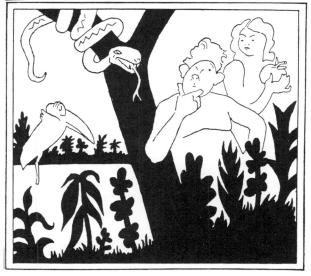

© 1993 by **Jim Hogshire**

When they came for the Fourth Amendment I didn't say anything because I had nothing to hide.

When they came for the Second Amendment I didn't say anything because I wasn't a gun owner.

When they came for the Fifth and Sixth Amendments I didn't say anything because I had committed no crimes.

When they came for the First Amendment I couldn't say anything.

● ● ● ● ● ● ● ●

When we bemoan the horrors of the War on Drugs we always speak of how the Constitution "is being ripped to shreds." But even as we say these words we don't seem to comprehend just what this means. We just say it, and then, having said it (among friends, of course) we go back to demanding our cable TV rates be lowered.

The truth is, our rights are not being "eroded." Most have already been eliminated. And just like the above epigram suggests, your right to say so will be the last thing to go. When they start telling your what to say and how to thing, you'll know it's all over. Sadly, that is what's happening now. The ever-powerful police state has modified its laws to the point where it is downright profitable to go hunting citizen/suspects — someone who is growing even one marijuana plant, "loitering" too long in a single area, selling "paraphernalia," or saying the wrong things. The general acceptance of the police state has paved the way for the "War on Drugs" to expand — to porno dealers, religious groups, gun owners, foreigners, and "troublemakers" of every stripe.

This could never have happened without a stunning lack of resistance by the people — especially those who consider themselves at the forefront of the Drug War Resistance. We "resisters" have allowed ourselves to be stratified and fragmented to the point where nearly everyone — no matter how supposedly radical — agrees with at least some of the government's oppression. Pro-hemp people are among the worst offenders with their explicit pleas to allow the government to "regulate and tax" hemp. Faux pro-drug luminaries like Terrence McKenna (*Food of the Gods*, etc.) go a little further in advocating more use of psychedelic drugs, but would still outlaw opiates and cocaine — since these are "hard drugs." It might also be that these folks don't happen to like coke or smack too much and are thus willing to send their fellow man to jail in the hope that *their* particular drug will get the government's nod. But the government only reluctantly gives the slightest of nods to MDs and others with the proper credentials.

So far we have managed to believe that the various outrages (warrantless searches, asset forfeiture, preventive detention, military troops enforcing civilian laws, etc. ad nauseum) are temporary aberrations. Somehow we make ourselves believe reason will overcome this madness before it goes too far. Or maybe we each think it would never get around to us — after all, *I'm not doing any harm.* How could the police possibly be interested in me? Well, they are interested in you — and have demonstrated this time and again by compiling huge databases made up of information on nearly every citizen who owns a telephone.

First published in 1993 Main Catalog

(Continued next page) **177**

> *"Fighting drugs" has given our government just the excuse they need to send troops to foreign countries and to police our borders and even our cities.*

The War on Drugs was never meant to alter anyone's drug use — it was a money and power scam from the start. "Fighting drugs" has given our government just the excuse they need to send troops to foreign countries and to police our borders and even our cities. The litany of atrocities is long and runs the gamut from wholesale human sacrifices overseas, to the theft of a few hundred dollars from a guy in an air-port who can't immediately prove it wasn't earned illegally.

And now they have come for the First Amendment.

A gardening supply shop just handed over $100,000 to the government rather than prove it was not involved in a conspiracy to grow marijuana because it had placed ads for grow lights in two magazines. A famous author is forced to use a pen name on his latest books because his real name is too associated with drugs and book dealers often refuse to carry any book that can be construed as promoting drug use. Even the word "marijuana" has caused a gardening book to be taken off the shelves in fear of the cops raiding, then seizing the whole store.

When cops in Indiana ran out of names gleaned from confiscated garden supply store customer lists and busted every hydroponic gardener they could, they set up their own hydroponics equipment stores, charged low prices, then calmly talked with customers while copying down names and license plate numbers. The monetary gains from this operation were measly, but the number of people going to prison and the fear injected into the community as a whole must have been worth it.

The War on Drugs has been highly successful in cowing the population, and increases its control every day. Once again, what is most disturbing is the complicity of the people. From turn-in-your-parents campaigns to NORML's obsequious "legalize, then tax and regulate!" proposals, to the idea that even marijuana should be illegal if it exceeds a certain arbitrary quantity, even "libertarian" types are tripping over themselves to help the cops. When we are not busy validating portions of the government's propaganda in the vain hope that we will be spared a pitiful ounce of weed, the rest of us are silent.

Today we live in a culture of fear and distrust, a culture that has taken fewer than ten years to create. The use of asset forfeiture laws was not very commonplace until after 1985. And the assault on speech only began in the last four years or so.

First, there is operation Green Merchant (it still continues, after collecting billions of dollars and destroying countless lives). In 1987, Ed Rosenthal first wrote with awe of some of America's pioneer indoor pot farms. Yet, he may not have realized that even thought he and his fellow pot-smokers had moved indoors, they were still in harm's way. After all, at that time the courts still recognized some modicum of privacy rights (helicopters were not allowed to hover just above a person's house taking infra-red pictures without a warrant, for instance). But by the end of 1988, nearly every state had mimicked federal statutes that not only relaxed the standards for probable cause but also increased the powers of search and seizure.

> *What is asset forfeiture? Basically it's this: The state seizes property under what they term "probable cause" and then keeps it, claiming it now belongs to the state...*

These last laws have come to be known under the heading of "asset forfeiture" and although they have been used vigorously in every state for at least the last five years many people still express shock that such a thing is legal. What is asset forfeiture? Basically it's this: The state seizes property under what they term "probable cause" and then keeps it, claiming it now belongs to the state because of a legal doctrine known as "relation back." Relation back says that once any thing, be it cash, car, or bass boat is used in an illegal way, it belongs to the state from that moment on. Thus if you lend your car to someone who uses it to bring drugs to a friend, the car is no longer yours. This is true even if the crime goes undetected for some time afterward. That car

(Continued next page)

belongs to the state and if it ever alleges that a crime took place in it, it can take possession of it.

This legal doctrine is not new; it harkens back to the Inquisition when those accused of heresy by the Church lost their property — half to the Church, half to the local secular official.

Normally, especially if the case is weak, the authorities will tell you to kiss your property goodbye or face prosecution. With the maximum penalties we have all voted for (or at least kept silent about) who wants to go to court? Most people just grind their teeth and let the government keep everything. One wonders what sort of marijuana tax could possibly compete with this as a source of revenue?

> *You can get your property back. You merely have to prove to a civil court by "a preponderance of evidence" that the state is wrong in its suspicion that the property was used in a crime.*

You *can* get your property back. You merely have to prove to a civil court by "a preponderance of evidence" that the state is wrong in its suspicion that the property was used in a crime. Now the burden of proof is shifted to the defendant, and it is a difficult burden to boot. Preponderance of evidence constitutes 51% or more (in the judge's opinion) of the evidence. Probable cause requires only suspicion. Thus, the state takes by probable cause, then requires a higher standard of proof from you, the ex-owner, to get it back.

Yes, this is the exact reverse of the doctrine of "innocent until proven guilty." But they get away with it because no human is charged with any crime. The case is against the confiscated property. That's why you see cases such as The State of California vs. $5,000 cash. You see, property doesn't have as many rights as people. Even if you are acquitted of any crime, your car, cash or bass boat will still have to prove its innocence.

By the way, this is nothing new either. This legal fiction harkens back to at least the 12th Century when a kettle was once tried for murder after it fell off a shelf on someone's head and killed him.

Obviously, this has made for some easy pickin's for state cops who often get into humorous court battles with each other over which jurisdiction gets how much seized property and bank accounts. It also invites the government to play even faster and looser with any "rights" Joe Citizen might have left. Thus, we have "paraphernalia laws" that are sporadically enforced to scare off certain people or to drum up some quick money. Paraphernalia laws spawned still others that make it illegal to even talk about drugs in such a way as could be construed as "promoting their use and or manufacture." The Analog Substance Act has even made certain compounds illegal that haven't yet been made or used by anyone. Indeed, these drugs exist only in theory. This last bit is truly a new twist on legal reality. Even the harshest medieval minds concerned themselves only with things generally recognized as real and did not make that which did not exist illegal.

Now, search warrants issued on phoned-in "anonymous tips," "pre-trial detention" based on a prosecutor's allegation, probable cause based on "profiles" that include several million people, are all commonplace. Things that didn't used to be illegal are now felonies. In some states it is a crime to have prescription drugs stored in anything but their original container. At least one dissenting judge noted this made a pill illegal for the time it took to remove it from the bottle and swallow it.

> *The War on Drugs brought us our first true thought crime when it introduced the idea of a conspiracy of just one person.*

The War on Drugs brought us our first true thought crime when it introduced the idea of a *conspiracy of just one person.* Unlike any other federal conspiracy charge, the War on Drugs does not require you to do a single thing in furtherance of your conspiracy. In other words, if you consider selling drugs — that is itself a crime. For any other crime you have to *do something*. Today we are seeing the first cases where speech — the transfer of information — has become illegal. If someone asks you how to grow marijuana, you will be guilty of a crime if you tell him.

Good thing for me I don't smoke pot, huh? Hope nobody asks me how to forge a prescription. Or decides ephedrine is an analogue of speed. Or

(Continued next page) **179**

decides a novel I write inspires thoughts contrary to the State's interests. This is the application of "thought crime" and nothing less. To police our thoughts, the cops keep extensive files on anybody, and everybody.

In some states, each and every prescription filled is noted by a computer and kept in an enormous database. When, in the computer's estimation, something appears "suspicious," the cops are dispatched to investigate — if not make an arrest. In Ohio, cops don't leave such crucial decisions up to a computer. There, the police have free access to any pharmacy's records and are allowed to even store this information at various police stations. And urine testing has subjected the majority of Americans to lifestyle investigations by almost anyone. Scrutinizing pee yields all kinds of information about a person besides "drug use."

Each and every person traveling on an airplane is now noted by law enforcement agencies, and even small bank transactions are reported to the government. Police databases now make available extensive information on any citizen.

So far, our attempts at solutions to this problem have been utter failures. I think that's because they rest on asking the system to change itself in a way that is clearly not in the interest of the system at all. All this is due to our silence and bleating for mercy. And Big Brother loves bleating sheep. He loves the sheep who agree there is such a thing as a "hate crime," the sheep who believe there are such things as "hard drugs" or drugs that "really should be controlled" or that certain religious outlooks aren't "real churches." And of course he loves the majority of sheep who are willing to part with "some of their rights" and convince themselves they won't regret it.

> *The pro-hemp sheep are perhaps the worst of all. They have been suckered into arguing for marijuana legalization on the basis of its value as an agricultural crop!*

The pro-hemp sheep are perhaps the worst of all. They have even been suckered into arguing for marijuana legalization on the basis of its value as an agricultural crop! About the only use for marijuana *not* mentioned by pro-hempists these days is that you can get high from it! Pro-hemp sheep love to tell stories about how the Founding Fathers wrote our Declaration of Independence on hemp paper. Some even go so far as to say that hemp can *save the world.* Please master, if you let us have our hemp, we'll back up the rest of your oppression. Here, you can even tax it, if you want.

But could the government ever expect to make as much money off taxation as it already does with asset forfeiture? In a world where a police dog "alerting" on a stack of cash results in a jackpot, or possession of any amount of drugs costs you your house, is this supposed to lure them into legalizing pot — the chance to regulate at a lower profit than which they already regulate?

> **High Times** *now "hates heroin, alcohol, speed and cocaine" according to a* USA Today *interview with* High Times *editor Steve Hagar.*

I know this is counter-culture heresy, but the fact is, no group has been more complacent about the War on Drugs than the pro-marijuana smokers. For all their self-righteous jabbering about freedom, they do little to secure it. They buy 90% of the government's anti-drug line and heartily condemn users of any other drugs. *High Times* now "hates heroin, alcohol, speed and cocaine" according to a *USA Today* interview with *High Times* editor Steve Hagar. "Now the only articles about heroin or cocaine you'll find in *High Times* will tell you where to get treatment," he says. Once a million circulation magazine devoted to all types of drug exploration, the magazine now essentially agrees with the Drug Warriors that coke and "crack" are scourges.

In return, *High Times* has suffered a concerted and sustained program of harassment by the DEA, which systematically drives away its advertisers and subjects it to threats of prosecution. But its hypocrisy remains transparent — some of their largest advertisers are companies that sell ephendrine and caffeine pills as fake speed. Both of these drugs, especially ephedrine, can be fatal in relatively small doses.

Some articles suggest *High Times* has come completely under DEA control when they run articles that teach growers to do their best to grow as little as

(Continued next page)

possible so, if busted, they won't be charged with dealing and face stiffer penalties. "If you grow, make sure you know the rules of the game," one article ends, "and play the game accordingly." Is this the magazine that published *The Encyclopedia of Recreational Drugs?* Advice on how to "play the game?"

Al Capone would be ashamed.

At least the coke dealers resist. They shoot back at governments that shoot at them. They put prices on judges' heads, they blow away cops and spring their pals from prison. In our country, no one fears a sheep with a grow light and a marijuana seedling. What is feared is physical abuse and death. This has been the punishment for people with nothing to confiscate for years. As a result, in areas where the punishment is not asset forfeiture, but incarceration, the Drug War really is fought with guns. Mostly this is in the inner city and on a few rural pot plantations. The propaganda has so far been able to hornswoggle us with the lies of "instantly addicting crack," PCP giving someone the strength of ten men, and the general fear of colored people at home and abroad.

The fear of the "Other" has led us to seriously limit firearms (semi-automatic weapons are supposedly favored by drug dealers when, in fact, they are most-favored by police departments), endorse pre-trial detention and the U.S. Army enforcing civilian laws (when will we have forced billeting of soldiers?). Oh, save us from those dark-skinned foreign druglords! We have now allowed our government to adopt truly fascistic "crime packages" that include the death penalty for destruction of government property, mandatory life sentences for small amounts of this or that substance and general mistreatment for anyone deemed a "kingpin" — an elastic definition which seems to mean "anyone accused of having drugs."

Before it's completely illegal, I would like to remind everyone that tyrants don't get disposed of by rational arguments or deal-making. In the end, it must become unprofitable and uncomfortable for The Establishment to continue to wage their Drug War. To this end it is obvious that mere talk is not enough (but, by all means SPEAK OUT — without that all is lost) but action is required. The simplest means of action is to turn the monster on its creators.

As the drug warriors become increasingly rapacious, as their SWAT teams blow away more and more innocent people, the public's perception of them is going to sour. So one of the best ways to fight the oppression is to bring the war home to those who love it so much. Why not report your kindly family doctor for drug-dealing?

Without much prodding you can get the polilce to tear his place apart, and perhaps ruin his practice. The doc will see he has more to fear from his government than anyone else, and so will all his friends.

> *Throw pot seeds on a politician's lawn. As the richer-and-more-powerful discover the joys of dealing with the man in blue they may come to listen to your logical arguments.*

Why not go ahead and help the cops with their turn-in-your-neighbor programs? Just make sure the neighbors you turn in are those with the smuggest attitudes and the juiciest assets. If those guys believe so heartily in the fairness of our criminal justice system, why not plant a little coke in their cars, then call the cops? Throw pot seeds on a politician's lawn. As the richer-and-more-powerful discover the joys of dealing with the man in blue they may come to listen to your logical arguments. But as long as they think they can escape the consequences of their own police state, they will continue to back it.

Take a tip from the IRS — terrorize just a few percent of the insulated middle class and the rest will readily do whatever it takes to escape the same treatment. After a slew of millionaires lose their houses, and some regular folks lose their bass boats and enough regular white folks see their children off to ten-year stretches in prison for non-crimes, the Drug War will cease. But not before.

Otherwise, never miss a chance to expose the drug war for what it is. If you have children, encourage them to challenge their teachers whenever their anti-drug messages come up. Teach them to teach their classmates that the teachers are lying. You don't have to promote drug use to promote your Constitution. All you have to do is promote freedom.●

Jim Hogshire is a freelance writer living in Seattle. He is the author of *Sell Yourself To Science: The Complete Guide to Selling Your Organs, Body Fluids, Bodily Functions and Being a Human Guinea Pig.*

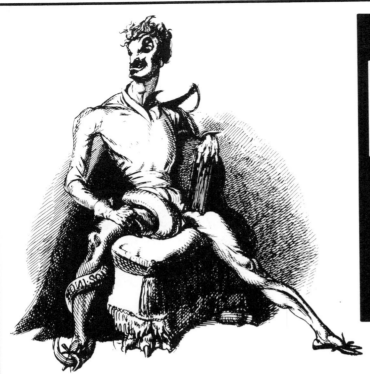

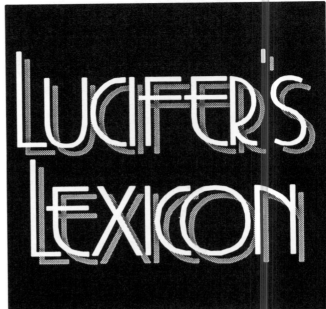

© *1993 by L.A. Rollins*

Amicus Curiae, *n.* A friend of the court and, therefore, an enemy of the people.

Armageddon Theology, *n.* That End-Time Religion. The optimistic Christian belief that the future looks bright, indeed, brighter than a thousand suns.

Armed Robbery, *n.* A form of practical alchemy by which lead can be transformed into gold.

Bay of Pigs, *n.* Pigs at bay.

Belief, *n.* A fig leaf used to cover up one's ignorance.

Broadcasting, *n.* Widely disseminating a narrow point-of-view.

Campaign, *n.* In politics, a race in which a horse's hind end always wins.

Check Your Premises, Don't check Ayn Rand's premises.

Civilization, *n.* The most advanced state of savagery.

Conspiracy, *n.* Piracy on the secret sea.

Conspiriologist, *n.* A Brussel sprout, a vegetable with a vendetta against sauerkraut. One who knows that the Nazis won World War II.

Communion Group, *n.* A close-encounter group.

Cryonic Suspension, *n.* The suspension of one's disbelief in cryonics.

Dumpster Diver, *n.* A practitioner of Discardianism, a religion based on worship of the Goodies. For more information, see the Bible of Discardianism, *Principia Discardia or How I Found the Goodies and What I Did With Them After I Found Them.*

Existence exists, A truism considered truly profound by those who do not understand that tautologies are tautological.

Freethinker, *n.* One who is not free to think any thoughts regarded as heretical by other freethinkers.

Gay-Basher, *n.* A bully willing to risk AIDS for the fun of beating up a guy who fights like a girl.

Gay Rights Movement, *n.* Strange bedfellows making politics.

Hemp, *n.* One of the world's most valuable and versatile plants. It can be used to make canvas sails, textiles (and if you outgrow your hemp shirt, no problem, just smoke it!), paper, construction boards (of course, people who live in grass houses should watch out for giant lawnmowers), paints, varnishes, oils, food (hemp can be used as an ingredient in

(Continued next page)

brownies, for example) medicine (for example, hemp can be used to induce uncontrollable laughter and, as *Reader's Digest* will tell you, laughter is the best medicine), rope (useful for lynching marijuana-crazed Negroes who rape White women, for example), and other things too numerous to remember. For more information, see the book, *The Emperor Could Wear Hemp Clothes.*

Homophobe, *n.* An ignorant bigot who regards gays as a bunch of fucking assholes. On second thought, gays *are* a bunch of fucking assholes, aren't they?

Ideologue, *n.* One who has an axiom to grind.

Identity Christian, *n.* A Fake-Identity Christian; an Aryan trying to pass as an Israelite.

Libertarian, *n.* One who believes in liberty and lives in slavery.

Logic, *n.* A fetter for free minds. The laws of thought, the violation of which makes one a thought criminal.

Market, the, *n.* A spook to which cowardly capitalists attribute the responsibility for their own actions.

Melodramamine, *n.* Trade name for a substance used to control the nausea and vomiting of motion-picture sickness.

MIAs, *n.* Mirages in Asia. Chicken bones in Communist captivity.

Multiculturalist, *n.* A Rainbow Supremacist.

Nietzchean, *n.* One who is a self-rolling wheel in his own head.

Objective Reality, *n.* A subjective fantasy produced by Ayn Rand's wishful thinking.

Objectivist, *n.* One who wants to fill all skyscapes with skyscrapers. One who hates poor looters, but loves polluters. One who opposes all tribalism, except that of the Thirteenth Tribe.

Open Borders, *n.* Hispanics Unlimited.

Politician, *n.* One who wishes to serve the public — to his supporters on a silver platter.

Polygamy, *n.* The more the marriers, the merrier. Polygamy does have a major drawback, though — too many mothers-in-law.

Potsdam Conference, *n.* The conference in 1945 at which the Allied pots damned the German kettles for being black.

Psilocybe cubensis, *n.* A mushroom with a view.

Rational Self-Interest, *n.* One's self-interest, not as determined by oneself, but by some uptight asshole in New York. Galtruism.

Reliable Sources, *n.* Sources able to lie repeatedly.

Responsible Journalism, *n.* The journalism which is responsible for censoring certain kinds of ideas and information from the mass media.

Self-censorship, *n.* The sort of censorship preferred by self-reliant Americans.

Shiftless, *adj.* Working no shift, neither the day shift, nor the swing shift, nor the graveyard shift.

Skeptic, *n.* One who doubts what he does not want to believe, and believes what he does not want to doubt.

Sour Grapes, *n.* The type of grapes used to make fine whines.

Television, *n.* An airhead-conditioner; a stupidifier. A friend to the friendless; a babysitter to the babysitterless; a mind to the mindless; and a god to the godless.

University, *n.* The antithesis of diversity.

U.S. Government, *n.* The policeman of the world, with a record of police brutality way worse than Dirty Harry's.

Wannsee Protocol, *n.* The Protocol of the Wise Men of Zyklon.

Womyn, *n.* Femyle pyrsyns who spyll wyrds stryngyly.

Work, *n.* Another day, another dolor. Remember, you lazy Americans: Work is for Japs!

Yellow Ribbon, *n.* A self-awarded war decoration for cowardice.

Zen, *n.* The sound of two lips flapping.

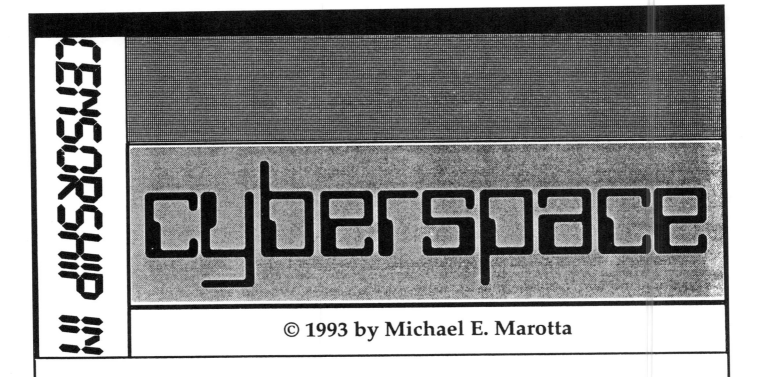

© 1993 by Michael E. Marotta

The sum total of all computer-to-computer connections is called "cyberspace" and in this artificial geography you will find Christians and Objectivists, golfers and Gulf War veterans, lesbians and thespians. This diversity creates a challenge for tolerance. As Ayn Rand noted, when people abandon money, their only alternative when dealing with each other is to use guns. Yet, the anti-capitalist mentality permeates cyberspace. Most public systems and networks actually forbid commercial messages. So, computer sysops and network moderators are reduced to cavalier enforcement of their personal quirks.

When Tom Jennings created Fidonet, *Omni* magazine called him an "online anarchist." Since then, Fidonet has developed a governing council and lost Jennings. Over the last two years, I have been banished from these Fidonet echoes:

- Stock Market for saying that Ivan Boesky is a political prisoner
- Virus for saying that viruses could be useful
- Communications for saying that telephone service should not be regulated by the government
- International Chat for asking "How are you" in Hebrew and Japanese.

Niggardly Attitudes

Kennita Watson, whom I met on Libernet, told me this story:

> When I was at Pyramid, I came in one day and "fortune" had been disabled. I complained to Operations, and ended up in a personal meeting with the manager. He showed me a letter from the NAACP written to Pyramid threatening to sue if they didn't stop selling racist material on their machines. They cited a black woman who had found the "...there were those whose skins were black... and their portion was niggardly...'Let my people go to the front of the bus'..." fortune, and complained to the NAACP. I suspect that she (and the NAACP) were clueless as to the meaning of the term "niggardly". I (as a black woman) was embarrassed and outraged. Because of the stupidity of a bunch of paranoid people, I couldn't read my fortune when I logged out any more.

Carl M. Kadie of the Electronic Frontier Foundation provided me with a very long list of similar material from Computers and Academic Freedom News. Typical examples are:

First published in 1993 Main Catalog (Continued next page)

- Steve Brack meant to post a note to the alt.flame newsgroup but also accidentally posted to rec.aquaria. Brack was permanently expelled from Ohio State U's Academic Computer Services.

- The National Center for Supercomputer Applications (NCSA) created rules that allowed searches of user email if they suspected that the email criticized the NCSA or the University of Illinois.

- On-line rudeness is prohibited at Iowa State. So is on-line discussion of sex and drugs.

Glenn Tenney, whom I met on The Well, sent me this:

I am candidate to U.S. Congress running an online campaign. One of my campaign announcements went to telecom-priv mailing list. The moderator of this mailing list works for the Army, and has so far refused to allow re-distribution of my announcement on "his" mailing list.

Parlez Vous Fascist?

I have a special interest in languages. I was raised in a bilingual household. (My mother's parents were Hungarian.) I took eight years of German from 7th grade through college. Since then, I've had two semesters of Japanese and one semester of Arabic. English is the "official" language of Fidonet, but there is no rule *requiring* English. However, when I used Hebrew and Japanese on the International Chat Echo, the local sysop created a new rule: English only on her BBS. I met similar resistance when using different languages on other echos.

I discussed my views with other Fidonet users. I suggested that Pascal programmers in New York City, Miami and Los Angeles might want to discuss their craft via the Pascal echo but en espanol. I was told that they could "start a Spanish language echo." This would mean, I countered, that every topic under the sun would be included on the same echo merely because they take place in the same language. It is true that, worldwide, English is the commonest *second* language. As telecomputering spreads, English cannot remain the *only* language. I found no sympathy for this on Fidonet. And those Anglophilic views came from most moderators, sysops, and users.

I took the issue to the Electronic Frontier Foundation. Their legal counsel, Mike Godwin (mnemonic-@eff.org), told me that this was a matter of "Marotta and one sysop" and not a free speech issue at all.

The Banality Of Evil

It is important to bear in mind that to the censor, censorship, like all evils, is always an unpleasant but necessary means to achieve a good result. Robert Warren is a sysop who replied to an article of mine on Computer Underground Digest. He said:

Several years ago, I posted a message on a board flaming another user on subject XYZ, the message was deleted and next day a letter from the sysop explained that my message was deleted because I was acting like an idiot. Looking back, I would have done the same thing in his shoes. Today, I'm the sysop of a BBS and the main host of a Network in Canada. ...I have not done it often, some three times for posting commercial ads on the net and 2 other times I've booted people off the net for saying "bunch of losers... ...cheap net..."

You get the idea. While some will say that censorship is a crime and some similar crud, I say that since I provide a service for free at MY expense with MY hardware, I expect a minimum of say on what gets posted. Posting a "white-power" or some other balderdash message will get you on a fast train to file 13... People have a right to say what they want in public, but some don't care about the responsibility that comes with it. So you zap 'em.

Now, there is no argument with his basic premise: Since he owns the equipment, he has the final say in its use. This is his right. Likewise, the administrators of publicly-funded university computers also engage in censorship under a mandate to serve the people who pay taxes. "All power tends to corrupt and absolute power corrupts absolutely," the historian John E. E. Acton said. It is no surprise that this applies in cyberspace.

Political and social freedom have little to do with constitutions or elections. Congress could choose a new prime minister every day or the people could elect the secretary of state to a three year term. The details are unimportant. Some places are free and some places are controlled because the people in those places need freedom or accept oppression. It always comes back to the individual.

A sysop who lowered my access told me: "You can start your own BBS and enforce your own rules." Of course, as a law enforcement professional, she lives for rules. Power corrupts. The opposite of Power is Market. Yet in cyberspace, the market for liberty falters.

Prodigy is a BBS service operated by Sears and IBM. In order to avoid alienating customers who make airline reservations and play the stock markets Prodigy enforces strict rules. The rules are so strict that Prodigy censored a Jew who complained about Nazis because his message included the original anti-Semitic remarks — and this was in "private" e-mail. Prodigy has received several such black eyes in the press over the last three years and shows absolutely no intention of changing. They profit from the market for tyranny or at least from the market for banality.

Anarchist Techno-Guerrilla

I announced my candidacy for Congress on several echoes for programmers: C, C++, Pascal, dBase, QuickBasic, 80xxx. The C and C++ moderators complained to the sysop of the computer I logged in on and he warned me not to do this again. I announced my candidacy on the History echo and got the same response. To me, "Programmer runs for Congress," is of interest to programmers and historians.

While complaining loudly about my "off-topic" posts, however, the moderators of those echoes allowed all kinds of off-topic posts. For instance, on the History echo there was an exchange about the Oxford English Dictionary CD-ROM — not about the history of the OED, but what a great buy the CD was. What is off topic, annoying or abusive, is totally up to one person who may never state their standard of conduct. Even if the rules were posted every day, unless you cover every possible situation, rules must be interpreted.

Bat Lang moderates the Communications echo and is far and away the most heavy-handed moderator in cyberspace. He objected to my *GridNews* (ISSN 1054-9315) uploads. Each issue runs 50-60 lines and begins with a three-line text banner which states the title, issue number, and length. *GridNews* comes out once or twice a month. This moderator's own rules specifically allow discussion of telecom service and policies. However, we were locked in an entirely different conflict. He threatened to disconnect all Lansing BBSes from "his" echo unless I stopped uploading *GridNews*. So, I registered on BBSes in Seattle, Buffalo and Baltimore. He wasn't amused

and again sent netmail to the Lansing sysops threatening to refuse them service if I did not stop. So I did. I stopped uploading *GridNews* to the Communications echo as a favor to those who favor me. If I did not value these hostages, I could continue to barrage this echo from five continents under any name I choose. The irony here is that the previous echo moderator had encouraged me to upload *GridNews*. When the ruler changed, the interpretation of the rules changed.

A New Liberty

The Stock Market echo moderator who objected to my posts about Ivan Boesky also complained about my uploads on gold and silver. (He allowed discussions about life insurance, however.) Today, this echo has a new moderator with a much smaller list of rules. As a result, the range and depth of discussion centered on the Stock Market is much improved.

Dehnbase Emerald BBS is home to libertarian and objectivist discussions and is a vital link in Libernet. The number is (303) 972-6575. Joseph Dehn is not interested in enforcing rules.

When I posted an article on multipole clamping devices in German on the Electronics echo, I received a reply from another user in German — and no flame from the moderator.

Three years ago, the Secret Service attempted to protect the money supply and the President by busting Phrack (an online news digest) and Steve Jackson Games, operator of a BBS for gamers. The Feds lost their case in court. The prosecutor resigned. The Secret Service and Bellcore are being sued. These wins came only because Mitch Kapor, Steve Wozniak and a handful of dedicated people pledged their personal resources. They created the Electronic Frontier Foundation, met the Feds head-on, and won.

They could beat the Secret Service in court. They cannot change individuals who fear. Censorship still exists in the physical world and in the virtual reality of cyberspace. However, the collapse of communism has discredited centralized authority and for the near future new ideas will continue to take root and flourish. Albert Gore and George Bush agreed on the need for a "data superhighway." The Electronic Frontier Foundation has recommended that this national network be open to commercial enterprises. This is good. An open market is the best protection against power and corruption. •

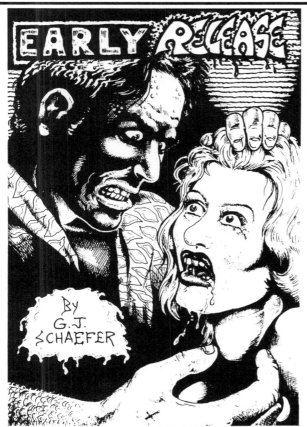

Illustration by Nick Bougas

The bus crawled through the darkening Florida countryside, the soft hum of rubber on macadam floating up from under the wheels. I was sitting in the back of the thing feeling edgy and impatient, smoking my RIP and contemplating the coming evening. I'd done sixteen years in the slam, straight up. One day the fucking warden says, "Pack your shit, Boy, you're being turned out. Early release. Prisons are full. Gotta push some of you oldtimers out, got too many newcocks coming in."

I packed my shit. It fit in the front pocket of my jeans. They gave me a hundred bucks and offered me a bus ticket to any city in Florida. I picked Tampa. What the fuck? One place is the same as another, ain't it?

I reached down and stroked the hilt of my shank. It was jammed in my boot convict style. I'd feel naked without it. In prison a man learns to rely on himself and the comforting presence of cold steel next to his leg on a hot summer night. My shank had saved my ass more than once from the wolf packs of asshole bandits that prey on the weak after lights out. Only the fittest survive the brutality of prison with their manhood intact.

The only other person I knew on the Trailways was a baby-faced punk from Florida State Prison at Starke, known among the criminal brotherhood as the East Unit, or just the Unit. There is no tougher prison in the U.S. of A. — only Folsom Prison in California comes close in terms of murderous reputation. The only question in my mind was whether the slender boy with the shaved legs was a fuck-boy or a killer queen. The kid had himself a copy of *Hustler,* and was sipping liquor from a bottle concealed in a paper bag. I was feeling high with freedom and I needed to bat the breeze a bit.

I leaned over toward the punk and gave him a wolfish grin.

"Hey, Boy. Whatcha got there inside that tote sack? Think I can't smell free-world hooch when it's uncorked?"

The punk had thick light-brown hair; he glanced up and over, blinking his watery no-color eyes. They were white trash convict eyes: guarded, fearful, ancient. Eyes that had known pain, and expected to know it again. The eyes of a prison fuck-boy. His answer was an apology.

"Sorry. I didn't catch what you said."

"I *said,* I want to know what's in that fucking sack you're sucking on, Kid."

The punk shifted in his seat, quickly looked around, then offered me a sly, shit-eating smile. "This here is Jim Beam Whiskey. Scored it right at Big Bad Daddy's Lounge in Starke. Five finger discount."

"Stole it?"

"I gave that lonely little feller a new home, is all," he drawled in his cracker, grit-sucking voice. "He was just sitting there with nobody paying him a lick of attention, so I boosted him up under my arm and here he is. Besides, tastes better when you steal it."

"Think so?"

"Sure. Wanna try a little snort?"

"Fucking-A on that, Kid."

The wheels squeaked and hummed along the cement pavement, the tropical countryside oozed past. It was so green — a wondrous world of a million different shades of green after sixteen years of solid gray. I took up the bag, wiped the neck of the bottle with my hand and belted down a healthy slug.

"That's damn fine shit there. Beats plum wine all to hell and gone. Fiery. Sets the sparks to jumping, don't it?"

(Continued next page)

"You betcha," the punk said.

"Got me some Bar-B-Cue corn chips here. Got 'em at the Kash-N-Karry store. Walked right into the little joint. Ten thousand kinds of shit to choose from. I didn't know what to do. It made me nervous seeing all that stuff, so I grabbed the first sack on the rack and hauled ass. Paid my kash; and karried the shit away, just like it said up there on the sign. Little girl at the money taking place up front had tits out front like Jane Fonda in Barbarella. I stared right at 'em. She smelt like a whore. I liked to skeeted in my drawers." I passed the bottle back to him, my eyes automatically scanning for a guard as I made the pass.

"I'll slide on the munchies, Oldcock. I'd probably just puke those corn chips up. I'm aiming to get drunk." He took another pull on his bottle and gave me a grin. His eyes were already slightly tinged with crimson from the powerful 90 proof hooch. Niggers had been at him. It was in his eyes; it came off him like a bad case of B.O. He'd be a walking death factory full of AIDS. I knew that for a fact. Mess with a pussy-boy in the joint and it's like Russian Roulette. Hell, play Russian Roulette with a pistol, your odds are safer. I was looking at a walking dead man. I motioned to the magazine open on his lap.

"You read that pervo shit or just look at the pictures? That Larry Flynt is the sickest fucker that ever put out a skin rag; I never have understood his brand of humor."

The punk picked up the magazine and set it on his knee, leaving me to see his dick stuck up like a flagpole. He opened the rag to the centerfold where a bare-assed lady was showing her Vaseline-slickened tunnel of love. The punk bent over and ran his tongue over the page, leaving a wet trail between the model's legs. He made a growl like a hound dog and said, "I like it when the girlies show the pink. *Hustler* gets my blood moving around, heats me up, ya know: I don't read it — I don't look at the cartoons. I just stare at those titties and those gorgeous hairy cunts and jack my dick. Doesn't everyone? Ain't that the reason they show them in the fucking thing?"

I grinned back at him, wondering what an asshole bandit would see in a naked whore. Maybe the same as anyone else; who can tell what goes on in a faggot's twisted mind? I'd been around them for sixteen years straight now, and never could figure them out. "So it heats you up and now you're hot stuff."

The punk nodded agreeably and took another pull on the bottle.

I snapped my finger at him and he quickly handed the jug back my way. "Here you go," he said. Nice polite kid.

I drank his whiskey, felt it burn down inside me. It brightened me up, made me more aware of myself. Shit. Maybe stolen booze was better. I closed my eyes for a minute. Felt the sonorous hum of the bus all around me. Heard the snick-snack of the tires snapping across the expansion cracks in the rural highway. It was a pleasant sound. I was tense. I needed to ease up, relax a little. Too many changes too fast. I wasn't used to it. Riding this fucking bus with no mesh welded over the windows was making me nervous. I realized I could simply throw open the window and leap out. I had a crazy fleeting urge to do just that. I saw the big headlines: *Man Dies Jumping From Window of Moving Bus*. Nobody would ever know why. It would be another unsolved mystery. I smiled at the thought.

I opened my eyes again, glanced at the kid. His eyes stared at nothing. He was leaning back against the bus seat, his hand playing with his dick. He smiled in a self-contained, distant manner at visions only he could see. He scratched at his balls like a whipped cur. I wondered if he was insane. I decided to chat him up and see what sort of worms came to the surface.

"Hey, Boy." He turned to me. "Yeah?"

"They give you that early release thing?"

He perked up. "Yeah. I got one of those. I earned day for day gain time working in the broom factory. Maxed my nickel with a deuce, two months and six days. I kept close watch on it."

"Listen. You a street queen?"

"Naw. Bi."

"Niggers turn you out?"

"That's it. Turned my cracker ass out all right. First night too," the kid sighed.

"Bad shit there."

The kid giggled, a high screechy sound, his slim girlish body wriggling with grim recollection as I passed back his little jug. He needed a hit. Drank. Wiped his mouth with the back of his hand.

"Mama Herk comes up to me. The biggest fucking nigger I ever saw in my entire life. I figure I'm gonna die, right?" I nodded his way. "Mama Herk says, 'White Boy, I want to suck your dick.' I figured I'd heard the fucker wrong, like he wanted me to suck his dick, but no. He

(Continued next page)

wanted to suck mine. And then I had to fuck him in the ass. You believe that shit?"

"Sure. Mama Herk is famous for it."

"He's a 280 pound queen."

"I know. I've *seen* Herk. I've been in sixteen fucking *years* and you want to tell *me* about Mama Herk? I've done more time in the *box* than you've done in the joint." The kid gave me a worried look.

"Herk turned me out, but I got protection too."

"You sucked nigger cock. Herk pimped you."

"OK, sure. That's it."

"What'd you get for two and a half years of swallowing black cock? AIDS? Clap?"

"I got half of everything."

"Niggers let you keep it?"

"Yeah. Herk made them let me keep it."

"Herk would be the only one who could help a little stringbean like you hold green money at The Unit."

"Oh, I made plenty. I made fucking plenty." He patted a fat roll in the front pocket of his jeans. "It all adds up, Oldcock."

I leaned back enjoying the heat of the booze. What it added up to was AIDS. But for him, not for me. "So now you are one loaded white boy."

The punk giggled again. His face was flushed and almost trusting. "I got me a big roll of green, and I'm on my way to spend it. I tell myself I earned it. That's how I see it."

He obviously hadn't learnt his lessons at Starke. The first one is to keep your mouth shut — tight. The boy was no convict, not yet he wasn't. I mulled over the news about the fat bankroll while I squinted out the dirty window as the clapboard nigger shacks of drab, impoverished West Tampa slid past. Pest holes of crime. Nigger comes out of a place like that and prison life looks damned good by comparison. Steady meals, basketball, TV in the evening, some piss-ass job in a grungy prison factory, and all the white ass a coon can pump at night. Correctional officer asleep in a locked office and a dorm full of sex-crazed criminal perverts running wild all night. Rehabilitation. I felt the wheels swish along the pavement; the bus swayed

from side to side, rocking along at a steady clip. I looked back at the Kid and said, "Yeah. You might as well enjoy it while you still got it. You get the AIDS and you're through dealing." I waited for him to argue around that one.

"I know. I figure I've got those AIDS things swimming around up in me somewheres. But it takes awhile for them to breed enough to where they kill you. So I'm gonna hit that fucking Tampa on the run and I'm gonna get drunk and suck me some pussy, and then maybe I'll jump off the Sunshine Skyway Bridge right into Tampa Bay. Hey, I just don't give a fuck. OK?"

The punk gave me his best killer-convict junkyard-dog stare. He looked like Garfield. I was trying not to laugh, so I said, "You ever sucked a pussy before in your whole damn life, Boy?"

He shrugged. "Never did, I admit it. Gonna start learning how to do it today. Heard me a lot of talk in The Unit about it, told myself I ought to give it a try. Hey, I sucked plenty of cock. Why not try a pussy?"

At least the kid had a sense of reality about life — or so it seemed. "How you figure to get ahold of this pussy? You gonna walk up to some lady and say, 'Excuse me, Ma'am, I'm fresh out of prison. Heard talk of pussy-sucking while I was in the joint, and figured I'd like to have me a try at it; would you be agreeable to lower your drawers and let me have a lick or three?' Or maybe you just knock her down, put a knife to her throat and tell her to fuck or die. About like that? Out where we're heading, Kid, is a thing called polite society."

"Just can't ask 'em flat out?"

"Well I reckon you can ask, but it's probably against the law to ask someone to commit a sex crime. Solicitation for criminal acts or something. I ain't no fucking lawyer."

"What's the criminal part?"

"Sucking pussy is a goddamned crime, Kid! It's called oral sodomy. You'd be right back there with Mama Herk in two shakes."

"You shittin' me? It's a *crime* to suck pussy?"

"No lie, Boy. It's a crime in the State of Florida."

I put the bag to my lips and sucked some liquid fire, let it trickle down my throat. I belched. Tasted corn chips at the back of my throat. I wondered if I could get AIDS from the neck of a whiskey bottle. Damn depressing thought. I dismissed it. Quickly handed the Kid back his bottle.

(Continued next page) **189**

I watched him take a pull, then closed my eyes and suddenly I was back in the darkness of the Hole. I saw the big brown sewer rats come out of the toilet hole in the floor, heard the dry rustle of thousands of cockroaches, the screams of insane and desperate men. Seven years in the Hole. Then the bus began to slow down. I looked out the grimy window, saw the terminal, a big sign reading *Trailways*. End of the fucking line.

"I'm getting excited," the Kid said.

I knew what he meant. The feeling was as contagious as his AIDS. The kid closed one eye and peered into the empty bottle. "Dead soldier," he remarked as he dropped the empty. It hit the floor with a dull clunk. An old lady gave him a dirty look. Started to speak, but held her tongue.

I got to my feet. Ran my hand down the side of the Kid's face and gave it a meaningful pat. He looked at me with new eyes, asking the unspoken question. He was borderline drunk.

"Got your heart set on sucking pussy, Kid?"

He nodded, "I did. Now I'm not so sure what I want to do."

"Yeah, but I know what to do."

"You do?" the Kid brightened.

"Damn right. Stick with me. I know Tampa pretty good. Worked armed robberies along Dale Mabry during the early seventies."

"You did?"

"Sure. And I've got phone numbers for a pair of cunts who done time down to Lowell. And you know what they fell on?"

"No. What?"

"Organized prostitution. I've got me a pair of whores on the line here. A pair is *two,* Kid. What do you say we call them up and I ask them to teach my homeboy from the Unit to suck honest-to-god pussy. I figure any girl come out of Lowell, she's got to be an expert at that happy pastime. Way I heard it, they don't do nothing else but lay around and lick each other's titties and suck those cunts. Now do you wanna tag along, or go to a motel and jack your dick?"

The punk gave me a look of gratitude. "Hey. That's OK! You really don't mind?"

"Hey. I done 16 years, Kid. I *dig* young boys, I just don't advertise it."

"What about the AIDS?"

"What about it?"

"...if you tell those girls I've been . . . you know."

"I ain't telling them double-barreled bags of shit nothin'. Are you?"

The punk smiled from ear to ear. "Fuck 'em!" he said.

"So what do you say?"

"I say DO it!"

So we hit the streets of Tampa running.

It cost me a quarter to get one of the whores on the phone. She said they were French teachers and could we meet them at the Blind Pig for our lessons? She said to look for her in a red dress with a big black flower at the waist. She'd bring her friend.

The next quarter went to call a cab. I didn't want to waste a minute getting to our first class.

The air in the Blind Pig was thick with the smoke of a thousand cigarettes. The people inside were loose and un-inhibited. We stood just inside the door and watched everyone shouting and laughing. The lighting was subdued. Smoke swirled around the room, turning the air into a layered blue haze. The punk was agog.

"Outta sight!" he breathed.

We inched our way into the lounge and walked up to the bar like free men. Nobody tried to stop us. We weren't arrested or searched for contraband. Buying a drink without being searched for loose canteen coupons was a novelty. So was the selection. The faggot bought the first round. Dickel on the rocks. First ice cubes I'd seen in sixteen years. They were little tiny things, curved on one side and flat on the other. Sparkling and tinkling as I swirled them in the glass.

I checked out the Kid's fat wad of cash. He'd sucked him a lot of black cock to get that stash. I hoisted my glass.

"To survival, Kid."

He nodded. We clicked glasses and drank, glancing around the place and checking out the action. It was a honky-tonk kind of joint. Country music going wide open

(Continued next page)

on the juke box. Cheap wooden tables with low benches. The room was three-quarters full and the conversation was roaring along. The tables were piled high with empty beer bottles and ashtrays overflowing with butts. The crap was falling onto the floor and being trampled underfoot. It was a real dump. It reminded me of the open dorms at the Unit. Sloppy as hell but as alive as an anthill. I decided I liked it. The punk loved the shit out of it. We'd been there 15 minutes already and nobody had cracked on him for some ass. For him, that was a whole new way of life.

But there was one thing at the Blind Pig that the Unit never had: real whores. Not chain gang pussy boys, but genuine double-barreled, ass-swinging cunts. There were whores wandering around the joint smiling at everyone. Big wide smiles to pull in them big stiff dicks. Same smiles you see on the queens at the Unit. A lot of them in red dresses, but I was looking for that black flower.

A bitch with a mop of tangled hair dyed three separate shades sauntered past with a bottle of Pabst Blue Ribbon in one hand and a pickled pigfoot in the other. She smelled real fucking sweet.

"Check out that real live snatch," I said to the queer.

"What about her?"

"She's trolling for dick. Down here at the Blind Pig twitching her fanny at us. That's your basic working girl. Needs to pay her rent same as us. Look at her move. You like whores, Kid?"

"I like 'em. I like how they move in those tight little skirts... Whooooeee! If she'd bend over a little, I could see clear up to where the sun don't shine. Maybe see the wet spot!"

"What wet spot?"

"There was this old con down on M-Wing. For some money or some canteen, didn't matter which, he'd tell about a gal he saw get 'lecrocuted up in Alabama. Told me all about it. He looked up her dress and there was a big roll of pussy up there and the crack part was wet. He said it was the girlie's wet spot and they all got one. Reckon she's got one up under there?" The punk seemed genuinely curious.

"That sounds like old Curly Bill's yarn."

"That was the guy: Curly Bill. A nasty old fucker with long yellow teeth, and not too many of them. I had to give him a whole jar of Maxwell House to hear his story."

"Was it worth it?"

"Hell yeah! Best story I ever heard."

"You heard some others?"

"Sure, plenty. I saw Ted Bundy, Murf-the-Surf, the Catch-Me Killer, and the Ghoul."

"The Ghoul?"

"Sure. You know, that cop that killed the 34 women down around Oakland Park. Cut 'em up. Drank their blood. Fucked 'em when they were dead."

"Go on! You saw this guy?"

"Walking around on two feet."

"Wha'd he look like?"

"Big ole scary looking fucker. Looks like Hoss Cartwright."

"You say he killed 34 women?"

"Men, women, kids. Nobody knows for sure. I read the whole true story in *Inside Detective*. It had pictures of two girls he ate, plus one he hung by the neck. That one was drawing flies."

"Showed a picture of *that!?*"

"God's truth."

"You talk to this Ghoul?"

"Are you crazy? I seen that fucker coming and I got the hell out of the way. I wasn't gonna piss him off and become Number 35. Know what I mean?"

I laughed. The Ghoul. I wondered who had come up with that one. Some media asshole no doubt. Last I heard it was the Sex Beast. Now it's the Ghoul. Christ on a *stick*.

I finished my whiskey; went up by the barmaid and ordered two more. We knocked them back. The night was young. The cigarette smoke and music swirled around us. The voices banged away at our ears. We took it all in, feeling right at home with the ear-splitting din.

I felt like talking. The booze was loosening me up, and the night was starting to glitter in my brain. I checked my watch, then felt foolish for wanting to see how long we had before count.

(Continued next page) **191**

No count to stand at 8:00 p.m. Stand to attention, rattle off your number like a robot. No name, just your number. No nigger jive blasting from those black boom boxes. No prancing homos swishing off to the shithouse to suck black cock. The Unit — a place of rehabilitation. If the taxpayers only knew the truth.

I leaned closer to the pussy boy, put my elbow on the bar, and took a knock of bourbon. Damn good stuff.

"I done more than fifteen years, hard time. They bum-rapped me. I ain't no altar boy but you know a bum rap, it don't sit too well in a man. Festers in there like a cancer. A convict does his time. You get caught and you take the fall and you pull the time and you come out and you go back to work. You don't cry, you don't snitch for a plea. You've heard it said, if you can't do the time, don't pull the crime."

The punk nodded sagely into his drink. "What you fall on, Oldcock?"

"Murder! Bloody... fucking... murder."

"Jesus."

"Yeah. Chopped them up with a machete, they said. So when I get to Butler I go straight into Solitary. You know the drill."

The punk nodded.

"And for nothing, on the house, I get four years in the Box. Can you believe such shit?"

The punk's eyes widened as he shook his head in sympathetic understanding. "I know a guy. He raped the Warden's secretary. He got two years in the Box. This other guy, he got caught with a .38 caliber pistol inside the prison. He did maybe five years in the Box. So if you get four years in the Box from jump street, I figure the Warden plain don't like you, or a buddy of the Warden don't like you. That's it, couldn't be nothing else."

"Good, you understand. So you can see how I might be tempted to get me a machete and settle a few old scores."

"I can understand the temptation."

"I ain't saying I'm gonna do it. But after that first four years in the Box, you could say my attitude turned a tad radical."

"But you did manage to get out of the Box, right?"

"Right. And here's what happened. Along comes this new warden, Braselton. Big fucking gorilla runs about 280. Lifts weights. Came down from Cook County. You know, Chicago. Me, I'm from the Windy City, grew up on the Northside. That was back when Old Man Daley was Mayor and the cops were real mean. Capone, he came out of Chicago. Word I got was that Capone had Cermak bumped off down on Miami Beach..."

"What? You lost me. Who's Cermak?"

"Mayor Anton Cermak. He got killed in Miami. They said it was an attempt to kill that Jew Roosevelt."

"Roosevelt? Hey, that was before I was born, Home. Tell me how you got out of the Box," the punk groused.

"Well I done a few short stretches at Statesville, one longer at Menard. Braselton knew me there. He comes down here to Florida and finds me in the Box. He takes a look at my jacket, sees I ain't got a single write-up, so he decides to give the homeboy a break. Gets me a transfer out of the Box right over to Union County, Raiford Prison. I go straight to the Rock. F-Floor. Nasty grungy place. Then I get assigned a job. Put me in the packing plant. Ever been in the packing plant, Kid?"

"Never was." He took a knock at his drink.

"Well it's a place you wouldn't forget. You know that bacon they serve in the chow hall with the hog bristles still in it?"

"Yeah. Not that you'd see me eating it. I do admit the niggers scarf it right up. They'll snatch it right off your tray if you so much as blink an eye."

"OK. That's the bacon I'm talking about. The packing plant is where that crap is made and the noise alone is enough to drive you fucking insane. Machinery crashing and slamming all day long. The squealing pigs."

"Is that four-legged or two-legged pigs?"

"Very funny. This is serious. Now pay attention."

"OK, run it."

"So Benny drives down to Avon Park for a truckload of pigs. Great big fucking sows maybe three hundred, four hundred pounds. He comes back and we run them out of the truck and into a pen."

(Continued next page)

"A pigpen."

"Right. Then someone gives 'em a jab on the ass with an electric prod and they go running up a narrow chute. They're lined up in there snout to asshole; squealing like mad. crapping all over each other, just like the poor slobs on their way to Sparky. Same exact thing. Joe fastens some iron shackles around the rear hocks and this other fella gives the porker a pop on the noggin with a sledgehammer."

"Jesus."

"Yeah. Wham! Then they press a button and the hoist jerks the pig up into the air. The fuckers ain't even dead, just stunned, and they come to while they're hanging upside down. You never heard such screaming. The hog comes swinging down from the slaughter chute toward the killing floor and the thing is spewing shit and piss out its ass like a volcano."

"Gross."

"You ain't heard it all yet. Bobby Batson is there with this huge fucking knife and he slits their throats. The blood comes splashing out all over the place. They spray blood from the front and crap from the rear, and there's four hundred pounds of bucking meat writhing in the chains, gurgling and squealing and screaming like hell."

"So what was your job?"

"I gutted them. Slashed their fucking bellies open and got a snoot full of stench for my trouble. Let me tell you, Kid, there ain't no rehabilitation in the packing plant. Raw meat. Yellow tallow. Greasy coils of spilling guts. And the stench. I came out of four years in the Hole and walk into that. They told me it was supposed to be job training. Educational. Yeah, teach me the Work Ethic. The parole man would like it, they said. I'd have a skill to take with me to the streets. Make me a good parole risk. You've heard that story?"

The punk nodded. Caught the bartender for two more Dickels with ice. Good sipping whiskey. We sloshed them down. A whore rubbed her tits against the pussy-boy as she pressed through to the bar. He gave me a look. Big eyes, big wet smile. Thinking about a little cooze, he was. It was around. All around.

"Where are those French whores, Oldcock?"

"Don't cum in your drawers, Kid. They'll be around. You think you're the only stiff they got lined up to bury tonight? We got 'call girls' coming. They ain't like some snaggletooth rummy you find in a tonk. Call girls — you call 'em on the phone, make you an appointment. They get top dollar. But you've got a wad of green to spend."

"Damn right. Top-notch pussy, that's what we want!"

"Yeah, that packing plant was a real trip. Every time I see a cop I think of it. Never could get the blood washed off me. It'd be under my fingernails, my toenails, between my toes. Slice one of those sows and she squirts blood and crap right in your face. It's in your hair, dripping down your arms, soaked into your clothes. August, September — it was hotter than hell in there. Sixty million flies buzzing around eating that liquid pigshit mixed with blood. We were drowned in that slime, Kid. We died. Our souls flew out and went away."

"Sounds bad, Home."

"You don't know the half of it, Kid. The old Rock was nothing but fucking madness. The noise and the stench alone was enough to drive any man insane. They built the place about 1920, so there's 60 to 70 years of sweat and piss soaked into the cement. August comes around and you can't hardly breathe for the stink of the place. We'd put in a day in the packing plant and then the screws would herd us back to the cellblocks. F-Floor, H-Floor, G-Floor, all that was the packing plant crew."

"Big gang down there, huh?"

"Oh, hell yes. There was goddamned niggers in the cells too. Nasty fucking dirty black-assed niggers that never had a bath in their whole sorry lives. Filthy animals."

"Mama Herk was OK."

"Some are OK, some ain't. And that's a fact."

"Where are our whores? You think they'll be here soon?"

"Forget the whores for a minute. I'm getting to the part about when they cut off Newcock Benson's head."

"Cut the guy's head off? What was it, an accident?"

"Not exactly. Those niggers, you know they were bad, but at least they speak English and they understand when you tell them to hit the showers. Then we started getting

them Cuban assholes, Marielito scum. Castro opens the door to his insane asylums and lets all the nuts go to Florida. Guess where they end up?"

"The Rock?"

"Fucking-A. And these are crazy insane fuckers, not convicts. No habla ingles. No comprendo. Let me tell you what they comprendo, is a big fucking knife. And even normal guys were driven mad by the stench and the filth and the blood-sodden clothes stinking up the whole cellblock. Guys were bugging up every day — regular white guys. You never knew when it would happen. It was a 24-hour red alert just to stay alive. Bad on the nerves, Kid, I can tell you that."

"What about cutting off the head?"

"Shit. Some guy would pull out a knife — a hog slasher, pig sticker, even a meat cleaver. And he'd start swinging. Slaughter guys in the cell just like they were pigs coming off the chute, hanging from a chain. Get the picture?"

"I'm seeing it. Living color."

"OK. One day we are in this 20-man cell and a shiteater name of Dennison comes along with this newcock to put him in our cell. Swede Perkins, who was the boss coon of the cell, tells Dennison we ain't got no more room, the cell is full. Twenty bunks, twenty guys: White, Nigger, Cuban. Dennison tells Swede the newcock is coming in as number 21, and we ain't got jack-shit to say about it. So Swede tells Dennison if he puts the newcock in the cell, we're cutting off his damn head. Dennison just laughs and opens the door. He pushes the newcock into the cellblock and walks away. An hour later he comes back for a security count and the head is laying out on the tier."

"No shit?"

"No shit."

"So what happened?"

"We didn't get more guys than bunks, that's what happened. Every other cell was stacked up with guys like they're sardines in a damn can. Cell H4 has twenty guys, just what it's supposed to have."

"What'd the cops do?"

"Nothing. Every guy in the cell said he killed the newcock. Twenty guys. Twenty confessions. So the State said fuck it and put it under the rug. Called it a suicide or

some such shit. Suicide my ass. Dennison was told. He murdered that newcock. That was the old chain gang, Sonny. Pussy-boys don't have that kind of solidarity. No snitches stayed alive in them days. Ain't like now."

"What about the screw, Dennison. Did he get fired?"

"Dennison got fucking killed, Kid."

"Whaaaat?"

"Time goes by. The cons seen the cop who was responsible for the murder is still around. One day they caught him in the hallway and gutted him like a porker."

"But... *why?*"

"Because Swede told him, *IF* you put the newcock in the cell he's dead meat. Dennison put him in. The newcock had to die. Real convicts don't run off at the mouth, Kid. Dennison killed him. The State should have fried Dennison same as they fried Aubrey Adams, that baby-raping pig from Marion C.I. Since nothing was gonna be done officially, it got done unofficially. A lot more of them shiteating D.O.C. motherfuckers are gonna die before it's all over. You watch and see."

"Home, it sounds even worse than the Unit"

"It was." I took a drink and leaned closer to the Kid.

"Check this out: I lasted one week. Then I walked down to Classification, asked that old shithook Parks for a job change. Kitchen, laundry, farm squad, anything. Parks pulls out my jacket. He scans through it. Looks me dead in the eye and tells me his paperwork says I'm a butcher. I tell the fucker, 'I never done no butcher job on the street. Armed robbery, button work. That was my trade. Never done an honest day's work in my life, at least not in no straight john detail. What the fuck is this butcher trade crap?'

"Parks, that miserable shit, he says: 'Right here in your sheet, Boy, says The Butcher of Blind Creek. Got you some experience, says here. Hung 'em by their ankles and opened up their bellies. Figured you'd like it in the packing plant since that's your style. Heard it said them sows scream like real women. Hang 'em, gut 'em, listen to 'em scream. Talk about hog heaven, says right here you get off on that shit. Now get the hell out of my office.' "

The kid groaned. "Fucking Parks! I know him. What an asshole. Kept a bottle right in his desk. I went to a Progress Review with him once, and he was drunk on his ass. Parks. Sweet Jesus. Everybody hates that fucker."

(Continued next page)

"I seen it my own self, Kid. I seen a lot. Parks and plenty more just like him. I don't know where the State dredges up the human shit they have running these prisons.... Someone must tack job opportunity notices up in gay bars. Half the staff of the Unit is faggot. The citizens say they want rehabilitation. I've seen their program. What it is, see, this rehabilitation program, it's a flip-flop deal. You flip into the system one way and flop out another way. You know? Go in straight, come out queer. Go in healthy, come out diseased. Go in normal, come out perverted. Flip-flop rehabilitation theory. An educated man could write a book about it."

The faggot nodded his agreement. How could he argue? His program might have been a little different, but he knew what I meant. The dickeater never had to ask a silly question about rehabilitation. He understood.

I watched his pretty-boy long-lashed eyes surveying the action. A covert oblique swing of the eyeballs, always on the alert for the sudden move, the danger of the knife in the back. He slid up to the bar, copped two more bourbons, and paid for them. We slurped them down, the heat of the alcohol exciting our senses.

"Where's those fucking whores?" the Kid moaned.

"Home douching out their cunts getting ready for two hardheads out on early release. They squirt perfume on their tits, powder their assholes, use cherry-flavored juice up in their pussies to make them taste nice when you suck on 'em."

"Cherry flavored pussy?" The punk was in awe.

"As I live and breathe."

"Real call girls."

"The McCoy. Call 'em and they come."

"Like a couple of bitches. Here, Girl! Here, Girl!" He was getting giddy.

"You got the picture, now hold it."

"I've been holding it. Now I want to stick it in one of them pussy rolls."

"Don't worry, you will. Tonight. Now listen to my philosophy. "

"You make up a philosophy in the Box?"

"I did. Now listen."

"Tell me."

"Blood," I said, "that's where it all starts. I was up to the Unit during the riot back in '79. There was plenty of blood to see there. The shiteaters came in on us with clubs and mace and spilled our blood. They broke our bones, bruised our meat. All you are to them, Kid, is an animated bag of meat and blood. I seen it go down. I had a vision. Teeth were all over the quarterdeck. Smashed teeth. Step on them, they crunch like gravel. They'd run you down to Q-Wing and work on you with those clubs and cattle prods. Obedience training. Attitude adjustment. Rehabilitation. The beginning and the end of it is blood. The blood fills your mama's insides. She squats and squeezes you out her cunt like a lump of crap. You come sliding down her chute right between her piss and her shit. There's a cosmic message there, if you study on it. We eat shit and die. Just like it says on the back of the Scooter Tramps jackets."

"That's your philosophy?"

"That's it... blood. That's where it starts and that's where it ends."

"Makes sense."

"You gotta let it all out, Kid. You can't keep it locked up in the Box in your brain any more. To the public you ain't no more than a carcass on a hook. They don't know nothin'. They don't want to know nothin'. They think we live at some kind of summer camp. Tell Joe Sixpack what goes on inside a prison and he'll just call you a liar. But now we're out. First we're gonna have us some fun and then I don't know about you, but I've got some people to look up. A few folks who owe me."

I lifted my glass and realized it was empty. I started to order another round when I saw a hooker in a red dress come swinging through the door with a jaunty black silk flower pinned to her waist. She had her blonde hair up in a French twist. The other French teacher was right behind her, a brunette with fluffed-out hair in a shiny royal blue number. I gave them the high sign and nudged the punk, "Here comes our French lesson."

The two bimbos bounced over to a table and sat down. I took the cocksucker by the arm and steered him through the crowd. We walked up to the women and sat down, just like free men.

The women were both obviously professionals, with painted crimson lips slick and wet. Their cheeks were rouged, their noses powdered. They were ready. I gave them a sharp, knowing grin. The women smiled back with

avaricious eyes. They studied me and the punk, looking us up and down. I stared directly at their tits. They both had nice big ones. The punk snickered and sucked up some booze. His eyes were as red as a vampire's. His baby face was pink and greasy. He gave me a callow grin. A full boner curved up toward his navel. He was a randy boy.

"I'm Jerry, and this my road dog, Danny." The whores looked at him and smiled to each other. They knew easy money when they saw it, and they were both licking their lips.

Danny gave up a self-conscious giggle. "You ladies the schoolteachers we called about private tutoring in French?"

"Oui-oui. I'm Candy," said the blonde.

"And I'm Tiffany," chimed in the brunette.

"You guys afford lessons?" asked Candy.

The kid flashed his roll and asked, "Can I buy you ladies a drink?"

"French champagne," Candy gushed. "The French lessons are two hundred an hour. Each."

The punk blanched.

Tiffany arched an eyebrow. "Can you handle it, Big Daddy?"

"Sure — no problem." The kid put on a lopsided grin and shoved off toward the bar for a round of drinks.

"A couple of twenty-dollar hookers fleecing a lamb. Shame on you!" I grinned.

"Lambs were born to be shorn," Tiffany snapped.

Candy nudged me. "How'd you get our number?"

"Willy the Weasel."

"What'd Willy fall on last time — he tell you?"

"Murder Two. Willy has him a wart right here." I touched my finger to the side of my nose.

"So you know Willy."

"Sure. You think I'm vice squad?"

"Just being careful."

"Yeah? Willy told me you two pulled time at Lowell."

Candy groaned. "I did ten months on a bar-tack machine in the garment factory. Job training for the street, you know?"

"I know."

"Tiffany pulled a deuce at Broward. Armed robbery. She ain't as genteel as she looks. Where'd you pull yours?"

"Raiford — the Rock."

"Did you see Andrea when they took her up there?" Tiffany asked.

"Didn't see her but I damn sure heard her. Bitch screamed her lungs out. Took four matrons to get her down the mainline. It was a real show. I got the story from the Deathwatch Commander, Mr. Crowe."

The two hookers exchanged a glance and laughed.

"What's the joke?"

The kid came back just then with a fifth of Dickel and a big green bottle of champagne. He popped the cork. While he was pouring a round, I asked the kid if he was around the Unit when the Jackson bitch came up for a ride on the lightning. He said he was.

"Did she scream?" Tiffany asked.

"Screamed like she was being murdered. Everyone in the Unit heard her. The Captain told me there would have been a shit trail from the back ramp to the death cell, except they had her in sanitary briefs."

The two whores laughed some more.

"What's the joke?" Danny asked.

"My exact same question," I added.

"Tiffany saw when they put her on the transport van to ride her up to the Chair," Candy said.

"She was shrieking like a maniac," Tiffany giggled. "Old Lady Venziano, she's the Warden down there, goes trooping down to Andrea's cell and reads her the Death Warrant and Transport Order. The goon squad is there with chains and locks. The nurse is standing by with the old-fashioned Kotex on a belt, and a green diaper."

"What's that about?" Danny asked.

(Continued next page)

Tiffany arched an eyebrow his way. "The electric chair is at Starke. The Women's Death Row is west of Lauderdale, out in a swamp next to the County Dump. It's a 6 to 8 hour ride to Starke. Maybe you think they'll stop and let her pee at a gas station?"

The kid shrugged, blushed a bit. "What they do is strap a piss sop to your cunt, Honey, so you can piddle in it if you take a notion to go. The diaper is just in case you get real scared and start to shit. A girl on the way to the Chair might get the urge, don't you think?"

The kid obviously didn't know what to say.

"Any more dumb questions?" Tiffany huffed.

"Lighten up, Babe," Candy quipped, then turned to the Kid and said, "She's only been on the street three weeks. Takes awhile to shrug off the stresses and tensions of that lousy joint. Women screaming and hollering, sex-crazy for a man, everybody angling for the cutest dykes and trying for early release. It's insane."

Tiffany's ire subsided. She said, "Andrea came back to Broward on a Federal stay. She told us she took the mainline by storm. Went down with a tail-swinging strut and at least five hundred men calling out for her to fuck them."

"Her fantasy," I said.

Tiffany continued, "Then they gave her a cell next to that Adams guy and they talked."

"That part could be true," the punk said.

I nodded.

"Then they took Adams and burned him up in the Chair, and that was the end of him."

Candy said, "Then when she came back to Broward she was full of shit about how she had charmed the whole Unit. True or false?"

"A little of both," I allowed. "The guards had the Unit on lockdown when she made her walk on the mainline. Cruise said she was crying and screaming. We heard that in the cellblocks."

"Lying damn bitch," hissed Tiffany.

We all drank up. The girls were originally from Atlanta and both were kicked out on early release. They were working the senior citizen trade at the condos. Lonely old men paid a mighty sweet dollar for juicy young snatch.

Business was booming. I told them about the Rock. The rehabilitation. The packing plant. The early release.

The pussy was telling them about Ted Bundy, the Catch-Me Killer and the Ghoul. The drone of conversation hummed around us and the caustic smoke stung our eyes. We discussed the mindless violence, the bloody murder, the sexual slavery of men and women in prison. How their bodies were bought and sold to the highest bidders, unleashing the perverted lusts that gave hopeless men and women a reason to live from day to day.

The blonde put her hand on my crotch. Sighed with anticipation as she rubbed her hand along my ready shaft. Tiffany snuggled with the punk, her professional hands busy under the table. The sluts were already beginning to stink of rut. They gurgled and moaned, their minds clouded by the sexual business they needed to conclude. I looked at them with both contempt and lust. I slapped my empty tumbler onto the table and announced to the steamy group, "So let's get laid!" Everyone understood that. We got right up and off we went.

The fuck-boy was giddy. He couldn't believe his luck. We left the Blind Pig with the early release whores on our arms and lurched out into the humid warmth of the summer night. Nebraska Avenue was blazing with light. Cars with glaring headlights cruised up and down the Strip, their makes, models and styles all foreign and unrecognizable to me. Neon signs flashed and blinked, advertising places and products I'd never heard of.

Music throbbed and boomed from the doorways of bars and clubs. The whole city of Tampa was a gaudy whorehouse catering to the pleasures of tourist flesh.

A stinking coal-black nigger in a dirty T-shirt rattled a paper bag in the shadows of a doorway. "White Lady, White Lady," he sang out, "Crack."

"Get fucked, Nigger!" I snarled.

Candy giggled. The dope dealer retreated into his lair.

We turned off Nebraska. The side street was in darkness. The whores had them an old two-story flophouse trick pad. Danny was anxious to get it on. He was almost dragging Tiffany up the stairs. The stairwell stank of dry rot and stale piss. Familiar smells — prison smells. The stairs led up a landing. There were rooms on the right and left. Whores and transients.

Candy fished a key out of her clutch purse. She unlocked a door and flipped on a light. Hundreds of cockroaches fled, scuttling for the cracks. There were a pair of unmade

(Continued next page) **197**

ratty beds along the far wall, an aluminum chair, a Formica table strewn with Big Mac wrappers, cigarette butts and black ants.

"Home sweet home," Tiffany announced blithely.

"Fucking pig pen," I said.

"You don't like it, hit the road, Jack," Candy spat.

Danny toppled onto a bed. There was a half bottle of Dickel in his hand. He unscrewed the cap. Tiffany grabbed the bottle, drank up, handed it to me and began pulling off Danny's clothes. His trousers were hung up on his boner. We all laughed. I took a hit on the bottle, and passed it on to Candy. She drained it, tossed it in a corner and unzipped her dress. The cheap red fabric fell in a puddle at her feet. She caught it with her foot and kicked it into the same corner with the Dickel bottle. The bedraggled black silk flower was twisted and broken off its stem. It lay on the floor by the naked feet of the blonde whore. I watched her strip, burning with a puritanical rage as she shook her creamy udders free of her lacy black brassiere.

The punk and his dark-haired whore were wrestling on the bed. The blonde pulled off her black silk panty, put it to her nose and sniffed it, made a wry face and tossed it. She cleared her throat. "Straight French, half-and-half or around-the-world?"

"French for me," I said.

"Pay up!" the blonde said, holding out her mitt.

"You don't trust me?"

"Fuck no!"

I laughed. Fished out Danny's roll from his pants and paid the freight. The whore nodded. Put the four hundred in her shoulder bag.

Danny gasped and giggled on the bed. The dark-haired slut on top of him was naked. She had tapered fingers with the color of fresh blood glistening on the long enameled nails. Her hands fluttered around the boy's dick with professional skill. They knew what to do and were busily going about it.

The nude blonde stood there like a cow in a slaughter chute. Her eyes were bovine and dumb. She scratched absently at her pubic hair as we watched Tiffany work her magic on the fuck-boy's dick. What a pro. The queer was gasping. The slut was straddling his cock, her white legs spread wide. A lavish mop of dark pubic hair hung down between her legs. She took the punk's boner in her right hand and carefully angled it into her hole. She lowered herself with a grunt of pleasure. Danny's hands clenched the pillowy white buttocks, his fingers kneading the soft flesh. The impaled woman levered herself up and down on his pole growling deep in her throat. Her eyes were closed. A ropy tendril of saliva hung from her chin. We listened to the building tempo of passion, the wet smack of sweaty flesh meeting. The brunette kept sliding up and down Danny's cock until he arched his back and emptied his load, leaving her infected with the AIDS plague.

I unzipped my jeans, took out my own stiff boner, turned to the naked blonde and commanded her, "On your knees, Bitch!"

The whore did as she was told. She took my root in her mouth and sucked on it. She'd done it before and was just fine. I let her work. I stood there and looked down at the dandruff on her head. It looked like she might have lice as well.

I listened to the slurping, sucking sounds she made as they mingled with the whimpers coming from Danny. I felt the head of my dick rub the back of her throat. I relished the slippery warmth of her spit, heard the gurgle and mewl of her efforts. I caressed Candy's blonde, dandruffed hair. It had a greasy feel. She hummed as she sucked. It was a nice touch. I tried to pick up the tune, but couldn't recognize it. Must be a new one.

Outside there was the distant whoop of a police siren. Trouble for somebody, but not for me. The thought of being free was exciting. I speeded up my thrusts. Finally I held the blonde whore's head steady, shuddered and came in her mouth. She struggled to break free. I wrapped her hair around my hand and held her head tight on my cock. Danny was amused. He caught my eye as he giggled; probably remembering his own head locked on a man's spurting dick.

Tiffany wiped her cunt with a big wad of kleenex and dropped it on the floor. "Ride 'em, Cowgirl!" she yelped at Candy.

I felt the blonde's teeth close around my dick, and I shoved her away from me. It was the only thing to do. She fell back on the floor landing on her backside, gagging and heaving. She spat a gobbet of semen on the grimy floor.

"You motherfucker!" she shrieked.

I kicked her hard in the stomach and she doubled up. "Teach you to bite my dick, Bitch!" Bloody vomit spewed

(Continued next page)

up from her gut and splashed from her mouth onto the black flower on the floor. She retched and gasped. Her eyes were swimming with fear and disgust. Two tendrils of slick puke ran from her nose. "Like to bite my dick? I'll teach you to bite!" I kicked her in the face. Teeth flew from her mouth. The force slammed her back into the wall. She bounced off and collapsed onto her side. Her head thumped the floor.

Tiffany screamed. Danny sucked in his breath and jerked upright, suddenly alert, his prison instincts over-riding the alcoholic haze. The naked brunette made a lunge for her skirt. As she made her reach I drop-kicked her in the jaw. She spun around and crashed into the bedpost and flopped down to the floor into Candy's champagne-laced vomit. I leaped in the air and came down full force on Tiffany's chest with my knees. Her rib cage collapsed under my weight.

She coughed, her chin slick with glistening blood. Gurgling rasps were her only sound. Her body stiffened slightly, and a thin bubbling sound came up from deep in her throat. The breath snagged and then stopped. Her legs began to jerk in spasms and a pool of yellow urine widened around her hips. The breath came back with a start. A few rapid gasps rattled in the back of her throat. Pink frothy lung blood gushed from her mouth, and she was dead.

"Jerry! Jerry!" Danny yelled.

"Fucking sluts," I growled.

The punk's face was fishbelly white. The gray eyes widened with sudden terror. I smiled. Pulled my knife from my boot. Strode toward him. Danny cringed back against the wall, his delicate fag hands waving before him. Cowardly little AIDS-ridden queer.

"Jerry! No! Please!" he blubbered.

I swung the blade in with a sharp upward motion. It glanced off a rib and sliced up into the faggot's yellow heart. I pulled the shank out and chopped it across his face. A fountain of blood erupted. He started sliding down the wall. I held him up with my left hand and drove the shank into him again. And again. And again. His body slumped sideways, toppled over and hit the deck. I sank a kick into his balls. "Cocksucker!" I hissed. He never heard me. He was dead.

The blonde whore had rolled onto her back. Her face was bloody and broken, her eyes rolled in their sockets with the pain. Vomit and blood streamed from the corners of her mouth. Bloody bubbles formed and burst at her nostrils as she attempted to breathe.

I felt the pounding of my heart as the excitement fanned my rage. The coppery smell of whoreblood had me sweating and my nerves on fire. The blonde bitch groaned. The brunette was splayed across the floor in a ghastly pool of blood and urine and vomit.

I walked over to her to get a closer look. Her open eyes were dilated. The blood oozing from her nose and ears was beginning to thicken. She looked dead. I leaned over and punched the blade into her heart, just to be sure.

I picked up Danny's discarded trousers and removed the still-fat wad of cash from his front pocket. I searched the pocketbooks of the two hookers and came up with a couple of C-notes, in addition to my own four hundred. Chump change.

I heard the blonde whore groan. She was still on her back, lips swollen, eyes puffy and blackened. I walked over to her. I could see the cheesy crack between her legs, with the cooties crawling in her bush. She wasn't a natural blonde. I examined her ruined face and noticed that some-how her narrow, aristocratic nose had remained unbroken. I lifted the heel of my heavy boot and brought it down smartly on her snot locker, driving it up into her brain.

The whore didn't move and made no further sound. I set the point of the blade into the hollow of her white throat and shoved it in until I felt it grate bone. Then I twisted it. I picked up the sodden black flower and placed it in her evil mouth. It looked just right .

I opened the door to the flophouse flat. The hallway was dusty and empty. I walked down the rotting stairs to the street, with Danny's roll to keep me company. I thought of Canada, the Bahamas, the coast of North Africa. Then I thought of the cop who had framed me for murder sixteen years ago. Within an hour I was on a bus to Miami. •

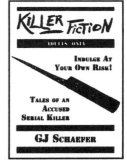

YOU WILL ALSO WANT TO READ:

☐ **94146 LOOMPANICS' GREATEST HITS: Articles and Features from the Best Book Catalog in the World,** *Edited by Michael Hoy.* A collection of articles and essays, cartoons and rants, gleaned from the pages of the Loompanics Unlimited book catalog. For over a decade, the Loompanics Catalog has served as a kiosk for writers from the far left, the far right and the "far out." A compendium of counterculture thought, this provocative book contains more than 75 features in all. *1990, 8½ x 11, 300 pp, Illustrated, soft cover.* **$16.95.**

☐ **94096 THE ABOLITION OF WORK: And Other Essays,** *by Bob Black.* Bob Black's opposition to work has landed him on the pages of "USA Today," "The Wall Street Journal," and "The Village Voice," among others. His writings have appeared in hundreds of counter-culture publications. The title essay in this collection is probably the most well-thought-out condemnation of wage labor ever to appear in print. The other essays are equally provocative and include the now-famous "Feminism as Fascism" and "Theses on Groucho Marxism." *1986, 5½ x 8½, 159 pp, soft cover.* **$9.95.**

☐ **94132 RANTS AND INCENDIARY TRACTS,** *Edited by Bob Black & Adam Parfrey.* Subtitled "Voices of Desperate Illumination 1558 to Present," "Rants and Incendiary Tracts" is a collection of very loud outcries from very disturbed writers. Timothy Leary, the Marquis de Sade, Judge Roy Bean, Ezra Pound, Wilhelm Reich, the Ayatollah Khomeini, Max Stirner, Valerie Solanas, Rabbi Meir Kahane, Anton Szandor La Vey, Kerry Wendell Thornley, Earth First!, and dozens more. "Why is a rant so important? Because no one dares speak his mind anymore." *1989, 5½ x 8½, 220 pp, Illustrated, soft cover.* **$9.95.**

☐ **85120 TWISTED IMAGE,** *by Ace Backwords.* This is the first collection of comic strips by America's funniest underground cartoonist. Ace Backwords takes on the controversial topics of sex, drugs and modern culture. His strips have appeared in more than 200 "marginal" publications including "High Times," "Maximum Rock'n'Roll," "Screw" and the Loompanics Catalog. For adults only. *1990, 8½ x 11, 128 pp, more than 200 strips, soft cover.* **$12.95.**

☐ **64129 SELL YOURSELF TO SCIENCE: The Complete Guide to Selling Your Organs, Body Fluids, Bodily Functions and Being a Human Guinea Pig,** *by Jim Hogshire.* This book shows exactly what your body is worth and how to sell it, in whole or in part. Your body is your business when you sell renewable resources such as blood, sperm, milk and hair. You can also arrange to sell your heart, lungs and other vital organs in the most unusual "going out of business" sale you've ever heard of. This amazing "career guide" also reveals what it's like to work as a guinea pig for drug companies. It pays up to $100 a day, and this book lists more than 150 active test sites. *1992, 5½ x 8½, 168 Illustrated, soft cover.* **$16.95.**

☐ **14099 THE ART & SCIENCE OF DUMPSTER DIVING,** *by John Hoffman.* This amazing book will show you how to get just about "anything" you want or need — food, clothing, furniture, building supplies, entertainment, luxury goods, tools, toys — you name it — "ABSOLUTELY FREE!" Includes: Step-by-step, illustrated dumpster diving techniques, Recipes for food salvaged from dumpsters, The "Big Three" dumpster hot spots, The "Lucky Seven" dive spots, How to convert trash to cash, and much, much more, including 14 original comic strips and a glorious full-color cover by Ace Backwords. *1993, 8½ x 11, 152 pp, Illustrated, soft cover.* **$12.95.**

☐ **34050 HUNTING HUMANS: An Encyclopedia of Modern Serial Killers,** *by Michael Newton.* More than 500 detailed case histories of serial killers from the 20th Century. This disturbing book describes their lives and their exploits without any varnish or puffery — the chilling details speak for themselves. More than 60% of the killers described here have never been mentioned in a published book before. This huge book is an unforgettable chronicle of the world's most deranged homicidal maniacs. *1990, 8½ x 11, 353 pp, Illustrated, hard cover.* **$34.95.**

⚜⚜⚜⚜⚜⚜⚜⚜⚜⚜⚜⚜⚜⚜⚜⚜⚜⚜⚜⚜⚜⚜⚜⚜⚜⚜⚜⚜⚜⚜⚜

LOOMPANICS UNLIMITED / PO BOX 1197 / Port Townsend, WA 98368   LGR

Please send the books I have checked above. I am enclosing $ _____ (including $4.00 for shipping and handling of 1 to 3 titles, $6.00 for 4 or more).

Name _____

Address _____

City _____

State/Zip_____

(Washington residents please include 7.8% sales tax.)

"Yes, there are book about the skills of apocalypse —spying, surveillance, fraud, wiretapping, smuggling, self-defense, lockpicking, gunmanship, eavesdropping, car chasing, civil warfare, surviving jail, and dropping out of sight. Apparently writing books is the way mercenaries bring in spare cash between wars. The books are useful, and it's good the information is freely available (and they definitely inspire interesting dreams), but their advice should be taken with a salt shaker or two and all your wits. A few of these volumes are truly scary. Loompanics is the best of the Libertarian suppliers who carry them. Though full of 'you'll-wish-you'd-read-these-when-it's-too-late' rhetoric, their catalog is genuinely informative."

— **The Next Whole Earth Catalog**

THE BEST BOOK CATALOG IN THE WORLD!!!

We offer hard-to-find books on the world's most unusual subjects. Here are a few of the topics covered IN DEPTH in our exciting new catalog:

- *Hiding/Concealment of physical objects! A complete section of the best books ever written on hiding things.*
- *Fake ID/Alternate Identities! The most comprehensive selection of books on this little-known subject ever offered for sale! You have to see it to believe it!*
- *Investigative/Undercover methods and techniques! Professional secrets known only to a few, now revealed to you to use! Actual police manuals on shadowing and surveillance!*
- *And much, much more, including Locks and Locksmithing, Self-Defense, Intelligence Increase, Life Extension, Money-Making Opportunities, Human Oddities, Exotic Weapons, Sex, Drugs, Anarchism, and more!*

Our book catalog is 280 pages, 8½ x 11, packed with over 820 of the most controversial and unusual books ever printed! You can order every book listed! Periodic supplements keep you posted on the LATEST titles available!!! Our catalog is $5.00, including shipping and handling.

Our book catalog is truly THE BEST BOOK CATALOG IN THE WORLD! Order yours today you will be very pleased, we know.

LOOMPANICS UNLIMITED
PO BOX 1197
PORT TOWNSEND, WA 98368
USA